J. S. MILL'S PHILOSOPHY

OF SCIENTIFIC METHOD

The Hafner Library of Classics

[Number Twelve]

John Stuart Mill's Philosophy of Scientific Method

Edited with an Introduction by

ERNEST NAGEL

Professor of Philosophy, Columbia University

HAFNER PUBLISHING CO.

NEW YORK

CONTENTS

BAT 3. 95+ 160 4(14(2)

BOOK III: OF INDUCTION

BOOK FOUR:

OF OPERATIONS SUBSIDIARY TO INDUCTION

BOOK V:

ON THE LOGIC OF THE MORAL SCIENCES [Bk. VI]

FROM AN EXAMINATION
OF SIR WILLIAM HAMILTON'S PHILOSOPHY

INTRODUCTION

I

Like many other major works in philosophy, the contributions of John Stuart Mill to logic, scientific method, and the theory of knowledge are the clarified and matured expressions of an intellectual tradition that did not begin with him. Mill was not a thinker gifted with great originality, and while he modified and expanded the ideas he acquired from his predecessors, he did not radically transform them. He was the heir and champion of a philosophy that has its source in Locke, Berkeley, and Hume, and that was developed further by Hartley, Bentham, and his own father, James Mill. And though he was sensitive to winds of doctrine for which his teachers showed little sympathy, his writings on logic and related subjects were primarily an articulate and systematic formulation of the principles involved in the philosophy of British sensationalistic empiricism and utilitarianism.

However, Mill was not a secluded academic thinker, intellectually aloof from the political, economic, and religious issues that agitated his age. On the contrary, most of his published work was the fruit of discussions and controversies centering around burning practical problems, and even his more technical theoretical analyses were controlled by the aim of removing the obstacles which false philosophies placed in the path of social progress. His intense and abiding preoccupation with public questions explains many of the specific turns of his philosophical writings, and is the source of much of their strength as well as of their limitations.

Mill's life fell into the period when modern science was producing not only basic alterations in the outlook of a relatively small group of professional thinkers, but through its alliance with industrial technology was changing the physical face of England and effectively modifying the positions of masses of people in the social economy. Conceptions of nature, man, and society that had been developed in earlier centuries and had come to be regarded as axiomatic, were challenged in a manner and on a scale that was unprecedented. But the new order of institutions and ideas required a theoretical interpretation and defense — in part to make the altered world intelligible to those who were active in bringing it to birth, in part to serve as a weapon against those who stood in the way of further alterations. It was the historical mission of sensationalistic empiricism — the "philosophy of experience," as Mill called it — to perform just this function. It was this philosophy which had been used to consolidate the victories won in the bloodless revolution of 1688, which formed a major prop for the French Enlightenment and its sequel, and which in the nineteenth century helped the industrial class coming into power to undermine the system of ideas associated with a feudal economy and to justify its scheme of social policy.

The philosophical school with which Mill was connected regarded its doctrines as the explicit formulation of a conception of things demanded by modern science, and its members identified themselves with the "party of Progress" that was struggling to bring about basic political and social changes. But conversely, defenders of the passing order of ideas, in addition to employing other means, attempted to stem the tide of events by directing their fire on the weaknesses and inadequacies of the "negative" philosophy of their opponents, and by recasting the theoretical foundations of their own ancient faiths. The French Revolution and its consequences produced a powerful reaction throughout Europe against the ideas associated with the Enlightenment — a reaction that was nourished by the social groups in the process of being displaced from their traditional positions of dominance, but also by the widespread social evils that accompanied the maturing of the industrial revolution. An important fraction of nineteenth century philosophic writing was devoted, on the one hand, to a vigorous criticism of the philosophy of experience, and on the other hand to a reinterpretation of age-old beliefs and institutions so as to win for them a secure place in the new order of things.

Adherents of the philosophy of experience were thus faced with a double task: the continuation of their assault on what they believed were unworthy survivals from older social and intellectual systems; and the reformulation of their own principles with a view to meeting the philosophical criticisms levelled against them. In this warfare between opposing social ideals and philosophies Mill played a prominent role. For several years after the establishment in 1823 of the Benthamite *Westminster Review* he was its most frequent contributor, and the analyses of current political abuses which he and others published in it had some part in bringing about the passage of the Reform Bill of 1832. The prospects of the "philosophical Radicals," the name subsequently given to Mill and his associates, now appeared to be bright. A number of them won seats in the first reformed Parliament, and in several periodicals — especially in the *London and Westminster Review*, the newly founded organ of the group — Mill became the leading spokesman for Radical objectives: representative government based on universal suffrage and complete freedom of public discussion, supported by arguments derived from Bentham's utilitarian ethics, Malthusian population theory, Ricardian economics, and Hartleian psychology. However, for various reasons philosophical Radicalism declined into obscurity. In his disappointment with the performance of the Radicals in Parliament and with the turn of political events both at home and on the continent of Europe, Mill severed his connections with the *London and Westminster* and turned to more technical philosophic writing. He now took the view that "the mental regeneration of Europe must precede its moral regeneration," and believed that there was nothing better for him to do than to complete his long-postponed treatise on logic which he thought was "destined to do its little part toward straightening and strengthening the intellects which have this great work to do."[1] But Mill did not permanently withdraw from political journalism, and soon resumed writing on subjects of general public interest. Eventually, in 1865, he consented to be a candidate for a seat in Parliament, where his courageous support of unpopular causes made him a distinguished though not always an effective figure.

But it was the publication in 1843 of his *System of Logic* that established him as the philosophical leader of his school. It was the "best attacked" book of the time, provoking not only detailed critical comment from influential philosophic adversaries such as

[1] Caroline Fox, *Memories of Old Friends*, London, 1883, p. 434.

Whewell, but also extensive discussion from prominent theologians such as W. G. Ward, a leading member of the conservative Oxford Movement. However, the book was widely hailed as a signal contribution to its subject, and rapidly achieved the status of a classic in the philosophic literature of utilitarianism. It went through eight editions during Mill's life, and Mill used the opportunity thus given him to reply with care to many of his critics and to record a number of substantial changes in his original analyses. An important supplement to the *Logic* appeared in 1865, with the title *Examination of Sir William Hamilton's Philosophy*. The aim of this later work was to review in detail the philosophic doctrines of Hamilton (professor of Logic and Metaphysics at Edinburgh), whom Mill regarded as the chief pillar of the "intuitional" philosophy. It is a highly polemical book, and Mill hoped in it to settle scores once for all with his philosophical opponents — the five editions of the work he saw through the press enabled him to broaden his attack by including criticisms of many British and American defenders of Hamilton. But the book has more than a polemical interest, for it treats fully a number of questions which are barely mentioned in the *Logic*, and it makes explicit fundamental aspects of Mill's philosophy that he did not develop elsewhere.

Meanwhile, in 1844, Mill published his five *Essays on Some Unsettled Questions of Political Economy*, the terminal essay "On the Definition of Political Economy" being one of the best statements and defenses of the method of Ricardian economics. In 1848, his *Principles of Political Economy* appeared, in which he achieved for the social theory of philosophical Radicalism what in the *Logic* he did for its method and theory of knowledge. Mill's most mature reflections on theoretical ethics were incorporated into his *Utilitarianism*, published in 1861, a brief book that made explicit his divergences from orthodox Benthamism. His posthumous *Three Essays on Religion* dismayed some of his followers who retained the original Radical appraisal of religious belief as being simply a tissue of superstition; the essays nonetheless exerted some influence, for they contained suggestions as to how far it was possible to be an unregenerate empiricist and yet subscribe to a theology.

In the process of adjusting the central tenets of his philosophy to the requirements of the contemporary science, Mill was thus led to revise some of them, and to make concessions (especially in the theory of morals and politics) that disturbed his friends — "Much as I admire John Mill," George Grote the historian of Greece and staunch utilitarian is reported to have remarked, "my admiration is always mixed with fear."[2] But in this process Mill also was compelled to make explicit the assumptions of that philosophy, to develop their implications and indicate in detail their applications, with a thoroughness unequalled in the writings of his predecessors. He was perhaps the foremost political pamphleteer of English utilitarianism; he was undoubtedly the most systematic expounder of its basic theory.

II

Mill's education as a youth was a careful preparation for his subsequent role as philosophical leader of his school. He was born in London on May 20, 1806, the oldest child of James Mill, Bentham's chief disciple and ally, intimate friend of Ricardo, and in his own right a major figure in the history of English utilitarianism. As the father once wrote Bentham, he hoped to make of the young boy a "successor worthy of us"; and since he was also convinced by his reading of Helvetius that all differences between the characters and capacities of men are the product of environmental influences, he supervised the education of his son himself. Except for a year spent in France during his fifteenth year with the family of Sir Samuel Bentham, brother of the philosopher, John Mill received his entire formal training at home from his father. From the age of three until he obtained employment with the East India Company in 1823, he was subjected to a remarkable intellectual discipline, directed toward making him an adherent of his father's ideas, but at the same time an independent thinker who would never accept conclusions on the basis of mere authority. By his sixteenth year he was thoroughly adept in the principles of sensationalistic empiricism, utilitarian ethics, Ricardian economics, and the politics of Radicalism. "If I have accomplished

[2] Alexander Bain, *John Stuart Mill*, New York, 1882, p. 83.

anything," he wrote in his *Autobiography*, "I owe it, among other fortunate circumstances, to the fact that through the early training bestowed on me by my father, I started, I may fairly say, with an advantage of a quarter of a century over my contemporaries."[3]

On Mill's return from France he was given to read Dumont's *Traité de législation*, a digest of Bentham's philosophy of law; and although he had seen much of Bentham personally and was familiar with Benthamite ideas, the study of this work marked an epoch in his life. As he later declared,

What thus impressed me was the chapter in which Bentham passed judgment on the common modes of reasoning in morals and legislation deduced from phrases like "the law of nature," "right reason," "the moral sense," "natural rectitude," and the like, and characterized them as dogmatism in disguise, imposing its sentiments upon others under cover of sounding expressions which convey no reason for the sentiment, but set up the sentiment as its own reason. . . . The "principle of utility" understood as Bentham understood it, and applied in the manner in which he applied it through these three volumes, fell exactly into its place as the keystone which held together the detached and fragmentary component parts of my knowledge and beliefs. It gave unity to my conceptions of things. I now had opinions; a creed, a doctrine, a philosophy; in one among the best senses of the word, a religion; the inculcation and diffusion of which could be made the principal outward purpose of a life.[4]

Mill subsequently qualified his early acceptance of the Benthamite principle of utility. But his esteem for what he regarded as Bentham's great contribution to philosophy did not diminish, and he took permanently for his own Bentham's conception of the correct method to be employed in philosophy. Years later, at the height of his own intellectual powers, he evaluated Bentham's place in history as follows:

If we were asked to say, in the fewest possible words, what we conceive to be Bentham's place among these great intellectual benefactors of humanity; what he was, and what he was not; what kind of service he did and did not render to truth; we should say — he was not a great philosopher, but he was a great reformer of philosophy. He brought into philosophy something which it

---

[3] *Autobiography of John Stuart Mill*, New York, 1924, p. 21.
[4] *Ibid.*, pp. 45-7.

greatly needed, and for want of which it was at a stand. It was not his doctrines which did this, it was his mode of arriving at them. He introduced into morals and politics those habits of thought and modes of investigation, which are essential to the idea of science; and the absence of which made those departments of inquiry, as physics had been before Bacon, a field of interminable discussion, leading to no result. It was not his opinion, in short, but his method, that constituted the novelty and the value of what he did; a value beyond all price, even though we should reject the whole, as we unquestionably must a large part, of the opinions themselves.

Bentham's method may be shortly described as the method of detail; of treating wholes by separating them into their parts, abstractions by resolving them into Things, — classes and generalities by distinguishing them into the individuals of which they are made up; and breaking every question into pieces before attempting to solve it. . . .[5]

Mill's formal education came to an end in 1823, upon his entering the India House as an employee. He remained with the East India Company until its dissolution in 1858, then retiring on a handsome pension. He was thus assured throughout his life of a secure income and ample leisure. In addition to the steady flow of reviews and books that came from his pen, he found time to participate in a number of discussion and debating circles. Of these, the most important for his own development was the small group that met twice weekly at the home of George Grote for several years, in order to read critically various books in economic theory, logic, and analytic psychology. "I have always dated from these conversations," he maintained, "my own real inauguration as an original and independent thinker." At any rate, it was out of these discussions that two of Mill's major literary projects developed, his *Essays on Some Unsettled Questions of Political Economy*, and his *Logic*.

Meanwhile, however, he experienced an intellectual and emotional crisis that profoundly affected his outlook and his subsequent relations with his contemporaries. Until 1826 he gave his complete assent to the ideas of his father, sharing as well the latter's sectarian bias, and subsequently confessed that up to this time he had been

[5] John S. Mill, *Dissertations and Discussions*, London, 1859–75, Vol. I, pp. 339–40.

"a mere reasoning machine," conforming to the popular conception of a faithful Benthamite. In that year, he fell prey to a long and deep despondency which led him to question the fundamental aim he had set for himself, to be a reformer of the world. His *Autobiography* gives a vivid description of this poignant moment:

It occurred to me to put the question directly to myself: "Suppose that all your objects in life were realized; that all the changes in institutions and opinions which you are looking forward to, could be completely effected at this very instant: would this be a great joy and happiness to you?" And an irrepressible self-consciousness distinctly answered "No!" At this my heart sank within me: the whole foundation on which my life was constructed fell down. All my happiness was to have been found in the continual pursuit of this end. The end had ceased to charm, and how could there ever again be any interest in the means? I seemed to have nothing left to live for.[6]

He recovered from this melancholy only slowly, crediting his final release from it to Wordsworth, whose poetry he read at this time. The immediate effect of the entire experience on Mill's thought was to make "the cultivation of feelings" central to his ethical philosophy, and to lead him to cease attaching exclusive importance to the training of human beings for speculation and action. The admiration he acquired for Wordsworth's poetry also inclined him to greater sympathy toward the ideas of other members of Coleridge's circle. He thus came to find merit in men and doctrines that were the objects of suspicion if not hostile contempt of orthodox utilitarians: in Coleridge himself, and his disciples Frederick Maurice and John Sterling, from whom he learned to interpret the meaning of traditional beliefs in a less literal and more catholic spirit; in Carlyle, with whom he formed for many years a warm friendship, and with many of whose indictments of the social evils of unrestrained individualism he found himself in agreement; in the St. Simonians and Comte, from whom he acquired, among other ideas, a belief in a fixed order of social progress; and in Continental historians such as Niebuhr, Guizot, and Michelet, who taught him that political institutions should be judged not "absolutely," on the basis of a fixed political theory, but "rela-

---

[6] *Autobiography* (New York, 1924), p. 94.

tively," in terms of the functions they perform in different historical epochs.

It is noteworthy, however, that though under the impact of these influences Mill revised some of his ethical and political convictions, he did not surrender any of the basic premises of his general philosophy of experience. He admitted that eighteenth century followers of Locke (especially the school of Condillac) had effectively debased Locke's doctrines, so that these latter stood in need of renovation. But his reading of the Coleridgians and their German sources only deepened his conviction that their conception of intellectual method and their theory of knowledge were false, and were fraught with dangerous social implications.

One remaining influence in Mill's life requires brief mention — his relations with Mrs. Harriet Taylor, who became his wife in 1851 after the death of her first husband. His intimate friendship over a period of twenty years with a married woman scandalized his own family and many of his other friends, and in consequence he withdrew from nearly all social intercourse. Of Mrs. Taylor's character and intellectual powers he entertained the highest possible estimate; and he claimed to be indebted to her both for much in his ethical and political philosophy, as well as for a "wise scepticism" in theoretical speculation. Mill's account of his intellectual obligations to his wife is generally discounted as largely a lover's exaggeration. Her sudden death in 1858 made him more than ever a social recluse. He spent a considerable portion of his remaining years at Avignon, the place of her death, completing and publishing many literary projects which he had begun jointly with her. He died at Avignon on May 8, 1873.

III

The final draft of the *System of Logic* was completed by Mill in about two years; but the ideas which entered into it were the result of a dozen years of intellectual groping and growth.

Most of what is contained in the First Book of the work was stimulated by reading with his friends at Grote's home Whately's *Logic*, Hobbes' *Computatio sive Logica*, and a scholastic manual on logic by the Jesuit father Du Trieu. Mill was critical of traditional formal logic, but he did not spurn it as did many of his contemporaries — his original aim in projecting a work on logic was merely "to rationalize and correct the principles and distinctions of the school logicians, and to improve the theory of the Import of Propositions."

However, when, in 1830, he began to set his ideas on paper, the scope of the project was enlarged under the stimulus of Macaulay's attack on James Mill's "Essay on Government." Macaulay, a thoroughgoing Baconian in his conception of the nature of scientific method, criticized severely the elder Mill's reliance on deduction from first principles in developing a theory of politics; and he urged the superiority of using history and observation as the basis for political analysis. Mill believed that both his father and Macaulay were wrong:

> I felt that politics could not be a science of specific experience; and that the accusations against the Benthamic theory of *being* a theory, of proceeding *a priori* by way of general reasoning, instead of Baconian experiment, showed complete ignorance of Bacon's principles, and of the necessary conditions of experimental investigations. . . . I saw that Macaulay's conception of the logic of politics was erroneous; that he stood up for the empirical mode of treating political phenomena, against the philosophical; that even in physical science his notions of philosophizing might have recognized Kepler, but would have excluded Newton and Laplace. But I could not help feeling that . . . there was truth in several of his strictures on my father's treatment of the subject; that my father's premises were really too narrow, and included but a small number of the general truths, on which, in politics, the important consequences depend. . . . This made me think that there was really something more fundamentally erroneous in my father's conception of philosophic method, as applicable to politics, than I had hitherto supposed there was. But I did not at first see clearly what the error might be. . . . In attempting to fathom the mode of tracing causes and effects in physical science, I soon saw that in the more perfect of the sciences, we ascend, by generalization from particulars, to the tendencies of causes considered singly, and then reason downward from those separate tendencies, to the effect of the same causes when combined. I then asked myself, what is the ultimate analysis of this deductive process; the common theory of the syllogism evidently throwing no light upon it . . . The Composition of Forces, in dynamics, occurred to me as the most complete example of the logical process I was investigating.

On examining, accordingly, what the mind does when it applies
the principle of the Composition of Forces, I found that it performs
a simple act of addition. It adds the separate effect of the one
force to the separate effect of the other, and puts down the sum
of these separate effects as the joint effect. But is this a legitimate
process? In dynamics, and in all the mathematical branches of
physics, it is; but in some other cases, as in chemistry, it is not;
and I then recollected that something not unlike this was pointed
out as one of the distinctions between chemical and mechanical
phenomena, in the introduction to that favourite of my boyhood,
Thompson's System of Chemistry. This distinction at once made
my mind clear as to what was perplexing me in respect to the
philosophy of politics. I now saw, that a science is either deductive
or experimental, according as, in the province it deals with, the
effects of causes when conjoined, are or are not the sums of the
effects which the same causes produce when separate. It followed
that politics must be a deductive science. It thus appeared, that
both Macaulay and my father were wrong; the one in assimilating
the method of philosophizing in politics to the purely experimental
method of chemistry; while the other, though right in adopting
a deductive method, had made a wrong selection of one, having
taken as the type of deduction, not the appropriate process, that
of the deductive branches of natural philosophy, but the inappro-
priate one of pure geometry, which, not being a science of causation
at all, does not require or admit of any summing-up of effects. A
foundation was thus laid in my thought for the principal chapters
of what I afterwards published on the Logic of the Moral
Sciences. . . .[7]

However, the composition of the book was interrupted, and not
resumed until 1832. Mill now began to struggle with "the great
paradox of the discovery of new truths by general reasoning."
He was perfectly convinced that all reasoning is resolvable into
a series of syllogisms, and that in every syllogism the conclusion
is "actually contained and implied in the premises." But, as he
explained in the *Autobiography*,

How, being so contained and implied, it could be new truth, and
how theorems of geometry, so different in appearance from the
definitions and axioms, could be all contained in these, was a
difficulty which no one, I thought, had sufficiently felt, and which
at all events, no one had succeeded in clearing up. . . . At last,
when reading a second or third time the chapters on Reasoning

[7] *Ibid.*, pp. 110–13.

in the second volume of Dugald Stewart, . . . I came upon an idea of his respecting the use of axioms in ratiocination, which I did not remember to have before noticed, but which now, in meditating upon it, seemed to me not only true of axioms, but of all general propositions whatever, and to be the key of the whole perplexity. From this germ grew the theory of the syllogism, propounded in the Second Book of the Logic; which I immediately fixed by writing it out. And now, with greatly increased hope of being able to produce a work on Logic, of some originality and value, I proceeded to write the First Book, from the rough and imperfect draft I had already made. What I now wrote became the basis of that part of the subsequent Treatise; except that it did not contain the Theory of Kinds, which was a later addition suggested by otherwise inextricable difficulties which met me in my first attempt to work out the subject of some of the concluding chapters of the Third Book.[8]

But Mill was again compelled to lay the book aside because he could make "nothing satisfactory" out of Induction, upon which his proposed resolution of "the great paradox of general reasoning" ultimately rests. The only natural science with which he had first-hand familiarity was classificatory botany, for which he acquired a permanent taste during his early sojourn in France; and he was therefore acutely conscious of his lack of a comprehensive perspective upon the physical sciences. When Whewell's *History of the Inductive Sciences* appeared in 1837, he read it eagerly and with the sense that the book supplied him with what he had long wanted. He also re-read Sir John Herschel's *Discourse on the Study of Natural Philosophy*, and now found in it important aids toward formulating a theory of induction. He felt confident that he had finally unraveled all the really hard knots in the subject, and that the completion of the *Logic* was merely a question of time. In any event, he was able to write out at a rapid pace the crucial chapters on the demonstrative sciences in the Second Book, as well as most of the Third Book devoted to induction.

At about this time Mill was reading Comte's *Philosophie Positive*, and was enormously impressed by it. Indeed, he adopted some of its analyses for the final Book of the *Logic* dealing with the social sciences. Thus, he took over Comte's distinction between social statics and social dynamics, and he felt particularly indebted

[8] *Ibid.*, p. 127.

to Comte for what Mill called the "Inverse Deductive or Historical Method" as unusually pertinent for the study of social phenomena. Nevertheless, Mill found that Comte had nothing to teach him on the subject of induction. For Comte did not, as Mill believed himself to have done, try to reduce inductive inference to strict rules of procedure, analogous to those which syllogistic theory supplies for deductive reasoning. During the following year, in 1838, he succeeded in filling out what he thought were the remaining gaps in his draft of the Third Book. He found, in particular, that in order to deal satisfactorily with laws of nature that are not laws of causation he had to recognize that "kinds are realities in nature, and not mere distinctions for convenience." And in working out the consequences of this shift in point of view, he was compelled to modify several chapters in the First Book of his treatise. However, it was not until 1840, upon severing his relations with the *London and Westminster Review*, that Mill found time to complete the work. He rewrote it from the beginning, added a fourth Book on language and classification (into which, as he once remarked, he placed subjects for which there was no convenient room elsewhere), and another Book on fallacies; and by the end of 1841 it was ready for the printer.

But though the *Logic* took long to write, its composition was controlled by a central idea, and its various parts were integrated by a common thesis: sound action is possible only on the basis of sound theory, and sound theory (whether in the natural or in the social sciences) is the product of a sound logic. As a follower of Locke, Mill was convinced that every philosophy must take its starting point from a theory concerning both the sources and the possible objects of knowledge; and it was therefore clear to him that all conflicts between fundamental beliefs have their ultimate origin in differences in logical theory. But as Mill viewed the philosophic scene, a deep gulf separates those who accept "experience" as the final and exclusive authority, from those who rely on "intuition" for certifying beliefs — this latter label serving to cover, with a none too delicate power of discrimination, various forms of apriorism, such as the rationalist philosophies of the seventeenth century, the views of Kant and his followers, and the doctrines of Reid and the Scottish Realists. To support and substantiate the philosophy of experience, and to expose the shortcomings of the intuitional philosophy and thereby undermine its influence, were the ultimate objectives Mill had before him in writing both the *Logic* and his later polemic against Hamilton. On this point nothing could be more explicit than Mill's own statement:

The German, or *a priori* view of human knowledge, and of the knowing faculties, is likely for some time longer (though it may be hoped in a diminishing degree) to predominate among those who occupy themselves with such inquiries, both here and on the Continent. But the "System of Logic" supplies what was wanted, a text-book of the opposite doctrine — that which derives all knowledge from experience, and all moral and intellectual qualities principally from the direction given to the associations. I make as humble an estimate as anybody of what either an analysis of logical processes, or any possible canons of evidence, can do by themselves, toward guiding or rectifying the operations of the understanding. Combined with other requisites, I certainly do think them of great use; but whatever may be the practical value of a true system of philosophy of these matters, it is hardly possible to exaggerate the mischiefs of a false one. The notion that truths external to the mind may be known by intuition or consciousness, independently of observation and experience, is, I am persuaded, in these times, the great intellectual support of false doctrines and bad institutions. By the aid of this theory, every inveterate belief and every intense feeling, of which the origin is not remembered, is enabled to dispense with the obligation of justifying itself by reason, and is erected into its own all-sufficient voucher and justification. There never was such an instrument devised for consecrating deep-seated prejudices. And the chief strength of this philosophy in morals, politics, and religion, lies in the appeal which it is accustomed to make to the evidence of mathematics and of the cognate branches of physical science. To expel it from these, is to drive it from its stronghold: and because this had never been effectually done, the intuitive school, even after what my father had written in his Analysis of Mind, had in appearance, and as far as published writings were concerned, on the whole the best of the argument. In attempting to clear up the real nature of the evidence of mathematical and physical truths, the "System of Logic" met the intuitive philosophers on ground on which they had previously been deemed unassailable; and gave its own explanation, from experience and association, of that peculiar character of what are called necessary truths, which is adduced as proof that their evidence must come from a deeper source than experience.

Whether this has been done effectually, is still *sub-judice;* and even then, to deprive a mode of thought so strongly rooted in human prejudices and partialities, of its mere speculative support, goes but a very little way towards overcoming it; but though only a step, it is a quite indispensable one; for since, after all, prejudice can only be successfully combated by philosophy, no way can really be made against it permanently until it has been shown not to have philosophy on its side.[8a]

Mill gave an even clearer expression to the social significance he attached to a correct philosophy in his explanation of the reasons that prompted his minute dissection of Hamilton's ideas.

The difference between these two schools of philosophy, that of Intuition, and that of Experience and Association, is not a mere matter of abstract speculation; it is full of practical consequences, and lies at the foundation of all the greatest differences of practical opinion in an age of progress. The practical reformer has continually to demand that changes be made in things which are supported by powerful and widely-spread feelings, or to question the apparent necessity and indefeasibleness of established facts; and it is often an indispensable part of his argument to show, how those powerful feelings had their origin, and how those facts came to seem necessary and indefeasible. There is therefore a natural hostility between him and a philosophy which discourages the explanation of feelings and moral facts by circumstances and association, and prefers to treat them as ultimate elements of human nature; a philosophy which is addicted to holding up favorite doctrines as intuitive truths, and deems intuition to be the voice of Nature and of God, speaking with an authority higher than that of our reason. In particular, I have long felt that the prevailing tendency to regard all the marked distinctions of human character as innate, and in the main indelible, and to ignore the irresistible proofs that by far the greater part of those differences, whether between individuals, races, or sexes, are such as not only might but naturally would be produced by differences in circumstances, is one of the chief hindrances to the rational treatment of great social questions, and one of the greatest stumbling blocks to human improvement. This tendency has its source in the intuitional metaphysics which characterized the reaction of the nineteenth century against the eighteenth, and it is a tendency so agreeable to human indolence, as well as to conservative interests generally, that unless attacked at the very root, it is sure to be carried to even a greater length than is really justified by the more moderate

[8a] *Ibid.*, pp. 157–9.

forms of the intuitional philosophy. That philosophy, not always in its moderate forms, had ruled the thought of Europe for the greater part of a century. My father's Analysis of the Mind, my own Logic, and Professor Bain's great treatise, had attempted to re-introduce a better mode of philosophizing, latterly with quite as much success as could be expected; but I had for some time felt that there ought to be a hand-to-hand fight between them, that controversial as well as expository writings were needed, and that the time was come when such controversy would be useful. Considering then the writings and fame of Sir W. Hamilton as the great fortress of the intuitional philosophy in this country, a fortress the more formidable from the imposing character, and the in many respects great personal merits and mental endowments, of the man, I thought it might be a real service to philosophy to attempt a thorough examination of all his most important doctrines, and an estimate of his general claims to eminence as a philosopher, and I was confirmed in this resolution by observing that in the writings of at least one, and him one of the ablest, of Sir W. Hamilton's followers, his peculiar doctrines were made the justification of a view of religion which I hold to be profoundly immoral — that it is our duty to bow down in worship before a Being whose natural attributes are affirmed to be unknowable by us, and to be perhaps extremely different from those which, when we are speaking of our fellow creatures, we call by the same names.[9]

[9] *Ibid.*, pp. 191–3. Mill felt particularly strongly on the last point mentioned in the above citation. He was shocked not only by what he regarded as the bad logic of Hamilton's followers when dealing with theological questions that affect mankind most intimately, but also by the pernicious abuse of the ethics of language of which he believed they were guilty. One of the most eloquent pleas he ever wrote for clarity and integrity in the use of language is contained in the severe condemnation of H. L. Mansel's *Limits of Religious Thought* that he included in his book on Hamilton: "Here, then, I take my stand on the acknowledged principle of logic and of morality, that when we mean different things we have no right to call them by the same name, and to apply to them the same predicates, moral and intellectual. Language has no meaning for the words Just, Merciful, Benevolent, save that in which we predicate them of our fellow-creatures; and unless that is what we intend to express by them, we have no business to employ the words. If in affirming them of God we do not mean to affirm these very qualities, differing only as greater in degree, we are neither philosophically nor morally entitled to affirm them at all. . . . If in ascribing goodness to God I do not mean what I mean by goodness; if I do not mean the goodness of which I have some knowledge, but an incomprehensible attribute of an incomprehensible substance, which for aught I know may be a totally different quality from that which I love and venerate — and even must, if Mr. Mansel is to be believed, be in some important

Mill maintained that no proposition in the *System of Logic* had been adopted by him for the sake of supporting any preconceived philosophy. Nevertheless, he concealed neither from himself nor from his readers what were the ultimate practical goals of his technical analyses. The historical significance of the work thus derives not only from the fact that it formulates systematically the logical credo of an influential philosophical school, but also from the fact that it served as an important instrument in the political and social struggles of the nineteenth century.

IV

The specific aim of the *System of Logic* was to present a general theory of proof. However, Mill rejected the traditionally influential view according to which the only general rules of logic are the principles of syllogistic or demonstrative reasoning. For he defined logic as the study of the intellectual operations that are instrumental to the evaluation of evidence. And while he recognized the important function of formal logic in this process of evaluation, he nevertheless believed that there is a "larger Logic,

particulars opposed to this — what do I mean by calling it goodness? and what reason have I for venerating it? If I know nothing about what the attribute is, I cannot tell that it is a proper object of veneration. To say that God's goodness may be different in kind from man's goodness, what is it but saying, with a slight change in phraseology, that God may possibly not be good? To assert in words what we do not think in meaning, is as suitable a definition as can be given of moral falsehood. . . . If, instead of the 'glad tidings' that there exists a Being in whom all the excellencies which the highest human mind can conceive, exist in a degree inconceivable to us, I am informed that the world is ruled by a being whose attributes are infinite, but what they are we cannot learn, nor what are the principles of his government, except that 'the highest human morality which we are capable of conceiving' does not sanction them; convince me of it, and I will bear my fate as I may. But when I am told I must believe this, and at the same time call this being by the names which express and affirm the highest human morality, I say in plain terms that I will not. Whatever power such a being may have over me, there is one thing which he shall not do: he shall not compel me to worship him. I will call no being good, who is not what I mean when I apply that epithet to my fellow-creatures; and if such a being can sentence me to hell for so calling him, to hell I will go" (*An Examination of Sir William Hamilton's Philosophy*, London, 1867, pp. 122–24).

which embraces all the general conditions of the ascertainment of truth," of which formal logic, "the smaller Logic, which only concerns itself with the conditions of consistency," is but a part.[10] In this conception of the scope of logic Mill had many predecessors; but in any event, his book became a primary stimulus to subsequent writers to identify logical theory with the analysis of scientific methods.

In spite of the ulterior social objectives which Mill frankly acknowledged as controlling the composition of the *Logic*, he claimed that logic is common ground upon which divergent schools of thought can join hands; and he maintained that most of the conclusions advanced in his treatise have no inherent connection with any special philosophy. Later writers, not committed to Mill's distinctive philosophic ideas, have indeed come to conclusions on detailed issues of scientific method which are not essentially different from his. Nevertheless, there can be little doubt that the "connected view of the principles of evidence and the methods of scientific investigation" he presented in his book is highly colored by the assumptions of Mill's philosophical heritage.

The chief emphasis of the *Logic* is upon the final authority of experience as the general warrant for beliefs, and upon the necessity for verifying propositions by observation of facts if futile speculation is to be avoided. The detailed discussions of special points contained in the book are simply analyses of methods by which the appeal to fact and experience can be made effective. However, this general insistence upon the role of observation and experience is not distinctive of Mill's position, and is one to which philosophies at serious variance with his have often subscribed. What is characteristic of Mill is his conception of what the *basic facts* are to which beliefs should be subjected for testing, and what are the essential requirements for the process of testing them. The theoretical grounds of logic, he explicitly argued, "are wholly borrowed from Psychology";[11] and it is the psychological assumptions of sensationalistic empiricism that are made to support the principles of evidence which emerge in the *Logic*.

[10] J. S. Mill, *An Examination of Sir William Hamilton's Philosophy*, London, 1867, p. 461.
[11] *Ibid.*, p. 445.

In this matter, Mill's point of departure is similar to that of Locke and Berkeley. "Of nature, or anything whatever external to ourselves," he declared in describing the central assumptions of his philosophy of experience, "we know . . . nothing, except the facts which present themselves to our senses, and such other facts as may, by analogy, be inferred from these. . . . Sensation, and the mind's consciousness of its own acts, are not only the exclusive sources, but the sole materials of our knowledge."[12] Accordingly, some things we come to know directly or by "consciousness" — these are our own bodily sensations and mental feelings; all else can be known only indirectly or through inference. Moreover, whatever thus falls into the "content of consciousness" and is therefore immediately intuited, is "known beyond possibility of question,"[13] even though we often err as to what it is we directly sense or feel. The facts upon which warranted beliefs must ultimately rest were thus assumed by Mill to be the indubitable but "subjective" data of direct awareness. And Mill's philosophy required him to show, in consequence, that these data do provide a necessary and sufficient *evidential* basis for all warranted propositions and principles — of the everyday view of things as well as of the most refined sciences, of mathematics as well as of physics, of formal logic as well as of the logic of induction.

But there is another crucial assumption that Mill made. As he saw it, there are two principal psychological systems, which he characterized as the aposteriori and the apriori schools. The chief difference between these schools, according to him, relates "not to the facts themselves, but to their origin. Speaking briefly and loosely, we may say that the one theory concedes the more complex phenomena of the mind to be products of experience, the other believes them to be original."[14] As a firm adherent of the aposteriori school, Mill was therefore committed to the task of tracing all beliefs and ideas back to their alleged *sources* in the indubitable data just described. And though in the *Logic* he was nominally occupied with constructing a general theory of *proof*, the consideration of the *origins* of ideas looms large in discussions ostensibly

---

[12] *Dissertations and Discussions*, Vol. I, p. 404.

[13] J. S. Mill, *A System of Logic*, London, 1879, Introduction, §4.

[14] *Dissertations and Discussions*, Vol. IV, p. 107.

devoted to questions of their validity. He does not always clearly disentangle issues that belong to empirical psychology from those that involve questions of logical warrant. And the predominantly psychological cast of Mill's account of the principles of evidence is a consequence of his assumption — with which his actual practice is, however, frequently at variance — that beliefs are warranted if they can be shown to have been derived from the data of sense and feeling.

These two assumptions, the assumption concerning the nature of indubitable data and the assumption concerning the need to investigate the origin of ideas, controlled in large measure the structure of Mill's thought. Though he frequently transcended them, they are the source of many of his difficulties and failures. The first assumption compelled him to reinterpret beliefs ostensibly about substantial things and unified minds so as to exhibit them as beliefs about series of independent sensations and feelings; and whatever success he may have had in accomplishing part of this task, he was burdened with problems (such as that of explaining how a mind that is no more than a series of feelings can nevertheless become conscious of its own unified totality) which he was not equipped to solve. The second assumption played havoc with his account of the principles of evidence, since quite clearly *all* beliefs, and not only true ones, have causes and antecedents; and Mill was able to escape complete intellectual shipwreck only by tacitly surrendering the principle of explaining validity in terms of origins. His acceptance of both assumptions helps to render more intelligible his account of the import of propositions, his doctrine of real kinds, his puritanical conception of mathematics, his psychological interpretation of the notion of necessity, his exaggerated claims for his rules of induction, as well as his strong conviction that analytic psychology must supply the ultimate premises for a science of society.

But however this may be, the fundamental principles upon which Mill relied for explaining the formation of the "complex phenomena of the mind" were the laws of the association of ideas he took over from Hartley and his own father. In the *Logic* he generally took for granted that the major ideas, beliefs, and principles operative in the ordinary affairs of life and in the sciences had already been constructed in accordance with these laws. But even in that work he makes repeated use of the laws of association in order to show that at no point in the development of the sciences is there need for admitting any "intuitive" or apriori principles. For it was part of his aim to exhibit not only the innumerable special conclusions of inquiry as merely "generalizations" derived from an "experience" construed in accordance with the postulates of associationist psychology, but to do this for the allegedly "necessary" principles of logic as well. Mill's philosophy required him to show that the ideas which the mind employed in organizing the flux of fugitive sensations and feelings were themselves the product of the laws of association working upon such elements of experience.

In particular, Mill rejected the view that the "laws of thought" — the principles of contradiction and excluded middle — are either inherent laws of the thinking faculty or analytical propositions whose truth is involved in the meaning of their terms. He maintained, on the contrary, that like other axioms these laws are "among our first and most familiar generalizations from experience." Thus, he saw the foundation for the principle of contradiction in the fact that

Belief and Disbelief are two different mental states, excluding one another. This we know by the simplest observations of our minds. And if we carry our observation outwards, we also find that light and darkness, sound and silence, motion and quiescence, equality and inequality, preceding and following, succession and simultaneousness, any positive phenomenon whatever and its negative, are distinct phenomena, pointedly contrasted, and the one always absent where the other is present. I consider the maxim in question to be a generalization from all these facts.[15]

And though he declared that the principle of excluded middle, far from being a necessity of thought, is not even true "unless with a large qualification" (since "between the true and the false there is a third possibility, the Unmeaning"), he quoted with emphatic approval Herbert Spencer's view that the principle "is simply a generalization of the universal experience that some mental states are directly destructive of other states."

[15] *A System of Logic*, Book II, Chapter VII, §5.

More generally, the criticism to which Mill was especially sensitive was the charge that his philosophy made the very possibility of science inexplicable. "It is affirmed," he noted, "that the doctrine of Locke, Hartley, and Bentham [leads to the view that] even science . . . loses the character of science . . . , and becomes empiricism; a mere enumeration and arrangement of facts, not explaining nor accounting for them: since a fact is only then accounted for, when we are made to see in it the manifestations of laws, which, as soon as they are perceived at all, are perceived to be *necessary*. . . ."[16] The conviction that the laws of science are in some sense "necessary" was part of the intellectual climate of the day, and Mill did not seriously question it. But he did think that this belief could be interpreted so as to be consonant with his own brand of empiricism. The idea of necessity, according to him, *is* explicable in terms of the laws of association:

. . . if there be any one feeling in our nature which the laws of association are obviously equal to producing, one would say it is that. Necessary, according to Kant's definition, and there is none better, is that of which negation is impossible. If we find it impossible, by any trial, to separate two ideas, we have all the feeling of necessity which the mind is capable of. Those, therefore, who deny that association can generate a necessity of thought, must be willing to affirm that two ideas are never so knit together by association as to be practically inseparable. But to affirm this is to contradict the most familiar experience of life. Many persons who have been frightened in childhood can never be alone in the dark without irrepressible terrors. Many a person is unable to revisit a particular place, or to think of a particular event, without recalling acute feelings of grief or reminiscences of suffering. If the facts which created these strong associations in individual minds, had been common to all mankind from their infancy, and had, when the associations were fully formed, been forgotten, we should have had a necessity of Thought — one of the necessities which are supposed to prove an objective law, and an *a priori* mental connexion between ideas. Now, in all the supposed natural beliefs and necessary conceptions which the principle of Inseparable Association is employed to explain, the generating causes of the association did begin nearly at the beginning of life, and are common either to all, or to a very large portion of mankind.[17]

---

[16] *Dissertations and Discussions*, Vol. I, p. 406.
[17] *Examination of Sir W. Hamilton's Philosophy*, pp. 318f.

The basic glue which held together Mill's world of atomic sensations and feelings was supplied by the laws of association.

The formation of the "complex phenomena of the mind" which Mill took for granted in the *Logic*, he attempted to outline in his book on Hamilton. He undertook to show in this latter work how, through the association of the primitive data of sensation and introspection, there were generated such distinctions as that between the subjective and the objective, the mental and the physical, the primary and the secondary qualities of matter, causality and coincidence, and between conception, judgment and reasoning. Given Mill's premises, the occurrence of these distinctions presented serious problems which he could not evade. He devoted much effort to explaining them, and was particularly concerned with the question how, if the ultimate materials of knowledge are private and subjective, it is nevertheless possible to achieve and justify the familiar belief in an independent external world of physical objects and alien minds. Mill's account of the external world as constituted out of permanent possibilities of sensation has turned out to be an influential contribution to epistemological discussion — it has been revived in recent years, and supported by more powerful tools of formal analysis than were available to him. But as is not uncommon with Mill, his proposed solution of the problem suffers from his confusing the question how men *acquire* the belief in an independent external world, with the quite different question as to what such a belief *means* and how it may be *warranted*. He resolved the former question in terms of associationist psychology. But he went on to maintain that the belief in permanent possibilities of sensation includes all that is essential in the belief in substance:

I believe that Calcutta exists, though I do not perceive it, and that it would still exist if every percipient inhabitant were suddenly to leave the place, or be struck dead. But when I analyse the belief, all I find in it is, that were these events to take place, the Permanent Possibility of Sensation which I call Calcutta would still remain; that if I were suddenly transported to the banks of the Hoogly, I should still have the sensations which, if now present, would lead me to affirm that Calcutta exists here and now.[18]

[18] *Ibid.*, p. 229.

This further account, however, is obviously not addressed to the issue concerning the origin of a belief, but to the problem of its meaning and warrant; and it is especially noteworthy that the discussion is carried on in terms of the *consequences* which the belief involves. Accordingly, Mill's analysis of the meaning and ground of the belief in an external world can be fitted into a theory of knowledge that is based on psychological premises quite different from his. And indeed, it was by building logical theory upon an analysis of beliefs in terms of their effects and consequences, rather than their causes and antecedents, that a foundation for a philosophy of experience was eventually laid which proved to be sturdier than the one constructed by Mill.

V

The *System of Logic* is an account of induction, "the operation of discovering and proving general propositions." For Mill held that every deductive inference is at bottom an inductive one; and accordingly, even his detailed discussions of formal reasoning and of the demonstrative sciences are subordinated to the analysis of inductive procedures.

The central position assigned to induction in Mill's logical theory is an easy corollary from the premises of his empiricism. It has already been noted that for Mill whatever falls outside the immediate "contents of consciousness" can be known only by inference. But a detailed discussion of the possible import of a proposition also discloses, so he maintains, that every proposition, except those "verbal" or "analytical" ones which merely unfold the meanings of their terms, asserts either simple existence, or relations of coexistence, sequence, resemblance, or causality between attributes. This list obviously does not contain the alternative that a proposition might affirm a relation of strict logical implication between things or existences. There must therefore be an empirical warrant for the mind's passage in inference from premise to conclusion. But the foundation for reasoning is not the definitional truth contained in the ancient *dictum de omni et nullo;* it is supplied by the experiential truth that "two things which constantly coexist with the same third thing, constantly coexist with one another." The real foundation for all inference is therefore the *nota notae est nota rei ipsius,* a mark of the mark is a mark of the thing itself. In brief, the inferences through which knowledge is extended beyond immediately apprehended sensations and feelings can only be inductive ones; and it is the supreme task of logic to make explicit the principles through which such extension of knowledge is achieved.

It was Mill's aim to achieve for induction what traditional logic accomplished for the syllogism: to formulate a set of abstract rules, analogous to the rules of the syllogism, with the aid of which inductive inferences could be tested and established. However, both his conception of his task as well as his execution of it were controlled by the cardinal assumption of his philosophy that an idea is shown to be valid when it is traced back to acceptable origins. In consequence, his discussion of inductive procedures frequently involve him in insuperable difficulties, simply because of his failure to distinguish uniformly between the problem of finding rules of *discovery* and the problem of finding general criteria of *validity.* He maintained, on the one hand, that "if discoveries are ever made by observation and experiment without Deduction, the four methods are methods of discovery." But he also believed that his methods are "rules and models (such as the Syllogism and its rules are for ratiocination), to which if inductive arguments conform, those arguments are conclusive, and not otherwise."[19] The consequences of this double claim were disastrous to the clarity of his exposition and to the adequacy of much of his analysis. His critics were quick to note, though Mill failed to appreciate the force of their objection, that without guiding ideas required for working the methods but not provided by them, the methods are helpless to advance an inquiry. On the other hand, it was also pointed out against him that once such guiding ideas have been found for analyzing the specific problems under investigation, perhaps the most essential step in the discovery of new truths has already been taken, so that it is not as rules of discovery that the experimental methods are useful.

Mill was nevertheless explicitly aware of the difference between inference as a *process* and inference as the warranted *product* of

[19] *A System of Logic,* Book III, Chapter IX, §6.

deliberately instituted controls and tests. Indeed, his famous defense of the syllogism against the charge of *petitio principii* was based squarely on this distinction. For as he pointed out in his criticism of Hamilton,

the syllogism is not the form in which we necessarily reason, but a test of reasoning: a form into which we may translate any reasoning, with the effect of exposing all the points at which any unwarranted inference can have got in.[20]

The actual process of reasoning is quite different from the fixed schemata into which propositions are thrown when we wish to establish the validity of that process. Every actual inference, so Mill maintained, is from particulars to particulars, a process in which from the fact that an object possesses certain attributes it is concluded that it possesses another attribute. The major premise of the syllogism is thus not a premise *from which* conclusions are actually drawn, but is a formula (serving as a convenient memorandum of previous coincidences of these attributes) *in accordance with which* inferences are made. Had Mill employed these distinctions in discussing the canons of induction, and had he analyzed the function of those canons in a manner consistent with his defense of the syllogism, he would have saved himself from much deserved criticism and would also have advanced the state of logical theory by several decades. For in his interpretation of the function of general propositions as *guiding principles* of inference, Mill was on the track of a fertile idea that eventually transformed the traditional foundations of empirical philosophy.

If Mill's canons of induction are conceived so as to bring them into line with his account of the syllogism, they must be regarded as attempts at formulating principles for *checking* the adequacy of scientific investigations into causal laws. Although they need to be seriously qualified in various ways beyond those recognized by Mill, they constitute important principles of criticism and evaluation. They are not the foundation for a new kind of logic which can be significantly contrasted with the logic of demonstration — an "inductive logic" in the sense in which Mill frequently envisaged such a subject has proved to be a barren and romantic dream.

[20] *Examination of Sir W. Hamilton's Philosophy*, p. 487.

But if there is any sense in which causal inquiries may be distinguished from one another on the ground of their relative reliabilities and adequacies, and if the task of inductive logic is to formulate criteria for making such distinctions, then Mill has contributed to such an undertaking. His canons of induction cannot be applied easily or in routine fashion to test the worth of particular investigations, chiefly because his formulations of the canons tacitly assume an ideal analysis of the evidence for inductive conclusions. Nonetheless, the canons state at least in part what is *meant* by an adequate proof in certain types of experimental inquiries; and though they must be supplemented by special factual assumptions whenever they are applied to concrete cases, they do call attention to considerations that are indispensable in evaluating much empirical evidence.

However, Mill did not fully realize that his canons of proof expressed a highly idealized conception of experimental inquiry. He was a child of his times, and accepted the then current Laplacian view that

the state of the whole universe at any instant . . . [is] the consequence of its state at the present instant; inasmuch that one who knew all the agents which exist at the present moment, their collocation in space, and all their properties, in other words, the laws of their agency, could predict the whole subsequent history of the universe. . . .[21]

He therefore assumed that it is in principle possible to establish with finality and complete logical assurance, on the basis of a relatively small number of experimental data, causal laws that state invariable and unconditional sequences of phenomena. This assumption is all but explicitly avowed by him in the question in which he poses what is for him the fundamental problem of induction: "Why is a single instance, in some cases, sufficient for a complete induction, while in others, myriads of concurring instances, without a single exception known or presumed, go such a very little way towards establishing an universal proposition?"[22] Every actual inference as a process in time may indeed be from particulars to particulars; but Mill nevertheless believed that the conclusion so

[21] *A System of Logic*, Book III, Chapter V, §8.
[22] *Ibid.*, Book III, Chapter III, §3.

established is in effect a general or universal one: "Whenever the evidence which we derive from observation of known cases justifies us in drawing an inference respecting even one unknown case, we should on the same evidence be justified in drawing a similar inference with respect to a whole class of cases. The inference either does not hold at all, or it holds in all cases of a certain description."[23]

Mill was hard put to it to square his confidence in the possibility of attaining inductive certitude with the remainder of his atomistic empiricism. His doctrine of real kinds, which were "not mere distinctions for convenience" but "radical distinctions in the things themselves," was one part of his answer to his fundamental problem of induction. The principle of uniformity of nature, which he believed was tacitly assumed in every inductive inference and which he claimed to be warranted by our observation of the actual course of nature, was another portion of his reply. The obvious circularity involved in taking for the "ultimate major premise" of all particular inductions a principle which itself was alleged to be simply an inductive generalization, became an easy target for Mill's critics. The criticism is telling against Mill, but mainly because, like most of those who made it, he supposed that in some cases at least the sciences do achieve complete and final certainty concerning the laws of nature. Mill did indeed acknowledge that because of the "plurality of causes and the intermixture of effects" only probable conclusions are frequently obtainable. But such conclusions did not represent for him science at its best; and the theory of chances was for him, as it had been for Laplace, ultimately only a makeshift.[24] Mill does not appear to have been intimately familiar with Hume's analysis of the grounds of inductive certitude, and on this point at any rate he was less subtle and less consistent than had been his intellectual ancestor.

Mill's examination of the methods appropriate to the social sciences constitute not only the concluding Book of the *Logic*, but also the *terminus ad quem* of what precedes it. He was too well acquainted with the complexities of social phenomena to permit himself to suppose that their causal interrelations might

---

[23] *Ibid.*, Book III, Chapter I, §1.

[24] Mill was a severe critic of the Laplacian ideas on probability in the first edition of his *Logic*, but withdrew the essentials of his criticism in later editions.

be unraveled with the help of his experimental canons alone. Some of the most valuable and illuminating chapters in the treatise are therefore devoted to discussions of ways in which inquiries may be conducted when a purely experimental approach is out of the question. His analyses of the conditions under which sciences can achieve the form of a deductive theory, of the nature and limits of explanation, and of the place of theory and verification in scientific inquiry — though they all bear the stigmata of assumptions and confusions inherent in his philosophy of experience — develop distinctions that have been incorporated into subsequent thought on logical questions.

The final Book of the *Logic* is in the main a summary of conclusions previously reached, applied to materials specific to the social sciences. The focus of Mill's attention in the central chapters of this Book is upon the issue raised by the controversy between his father and Macauley, and the "concrete deductive method" (which embodied his interpretation of the logic of the natural sciences) contains his recommendations for the procedure to be followed in political science. Mill hoped for many years to make substantial contributions to ethology, the unborn but heralded deductive science of the formation of character, which he believed would provide the proximate basis for all the social sciences. But nothing ever came of his intentions, a fact that is perhaps not surprising in the light of Mill's belief that the propositions of ethology must themselves be corollaries from the "laws of the mind" — that is, from the principles of his individualistic psychology. The material assumptions Mill accepted in his discussion of the social sciences do not appear to be well-grounded in the light of present knowledge. Nevertheless, in his tireless insistence that social "laws" do not represent reliable knowledge if such laws are supported simply by gross empirical correlations without being incorporated into a body of tested theory, he was voicing a lesson taught by centuries of scientific investigation.

VI

The extraordinary prestige which Mill's logical writings enjoyed during his lifetime did not long endure. A number of factors contributed to the diminution of their influence, factors some of which are extraneous to the intrinsic merits of Mill's analyses, while others are of a more relevant technical nature.

A philosophy which is an effective instrument for leveling obstacles in the path of a social class struggling to power, is not necessarily the best tool for justifying the domination of that class once power has been won. As it turned out, once a part of Mill's political program was realized, the industrial and mercantile groups who benefited most by it were not inclined to support the remainder; and they found better grounds than those contained in utilitarianism upon which to defend the exclusion of other claimants for political recognition. On the other hand, Mill's political and economic philosophy had little to offer to the under-privileged masses clamoring for social justice, and these turned to other intellectual supports for their claims. In brief, Mill's philosophy ceased to be the evangel of either the dominant or the submerged classes in the new society; and the theoretical under-pinning which Mill's *Logic* supplied for a once militant social outlook no longer appeared to be of great importance.

Moreover, Mill's writings, with their studied appeal to first principles and the weight of evidence, were effective with audiences disciplined in the art of rational controversy and sharing common assumptions concerning social goals. But with the advance of the nineteenth century, the relatively homogeneous cultural standards to which Mill could tacitly appeal in addressing his readers were gradually uprooted. New intellectual fashions came into being, some of which explicitly contemned rational analysis; and the extensive social re-alignments which were going on, brought into the area of political discussion audiences with sharply divergent social objectives. A logical theory that appeared to one generation as the expression of the height of rationality, came to be viewed by a later one as an anachronistic survival.

But there were more specifically pertinent doctrinal reasons for the decline of Mill's authority in logical matters. Among these, one of the most important was the impact of Darwinian ideas on both psychology and philosophy. Evolutionary theory directed attention toward the historical development of the mental functions as instruments in the struggle for survival, and away from the supposed formation of concepts in the individual mind out of allegedly primitive sensations and feelings. The individual mind came to be conceived neither as a substance nor as a passive recipient of impressions, but as a phase or mode of organic behavior, instrumental in adjusting the organism to its environment. According to then current evolutionary doctrines, the explanation for various alleged necessities of thought was to be found in the inherited experiences of the race, rather than in the principles of associationist psychology; for these principles were believed to offer what was at best only a conjectural reconstruction of the development of individual minds. Accordingly, success in coping with the environment was taken as the ultimate test for the validity of ideas, not conformity to some antecedently fixed standards of rationality. These are views and emphases that were foreign to Mill's logical theory, though there is doubtless no necessary incompatibility between the evolutionary stress upon genetic method and Mill's preoccupation with psychological origins. Nevertheless, the sense of illumination which many obtained from the evolutionary accounts of the nature of the intellectual faculties, also persuaded them that much of Mill's analysis was superficial and outmoded.

The fresh winds of thought introduced by evolutionary theory were strengthened at many points by influences originating in German philosophy. Kantian and Hegelian ideas gradually became acclimatized to British soil, and under their stimulus a new generation of thinkers subjected Mill's psychological apparatus to an impressive and devastating critique. The superior dialectic of Mill's new opponents (especially T. H. Green's and F. H. Bradley's, at Oxford) not only exposed many of the inadequacies of his associationist psychology; it also made evident the role of organizing principles in the systematization of knowledge which were not readily accounted for by Mill's sensationalistic phenomenalism. Moreover, an important revolt was taking place, in part inspired by Hegelian ideas, against the method and the conclusions of Ricardian economics, and significant intellectual victories were being scored over utilitarian ethical and political theory. The combined effect of these critical reactions was to weaken permanently Mill's hold both in various outstanding universities in

Britain and America, as well as upon men who were influential in public affairs.

Developments within formal logic, mathematics, and physics, also contributed to the undermining of Mill's authority, and to make many of his analyses rapidly obsolete. The modern renaissance of formal logic that began with DeMorgan and Boole, with whose work Mill was at least superficially familiar, made no serious impression upon him; at any rate, he failed to appreciate the transforming power of the newer investigations upon traditional logical doctrines. He mentions George Peacock, and he may therefore have been acquainted with the conception of mathematics, of which Peacock was a leading exponent, according to which demonstrative mathematics is a purely formal discipline whose theorems can be established independently of any particular interpretation that may be given to its axioms. But if Mill was familiar with this view, its significance for a general theory of proof was not recognized by him; and in consequence Mill's discussion of the demonstrative sciences involved assumptions concerning their foundations that were being successfully challenged by professional workers in the subject. In any case, the discovery of non-Euclidian geometries, the reconstruction of mathematical analysis by Weierstrass and others, and the reformulation of arithmetic as a chapter of formal logic, made it impossible before long to regard Mill's psychologized account of mathematics as anything but a hopeless and outdated oversimplification.

Within physics, also, changes were taking place that challenged many of Mill's assumptions concerning the structure of science. The development of the statistical view of nature during the second half of the nineteenth century cast doubt on his version of what constitutes the ideal of scientific investigation. Moreover, increasing use was being made of highly abstract mathematical devices in the construction of physical theory. And it became apparent even to those who were not professional students of the natural sciences that Mill's account of the formation of scientific concepts and of their mode of validation in no way clarified the actual practice of physicists. Whatever value his canons of experimental method possess at a certain level of scientific inquiry, they appear to have little relevance for testing the complex intellectual structures that theoretical physicists were submitting for consideration.

Nonetheless, though philosophical criticism and advances in positive knowledge have reduced Mill's prestige as a logician, the influence of his contributions to the philosophy of logic and scientific method has not vanished entirely. His hatred of obscurantism, his love of clarity, and his passionate devotion to carefully reasoned analysis, have won him admirers and emulators even among those who reject many of his specific assumptions and conclusions. For example, though William James possessed philosophical interests and loyalties foreign to those of Mill, and though his work in psychology did much to discredit the latter's atomistic sensationalism, he dedicated his *Pragmatism* to Mill's memory, with the inscription "From whom I first learned the pragmatic openness of mind and whom my fancy likes to picture as our leader were he alive." The method of philosophizing which Mill cultivated, and the over-all scientific and empirical temper of his writings, have proved to be congenial to many thinkers; and at a number of important seats of learning — for example, at the University of Cambridge, which was once a hotbed of philosophical radicalism — the general spirit of his approach has continued to flourish. It is, moreover, no inconsiderable achievement for any thinker to effect a basic change in the content of treatises and textbooks dealing with his subject. Mill's canons of experimental method are given a place in most of the larger works on logic that have appeared subsequently to his own. And though his account of the methods is often severely qualified, and is shorn of some of the claims he made for them, they are standard features of texts through which most beginning students in Anglo-American countries are introduced to logic. Nor must one ignore the fact that Mill's comprehensive view of logic as the systematic presentation of the principles of evidence has continued to inspire influential groups of contemporary writers on the subject. There are doubtless no perfect Millians alive today; but many influential thinkers are still actively engaged in achieving, though with the hope of being more adequate to the task than was Mill, that connected account of the principles of evidence he wished to render.

Mill's chapter on the composition of causes, contained in the

Third Book of the *Logic*, is the classic source of current doctrines of emergent evolution, and contains what is still one of the most sober and valuable analyses of the logical issues involved in the widespread notion of emergence. That chapter, moreover, contains one of the important grounds for Mill's conviction that both the natural and the social sciences are subject to the authority of a common logic. This contention has been vigorously attacked by many recent historians and sociologists, and the issue has created a fundamental cleavage in contemporary social science research. The specific arguments by which Mill supported his belief do not play a role in the current debate, even though the distinctions he developed in the chapter on the composition of causes are by no means irrelevant to the question. However, the liveliness of the present debate makes evident that while Mill did not finally dispose of the issues involved, he was at any rate grappling with a central problem of social science method, and that his own resolutions of them continue to animate a significant portion of professional workers in the field.

NOTE ON THE TEXT

The abridged text of *A System of Logic* contained in this volume is based on the eighth edition (New York, 1881) of that work, the last one to be revised by Mill for publication. The present version of the *Logic* omits the whole of the original Book V (*On Fallacies*), as well as many chapters, numbered sections, and paragraphs from other books. These omissions have been made for the sake of a more compact statement of Mill's doctrines than he gave them; but in the judgment of the editor only materials of subordinate interest have been excluded, and nothing essential for the understanding of Mill's thought has been eliminated. Mill's numbering of the sections included in this edition has also been altered, but the titles for them, which in the complete edition were given only in the Table of Contents, have now also been inserted in the text. The references given in brackets in the Table of Contents indicate the number of the Book, Chapter, or Section, respectively, of the complete work. Furthermore, in order to facilitate cross references between the present edition and the complete work, the original Table of Contents has been reprinted at the end of this edition. Here the asterisks indicate the parts omitted in the present edition, whereas the numerals in brackets refer to the number of that part of the work in the present edition. Deletions within numbered sections are indicated in the body of the text in the customary manner. Mill's punctuation has been modernized, and his spelling changed to accord with American usage.

The selections from *An Examination of Sir William Hamilton's Philosophy* are taken from the third edition (1867) of that work. They contain a fuller account than are supplied by Mill's other writings of his views on a number of central issues in the theory of knowledge. The analyses they contribute supplement in an important way what he has to say on related matters in his *Logic*.

"On the Definition of Political Economy; and on the Method of Investigation Proper to It" is the concluding chapter of his first book on economics, *Essays on Some Unsettled Questions of*

Political Economy. Although it contains a vigorous defense of the method of classical economics and one of the best statements of Mill's conception of the logic of social science, it is not easily accessible. It is reprinted here in its entirety from the first edition (1844) of that book.

SELECTED BIBLIOGRAPHY

MILL'S MAJOR WORKS

A System of Logic (1843).
Principles of Political Economy (1848).
Dissertations and Discussions (1859–75).
On Liberty (1859).
Considerations on Representative Government (1861).
Utilitarianism (1863).
An Examination of Sir William Hamilton's Philosophy (1865).
The Subjection of Women (1869).

Posthumously published:

Autobiography, edited by Helen Taylor (1873).
Nature, the Utility of Religion, Theism, Being Three Essays on
    Religion (1874).
On Social Freedom (1907).

COLLATERAL READING

Jackson, Reginald, *An Examination of the Deductive Logic of John
    Stuart Mill.* London, 1942.
Jevons, William Stanley, *Pure Logic, or, the Logic of Quality Apart
    from Quantity, With Remarks on Boole's System and on the
    Relation of Logic and Mathematics.* London 1864.
Neff, Emery E., *Carlyle and Mill: An Introduction to Victorian
    Thought.* New York, 1926.
Stephen, Leslie, *The English Utilitarians.* 3 vols. New York,
    1900.

A SYSTEM OF LOGIC

RATIOCINATIVE AND INDUCTIVE

Being a Connected View of

the Principles of Evidence and

the Methods of Scientific Investigation

EIGHTH EDITION

[*Abridged*]

PREFACE TO THE FIRST EDITION

This book makes no pretense of giving to the world a new theory of the intellectual operations. Its claim to attention, if it possess any, is grounded on the fact that it is an attempt, not to supersede, but to embody and systematize, the best ideas which have been either promulgated on its subject by speculative writers or conformed to by accurate thinkers in their scientific inquiries.

To cement together the detached fragments of a subject, never yet treated as a whole, to harmonize the true portions of discordant theories by supplying the links of thought necessary to connect them, and by disentangling them from the errors with which they are always more or less interwoven, must necessarily require a considerable amount of original speculation. To other originality than this the present work lays no claim. In the existing state of the cultivation of the sciences, there would be a very strong presumption against anyone who should imagine that he had effected a revolution in the theory of the investigation of truth or added any fundamentally new process to the practice of it. The improvement which remains to be effected in the methods of philosophizing (and the author believes that they have much need of improvement) can only consist in performing more systematically and accurately operations with which, at least in their elementary form, the human intellect, in some one or other of its employments, is already familiar.

In the portion of the work which treats of ratiocination, the author has not deemed it necessary to enter into technical details which may be obtained in so perfect a shape from the existing treatises on what is termed the logic of the schools. In the contempt entertained by many modern philosophers for the syllogistic art, it will be seen that he by no means participates, though the scientific theory on which its defense is usually rested appears to him erroneous; and the view which he has suggested of the nature and functions of the syllogism may, perhaps, afford the means of conciliating the principles of the art with as much as is well grounded in the doctrines and objections of its assailants.

3

The same abstinence from details could not be observed in the First Book, on Names and Propositions, because many useful principles and distinctions which were contained in the old logic have been gradually omitted from the writings of its later teachers, and it appeared desirable both to revive these and to reform and rationalize the philosophical foundation on which they stood. The earlier chapters of this preliminary Book will consequently appear, to some readers, needlessly elementary and scholastic. But those who know in what darkness the nature of our knowledge and of the processes by which it is obtained is often involved by a confused apprehension of the import of the different classes of words and assertions will not regard these discussions as either frivolous or irrelevant to the topics considered in the later Books.

On the subject of induction, the task to be performed was that of generalizing the modes of investigating truth and estimating evidence by which so many important and recondite laws of nature have, in the various sciences, been aggregated to the stock of human knowledge. That this is not a task free from difficulty may be presumed from the fact that, even at a very recent period, eminent writers (among whom it is sufficient to name Archbishop Whately, and the author of a celebrated article on Bacon in the *Edinburgh Review*) have not scrupled to pronounce it impossible.[1] The author has endeavored to combat their theory in the manner in which Diogenes confuted the skeptical reasonings against the possibility of motion, remembering that Diogenes's argument would have been equally conclusive though his individual perambulations might not have extended beyond the circuit of his own tub.

Whatever may be the value of what the author has succeeded in

[1] In the later editions of Archbishop Whately's *Logic*, he states his meaning to be, not that "rules" for the ascertainment of truths by inductive investigation cannot be laid down, or that they may not be "of eminent service," but that they "must always be comparatively vague and general, and incapable of being built up into a regular demonstrative theory like that of the Syllogism." (Book iv., ch. iv., § 3.) And he observes that to devise a system for this purpose, capable of being "brought into a scientific form," would be an achievement which "he must be more sanguine than scientific who expects." (Book iv., ch. ii., § 4.) To effect this, however, being the express object of the portion of the present work which treats of induction, the words in the text are no overstatement of the difference of opinion between Archbishop Whately and me on the subject.

effecting on this branch of his subject, it is a duty to acknowledge that for much of it he has been indebted to several important treatises, partly historical and partly philosophical, on the generalities and processes of physical science, which have been published within the last few years. To these treatises and to their authors, he has endeavored to do justice in the body of the work. But as with one of these writers, Dr. Whewell, he has occasion frequently to express differences of opinion, it is more particularly incumbent on him in this place to declare that, without the aid derived from the facts and ideas contained in that gentleman's *History of the Inductive Sciences*, the corresponding portion of this work would probably not have been written.

The concluding Book is an attempt to contribute toward the solution of a question which the decay of old opinions and the agitation that disturbs European society to its inmost depths render as important in the present day to the practical interests of human life as it must, at all times, be to the completeness of our speculative knowledge — *viz.*, whether moral and social phenomena are really exceptions to the general certainty and uniformity of the course of nature, and how far the methods by which so many of the laws of the physical world have been numbered among truths irrevocably acquired and universally assented to can be made instrumental to the formation of a similar body of received doctrine in moral and political science.

INTRODUCTION

1. *Is logic the art and science of reasoning?*

LOGIC has often been called the art of reasoning. A writer[2] who has done more than any other person to restore this study to the rank from which it had fallen in the estimation of the cultivated class in our own country has adopted the above definition with an amendment. He has defined logic to be the science, as well as the art, of reasoning, meaning by the former term the analysis of the mental process which takes place whenever we reason, and by the latter, the rules grounded on that analysis for conducting the process correctly. There can be no doubt as to the propriety of the emendation. A right understanding of the mental process itself, of the conditions it depends on, and the steps of which it consists, is the only basis on which a system of rules fitted for the direction of the process can possibly be founded. Art necessarily presupposes knowledge; art, in any but its infant state, presupposes scientific knowledge; and if every art does not bear the name of a science, it is only because several sciences are often necessary to form the groundwork of a single art. So complicated are the conditions which govern our practical agency that to enable one thing to be *done*, it is often requisite to *know* the nature and properties of many things.

Logic, then, comprises the science of reasoning, as well as an art founded on that science. But the word "reasoning," again, like most other scientific terms in popular use, abounds in ambiguities. In one of its acceptations, it means syllogizing, or the mode of inference which may be called (with sufficient accuracy for the present purpose) concluding from generals to particulars. In another of its senses, to reason is simply to infer any assertion from assertions already admitted; and in this sense induction is as much entitled to be called reasoning as the demonstrations of geometry.

Writers on logic have generally preferred the former acceptation

[2] Archbishop Whately.

of the term; the latter and more extensive signification is that in which I mean to use it. I do this by virtue of the right I claim for every author to give whatever provisional definition he pleases of his own subject. But sufficient reasons will, I believe, unfold themselves as we advance why this should be not only the provisional but the final definition. It involves, at all events, no arbitrary change in the meaning of the word, for, with the general usage of the English language, the wider signification, I believe, accords better than the more restricted one.

2. *Logic is concerned with inferences, not with intuitive truths.*

. . . .

Truths are known to us in two ways: some are known directly and of themselves; some through the medium of other truths. The former are the subject of intuition or consciousness,[3] the latter, of inference. The truths known by intuition are the original premises from which all others are inferred. Our assent to the conclusion being grounded on the truth of the premises, we never could arrive at any knowledge by reasoning unless something could be known antecedently to all reasoning.

Examples of truths known to us by immediate consciousness are our own bodily sensations and mental feelings. I know directly and of my own knowledge that I was vexed yesterday, or that I am hungry today. Examples of truths which we know only by way of inference are occurrences which took place while we were absent, the events recorded in history, or the theorems of mathematics. The two former we infer from the testimony adduced, or from the traces of those past occurrences which still exist; the latter, from the premises laid down in books of geometry under the title of definitions and axioms. Whatever we are capable of knowing must belong to the one class or to the other; must be in the number of the primitive data, or of the conclusions which can be drawn from these.

With the original data or ultimate premises of our knowledge,

[3] I use these terms indiscriminately because, for the purpose in view, there is no need for making any distinction between them. But metaphysicians usually restrict the name intuition to the direct knowledge we are supposed to have of things external to our minds, and consciousness to our knowledge of our own mental phenomena.

with their number or nature, the mode in which they are obtained, or the tests by which they may be distinguished, logic, in a direct way at least, has, in the sense in which I conceive the science, nothing to do. These questions are partly not a subject of science at all, partly that of a very different science.

Whatever is known to us by consciousness is known beyond possibility of question. What one sees or feels, whether bodily or mentally, one cannot but be sure that one sees or feels. No science is required for the purpose of establishing such truths; no rules of art can render our knowledge of them more certain than it is in itself. There is no logic for this portion of our knowledge.

But we may fancy that we see or feel what we, in reality, infer. A truth or supposed truth, which is really the result of a very rapid inference, may seem to be apprehended intuitively. It has long been agreed by thinkers of the most opposite schools that this mistake is actually made in so familiar an instance as that of the eyesight. There is nothing of which we appear to ourselves to be more directly conscious than the distance of an object from us. Yet it has long been ascertained that what is perceived by the eye is, at most, nothing more than a variously colored surface; that, when we fancy we see distance, all we really see is certain variations of apparent size and degrees of faintness of color; that our estimate of the object's distance from us is the result partly of a rapid inference from the muscular sensations accompanying the adjustment of the focal distance of the eye to objects unequally remote from us, and partly of a comparison (made with so much rapidity that we are unconscious of making it) between the size and color of the object as they appear at the time and the size and color of the same or of similar objects as they appeared when close at hand, or when their degree of remoteness was known by other evidence. The perception of distance by the eye, which seems so like intuition, is thus, in reality, an inference grounded on experience, an inference, too, which we learn to make, and which we make with more and more correctness as our experience increases, though in familiar cases it takes place so rapidly as to appear exactly on a par with those perceptions of sight which are really intuitive — our perceptions of color.[4]

[4] This important theory has, of late, been called in question by a writer of deserved reputation, Mr. Samuel Bailey; but I do not conceive that the grounds

Of the science, therefore, which expounds the operations of the human understanding in the pursuit of truth, one essential part is the inquiry: What are the facts which are the objects of intuition or consciousness, and what are those which we merely infer? But this inquiry has never been considered a portion of logic. Its place is in another and a perfectly distinct department of science to which the name metaphysics more particularly belongs: that portion of mental philosophy which attempts to determine what part of the furniture of the mind belongs to it originally, and what part is constructed out of materials furnished to it from without. To this science appertain the great and much debated questions of the existence of matter, the existence of spirit and of a distinction between it and matter, the reality of time and space as things without the mind and distinguishable from the objects which are said to exist *in* them. For, in the present state of the discussion on these topics, it is almost universally allowed that the existence of matter or of spirit, of space or of time, is in its nature unsusceptible of being proved, and that, if anything is known of them, it must be by immediate intuition. To the same science belong the inquiries into the nature of conception, perception, memory, and belief, all of which are operations of the understanding in the pursuit of truth, but with which, as phenomena of the mind, or with the possibility which may or may not exist of analyzing any of them into simpler phenomena, the logician as such has no concern. To this science must also be referred the following, and all analogous questions: to what extent our intellectual faculties and our emotions are innate — to what extent the result of association: whether God and duty are realities, the existence of which is manifest to us *a priori* by the constitution of our rational faculty; or whether our ideas of them are acquired notions, the origin of which we are able to trace and explain, and the reality of the objects themselves a question not of consciousness or intuition, but of evidence and reasoning.

The province of logic must be restricted to that portion of our

on which it has been admitted as an established doctrine for a century past have been at all shaken by that gentleman's objections. I have elsewhere said what appeared to me necessary in reply to his arguments (*Westminster Review* for October, 1842; reprinted in *Dissertations and Discussions*, Vol. II).

knowledge which consists of inferences from truths previously known, whether those antecedent data be general propositions or particular observations and perceptions. Logic is not the science of belief, but the science of *proof or evidence*. Insofar as belief professes to be founded on proof, the office of logic is to supply a test for ascertaining whether or not the belief is well grounded. With the claims which any proposition has to belief on the evidence of consciousness — that is, without evidence in the proper sense of the word — logic has nothing to do.

3. *Relation of logic to the other sciences*

By far the greatest portion of our knowledge, whether of general truths or of particular facts, being avowedly matter of inference, nearly the whole, not only of science but of human conduct, is amenable to the authority of logic. To draw inferences has been said to be the great business of life. Every one has daily, hourly, and momentary need of ascertaining facts which he has not directly observed, not from any general purpose of adding to his stock of knowledge but because the facts themselves are of importance to his interests or to his occupations. The business of the magistrate, of the military commander, of the navigator, of the physician, of the agriculturist is merely to judge of evidence and to act accordingly. They all have to ascertain certain facts in order that they may afterward apply certain rules, either devised by themselves or prescribed for their guidance by others; and, as they do this well or ill, so they discharge well or ill the duties of their several callings. It is the only occupation in which the mind never ceases to be engaged and is the subject, not of logic, but of knowledge in general.

Logic, however, is not the same thing with knowledge, though the field of logic is co-extensive with the field of knowledge. Logic is the common judge and arbiter of all particular investigations. It does not undertake to find evidence, but to determine whether it has been found. Logic neither observes nor invents nor discovers, but judges. It is no part of the business of logic to inform the surgeon what appearances are found to accompany a violent death. This he must learn from his own experience and observation, or from that of others, his predecessors in his peculiar pursuit. But logic sits in judgment on the sufficiency of that observation and experience to justify his rules and on the sufficiency of his rules to justify his conduct. It does not give him proofs, but teaches him what makes them proofs and how he is to judge of them. It does not teach that any particular fact proves any other, but points out to what conditions all facts must conform in order that they may prove other facts. To decide whether any given fact fulfills these conditions or whether facts can be found which fulfill them in a given case belongs exclusively to the particular art or science, or to our knowledge of the particular subject.

It is in this sense that logic is what it was so expressively called by the schoolmen and by Bacon, *ars artium*, the science of science itself. All science consists of data and conclusions from those data, of proofs and what they prove; now logic points out what relations must subsist between data and whatever can be concluded from them, between proof and everything which it can prove. If there be any such indispensable relations, and if these can be precisely determined, every particular branch of science, as well as every individual in the guidance of his conduct, is bound to conform to those relations, under the penalty of making false inferences — of drawing conclusions which are not grounded in the realities of things. Whatever has at any time been concluded justly, whatever knowledge has been acquired otherwise than by immediate intuition, depended on the observance of the laws which it is the province of logic to investigate. If the conclusions are just and the knowledge real, those laws, whether known or not, have been observed.

BOOK I

Of Names and Propositions

"La scolastique, qui produisit dans la logique, comme dans la morale, et dans une partie de la métaphysique, une subtilité, une précision d'idées, dont l'habitude inconnue aux anciens, a contribué plus qu'on ne croit au progrès de la bonne philosophie." — CONDORCET, *Vie de Turgot.*

"To the schoolmen the vulgar languages are principally indebted for what precision and analytic subtlety they possess." — SIR W. HAMILTON, *Discussions in Philosophy.*

CHAPTER I

OF THE NECESSITY OF COMMENCING WITH AN ANALYSIS OF LANGUAGE

1. *Theory of names, why a necessary part of logic*

IT is so much the established practice of writers on logic to commence their treatises by a few general observations (in most cases, it is true, rather meagre) on terms and their varieties, that it will, perhaps, scarcely be required from me, in merely following the common usage, to be as particular in assigning my reasons as it is usually expected that those should be who deviate from it.

The practice, indeed, is recommended by considerations far too obvious to require a formal justification. Logic is a portion of the art of thinking; language is evidently, and by the admission of all philosophers, one of the principal instruments or helps of thought; and any imperfection in the instrument or in the mode of employing it is confessedly liable, still more than in almost any other art, to confuse and impede the process and destroy all ground of confidence in the result. For a mind not previously versed in the meaning and right use of the various kinds of words to attempt the study of methods of philosophizing would be as if someone should attempt to become an astronomical observer, having never learned to adjust the focal distance of his optical instruments so as to see distinctly.

Since reasoning or inference, the principal subject of logic, is an operation which usually takes place by means of words, and, in complicated cases, can take place in no other way, those who have not a thorough insight into the signification and purposes of words will be under chances, amounting almost to certainty, of reasoning or inferring incorrectly. And logicians have generally felt that unless, in the very first stage, they removed this source of error, unless they taught their pupil to put away the glasses which distort the object and to use those which are adapted to his purpose in such a manner as to assist, not perplex, his vision, he would not be in a condition to practice the remaining part of their discipline with any prospect of advantage. Therefore it is that an inquiry into language, so far as is needful to guard against the errors to which it gives rise, has at all times been deemed a necessary preliminary to the study of logic.

But there is another reason, of a still more fundamental nature, why the import of words should be the earliest subject of the logician's consideration because without it he cannot examine into the import of propositions. Now this is a subject which stands on the very threshold of the science of logic.

The object of logic, as defined in the introductory chapter, is to ascertain how we come by that portion of our knowledge (much the greatest portion) which is not intuitive, and by what criterion we can, in matters not self-evident, distinguish between things proved and things not proved, between what is worthy and what is unworthy of belief. Of the various questions which present themselves to our inquiring faculties, some receive an answer from direct consciousness; others, if resolved at all, can only be resolved by means of evidence. Logic is concerned with these last. But before inquiring into the mode of resolving questions, it is necessary to inquire what are those which offer themselves, what questions are conceivable, what inquiries are there, to which mankind have either obtained or been able to imagine it possible that they should obtain, an answer. This point is best ascertained by a survey and analysis of propositions.

2. *First step in the analysis of Propositions*

The answer to every question which it is possible to frame, must be contained in a proposition or assertion. Whatever can be an object of belief or even of disbelief must, when put into words, assume the form of a proposition. All truth and all error lie propositions. What, by a convenient misapplication of an abstract term we call truth, means simply a true proposition; and errors are false propositions. To know the import of all possible propositions would be to know all questions which can be raised, all matters which are suspectible of being either believed or disbelieved. How many kinds of inquiries can be propounded, how many kinds of judgments can be made, and how many kinds of propositions is it possible to frame with a meaning, are but different forms of one and the same question. Since then the objects of all belief and of all inquiry express themselves in propositions, a sufficient scrutiny of propositions and of their varieties will apprise us what questions mankind have actually asked themselves, and what, in the nature of answers to those questions, they have actually thought they had grounds to believe.

Now the first glance at a proposition shows that it is formed by putting together two names. A proposition, according to the common simple definition which is sufficient for our purpose, is *discourse in which something is affirmed or denied of something....*

Every proposition consists of three parts, the subject, the predicate, and the copula. The predicate is the name denoting that which is affirmed or denied. The subject is the name denoting the person or thing which something is affirmed or denied of. The copula is the sign denoting that there is an affirmation or denial, and thereby enabling the hearer or reader to distinguish a proposition from any other kind of discourse. . . .

Dismissing for the present the copula, of which more will be said hereafter, every proposition, then, consists of at least two names, brings together two names in a particular manner. This is already a first step towards what we are in quest of. It appears from this that for an act of belief *one* object is not sufficient; the simplest act of belief supposes, and has something to do with *two* objects, two names to say the least, and (since the names must be names of something) two *nameable things*. A large class of

thinkers would cut the matter short by saying two *ideas*. . . .
But this we are not yet in a condition to say; whether such be the
correct mode of describing the phenomenon is an after-consider-
ation. The result with which for the present we must be contented
is that in every act of belief *two* objects are in some manner taken
cognizance of, that there can be no belief claimed or question
propounded which does not embrace two distinct (either material
or intellectual) subjects of things, each of them capable or not of
being conceived by itself but incapable of being believed by itself.

. . . .

CHAPTER II

OF NAMES

1. *Names are names of things, not of our ideas*

"A name," says Hobbes,[1] "is a word taken at pleasure to serve
for a mark which may raise in our mind a thought like to some
thought we had before, and which, being pronounced to others,
may be to them a sign of what thought the speaker had[2] before
in his mind." This simple definition of a name as a word (or set
of words) serving the double purpose of a mark to recall to ourselves the likeness of a former thought and a sign to make it known
to others appears unexceptionable. Names, indeed, do much more
than this, but whatever else they do grows out of and is the result
of this, as will appear in its proper place.

Are names more properly said to be the names of things or of
our ideas of things? The first is the expression in common use;
the last is that of some metaphysicians who conceived that, in
adopting it, they were introducing a highly important distinction.

[1] *Computation or Logic*, chap. II.

[2] In the original "had, *or had not.*" These last words, as involving a subtlety
foreign to our present purpose, I have forborne to quote.

The eminent thinker just quoted seems to countenance the latter opinion. "But seeing," he continues, "names ordered in speech (as is defined) are signs of our conceptions, it is manifest they are not signs of the things themselves; for that the sound of this word *stone* should be the sign of a stone cannot be understood in any sense but this, that he that hears it collects that he that pronounces it thinks of a stone."

If it be merely meant that the conception alone, and not the thing itself, is recalled by the name or imparted to the hearer, this of course cannot be denied. Nevertheless there seems good reason for adhering to the common usage, and calling (as indeed Hobbes himself does in other places) the word *sun* the name of the sun and not the name of our idea of the sun. For names are not intended only to make the hearer conceive what we conceive, but also to inform him what we believe. Now, when I use a name for the purpose of expressing a belief, it is a belief concerning the thing itself, not concerning my idea of it. When I say, "the sun is the cause of day," I do not mean that my idea of the sun causes or excites in me the idea of day, or, in other words, that thinking of the sun makes me think of day. I mean that a certain physical fact, which is called the sun's presence (and which, in the ultimate analysis, resolves itself into sensations, not ideas), causes another physical fact, which is called day. It seems proper to consider a word as the *name* of that which we intend to be understood by it when we use it; of that which any fact that we assert of it is to be understood of; that, in short, concerning which, when we employ the word, we intend to give information. Names, therefore, shall always be spoken of in this work as the names of things themselves and not merely of our ideas of things.

But the question now arises, of what things? To answer this it is necessary to take into consideration the different kinds of names.

2. *Words which are not names, but parts of names*

It is usual, before examining the various classes into which names are commonly divided, to begin by distinguishing from names of every description those words which are not names but only parts of names. Among such are reckoned particles, as *of, to, truly, often;* the inflected cases of nouns substantive, as *me, him, John's;* and even adjectives, as *large, heavy.* These words do not express things of which anything can be affirmed or denied. We cannot say, "Heavy fell," or "A heavy fell"; "Truly," or "A truly was asserted"; "Of," or "An of was in the room." Unless, indeed, we are speaking of the mere words themselves, as when we say, "Truly is an English word," or, "Heavy is an adjective." In that case they are complete names — *viz.,* names of those particular sounds, or of those particular collections of written characters. This employment of a word to denote the mere letters and syllables of which it is composed was termed by the schoolmen the *suppositio materialis* of the word. In any other sense we cannot introduce one of these words into the subject of a proposition, unless in combination with other words, as "A heavy *body* fell," "A truly *important fact* was asserted"; "A *member* of *parliament* was in the room."

An adjective, however, is capable of standing by itself as the predicate of a proposition, as when we say, "Snow is white"; and occasionally even as the subject, for we may say, "White is an agreeable color." The adjective is often said to be so used by a grammatical ellipsis: "Snow is white," instead of "Snow is a white object"; "White is an agreeable color," instead of, "A white color," or, "The color white is agreeable." The Greeks and Romans were allowed, by the rules of their language, to employ this ellipsis universally in the subject as well as in the predicate of a proposition. In English this cannot, generally speaking, be done. We may say, "The earth is round," but we cannot say, "Round is easily moved"; we must say, "A round object." This distinction, however, is rather grammatical than logical. Since there is no difference of meaning between *round* and *a round object,* it is only custom which prescribes that, on any given occasion, one shall be used and not the other. We shall, therefore, without scruple, speak of adjectives as names, whether in their own right or as representative of the more circuitous forms of expression above exemplified. The other classes of subsidiary words have no title whatever to be considered as names. An adverb or an accusative case cannot, under any circumstances (except when their mere letters and syllables are spoken of), figure as one of the terms of a proposition.

Words which are not capable of being used as names, but only

as parts of names, were called by some of the schoolmen syncategorematic terms: from σὺν, with, and κατηγορέω, to predicate,
because it was only *with* some other word that they could be
predicated. A word which could be used either as the subject or
predicate of a proposition without being accompanied by any other
word was termed by the same authorities a categorematic term.
A combination of one or more categorematic and one or more
syncategorematic words, as "a heavy body," or "a court of justice,"
they sometimes called a *mixed* term, but this seems a needless
multiplication of technical expressions. A mixed term is, in the
only useful sense of the word, categorematic. It belongs to the
class of what have been called many-worded names.

For, as one word is frequently not a name but only part of a
name, so a number of words often compose one single name and
no more. These words, "The place which the wisdom or policy of
antiquity had destined for the residence of the Abyssinian princes,"
form, in the estimation of the logician, only one name, one categorematic term. A mode of determining whether any set of words
makes only one name or more than one is by predicating something
of it, and observing whether, by this predication, we make only
one assertion or several. Thus, when we say, "John Nokes, who
was the mayor of the town, died yesterday," by this predication
we make but one assertion, whence it appears that "John Nokes,
who was the mayor of the town," is no more than one name. It is
true that, in this proposition, besides the assertion that John Nokes
died yesterday there is included another assertion, namely, that
John Nokes was mayor of the town. But this last assertion was
already made; we did not make it by adding the predicate "died
yesterday." Suppose, however, that the words had been, "John
Nokes *and* the mayor of the town," they would have formed two
names instead of one. For when we say, "John Nokes and the
mayor of the town died yesterday," we make two assertions: one,
that John Nokes died yesterday; the other, that the mayor of the
town died yesterday.

It being needless to illustrate at any greater length the subject of
many-worded names, we proceed to the distinctions which have
been established among names, not according to the words they
are composed of, but according to their signification.

3. *General and singular names*

All names are names of something, real or imaginary, but all things have not names appropriated to them individually. For some individual objects we require and, consequently, have separate distinguishing names; there is a name for every person and for every remarkable place. Other objects of which we have not occasion to speak so frequently we do not designate by names of their own; but when the necessity arises for naming them, we do so by putting together several words, each of which, by itself, might be and is used for an indefinite number of other objects, as when I say, "this stone": "this" and "stone" being, each of them, names that may be used of many other objects besides the particular one meant, though the only object of which they can both be used at the given moment, consistently with their signification, may be the one of which I wish to speak.

Were this the sole purpose for which names that are common to more things than one could be employed, if they only served, by mutually limiting each other, to afford a designation for such individual objects as have no names of their own, they could only be ranked among contrivances for economizing the use of language. But it is evident that this is not their sole function. It is by their means that we are enabled to assert *general* propositions, to affirm or deny any predicate of an indefinite number of things at once. The distinction, therefore, between *general* names and *individual* or *singular* names is fundamental, and may be considered as the first grand division of names.

A general name is, familiarly defined, a name which is capable of being truly affirmed, in the same sense, of each of an indefinite number of things. An individual or singular name is a name which is only capable of being truly affirmed, in the same sense, of one thing.

Thus, *man* is capable of being truly affirmed of John, George, Mary, and other persons without assignable limit, and it is affirmed of all of them in the same sense, for the word "man" expresses certain qualities, and when we predicate it of those persons, we assert that they all possess those qualities. But *John* is only capable of being truly affirmed of one single person, at least in the same sense. For, though there are many persons who bear that name, it is not conferred upon them to indicate any qualities or any thing which belongs to them in common, and cannot be said to be affirmed of them in any *sense* at all, consequently not in the same sense. "The king who succeeded William the Conqueror" is also an individual name. For that there cannot be more than one person of whom it can be truly affirmed is implied in the meaning of the words. Even "*the* king," when the occasion or the context defines the individual of whom it is to be understood, may justly be regarded as an individual name.

It is not unusual, by way of explaining what is meant by a general name, to say that it is the name of a *class*. But this, though a convenient mode of expression for some purposes, is objectionable as a definition since it explains the clearer of two things by the more obscure. It would be more logical to reverse the proposition and turn it into a definition of the word *class*: "A class is the indefinite multitude of individuals denoted by a general name."

It is necessary to distinguish *general* from *collective* names. A general name is one which can be predicated of *each* individual of a multitude; a collective name cannot be predicated of each separately, but only of all taken together. "The seventy-sixth regiment of foot in the British army," which is a collective name, is not a general but an individual name, for though it can be predicated of a multitude of individual soldiers taken jointly, it cannot be predicated of them severally. We may say, "Jones is a soldier, and Thompson is a soldier, and Smith is a soldier," but we cannot say, "Jones is the seventy-sixth regiment, and Thompson is the seventy-sixth regiment, and Smith is the seventy-sixth regiment." We can only say, "Jones, and Thompson, and Smith, and Brown, and so forth (enumerating all the soldiers) are the seventy-sixth regiment."

"The seventy-sixth regiment" is a collective name, but not a general one; "a regiment" is both a collective and a general name — general with respect to all individual regiments of each of which separately it can be affirmed, collective with respect to the individual soldiers of whom any regiment is composed.

4. *Concrete and abstract*

The second general division of names is into *concrete* and *abstract*. A concrete name is a name which stands for a thing; an abstract name is a name which stands for an attribute of a thing. Thus *John, the sea, this table* are names of things. *White*, also, is a name of a thing, or rather of things. Whiteness, again, is the name of a quality or attribute of those things. Man is a name of many things; humanity is a name of an attribute of those things. *Old* is a name of things; *old age* is a name of one of their attributes.

I have used the words concrete and abstract in the sense annexed to them by the schoolmen who, notwithstanding the imperfections of their philosophy, were unrivaled in the construction of technical language and whose definitions, in logic at least, though they never went more than a little way into the subject, have seldom, I think, been altered but to be spoiled. A practice, however, has grown up in more modern times which, if not introduced by Locke, has gained currency chiefly from his example, of applying the expression "abstract name" to all names which are the result of abstraction or generalization, and consequently to all general names, instead of confining it to the names of attributes. The metaphysicians of the Condillac school — whose admiration of Locke, passing over the profoundest speculations of that truly original genius, usually fastens with peculiar eagerness upon his weakest points — have gone on imitating him in this abuse of language until there is now some difficulty in restoring the word to its original signification. A more wanton alteration in the meaning of a word is rarely to be met with; for the expression *general name*, the exact equivalent of which exists in all languages I am acquainted with, was already available for the purpose to which *abstract* has been misappropriated, while the misappropriation leaves that important class of words, the names of attributes, without any compact distinctive appellation. The old acceptation, however, has not gone so completely out of use as to deprive those who still adhere to it of all chance of being understood. By *abstract*, then, I shall always, in logic proper, mean the opposite of *concrete;* by an abstract name, the name of an attribute; by a concrete name, the name of an object.

Do abstract names belong to the class of general or to that of singular names? Some of them are certainly general. I mean those which are names not of one single and definite attribute but of a class of attributes. Such is the word *color*, which is a name common to whiteness, redness, etc. Such is even the word *whiteness*, in respect of the different shades of whiteness to which it is applied in common; the word *magnitude*, in respect of the various degrees of magnitude and the various dimensions of space; the word *weight*, in respect of the various degrees of weight. Such also is the word *attribute* itself, the common name of all particular attributes. But when only one attribute, neither variable in degree nor in kind, is designated by the name — as visibleness, tangibleness, equality, squareness, milk-whiteness — then the name can hardly be considered general; for though it denotes an attribute of many different objects, the attribute itself is always conceived as one, not many. To avoid needless logomachies, the best course would probably be to consider these names as neither general nor individual, and to place them in a class apart.

It may be objected to our definition of an abstract name that not only the names which we have called abstract, but adjectives which we have placed in the concrete class, are names of attributes; that *white*, for example, is as much the name of the color as *whiteness* is. But (as before remarked) a word ought to be considered as the name of that which we intend to be understood by it when we put it to its principal use, that is, when we employ it in predication. When we say "snow is white," "milk is white," "linen is white," we do not mean it to be understood that snow or linen or milk is a color. We mean that they are things having the color. The reverse is the case with the word *whiteness*; what we affirm to *be* whiteness is not snow but the color of snow. Whiteness, therefore, is the name of the color exclusively, white is a name of all things whatever having the color, a name, not of the quality whiteness, but of every white object. It is true, this name was given to all those various objects on account of the quality, and we may therefore say, without impropriety, that the quality forms part of its signification; but a name can only be said to stand for, or to be a name of, the things of which it can be predicated. We shall presently see that all names which can be said to have any signification, all names by applying which to an individual we give any information respecting that individual, may be said to *imply* an attribute of some sort, but they are not names of the attribute; it has its own proper abstract name.

5. *Connotative and non-connotative*

This leads to the consideration of a third great division of names, into *connotative* and *non-connotative*, the latter sometimes, but improperly, called *absolute*. This is one of the most important distinctions which we shall have occasion to point out and one of those which go deepest into the nature of language.

A non-connotative term is one which signifies a subject only, or an attribute only. A connotative term is one which denotes a subject and implies an attribute. By a subject is here meant anything which possesses attributes. Thus John, or London, or England are names which signify a subject only. Whiteness, length, virtue, signify an attribute only. None of these names, therefore, are connotative. But *white, long, virtuous*, are connotative. The word *white* denotes all white things, as snow, paper, the foam of the sea, etc., and implies, or in the language of the schoolmen, *connotes*,[3] the attribute *whiteness*. The word *white* is not predicated of the attribute, but of the subjects, snow, etc.; but when we predicate it of them, we convey the meaning that the attribute whiteness belongs to them. The same may be said of the other words above cited. Virtuous, for example, is the name of a class which includes Socrates, Howard, the Man of Ross, and an undefinable number of other individuals, past, present, and to come. These individuals, collectively and severally, can alone be said with propriety to be denoted by the word; of them alone can it properly be said to be a name. But it is a name applied to all of them in consequence of an attribute which they are supposed to possess in common, the attribute which has received the name of virtue. It is applied to all beings that are considered to possess this attribute, and to none which are not so considered.

All concrete general names are connotative. The word *man*, for example, denotes Peter, Jane, John, and an indefinite number of other individuals of whom, taken as a class, it is the name. But

---

[3]*Notare*, to mark; *connotare*, to mark *along with;* to mark one thing *with* or *in addition to* another.

it is applied to them because they possess, and to signify that they possess, certain attributes. These seem to be corporeity, animal life, rationality, and a certain external form which, for distinction, we call the human. Every existing thing which possessed all these attributes would be called a man; and anything which possessed none of them, or only one, or two, or even three of them without the fourth, would not be so called. For example, if in the interior of Africa there were to be discovered a race of animals possessing reason equal to that of human beings but with the form of an elephant, they would not be called men. Swift's Houyhnhnms would not be so called. Or if such newly-discovered beings possessed the form of man without any vestige of reason, it is probable that some other name than that of man would be found for them. How it happens that there can be any doubt about the matter will appear hereafter. The word *man*, therefore, signifies all these attributes and all subjects which possess these attributes. But it can be predicated only of the subjects. What we call men are the subjects, the individual Stiles and Nokes, not the qualities by which their humanity is constituted. The name, therefore, is said to signify the subjects *directly*, the attributes *indirectly;* it *denotes* the subjects, and implies, or involves, or indicates, or, as we shall say henceforth, *connotes*, the attributes. It is a connotative name.

Connotative names have hence been also called *denominative*, because the subject which they denote is denominated by, or receives a name from, the attribute which they connote. Snow and other objects receive the name white because they possess the attribute which is called whiteness; Peter, James, and others receive the name man because they possess the attributes which are considered to constitute humanity. The attribute, or attributes, may, therefore, be said to denominate those objects or to give them a common name.[4]

It has been seen that all concrete general names are connotative.

[4]Archbishop Whately, who, in the later editions of his *Elements of Logic*, aided in reviving the important distinction treated of in the text, proposes the term "attributive" as a substitute for "connotative" (p. 22, 9th ed.). The expression is, in itself, appropriate; but as it has not the advantage of being connected with any verb of so markedly distinctive a character as "to connote," it is not, I think, fitted to supply the place of the word connotative in scientific use.

Even abstract names, though the names only of attributes, may, in some instances, be justly considered as connotative; for attributes themselves may have attributes ascribed to them, and a word which denotes attributes may connote an attribute of those attributes. Of this description, for example, is such a word as *fault*, equivalent to *bad* or *hurtful quality*. This word is a name common to many attributes and connotes hurtfulness, an attribute of those various attributes. When, for example, we say that slowness in a horse is a fault, we do not mean that the slow movement, the actual change of place of the slow horse, is a bad thing, but that the property or peculiarity of the horse, from which it derives that name, the quality of being a slow mover, is an undesirable peculiarity.

In regard to those concrete names which are not general but individual, a distinction must be made.

Proper names are not connotative; they denote the individuals who are called by them, but they do not indicate or imply any attributes as belonging to those individuals. When we name a child by the name Paul or a dog by the name Caesar, these names are simply marks used to enable those individuals to be made subjects of discourse. It may be said, indeed, that we must have had some reason for giving them those names rather than any others, and this is true, but the name, once given, is independent of the reason. A man may have been named John because that was the name of his father; a town may have been named Dartmouth because it is situated at the mouth of the Dart. But it is no part of the signification of the word John that the father of the person so called bore the same name, nor even of the word Dartmouth to be situated at the mouth of the Dart. If sand should choke up the mouth of the river or an earthquake change its course and remove it to a distance from the town, the name of the town would not necessarily be changed. That fact, therefore, can form no part of the signification of the word; for otherwise, when the fact confessedly ceased to be true, no one would any longer think of applying the name. Proper names are attached to the objects themselves and are not dependent on the continuance of any attribute of the object.

But there is another kind of names, which, although they are individual names — that is, predicable only of one object — are really connotative. For, though we may give to an individual a name utterly unmeaning, unmeaningful which we call a proper name — a word which answers the purpose of showing what thing it is we are talking about, but not of telling anything about it; yet a name peculiar to an individual is not necessarily of this description. It may be significant of some attribute or some union of attributes which, being possessed by no object but one, determines the name exclusively to that individual. "The sun" is a name of this description; "God," when used by a monotheist, is another. These, however, are scarcely examples of what we are now attempting to illustrate, being, in strictness of language, general, not individual names, for, however they may be *in fact* predicable only of one object, there is nothing in the meaning of the words themselves which implies this; and, accordingly, when we are imagining and not affirming, we may speak of many suns; and the majority of mankind have believed, and still believe, that there are many gods. But it is easy to produce words which are real instances of connotative individual names. It may be part of the meaning of the connotative name itself, that there can exist but one individual possessing the attribute which it connotes, as, for instance, "the *only* son of John Stiles"; "the *first* emperor of Rome." Or the attribute connoted may be a connection with some determinate event, and the connection may be of such a kind as only one individual could have, or may, at least, be such as only one individual actually had, and this may be implied in the form of the expression. "The father of Socrates" is an example of the one kind (since Socrates could not have had two fathers), "the author of the Iliad," "the murderer of Henri Quatre," of the second. For, though it is conceivable that more persons than one might have participated in the authorship of the Iliad or in the murder of Henri Quatre, the employment of the article *the* implies that, in fact, this was not the case. What is here done by the word *the* is done in other cases by the context; thus, "Caesar's army" is an individual name if it appears from the context that the army meant is that which Caesar commanded in a particular battle. The still more general expressions, "the Roman army," or "the Christian army," may be individualized in a similar manner. Another case

of frequent occurrence has already been noticed; it is the following:
The name, being a many-worded one, may consist, in the first
place, of a *general* name, capable therefore, in itself, of being
affirmed of more things than one, but which is, in the second place,
so limited by other words joined with it that the entire expression
can only be predicated of one object, consistently with the meaning
of the general term. This is exemplified in such an instance as the
following: "the present prime minister of England." "Prime
Minister of England" is a general name; the attributes which it
connotes may be possessed by an indefinite number of persons, in
succession, however, not simultaneously, since the meaning of the
name itself imports (among other things) that there can be only
one such person at a time. This being the case, and the application
of the name being afterward limited, by the article and the word
present, to such individuals as possess the attributes at one indivis-
ible point of time, it becomes applicable only to one individual.
And, as this appears from the meaning of the name without any
extrinsic proof, it is strictly an individual name.

From the preceding observations it will easily be collected that
whenever the names given to objects convey any information —
that is, whenever they have properly any meaning — the meaning
resides not in what they *denote* but in what they *connote*. The
only names of objects which connote nothing are *proper* names,
and these have, strictly speaking, no signification.[5]

If, like the robber in the Arabian Nights, we make a mark with
chalk on a house to enable us to know it again, the mark has a
purpose, but it has not properly any meaning. The chalk does not
declare anything about the house; it does not mean, "This is such

---

[5] A writer who entitles his book *Philosophy; or, the Science of Truth*, charges
me in his very first page (referring at the foot of it to this passage) with asserting that *general* names have properly no signification. And he repeats this
statement many times in the course of his volume, with comments, not at all
flattering, thereon. It is well to be now and then reminded to how great a
length perverse misquotation (for, strange as it appears, I do not believe that
the writer is dishonest) can sometimes go. It is a warning to readers, when they
see an author accused, with volume and page referred to, and the apparent
guarantee of inverted commas, of maintaining something more than commonly
absurd, not to give implicit credence to the assertion without verifying the
reference.

a person's house," or "This is a house which contains booty."
The object of making the mark is merely distinction. I say to
myself, "All these houses are so nearly alike that if I lose sight of
them I shall not again be able to distinguish that which I am now
looking at from any of the others; I must therefore contrive to
make the appearance of this one house unlike that of the others,
that I may hereafter know when I see the mark — not, indeed, any
attribute of the house — but simply that it is the same house
which I am now looking at." Morgiana chalked all the other
houses in a similar manner and defeated the scheme. How?
Simply by obliterating the difference of appearance between that
house and the others. The chalk was still there, but it no longer
served the purpose of a distinctive mark.

When we impose a proper name, we perform an operation in
some degree analogous to what the robber intended in chalking
the house. We put a mark, not, indeed, upon the object itself
but, so to speak, upon the idea of the object. A proper name is
but an unmeaning mark which we connect in our minds with the
idea of the object, in order that, whenever the mark meets our
eyes or occurs to our thoughts, we may think of that individual
object. Not being attached to the thing itself, it does not, like
the chalk, enable us to distinguish the object when we see it, but
it enables us to distinguish it when it is spoken of, either in the
records of our own experience or in the discourse of others, to know
that what we find asserted in any proposition of which it is the
subject is asserted of the individual thing with which we were
previously acquainted.

When we predicate of anything its proper name, when we say,
pointing to a man, "This is Brown or Smith," or pointing to a city,
"It is York," we do not, merely by so doing, convey to the reader
any information about them except that those are their names.
By enabling him to identify the individuals, we may connect them
with information previously possessed by him; by saying, "This is
York," we may tell him that it contains the Minster. But this is
in virtue of what he has previously heard concerning York, not by
anything implied in the name. It is otherwise when objects are
spoken of by connotative names. When we say, "The town is built
of marble," we give the hearer what may be entirely new infor-

mation, and this merely by the signification of the many-worded connotative name, "built of marble." Such names are not signs of the mere objects, invented because we have occasion to think and speak of those objects individually, but signs which accompany an attribute, a kind of livery in which the attribute clothes all objects which are recognized as possessing it. They are not mere marks but more, that is to say, significant marks, and the connotation is what constitutes their significance.

As a proper name is said to be the name of the one individual which it is predicated of, so (as well from the importance of adhering to analogy as for the other reasons formerly assigned) a connotative name ought to be considered a name of all the various individuals which it is predicable of, or, in other words, *denotes*, and not of what it connotes. But by learning what things it is a name of, we do not learn the meaning of the name; for to the same thing we may, with equal propriety, apply many names, not equivalent in meaning. Thus I call a certain man by the name Sophroniscus; I call him by another name, the father of Socrates. Both these are names of the same individual, but their meaning is altogether different. They are applied to that individual for two different purposes: the one merely to distinguish him from other persons who are spoken of; the other to indicate a fact relating to him, the fact that Socrates was his son. I further apply to him these other expressions: a man, a Greek, an Athenian, a sculptor, an old man, an honest man, a brave man. All these are, or may be, names of Sophroniscus, not, indeed, of him alone, but of him and each of an indefinite number of other human beings. Each of these names is applied to Sophroniscus for a different reason, and by each whoever understands its meaning is apprised of a distinct fact or number of facts concerning him; but those who knew nothing about the names except that they were applicable to Sophroniscus would be altogether ignorant of their meaning. It is even possible that I might know every single individual of whom a given name could be with truth affirmed and yet could not be said to know the meaning of the name. A child knows who are its brothers and sisters long before it has any definite conception of the nature of the facts which are involved in the signification of those words.

In some cases it is not easy to decide precisely how much a

particular word does or does not connote; that is, we do not exactly
know (the case not having arisen) what degree of difference in the
object would occasion a difference in the name. Thus it is clear
that the word man, besides animal life and rationality, connotes
also a certain external form, but it would be impossible to say
precisely what form; that is, to decide how great a deviation from
the form ordinarily found in the beings whom we are accustomed
to call men would suffice in a newly-discovered race to make us
refuse them the name of man. Rationality, also, being a quality
which admits of degrees, it has never been settled what is the
lowest degree of that quality which would entitle any creature to
be considered a human being. In all such cases, the meaning of
the general name is so far unsettled and vague; mankind have not
come to any positive agreement about the matter. When we come
to treat of classification, we shall have occasion to show under
what conditions this vagueness may exist without practical inconvenience, and cases will appear in which the ends of language are
better promoted by it than by complete precision, in order that,
in natural history for instance, individuals or species of no very
marked character may be ranged with those more strongly characterized individuals or species to which, in all their properties
taken together, they bear the nearest resemblance.

But this partial uncertainty in the connotation of names can
only be free from mischief when guarded by strict precautions.
One of the chief sources, indeed, of lax habits of thought is the
custom of using connotative terms without a distinctly ascertained
connotation and with no more precise notion of their meaning than
can be loosely collected from observing what objects they are used
to denote. It is in this manner that we all acquire, and inevitably
so, our first knowledge of our vernacular language. A child learns
the meaning of the words *man* or *white* by hearing them applied
to a variety of individual objects and finding out, by a process of
generalization and analysis which he could not himself describe,
what those different objects have in common. In the case of these
two words the process is so easy as to require no assistance from
culture, the objects called human beings and the objects called
white differing from all others by qualities of a peculiarly definite
and obvious character. But in many other cases, objects bear a

general resemblance to one another, which leads to their being familiarly classed together under a common name, while, without more analytic habits than the generality of mankind possess, it is not immediately apparent what are the particular attributes upon the possession of which in common by them all their general resemblance depends. When this is the case people use the name without any recognized connotation, that is, without any precise ·meaning; they talk and, consequently, think vaguely, and remain contented to attach only the same degree of significance to their own words which a child three years old attaches to the words brother and sister. The child, at least, is seldom puzzled by the starting up of new individuals on whom he is ignorant whether or not to confer the title, because there is usually an authority close at hand competent to solve all doubts. But a similar resource does not exist in the generality of cases, and new objects are continually presenting themselves to men, women, and children which they are called upon to class *proprio motu*. They, accordingly, do this on no other principle than that of superficial similarity, giving to each new object the name of that familiar object the idea of which it most readily recalls, or which, on a cursory inspection, it seems to them most to resemble, as an unknown substance found in the ground will be called, according to its texture, earth, sand or a stone. In this manner, names creep on from subject to subject until all traces of a common meaning sometimes disappear, and the word comes to denote a number of things not only independently of any common attribute but which have actually no attribute in common, or none but what is shared by other things to which the name is capriciously refused. Even scientific writers have aided in this perversion of general language from its purpose, sometimes because, like the vulgar, they knew no better, and sometimes in deference to that aversion to admit new words which induces mankind, on all subjects not considered technical, to attempt to make the original stock of names serve with but little augmentation to express a constantly increasing number of objects and distinctions, and, consequently, to express them in a manner progressively more and more imperfect.

To what a degree this loose mode of classing and denominating objects has rendered the vocabulary of mental and moral philos-

ophy unfit for the purposes of accurate thinking is best known to
whoever has most meditated on the present condition of those
branches of knowledge. Since, however, the introduction of a new
technical language as the vehicle of speculations on subjects belonging to the domain of daily discussion is extremely difficult to effect
and would not be free from inconvenience even if effected, the
problem for the philosopher, and one of the most difficult which
he has to resolve, is, in retaining the existing phraseology, how
best to alleviate its imperfections. This can only be accomplished
by giving to every general concrete name which there is frequent
occasion to predicate a definite and fixed connotation in order that
it may be known what attributes, when we call an object by that
name, we really mean to predicate of the object. And the question
of most nicety is how to give this fixed connotation to a name with
the least possible change in the objects which the name is habitually
employed to denote, with the least possible disarrangement, either
by adding or subtraction, of the group of objects which, in however
imperfect a manner, it serves to circumscribe and hold together,
and with the least vitiation of the truth of any propositions which
are commonly received as true.

This desirable purpose of giving a fixed connotation where it is
wanting is the end aimed at whenever any one attempts to give a
definition of a general name already in use, every definition of a
connotative name being an attempt either merely to declare, or to
declare and analyze, the connotation of the name. And the fact
that no questions which have arisen in the moral sciences have been
subjects of keener controversy than the definitions of almost all
the leading expressions is a proof how great an extent the evil to
which we have adverted has attained.

Names with indeterminate connotation are not to be confounded
with names which have more than one connotation, that is to say,
ambiguous words. A word may have several meanings, but all of
them fixed and recognized ones, as the word *post*, for example, or
the word *box*, the various senses of which it would be endless to
enumerate. And the paucity of existing names in comparison with
the demand for them may often render it advisable and even
necessary to retain a name in this multiplicity of acceptations,
distinguishing these so clearly as to prevent their being confounded

with one another. Such a word may be considered as two or more names, accidentally written and spoken alike.[6]

. . . .

[6] Before quitting the subject of connotative names, it is proper to observe that the first writer who, in our times, has adopted from the schoolmen the word *to connote*, Mr. James Mill, in his *Analysis of the Phenomena of the Human Mind*, employs it in a signification different from that in which it is here used. He uses the word in a sense co-extensive with its etymology, applying it to every case in which a name, while pointing directly to one thing (which is consequently termed its signification), includes also a tacit reference to some other thing. In the case considered in the text, that of concrete general names, his language and mine are the converse of one another. Considering (very justly) the signification of the name to lie in the attribute, he speaks of the word as *noting* the attribute, and *connoting* the things possessing the attribute, And he describes abstract names as being properly concrete names with their connotation dropped, whereas, in my view, it is the *de*notation which would be said to be dropped, what was previously connoted becoming the whole signification.

In adopting a phraseology at variance with that which so high an authority, and one which I am less likely than any other person to undervalue, has deliberately sanctioned, I have been influenced by the urgent necessity for a term exclusively appropriated to express the manner in which a concrete general name serves to mark the attributes which are involved in its signification. This necessity can scarcely be felt in its full force by anyone who has not found by experience how vain is the attempt to communicate clear ideas on the philosophy of language without such a word. It is hardly an exaggeration to say that some of the most prevalent of the errors with which logic has been infected, and a large part of the cloudiness and confusion of ideas which have enveloped it, would, in all probability, have been avoided if a term had been in common use to express exactly what I have signified by the term *to connote*. And the schoolmen to whom we are indebted for the greater part of our logical language gave us this also, and in this very sense. For though some of their general expressions countenance the use of the word in the more extensive and vague acceptation in which it is taken by Mr. Mill, yet when they had to define it specifically as a technical term and to fix its meaning as such, with that admirable precision which always characterizes their definitions, they clearly explained that nothing was said to be connoted except *forms*, which word may generally, in their writings, be understood as synonymous with *attributes*.

Now, if the word *to connote*, so well suited to the purpose to which they applied it, be diverted from that purpose by being taken to fulfill another for which it does not seem to me to be at all required, I am unable to find any expression to replace it but such as are commonly employed in a sense so much more general that it would be useless attempting to associate them peculiarly with this precise idea. Such are the words, to involve, to imply, etc. By employing these, I should fail of attaining the object for which alone the name

CHAPTER III

OF THE THINGS DENOTED BY NAMES

1. *Necessity of an enumeration of namable things. The categories of Aristotle*

Looking back now to the commencement of our inquiry, let us attempt to measure how far it has advanced. Logic, we found, is the theory of proof. But proof supposes something provable, which must be a proposition or assertion, since nothing but a proposition can be an object of belief or, therefore, of proof. A proposition is discourse which affirms or denies something of some other thing. This is one step; there must, it seems, be two things concerned in every act of belief. But what are these things? They can be no other than those signified by the two names which, being joined together by a copula, constitute the proposition. If, therefore, we knew what all names signify, we should know everything which, in the existing state of human knowledge, is capable either of being made a subject of affirmation or denial or of being itself affirmed or denied of a subject. We have, accordingly, in the preceding chapter, reviewed the various kinds of names, in order to ascertain what is signified by each of them. And we have now carried this survey far enough to be able to take an account of its results and to exhibit an enumeration of all kinds of things which are capable of being made predicates, or of having any thing predicated of them; after which to determine the import of predication, that is, of propositions, can be no arduous task.

. . . .

I. Feelings or States of Consciousness

2. *Feelings or states of consciousness*

A feeling and a state of consciousness are, in the language of philosophy, equivalent expressions: everything is a feeling of which is needed, namely, to distinguish this particular kind of involving and implying from all other kinds, and to assure to it the degree of habitual attention which its importance demands.

the mind is conscious; everything which it *feels*, or, in other words, which forms a part of its own sentient existence. In popular language feeling is not always synonymous with state of consciousness, being often taken more peculiarly for those states which are conceived as belonging to the sensitive, or to the emotional, phasis of our nature; and sometimes, with a still narrower restriction, to the emotional alone as distinguished from what are conceived as belonging to the percipient or to the intellectual phasis. But this is an admitted departure from correctness of language, just as, by a popular perversion the exact converse of this, the word mind is withdrawn from its rightful generality of signification and restricted to the intellect. The still greater perversion by which feeling is sometimes confined not only to bodily sensations but to the sensations of a single sense, that of touch, needs not be more particularly adverted to.

Feeling, in the proper sense of the term, is a genus, of which sensation, emotion, and thought, are subordinate species. Under the word thought is here to be included whatever we are internally conscious of when we are said to think — from the consciousness we have when we think of a red color without having it before our eyes to the most recondite thoughts of a philosopher or poet. Be it remembered, however, that by a thought is to be understood what passes in the mind itself, and not any object external to the mind which the person is commonly said to be thinking of. He may be thinking of the sun or of God, but the sun and God are not thoughts; his mental image, however, of the sun, and his idea of God, are thoughts, states of his mind, not of the objects themselves, and so also is his belief of the existence of the sun or of God, or his disbelief, if the case be so. Even imaginary objects (which are said to exist only in our ideas) are to be distinguished from our ideas of them. I may think of a hobgoblin, as I may think of the loaf which was eaten yesterday or of the flower which will bloom tomorrow. But the hobgoblin which never existed is not the same thing with my idea of a hobgoblin, any more than the loaf which once existed is the same thing with my idea of a loaf, or the flower which does not yet exist, but which will exist, is the same with my idea of a flower. They are all not thoughts but objects of thought, though at the present time all the objects are alike nonexistent.

In like manner, a sensation is to be carefully distinguished from the object which causes the sensation, our sensation of white from a white object, nor is it less to be distinguished from the attribute whiteness which we ascribe to the object in consequence of its exciting the sensation. Unfortunately for clearness and due discrimination in considering these subjects, our sensations seldom receive separate names. We have a name for the objects which produce in us a certain sensation, the word *white*. We have a name for the quality in those objects to which we ascribe the sensation, the name *whiteness*. But when we speak of the sensation itself (as we have not occasion to do this often except in our scientific speculations), language, which adapts itself for the most part only to the common uses of life, has provided us with no single-worded or immediate designation; we must employ a circumlocution and say, "The sensation of white," or "The sensation of whiteness;" we must denominate the sensation either from the object or from the attribute by which it is excited. Yet the sensation, though it never *does*, might very well be *conceived* to exist without anything whatever to excite it. We can conceive it as arising spontaneously in the mind. But if it so arose we should have no name to denote it which would not be a misnomer. In the case of our sensations of hearing we are better provided; we have the word sound and a whole vocabulary of words to denote the various kinds of sounds. For, as we are often conscious of these sensations in the absence of any perceptible object, we can more easily conceive having them in the absence of any object whatever. We need only shut our eyes and listen to music to have a conception of a universe with nothing in it except sounds and ourselves hearing them; and what is easily conceived separately, easily obtains a separate name. But, in general, our names of sensations denote indiscriminately the sensation and the attribute. Thus *color* stands for the sensations of white, red, etc., but also for the quality in the colored object. We talk of the colors of things as among their *properties*.

3. *Feelings must be distinguished from their physical antecedents. Perceptions, what*

In the case of sensations, another distinction has also to be kept in view which is often confounded, and never without mischievous consequences. This is the distinction between the sensation itself and the state of the bodily organs which precedes the sensation and which constitutes the physical agency by which it is produced. One of the sources of confusion on this subject is the division commonly made of feelings into bodily and mental. Philosophically speaking, there is no foundation at all for this distinction; even sensations are states of the sentient mind, not states of the body as distinguished from it. What I am conscious of when I see the color blue is a feeling of blue color, which is one thing; the picture on my retina, or the phenomenon of hitherto mysterious nature which takes place in my optic nerve or in my brain, is another thing of which I am not at all conscious and which scientific investigation alone could have apprised me of. These are states of my body, but the sensation of blue, which is the consequence of these states of body, is not a state of body; that which perceives and is conscious is called mind. When sensations are called bodily feelings, it is only as being the class of feelings which are immediately occasioned by bodily states; whereas the other kinds of feelings, thoughts, for instance, or emotions, are immediately excited not by anything acting upon the bodily organs but by sensations or by previous thoughts. This, however, is a distinction not in our feelings but in the agency which produces our feelings; all of them when actually produced are states of mind.

Besides the affection of our bodily organs from without and the sensation thereby produced in our minds, many writers admit a third link in the chain of phenomena which they call a perception and which consists in the recognition of an external object as the exciting cause of the sensation. This perception, they say, is an *act* of the mind, proceeding from its own spontaneous activity, while, in a sensation, the mind is passive, being merely acted upon by the outward object. And according to some metaphysicians, it is by an act of the mind, similar to perception except in not being preceded by any sensation, that the existence of God, the soul, and other hyperphysical objects, is recognized.

These acts of what is termed perception, whatever be the conclusion ultimately come to respecting their nature, must, I conceive, take their place among the varieties of feelings or states of mind. In so classing them, I have not the smallest intention of declaring or insinuating any theory as to the law of mind in which these mental processes may be supposed to originate, or the conditions under which they may be legitimate or the reverse. Far less do I mean (as Dr. Whewell seems to suppose must be meant in an analogous case[1]) to indicate that, as they are "*merely* states of mind," it is superfluous to inquire into their distinguishing peculiarities. I abstain from the inquiry as irrelevant to the science of logic. In these so-called perceptions or direct recognitions by the mind of objects, whether physical or spiritual, which are external to itself, I can see only cases of belief, but of belief which claims to be intuitive, or independent of external evidence. When a stone lies before me, I am conscious of certain sensations which I receive from it; but if I say that these sensations come to me from an external object which I *perceive*, the meaning of these words is that, receiving the sensations, I intuitively *believe* that an external cause of those sensations exists. The laws of intuitive belief and the conditions under which it is legitimate are a subject which, as we have already so often remarked, belongs, not to logic, but to the science of the ultimate laws of the human mind.

To the same region of speculation belongs all that can be said respecting the distinction which the German metaphysicians and their French and English followers so elaborately draw between the *acts* of the mind and its merely passive *states;* between what it receives from, and what it gives to, the crude materials of its experience. I am aware that, with reference to the view which those writers take of the primary elements of thought and knowledge, this distinction is fundamental. But for the present purpose, which is to examine not the original groundwork of our knowledge, but how we come by that portion of it which is not original, the difference between active and passive states of mind is of secondary importance. For us, they all are states of mind; they all are feelings, by which, let it be said once more, I mean to imply nothing of passivity but simply that they are psychological facts, facts which take place in the mind and are to be carefully distinguished from the external or physical facts with which they may be connected either as effects or as causes.

[1] *Philosophy of the Inductive Sciences*, I, 40.

4. *Volitions and actions, what*

Among active states of mind, there is, however, one species which merits particular attention, because it forms a principal part of the connotation of some important classes of names. I mean *volitions*, or acts of the will. When we speak of sentient beings by relative names, a large portion of the connotation of the name usually consists of the actions of those beings; actions past, present, and possible or probable future. Take, for instance, the words "sovereign" and "subject." What meaning do these words convey but that of innumerable actions done or to be done by the sovereign and the subjects to, or in regard to, one another reciprocally? So with the words "physician" and "patient," "leader" and "follower," "tutor" and "pupil." In many cases the words also connote actions which would be done under certain contingencies by persons other than those denoted, as the words "mortgager" and "mortgagee," "obliger" and "obligee," and many other words expressive of legal relation, which connote what a court of justice would do to enforce the legal obligation if not fulfilled. There are also words which connote actions previously done by persons other than those denoted, either by the name itself or by its correlative, as the word "brother." From these instances, it may be seen how large a portion of the connotation of names consists of actions. Now what is an action? Not one thing, but a series of two things: the state of mind called a volition, followed by an effect. The volition, or intention to produce the effect, is one thing; the effect produced in consequence of the intention is another thing; the two together constitute the action. I form the purpose of instantly moving my arm; that is a state of my mind. My arm (not being tied or paralytic) moves in obedience to my purpose; that is a physical fact, consequent on a state of mind. The intention followed by the fact, or (if we prefer the expression) the fact when preceded and caused by the intention, is called the action of moving my arm.

5. *Substance and attribute*

Of the first leading division of namable things, viz., feelings or states of consciousness, we began by recognizing three subdivisions:

sensations, thoughts, and emotions. The first two of these we have illustrated at considerable length; the third, emotions, not being perplexed by similar ambiguities, does not require similar exemplification. And, finally, we have found it necessary to add to these three a fourth species, commonly known by the name volitions. We shall now proceed to the two remaining classes of namable things, all things which are regarded as external to the mind being considered as belonging either to the class of substances or to that of attributes.

II. Substances

Logicians have endeavored to define substance and attribute, but their definitions are not so much attempts to draw a distinction between the things themselves as instructions what difference it is customary to make in the grammatical structure of the sentence, according as we are speaking of substances or of attributes. Such definitions are rather lessons of English, or of Greek, Latin, or German, than of mental philosophy. An attribute, say the school logicians, must be the attribute *of* something; color, for example, must be the color *of* something; goodness must be the goodness *of* something; and if this something should cease to exist or should cease to be connected with the attribute, the existence of the attribute would be at an end. A substance, on the contrary, is self-existent; in speaking about it, we need not put *of* after its name. A stone is not the stone *of* anything; the moon is not the moon *of* anything but simply the moon. Unless, indeed, the name which we choose to give to the substance be a relative name; if so, it must be followed either by *of* or by some other particle, implying, as that preposition does, a reference to something else; but then the other characteristic peculiarity of an attribute would fail; the *something* might be destroyed, and the substance might still subsist. Thus, a father must be the father *of* something, and so far resembles an attribute in being referred to something besides himself; if there were no child, there would be no father, but this, when we look into the matter, only means that we should not call him father. The man called father might still exist though there were no child, as he existed before there was a child, and there would be no contradiction in supposing him to exist though the whole universe except himself were destroyed. But destroy all white substances and where would be the attribute whiteness? Whiteness, without any white thing, is a contradiction in terms.

This is the nearest approach to a solution of the difficulty that will be found in the common treatises on logic. It will scarcely be thought to be a satisfactory one. If an attribute is distinguished from a substance by being the attribute *of* something, it seems highly necessary to understand what is meant by *of*, a particle which needs explanation too much itself to be placed in front of the explanation of anything else. And as for the self-existence of substance, it is very true that a substance may be conceived to exist without any other substance, but so also may an attribute without any other attribute, and we can no more imagine a substance without attributes than we can imagine attributes without a substance.

Metaphysicians, however, have probed the question deeper and given an account of substance considerably more satisfactory than this. Substances are usually distinguished as bodies or minds. Of each of these, philosophers have at length provided us with a definition which seems unexceptionable.

6. *Body*

A body, according to the received doctrine of modern metaphysicians, may be defined the external cause to which we ascribe our sensations. When I see and touch a piece of gold, I am conscious of a sensation of yellow color, and sensations of hardness and weight; and by varying the mode of handling, I may add to these sensations many others completely distinct from them. The sensations are all of which I am directly conscious, but I consider them as produced by something not only existing independently of my will but external to my bodily organs and to my mind. This external something I call a body.

It may be asked how come we to ascribe our sensations to any external cause? And is there sufficient ground for so ascribing them? It is known that there are metaphysicians who have raised

a controversy on the point, maintaining that we are not warranted
in referring our sensations to a cause such as we understand by
the word body, or to any external cause whatever. Though we
have no concern here with this controversy nor with the metaphysical niceties on which it turns, one of the best ways of showing what is meant by substance is to consider what position it is
necessary to take up in order to maintain its existence against
opponents.

It is certain, then, that a part of our notion of a body consists
of the notion of a number of sensations of our own, or of other
sentient beings, habitually occurring simultaneously. My conception of the table at which I am writing is compounded of its
visible form and size, which are complex sensations of sight, its
tangible form and size, which are complex sensations of our organs
of touch and of our muscles, its weight, which is also a sensation
of touch and of the muscles, its color, which is a sensation of sight,
its hardness, which is a sensation of the muscles, its composition,
which is another word for all the varieties of sensation which we
receive under various circumstances from the wood of which it is
made, and so forth. All or most of these various sensations frequently are and, as we learn by experience, always might be
experienced simultaneously, or in many different orders of succession at our own choice; and hence the thought of any one of them
makes us think of the others, and the whole becomes mentally
amalgamated into one mixed state of consciousness, which, in the
language of the school of Locke and Hartley, is termed a complex
idea.

Now there are philosophers who have argued as follows: if we
conceive an orange to be divested of its natural color without
acquiring any new one, to lose its softness without becoming hard,
its roundness without becoming square or pentagonal, or of any
other regular or irregular figure whatever, to be deprived of size,
of weight, of taste, of smell, to lose all its mechanical and all its
chemical properties and acquire no new ones, to become, in short,
invisible, intangible, imperceptible, not only by all our senses but
by the senses of all other sentient beings, real or possible, nothing,
say these thinkers, would remain. For of what nature, they ask,
could be the residuum? and by what token could it manifest its

presence? To the unreflecting, its existence seems to rest on the evidence of the senses. But, to the senses, nothing is apparent except the sensations. We know, indeed, that these sensations are bound together by some law; they do not come together at random but according to a systematic order, which is part of the order established in the universe. When we experience one of these sensations, we usually experience the others also, or know that we have it in our power to experience them. But a fixed law of connection, making the sensations occur together, does not, say these philosophers, necessarily require what is called a substratum to support them. The conception of a substratum is but one of many possible forms in which that connection presents itself to our imagination, a mode of, as it were, realizing the idea. If there be such a substratum, suppose it at this instant miraculously annihilated, and let the sensations continue to occur in the same order, and how would the substratum be missed? By what signs should we be able to discover that its existence had terminated? Should we not have as much reason to believe that it still existed as we now have? And if we should not then be warranted in believing it, how can we be so now? A body, therefore, according to these metaphysicians, is not anything intrinsically different from the sensations which the body is said to produce in us; it is, in short, a set of sensations, or rather, of possibilities of sensation, joined together according to a fixed law.

The controversies to which these speculations have given rise, and the doctrines which have been developed in the attempt to find a conclusive answer to them, have been fruitful of important consequences to the science of mind. The sensations (it was answered) which we are conscious of, and which we receive, not at random but joined together in a certain uniform manner, imply not only a law or laws of connection but a cause external to our mind, which cause, by its own laws, determines the laws according to which the sensations are connected and experienced. The schoolmen used to call this external cause by the name we have already employed, a *substratum*, and its attributes (as they expressed themselves) *inhered*, literally *stuck*, in it. To this substratum the name matter is usually given in philosophical discussions. It was soon, however, acknowledged by all who reflected on the subject that the existence of matter cannot be proved by extrinsic evidence. The answer, therefore, now usually made to Berkeley and his followers is that the belief is intuitive; that mankind, in all ages, have felt themselves compelled, by a necessity of their nature, to refer their sensations to an external cause; that even those who deny it in theory yield to the necessity in practice, and both in speech, thought, and feeling, do, equally with the vulgar, acknowledge their sensations to be the effects of something external to them; this knowledge, therefore, it is affirmed, is as evidently intuitive as our knowledge of our sensations themselves is intuitive. And here the question merges in the fundamental problem of metaphysics properly so called, to which science we leave it.

But although the extreme doctrine of the idealist metaphysicians, that objects are nothing but our sensations and the laws which connect them, has not been generally adopted by subsequent thinkers, the point of most real importance is one on which those metaphysicians are now very generally considered to have made out their case, viz.: that *all we know* of objects is the sensations which they give us, and the order of the occurrence of those sensations. Kant himself, on this point, is as explicit as Berkeley or Locke. However firmly convinced that there exists a universe of "Things in themselves," totally distinct from the universe of phenomena, or of things as they appear to our senses, and even when bringing into use a technical expression (*Noumenon*) to denote what the thing is in itself, as contrasted with the *representation* of it in our minds, he allows that this representation (the matter of which, he says, consists of our sensations, though the form is given by the laws of the mind itself) is all we know of the object; and that the real nature of the thing is, and by the constitution of our faculties ever must remain, at least in the present state of existence, an impenetrable mystery to us. "Of things absolutely or in themselves," says Sir William Hamilton,[2] "be they external, be they internal, we know nothing, or know them only as incognizable; and become aware of their incomprehensible existence only as this is indirectly and accidentally revealed to us, through certain qualities related to our faculties of knowledge,

[2] *Discussions on Philosophy*, etc. Appendix I., pp. 643, 644.

and which qualities, again, we cannot think as unconditional, irrelative, existent in and of ourselves. All that we know is therefore phenomenal — phenomenal of the unknown."[3] The same doctrine is laid down in the clearest and strongest terms by M. Cousin, whose observations on the subject are the more worthy of attention as, in consequence of the ultra-German and ontological character of his philosophy in other respects, they may be regarded as the admissions of an opponent.[4]

[3] It is to be regretted that Sir William Hamilton, though he often strenuously insists on this doctrine, and though, in the passage quoted, he states it with a comprehensiveness and force which leave nothing to be desired, did not consistently adhere to his own doctrine, but maintained along with it opinions with which it is utterly irreconcilable. See the third and other chapters of *An Examination of Sir William Hamilton's Philosophy.*

[4] "Nous savons qu'il existe quelque chose hors de nous, parceque nous ne pouvons expliquer nos perceptions sans les rattacher à des causes distinctes de nous mêmes; nous savons de plus que ces causes, dont nous ne connaissons pas d'ailleurs l'essence, produisent les effets les plus variables, les plus divers, et même les plus contraires, selon qu'elles rencontrent telle nature ou telle disposition du sujet. Mais savons-nous quelque chose de plus? et même, vu le caractère indéterminé des causes que nous concevons dans les corps, y a-t-il quelque chose de plus à savoir? Y a-t-il lieu de nous enquérir si nous percevons les choses telles qu'elles sont? Non évidemment. . . . . Je ne dis pas que le problème est insoluble, *je dis qu'il est absurde et enferme une contradiction.* Nous *ne savons pas ce que ces causes sont en elles-mêmes,* et la raison nous défend de chercher à le connaître: mais il est bien évident *à priori,* qu'*elles ne sont pas en elles-mêmes ce qu'elles sont par rapport à nous,* puisque la présence du sujet modifie nécessairement leur action. Supprimez tout sujet sentant, il est certain que ces causes agiraient encore puisqu'elles continueraient d'exister; mais elles agiraient autrement; elles seraient encore des qualités et des propriétés, mais qui ne ressembleraient à rien de ce que nous connaissons. Le feu ne manifesterait plus aucune des propriétés que nous lui connaissons: que serait-il? C'est ce que nous ne saurons jamais. *C'est d'ailleurs peut-être un problème qui ne répugne pas seulement à la nature de notre esprit, mais à l'essence même des choses.* Quand même en effet on supprimerait par le pensée tous les sujets sentants, il faudrait encore admettre que nul corps ne manifesterait ses propriétés autrement qu'en relation avec un sujet quelconque, et dans ce cas *ses propriétés ne seraient encore que relatives:* en sorte qu'il me paraît fort raisonnable d'admettre que les propriétés déterminées des corps n'existent pas indépendamment d'un sujet quelconque, et que quand on demande si les propriétés de la matière sont telles que nous les percevons, il faudrait voir auparavant si elles sont en tant que déterminées, et dans quel sens il est vrai de dire qu'elles sont." — *Cours d'Histoire de la Philosophie Morale au 18me siècle,* 8me leçon.

There is not the slightest reason for believing that what we call the sensible qualities of the object are a type of anything inherent in itself, or bear any affinity to its own nature. A cause does not, as such, resemble its effects; an east wind is not like the feeling of cold, nor heat like the steam of boiling water. Why, then, should matter resemble our sensations? Why should the inmost nature of fire or water resemble the impressions made by those objects upon our senses?[5] Or on what principle are we authorized to deduce from the effects anything concerning the cause, except that it is a cause adequate to produce those effects? It may, therefore, safely be laid down as a truth both obvious in itself, and admitted by all whom it is at present necessary to take into consideration, that, of the outward world, we know and can know absolutely nothing except the sensations which we experience from it.[6]

[5] An attempt, indeed, has been made by Reid and others to establish that, although some of the properties we ascribe to objects exist only in our sensations, others exist in the things themselves, being such as cannot possibly be copies of any impression upon the senses; and they ask from what sensations our notions of extension and figure have been derived? The gauntlet thrown down by Reid was taken up by Brown, who, applying greater powers of analysis than had previously been applied to the notions of extension and figure, pointed out that the sensations from which those notions are derived are sensations of touch, combined with sensations of a class previously too little adverted to by metaphysicians, those which have their seat in our muscular frame. His analysis, which was adopted and followed up by James Mill, has been further and greatly improved upon in Professor Bain's profound work, *The Senses and the Intellect*, and in the chapters on "Perception" of a work of eminent analytic power, Mr. Herbert Spencer's *Principles of Psychology*.

On this point M. Cousin may again be cited in favor of the better doctrine. M. Cousin recognizes, in opposition to Reid, the essential subjectivity of our conceptions of what are called the primary qualities of matter, as extension, solidity, etc., equally with those of color, heat, and the remainder of the so-called secondary qualities. — *Cours*, ut supra, 9me leçon.

[6] This doctrine, which is the most complete form of the philosophical theory known as the relativity of human knowledge, has, since the recent revival in this country of an active interest in metaphysical speculation, been the subject of a greatly increased amount of discussion and controversy, and dissentients have manifested themselves in considerably greater number than I had any knowledge of when the passage in the text was written. The doctrine has been attacked from two sides. Some thinkers, among whom are the late Professor Ferrier, in his *Institutes of Metaphysic*, and Professor John Grote, in his

7. *Mind*

Body having now been defined the external cause, and (according to the more reasonable opinion) the unknown external cause, to which we refer our sensations, it remains to frame a definition of Mind. Nor, after the preceding observations, will this be difficult. For, as our conception of a body is that of an unknown exciting cause of sensations, so our conception of a mind is that of an unknown recipient or percipient of them; and not of them alone, but of all our other feelings. As body is understood to be the mysterious something which excites the mind to feel, so mind is the mysterious something which feels and thinks. It is unnecessary to give in the case of mind, as we gave in the case of matter, a particular statement of the skeptical system by which its existence as a thing in itself, distinct from the series of what are denominated its states, is called in question. But it is necessary to remark that on the inmost nature (whatever be meant by inmost nature) of the thinking principle, as well as on the inmost nature of matter, we are and, with our faculties must always remain, entirely in

Exploratio Philosophica, appear to deny altogether the reality of Noumena, or things in themselves — of an unknowable substratum or support for the sensations which we experience and which, according to the theory, constitute all our knowledge of an external world. It seems to me, however, that in Professor Grote's case at least, the denial of Noumena is only apparent, and that he does not essentially differ from the other class of objectors, including Mr. Bailey in his valuable *Letters on the Philosophy of the Human Mind*, and (in spite of the striking passage quoted in the text) also Sir William Hamilton, who contend for a direct knowledge by the human mind of more than the sensations — of certain attributes or properties as they exist, not in us but in the things themselves.

With the first of these opinions, that which denies Noumena, I have, as a metaphysician, no quarrel; but, whether it be true or false, it is irrelevant to logic. And since all the forms of language are in contradiction to it, nothing but confusion could result from its unnecessary introduction into a treatise, every essential doctrine of which could stand equally well with the opposite and accredited opinion. The other and rival doctrine, that of a direct perception or intuitive knowledge of the outward object as it is in itself, considered as distinct from the sensations we receive from it, is of far greater practical moment. But even this question, depending on the nature and laws of intuitive knowledge, is not within the province of logic. For the grounds of my own opinion concerning it, I must content myself with referring to a work already mentioned — *An Examination of Sir William Hamilton's Philosophy*, several chapters of which are devoted to a full discussion of the questions and theories relating to the supposed direct perception of external objects.

the dark. All which we are aware of, even in our own minds, is (in the words of James Mill) a certain "thread of consciousness", a series of feelings, that is, of sensations, thoughts, emotions, and volitions, more or less numerous and complicated. There is a something I call myself, or, by another form of expression, my mind, which I consider as distinct from these sensations, thoughts, etc.; a something which I conceive to be not the thoughts, but the being that has the thoughts, and which I can conceive as existing forever in a state of quiescence, without any thoughts at all. But what this being is, though it is myself, I have no knowledge, other than the series of its states of consciousness. As bodies manifest themselves to me only through the sensations of which I regard them as the causes, so the thinking principle, or mind, in my own nature makes itself known to me only by the feelings of which it is conscious. I know nothing about myself save my capacities of feeling or being conscious (including, of course, thinking and willing); and, were I to learn anything new concerning my own nature, I cannot with my present faculties conceive this new information to be anything else than that I have some additional capacities, as yet unknown to me, of feeling, thinking, or willing.

Thus, then, as body is the unsentient cause to which we are naturally prompted to refer a certain portion of our feelings, so mind may be described as the sentient *subject* (in the scholastic sense of the term) of all feelings; that which has or feels them. But of the nature of either body or mind, further than the feelings which the former excites and which the latter experiences, we do not, according to the best existing doctrine, know anything; and, if anything, logic has nothing to do with it or with the manner in which the knowledge is acquired. With this result we may conclude this portion of our subject, and pass to the third and only remaining class or division of namable things.

III. ATTRIBUTES: AND, FIRST, QUALITIES

8. *Qualities*

From what has already been said of Substance, what is to be said of Attribute is easily deducible. For if we know not and cannot know anything of bodies but the sensations which they excite in us or in others, those sensations must be all that we can, at bottom, mean by their attributes, and the distinction which we verbally make between the properties of things and the sensations we receive from them must originate in the convenience of discourse rather than in the nature of what is signified by the terms.

Attributes are usually distributed under the three heads of Quality, Quantity, and Relation. We shall come to the two latter presently; in the first place we shall confine ourselves to the former.

Let us take, then, as our example one of what are termed the sensible qualities of objects, and let that example be whiteness. When we ascribe whiteness to any substance, as, for instance, snow, when we say that snow has the quality whiteness, what do we really assert? Simply, that when snow is present to our organs, we have a particular sensation which we are accustomed to call the sensation of white. But how do I know that snow is present? Obviously by the sensations which I derive from it and not otherwise. I infer that the object is present because it gives me a certain assemblage or series of sensations. And when I ascribe to it the attribute whiteness, my meaning is only that, of the sensations composing this group or series, that which I call the sensation of white color is one.

This is one view which may be taken of the subject. But there is also another and a different view. It may be said that it is true we *know* nothing of sensible objects except the sensations they excite in us, that the fact of our receiving from snow the particular sensation which is called a sensation of white is the *ground* on which we ascribe to that substance the quality whiteness, the sole proof of its possessing that quality. But because one thing may be the sole evidence of the existence of another thing, it does not follow that the two are one and the same. The attribute whiteness (it may be said) is not the fact of receiving the sensation, but something in the object itself, a *power* inherent in it, something *in virtue* of which the object produces the sensation. And when we affirm that snow possesses the attribute whiteness, we do not merely assert that the presence of snow produces in us that sensation, but that it does so through and by reason of that power or quality.

For the purposes of logic it is not of material importance which of these opinions we adopt. The full discussion of the subject belongs to the other department of scientific inquiry, so often alluded to under the name of metaphysics; but it may be said here that, for the doctrine of the existence of a peculiar species of entities called qualities, I can see no foundation except in a tendency of the human mind which is the cause of many delusions. I mean the disposition, wherever we meet with two names which are not precisely synonymous, to suppose that they must be the names of two different things, whereas, in reality, they may be names of the same thing viewed in two different lights or under different suppositions as to surrounding circumstances. Because *quality* and *sensation* cannot be put indiscriminately one for the other, it is supposed that they cannot both signify the same thing, namely, the impression or feeling with which we are affected through our senses by the presence of an object; though there is at least no absurdity in supposing that this identical impression or feeling may be called a sensation when considered merely in itself, and a quality when looked at in relation to any one of the numerous objects, the presence of which to our organs excites in our minds that among various other sensations or feelings. And if this be admissable as a supposition, it rests with those who contend for an entity *per se* called a quality to show that their opinion is preferable, or is anything in fact but a lingering remnant of the old doctrine of occult causes, the very absurdity which Molière so happily ridiculed when he made one of his pedantic physicians account for the fact that opium produces sleep by the maxim, because it has a soporific virtue.

It is evident that, when the physician stated that opium has a soporific virtue, he did not account for, but merely asserted over again, the fact that it produces sleep. In like manner, when we say that snow is white because it has the quality of whiteness, we are only re-asserting in more technical language the fact that it excites in us the sensation of white. If it be said that the sensation must have some cause, I answer, its cause is the presence of the assemblage of phenomena which is termed the object. When we have asserted that, as often as the object is present and our organs in their normal state, the sensation takes place, we have stated all that we know about the matter. There is no need, after assigning a certain and intelligible cause, to suppose an occult cause besides, for the purpose of enabling the real cause to produce its effect. If I am asked, why does the presence of the object cause this sensation in me, I cannot tell; I can only say that such is my nature and the nature of the object; that the fact forms a part of the constitution of things. And to this we must at last come, even after interpolating the imaginary entity. Whatever number of links the chain of causes and effects may consist of, how any one link produces the one which is next to it remains equally inexplicable to us. It is as easy to comprehend that the object should produce the sensation directly and at once as that it should produce the same sensation by the aid of something else called the *power* of producing it.

But, as the difficulties which may be felt in adopting this view of the subject cannot be removed without discussions transcending the bounds of our science, I content myself with a passing indication and shall, for the purposes of logic, adopt a language compatible with either view of the nature of qualities. I shall say — what at least admits of no dispute — that the quality of whiteness ascribed to the object snow is *grounded* on its exciting in us the sensation of white; and adopting the language already used by the school logicians in the case of the kind of attributes called Relations, I shall term the sensation of white the *foundation* of the quality whiteness. For logical purposes the sensation is the only essential part of what is meant by the word, the only part which we ever can be concerned in proving. When that is proved, the quality is proved; if an object excites a sensation, it has, of course, the power of exciting it.

IV. RELATIONS

9. *Relations*

The *qualities* of a body, we have said, are the attributes grounded on the sensations which the presence of that particular body to our organs excites in our minds. But when we ascribe to any object the kind of attribute called a Relation, the foundation of the attribute must be something in which other objects are concerned besides itself and the percipient.

As there may with propriety be said to be a relation between any two things to which two correlative names are or may be given, we may expect to discover what constitutes a relation in general, if we enumerate the principal cases in which mankind have imposed correlative names and observe what these cases have in common.

What, then, is the character which is possessed in common by states of circumstances so heterogeneous and discordant as these: one thing *like* another; one thing *unlike* another; one thing *near* another; one thing *far from* another; one thing *before, after, along with* another; one thing *greater, equal, less,* than another; one thing the *cause* of another, the *effect* of another; one person the *master, servant, child, parent, debtor, creditor, sovereign, subject, attorney, client,* of another, and so on?

Omitting, for the present, the case of resemblance (a relation which requires to be considered separately), there seems to be one thing common to all these cases, and only one — that in each of them there exists or occurs, or has existed or occurred, or may be expected to exist or occur, some fact or phenomenon, into which the two things which are said to be related to each other both enter as parties concerned. This fact, or phenomenon, is what the Aristotelian logicians called the *fundamentum relationis.* Thus in the relation of greater and less between two magnitudes, the *fundamentum relationis* is the fact that one of the two magnitudes could, under certain conditions, be included in without entirely filling the space occupied by the other magnitude. In the relation of master and servant, the *fundamentum relationis* is the fact that the one has undertaken, or is compelled, to perform certain services for the benefit and at the bidding of the other. Examples might be indefinitely multiplied; but it is already obvious that whenever two things are said to be related, there is some fact, or series of facts, into which they both enter, and that, whenever any two things are involved in some one fact, or series of facts, we may ascribe to those two things a mutual relation grounded on the fact. Even if they have nothing in common but what is common to all things, that they are members of the universe, we call that a relation, and denominate them fellow-creatures, fellow-beings, or fellow-denizens of the universe. But in proportion as the fact into which the two objects enter as parts is of a more special and peculiar, or of a more complicated nature, so also is the relation grounded upon it. And there are as many conceivable relations as there are conceivable kinds of fact in which two things can be jointly concerned.

In the same manner, therefore, as a quality is an attribute grounded on the fact that a certain sensation or sensations are produced in us by the object, so an attribute grounded on some fact into which the object enters jointly with another object is a relation between it and that other object. But the fact in the latter case consists of the very same kind of elements as the fact in the former, namely, states of consciousness. In the case, for example, of any legal relation, as debtor and creditor, principal and agent, guardian and ward, the *fundamentum relationis* consists entirely of thoughts, feelings, and volitions (actual or contingent), either of the persons themselves or of other persons concerned in the same series of transactions; as, for instance, the intentions which would be formed by a judge, in case a complaint were made to his tribunal of the infringement of any of the legal obligations imposed by the relation, and the acts which the judge would perform in consequence; acts being (as we have already seen) another word for intentions followed by an effect, and that effect being but another word for sensations, or some other feelings, occasioned either to the agent himself or to somebody else. There is no part of what the names expressive of the relation imply that is not resolvable into states of consciousness, outward objects being, no doubt, supposed throughout as the causes by which some of those states of consciousness are excited, and minds as the subjects by which all of them are experienced, but neither the external objects nor the minds making their existence known otherwise than by the states of consciousness.

Cases of relation are not always so complicated as those to which we last alluded. The simplest of all cases of relation are those expressed by the words antecedent and consequent and by the word simultaneous. If we say, for instance, that dawn preceded sunrise, the fact in which the two things, dawn and sunrise, were jointly concerned, consisted only of the two things themselves; no third thing entered into the fact or phenomenon at all. Unless, indeed, we choose to call the succession of the two objects a third thing; but their succession is not something added to the things themselves; it is something involved in them. Dawn and sunrise announce themselves to our consciousness by two successive sensations. Our consciousness of the succession of these sensations is not a third sensation or feeling added to them; we have not first the two feelings and then a feeling of their succession. To have two feelings at all implies having them either successively or else simultaneously. Sensations, or other feelings, being given, succession and simultaneousness are the two conditions to the alternative of which they are subjected by the nature of our faculties, and no one has been able, or needs expect, to analyze the matter any further.

10. *Resemblance*

In a somewhat similar position àre two other sorts of relations, likeness and unlikeness. I have two sensations; we will suppose them to be simple ones; two sensations of white, or one sensation of white and another of black. I call the first two sensations *like*, the last two *unlike*. What is the fact or phenomenon constituting the *fundamentum* of this relation? The two sensations first, and then what we call a feeling of resemblance, or of want of resemblance. Let us confine ourselves to the former case. Resemblance is evidently a feeling, a state of the consciousness of the observer. Whether the feeling of the resemblance of the two colors be a third state of consciousness, which I have *after* having the two sensations of color, or whether (like the feeling of their succession) it is involved in the sensations themselves, may be a matter of discussion. But in either case, these feelings of resemblance and of its opposite, dissimilarity, are parts of our nature, and parts so far from being capable of analysis that they are presupposed in every attempt to analyze any of our other feelings. Likeness and unlikeness, therefore, as well as antecedence, sequence, and simultaneousness, must stand apart among relations, as things *sui generis*. They are attributes grounded on facts, that is, on states of consciousness, but on states which are peculiar, unresolvable, and inexplicable.

But, though likeness or unlikeness cannot be resolved into anything else, complex cases of likeness or unlikeness can be resolved into simpler ones. When we say of two things which consist of parts that they are like one another, the likeness of the wholes does admit of analysis; it is compounded of likenesses between the various parts respectively, and of likeness in their arrangement. Of how vast a variety of resemblances of parts must that resemblance be composed which induces us to say that a portrait or a landscape is like its original. If one person mimics another with any success, of how many simple likenesses must the general or complex likeness be compounded: likeness in a succession of bodily postures; likeness in voice, or in the accents and intonations of the voice; likeness in the choice of words, and in the thoughts or sentiments expressed, whether by word, countenance, or gesture.

All likeness and unlikeness of which we have any cognizance resolve themselves into likeness and unlikeness between states of our own, or some other, mind. When we say that one body is like another (since we know nothing of bodies but the sensations which they excite), we mean really that there is a resemblance between the sensations excited by the two bodies, or between some portions at least of those sensations. If we say that two attributes are like one another (since we know nothing of attributes except the sensations or states of feeling on which they are grounded), we mean really that those sensations or states of feeling resemble each other. We may also say that two relations are alike. The fact of resemblance between relations is sometimes called *analogy*, forming one of the numerous meanings of that word. The relation in which Priam stood to Hector, namely, that of father and son, resembles the relation in which Philip stood to Alexander, resembles it so closely that they are called the same relation. The relation in which Cromwell stood to England resembles the relation in which Napoleon stood to France, though not so closely as to be called the same relation. The meaning in both these instances must be that a resemblance existed between the facts which constituted the *fundamentum relationis*.

This resemblance may exist in all conceivable gradations, from perfect undistinguishableness to something extremely slight. When we say that a thought suggested to the mind of a person of genius is like a seed cast into the ground, because the former produces a multitude of other thoughts and the latter a multitude of other seeds, this is saying that between the relation of an inventive mind to a thought contained in it and the relation of a fertile soil to a seed contained in it there exists a resemblance; the real resemblance being in the two *fundamenta relationis*, in each of which there occurs a germ, producing by its development a multitude of other things similar to itself. And as, whenever two objects are jointly concerned in a phenomenon, this constitutes a relation between those objects, so, if we suppose a second pair of objects concerned in a second phenomenon, the slightest resemblance between the two phenomena is sufficient to admit of its being said that the two relations resemble, provided, of course, the points of resemblance are found in those portions of the two phenomena respectively which are connoted by the relative names.

While speaking of resemblance, it is necessary to take notice of an ambiguity of language against which scarcely anyone is sufficiently on his guard. Resemblance, when it exists in the highest degree of all, amounting to undistinguishableness, is often called identity, and the two similar things are said to be the same. I say often, not always, for we do not say that two visible objects, two persons, for instance, are the same, because they are so much alike that one might be mistaken for the other; but we constantly use this mode of expression when speaking of feelings, as when I say that the sight of any object gives me the *same* sensation or emotion today that it did yesterday, or the *same* which it gives to some other person. This is evidently an incorrect application of the word *same*, for the feeling which I had yesterday is gone, never to return; what I have today is another feeling, exactly like the former, perhaps, but distinct from it; and it is evident that two different persons cannot be experiencing the same feeling, in the sense in which we say that they are both sitting at the same table. By a similar ambiguity we say, that two persons are ill of the *same* disease; that two persons hold the *same* office; not in the sense in which we say that they are engaged in the same adventure or sailing in the same ship, but in the sense that they fill offices exactly similar, though, perhaps, in distant places. Great confusion of ideas is often produced and many fallacies engendered in otherwise enlightened understandings by not being sufficiently alive to the fact (in itself not always to be avoided) that they use the same name to express ideas so different as those of identity and undistinguishable resemblance. Among modern writers, Archbishop Whately stands almost alone in having drawn attention to this distinction and to the ambiguity connected with it.

Several relations, generally called by other names, are really cases of resemblance. As, for example, equality, which is but another word for the exact resemblance commonly called identity, considered as subsisting between things in respect of their *quantity*. And this example forms a suitable transition to the third and last of the three heads under which, as already remarked, Attributes are commonly arranged.

V. QUANTITY

11. *Quantity*

Let us imagine two things between which there is no difference (that is, no dissimilarity) except in quantity alone, for instance, a gallon of water, and more than a gallon of water. A gallon of water, like any other external object, makes its presence known to us by a set of sensations which it excites. Ten gallons of water are also an external object, making its presence known to us in a similar manner; and as we do not mistake ten gallons of water for a gallon of water, it is plain that the set of sensations is more or less different in the two cases. In like manner, a gallon of water and a gallon of wine are two external objects making their presence known by two sets of sensations, which sensations are different from each other. In the first case, however, we say that the difference is in quantity; in the last there is a difference in quality, while the quantity of the water and of the wine is the same. What is the real distinction between the two cases? It is not within the province of logic to analyze it, nor to decide whether it is susceptible of analysis or not. For us the following considerations are sufficient: It is evident that the sensations I receive from the gallon of water and those I receive from the gallon of wine are not the same, that is, not precisely alike; neither are they altogether unlike; they are partly similar, partly dissimilar; and that in which they resemble is precisely that in which alone the gallon of water and the ten gallons do not resemble. That in which the gallon of water and the gallon of wine are like each other and in which the gallon and the ten gallons of water are unlike each other is called their quantity. This likeness and unlikeness I do not pretend to explain, no more than any other kind of likeness or unlikeness. But my object is to show that when we say of two things that they differ in quantity, just as when we say that they differ in quality, the assertion is always grounded on a difference in the sensations which they excite. Nobody, I presume, will say that to see, or to lift, or to drink ten gallons of water does not include in itself a different set of sensations from those of seeing, lifting, or drinking one gallon, or that to see or handle a foot-rule and to see or handle a yard-measure made exactly like it are the same sensations. I do not undertake to say what the difference in the sensations is. Everybody knows, and nobody can tell, no more than anyone could tell what white is to a person who had never had the sensation. But the difference, so far as cognizable by our faculties, lies in the sensations. Whatever difference we say there is in the things themselves is, in this as in all other cases, grounded, and grounded exclusively, on a difference in the sensations excited by them.

VI. ATTRIBUTES CONCLUDED

12. *All attributes of bodies are grounded on states of consciousness*

Thus, then, all the attributes of bodies which are classed under quality or quantity are grounded on the sensations which we receive from those bodies, and may be defined: the powers which the bodies have of exciting those sensations. And the same general explanation has been found to apply to most of the attributes usually classed under the head of relation. They, too, are grounded on some fact or phenomenon into which the related objects enter as parts, that fact or phenomenon having no meaning and no existence to us, except the series of sensations or other states of consciousness by which it makes itself known, and the relation being simply the power or capacity which the object possesses of taking part along with the correlated object in the production of that series of sensations or states of consciousness. We have been obliged, indeed, to recognize a somewhat different character in certain peculiar relations, those of succession and simultaneity, of likeness and unlikeness. These, not being grounded on any fact or phenomenon distinct from the related objects themselves, do not admit of the same kind of analysis. But these relations, though not like other relations grounded on states of consciousness, are themselves states of consciousness: resemblance is nothing but our feeling of resemblance; succession is nothing but our feeling of succession. Or, if this be disputed (and we cannot, without transgressing the bounds of our science, discuss it here), at least our knowledge of these relations, and even our possibility of knowledge, is confined to those which subsist between sensations, or other states of consciousness; for, though we ascribe resemblance or succession or simultaneity to objects and to attributes, it is always in virtue of resemblance or succession or simultaneity in the sensations or states of consciousness which those objects excite, and on which those attributes are grounded.

13. *So also all attributes of mind*

In the preceding investigation we have, for the sake of simplicity, considered bodies only and omitted minds. But what we have said is applicable, *mutatis mutandis*, to the latter. The attributes of minds, as well as those of bodies, are grounded on states of feeling or consciousness. But in the case of a mind, we have to consider its own states as well as those which it produces in other minds. Every attribute of a mind consists either in being itself affected in a certain way or affecting other minds in a certain way. Considered in itself, we can predicate nothing of it but the series of its own feelings. When we say of any mind that it is devout or superstitious or meditative or cheerful, we mean that the ideas, emotions, or volitions implied in those words form a frequently recurring part of the series of feelings or states of consciousness which fill up the sentient existence of that mind.

In addition, however, to those attributes of a mind which are grounded on its own states of feeling, attributes may also be ascribed to it, in the same manner as to a body, grounded on the feelings which it excites in other minds. A mind does not, indeed like a body, excite sensations, but it may excite thoughts or emotions. The most important example of attributes ascribed on this ground is the employment of terms expressive of approbation or blame. When, for example, we say of any character, or (in other words) of any mind, that it is admirable, we mean that the contemplation of it excites the sentiment of admiration, and indeed somewhat more, for the word implies that we not only feel admiration, but approve that sentiment in ourselves. In some cases, under the semblance of a single attribute, two are really predicated: one of them, a state of the mind itself, the other, a state with which other minds are affected by thinking of it. As when we say of any one that he is generous. The word generosity expresses a certain state of mind, but being a term of praise, it also expresses that this state of mind excites in us another mental state called approbation. The assertion made, therefore, is twofold, and of the following purport: Certain feelings form habitually a part of this person's sentient existence, and the idea of those feelings of his excites the sentiment of approbation in ourselves or others.

As we thus ascribe attributes to minds on the ground of ideas and emotions, so may we to bodies on similar grounds, and not solely on the ground of sensations: as in speaking of the beauty of a statue, since this attribute is grounded on the peculiar feeling of pleasure which the statue produces in our minds, which is not a sensation, but an emotion.

VII. General Results

14. *Recapitulation*

Our survey of the varieties of things which have been, or which are capable of being, named — which have been, or are capable of being, either predicated of other things, or themselves made the subject of predications — is now concluded.

Our enumeration commenced with feelings. These we scrupulously distinguished from the objects which excite them, and from the organs by which they are, or may be supposed to be, conveyed. Feelings are of four sorts: sensations, thoughts, emotions, and volitions. What are called perceptions are merely a particular case of belief, and belief is a kind of thought. Actions are merely volitions followed by an effect.

After feelings we proceeded to substances. These are either bodies or minds. Without entering into the grounds of the metaphysical doubts which have been raised concerning the existence of matter and mind as objective realities, we stated as sufficient for us the conclusion in which the best thinkers are now for the most part agreed, that all we can know of matter is the sensations which it gives us and the order of occurrence of those sensations, and that while the substance body is the unknown cause of our sensations, the substance mind is the unknown recipient.

The only remaining class of namable things is attributes, and these are of three kinds, quality, relation, and quantity. Qualities, like substances, are known to us no otherwise than by the sensations or other states of consciousness which they excite; and while, in compliance with common usage, we have continued to speak of them as a distinct class of things, we showed that in predicating them no one means to predicate anything but those sensations or states of consciousness on which they may be said to be grounded and by which alone they can be defined or described. Relations, except the simple cases of likeness and unlikeness, succession and simultaneity, are similarly grounded on some fact or phenomenon, that is, on some series of sensations or states of consciousness, more or less complicated. The third species of attribute, quantity, is also manifestly grounded on something in our sensations or states of feeling, since there is an indubitable difference in the sensations excited by a larger and a smaller bulk, or by a greater or a less degree of intensity, in any object of sense or of consciousness. All attributes, therefore, are to us nothing but either our sensations and other states of feeling, or something inextricably involved therein: and to this even the peculiar and simple relations just adverted to are not exceptions. Those peculiar relations, however, are so important and, even if they might in strictness be classed among states of consciousness, are so fundamentally distinct from any other of those states, that it would be a vain subtlety to bring them under that common description, and it is necessary that they should be classed apart.[7]

As the result, therefore, of our analysis, we obtain the following as an enumeration and classification of all namable things:

1st. Feelings, or states of consciousness

2d. The minds which experience those feelings

3d. The bodies, or external objects which excite certain of those feelings, together with the powers or properties whereby they excite them; these latter (at least) being included rather in compliance with common opinion, and because their existence is taken for granted in the common language from which I cannot prudently deviate, than because the recognition of such powers or properties as real existences appears to be warranted by a sound philosophy

4th, and last. The successions and coexistences, the likenesses and unlikenesses, between feelings or states of consciousness. Those relations, when considered as subsisting between other things, exist in reality only between the states of consciousness which those things, if bodies, excite, if minds, either excite or experience.

This, until a better can be suggested, may serve as a substitute for the Categories of Aristotle considered as a classification of Existences. The practical application of it will appear when we commence the inquiry into the Import of Propositions, in other words, when we inquire what it is which the mind actually believes when it gives what is called its assent to a proposition.

These four classes comprising, if the classification be correct, all namable things, these or some of them must, of course, compose the signification of all names, and of these, or some of them, is made up whatever we call a fact.

For distinction's sake, every fact which is solely composed of

[7] Professor Bain (*Logic*, I, 49) defines attributes as "points of community among classes." This definition expresses well one point of view, but is liable to the objection that it applies only to the attributes of classes; though an object, unique in its kind, may be said to have attributes. Moreover, the definition is not ultimate, since the points of community themselves admit of, and require, further analysis; and Mr. Bain does analyze them into resemblances in the sensations or other states of consciousness excited by the object.

feelings or states of consciousness considered as such, is often called a psychological or subjective fact, while every fact which is composed, either wholly or in part, of something different from these, that is, of substances and attributes, is called an objective fact. We may say, then, that every objective fact is grounded on a corresponding subjective one, and has no meaning to us (apart from the subjective fact which corresponds to it), except as a name for the unknown and inscrutable process by which that subjective or psychological fact is brought to pass.

CHAPTER IV*

OF THE IMPORT OF PROPOSITIONS

1. *Doctrine that a proposition is the expression of a relation between two ideas*

An inquiry into the nature of propositions must have one of two objects: to analyze the state of mind called Belief, or to analyze what is believed. All language recognizes a difference between a doctrine or opinion and the fact of entertaining the opinion, between assent and what is assented to.

Logic, according to the conception here formed of it, has no concern with the nature of the act of judging or believing; the consideration of that act, as a phenomenon of the mind, belongs to another science. Philosophers, however, from Descartes downward, and especially from the era of Leibnitz and Locke, have by no means observed this distinction, and would have treated with great disrespect any attempt to analyze the import of propositions unless founded on an analysis of the act of judgment. A proposition, they would have said, is but the expression in words of a judgment. The thing expressed, not the mere verbal expression, is the important matter. When the mind assents to a proposition,

*[Chapter V of the eighth edition.]

it judges. Let us find out what the mind does when it judges, and we shall know what propositions mean, and not otherwise.

Conformably to these views, almost all the writers on logic in the last two centuries, whether English, German, or French, have made their theory of propositions, from one end to the other, a theory of judgments. They considered a proposition or a judgment, for they used the two words indiscriminately, to consist in affirming or denying one *idea* of another. To judge was to put two ideas together, or to bring one idea under another, or to compare two ideas, or to perceive the agreement or disagreement between two ideas; and the whole doctrine of propositions, together with the theory of reasoning (always necessarily founded on the theory of propositions), was stated as if ideas or conceptions, or whatever other term the writer preferred as a name for mental representations generally, constituted essentially the subject-matter and substance of those operations.

It is, of course, true that in any case of judgment, as for instance when we judge that gold is yellow, a process takes place in our minds of which some one or other of these theories is a partially correct account. We must have the idea of gold and the idea of yellow, and these two ideas must be brought together in our mind. But, in the first place, it is evident that this is only a part of what takes place, for we may put two ideas together without any act of belief, as when we merely imagine something, such as a golden mountain, or when we actually disbelieve; for in order even to disbelieve that Mohammed was an apostle of God, we must put the idea of Mohammed and that of an apostle of God together. To determine what it is that happens in the case of assent or dissent besides putting two ideas together is one of the most intricate of metaphysical problems. But, whatever the solution may be, we may venture to assert that it can have nothing whatever to do with the import of propositions, for this reason, that propositions (except sometimes when the mind itself is the subject treated of) are not assertions respecting our ideas of things, but assertions respecting the things themselves. In order to believe that gold is yellow, I must, indeed, have the idea of gold and the idea of yellow, and something having reference to those ideas must take place in my mind; but my belief has not reference to the ideas, it has reference to the things. What I believe is a fact relating to the outward thing, gold, and to the impression made by that outward thing upon the human organs, not a fact relating to my conception of gold, which would be a fact in my mental history, not a fact of external nature. It is true that, in order to believe this fact in external nature, another fact must take place in my mind, a process must be performed upon my ideas; but so it must in everything else that I do. I cannot dig the ground unless I have the idea of the ground and of a spade and of all the other things I am operating upon, and unless I put those ideas together.[1] But it would be a very ridiculous description of digging the ground to say that it is putting one idea into another. Digging is an operation which is performed upon the things themselves, though it cannot be performed unless I have in my mind the ideas of them. And, in like manner, believing is an act which has for its subject the facts themselves, though a previous mental conception of the facts is an indispensable condition. When I say that fire causes heat, do I mean that my idea of fire causes my idea of heat? No; I mean that the natural phenomenon, fire, causes the natural phenomenon, heat. When I mean to assert anything respecting the ideas, I give them their proper name; I call them ideas, as when I say that a child's idea of a battle is unlike the reality, or that the ideas entertained of the Deity have a great effect on the characters of mankind.

The notion that what is of primary importance to the logician in a proposition is the relation between the two *ideas* corresponding to the subject and predicate (instead of the relation between the two *phenomena* which they respectively express) seems to me one of the most fatal errors ever introduced into the philosophy of logic, and the principal cause why the theory of the science has made such inconsiderable progress during the last two centuries. The treatises on logic and on the branches of mental philosophy

[1]Dr. Whewell (*Philosophy of Discovery*, p. 242) questions this statement, and asks, "Are we to say that a mole cannot dig the ground, except he has an idea of the ground, and of the snout and paws with which he digs it?" I do not know what passes in a mole's mind, nor what amount of mental apprehension may or may not accompany his instinctive actions. But a human being does not use a spade by instinct, and he certainly could not use it unless he had knowledge of a spade and of the earth which he uses it upon.

connected with logic which have been produced since the intrusion of this cardinal error, though sometimes written by men of extraordinary abilities and attainments, almost always tacitly imply a theory that the investigation of truth consists in contemplating and handling our ideas or conceptions of things, instead of the things themselves, a doctrine tantamount to the assertion that the only mode of acquiring knowledge of nature is to study it at second hand, as represented in our own minds. Meanwhile, inquiries into every kind of natural phenomena were incessantly establishing great and fruitful truths on most important subjects by processes upon which these views of the nature of judgment and reasoning threw no light and in which they afforded no assistance whatever. No wonder that those who knew by practical experience how truths are arrived at should deem a science futile which consisted chiefly of such speculations. What has been done for the advancement of logic since these doctrines came into vogue has been done not by professed logicians but by discoverers in the other sciences, in whose methods of investigation many principles of logic, not previously thought of, have successively come forth into light, but who have generally committed the error of supposing that nothing whatever was known of the art of philosophizing by the old logicians because their modern interpreters have written to so little purpose respecting it.

We have to inquire, then, on the present occasion, not into judgment, but judgments; not into the act of believing, but into the thing believed. What is the immediate object of belief in a proposition? What is the matter of fact signified by it? What is it to which, when I assert the proposition, I give my assent, and call upon others to give theirs? What is that which is expressed by the form of discourse called a proposition, and the conformity of which to fact constitutes the truth of the proposition?

2. — *that it consists in referring something to, or excluding something from, a class*

Although Hobbes's theory of predication has not, in the terms in which he stated it, met with a very favorable reception from subsequent thinkers, a theory virtually identical with it and not by any means so perspicuously expressed may almost be said to have taken the rank of an established opinion. The most generally received notion of predication decidedly is that it consists in referring something to a class, that is, either placing an individual under a class, or placing one class under another class. Thus the proposition, "Man is mortal," asserts, according to this view of it, that the class man is included in the class mortal. "Plato is a philosopher," asserts that the individual Plato is one of those who compose the class philosopher. If the proposition is negative, then instead of placing something in a class, it is said to exclude something from a class. Thus, if the following be the proposition, "The elephant is not carnivorous," what is asserted (according to this theory) is that the elephant is excluded from the class carnivorous, or is not numbered among the things comprising that class. There is no real difference, except in language, between this theory of predication and the theory of Hobbes. For a class *is* absolutely nothing but an indefinite number of individuals denoted by a general name. The name given to them in common is what makes them a class. To refer anything to a class, therefore, is to look upon it as one of the things which are to be called by that common name. To exclude it from a class is to say that the common name is not applicable to it.

How widely these views of predication have prevailed is evident from this, that they are the basis of the celebrated *dictum de omni et nullo*. When the syllogism is resolved, by all who treat of it, into an inference that what is true of a class is true of all things whatever that belong to the class, and when this is laid down by almost all professed logicians as the ultimate principle to which all reasoning owes its validity, it is clear that, in the general estimation of logicians, the propositions of which reasonings are composed can be the expression of nothing but the process of dividing things into classes and referring everything to its proper class.

This theory appears to me a signal example of a logical error very often committed in logic, that of ὕστερον πρότερον, or explaining a thing by something which presupposes it. When I say that snow is white, I may and ought to be thinking of snow as a class, because I am asserting a proposition as true of all snow, but I am

certainly not thinking of white objects as a class; I am thinking of
no white object whatever except snow, but only of that and of the
sensation of white which it gives me. When, indeed, I have judged
or assented to the propositions that snow is white and that several
other things are also white, I gradually begin to think of white
objects as a class, including snow and those other things. But this
is a conception which followed, not preceded, those judgments and,
therefore, cannot be given as an explanation of them. Instead of
explaining the effect by the cause, this doctrine explains the cause
by the effect, and is, I conceive, founded on a latent misconception
of the nature of classification.

There is a sort of language very generally prevalent in these
discussions which seems to suppose that classification is an arrangement and grouping of definite and known individuals, that, when
names were imposed, mankind took into consideration all the individual objects in the universe, distributed them into parcels or
lists, and gave to the objects of each list a common name, repeating
this operation *toties quoties* until they had invented all the general
names of which language consists; which having been once done,
if a question subsequently arises whether a certain general name
can be truly predicated of a certain particular object, we have only
(as it were) to read the roll of the objects upon which that name
was conferred and see whether the object about which the question
arises is to be found among them. The framers of language (it
would seem to be supposed) have predetermined all the objects
that are to compose each class, and we have only to refer to the
record of an antecedent decision.

So absurd a doctrine will be owned by nobody when thus nakedly
stated, but if the commonly received explanations of classification
and naming do not imply this theory, it requires to be shown how
they admit of being reconciled with any other.

General names are not marks put upon definite objects; classes
are not made by drawing a line round a given number of assignable
individuals. The objects which compose any given class are perpetually fluctuating. We may frame a class without knowing the
individuals, or even any of the individuals, of which it may be
composed; we may do so while believing that no such individuals
exist. If by the *meaning* of a general name are to be understood

the things which it is the name of, no general name, except by accident, has a fixed meaning at all, or ever long retains the same meaning. The only mode in which any general name has a definite meaning is by being a name of an indefinite variety of things, namely, of all things, known or unknown, past, present, or future, which possess certain definite attributes. When, by studying, not the meaning of words but the phenomena of nature, we discover that these attributes are possessed by some object not previously known to possess them (as when chemists found that the diamond was combustible), we include this new object in the class, but it did not already belong to the class. We place the individual in the class because the proposition is true; the proposition is not true because the object is placed in the class.[2]

It will appear hereafter, in treating of reasoning, how much the theory of that intellectual process has been vitiated by the influence of these erroneous notions and by the habit which they exemplify of assimilating all the operations of the human understanding which have truth for their object to processes of mere classification and naming. Unfortunately, the minds which have been entangled in this net are precisely those which have escaped the other cardinal error commented upon in the beginning of the present chapter. Since the revolution which dislodged Aristotle from the schools, logicians may almost be divided into those who have looked upon reasoning as essentially an affair of ideas and those who have looked upon it as essentially an affair of names.

[2] Professor Bain remarks, in qualification of the statement in the text (*Logic*, i., 50), that the word Class has two meanings, "the class definite, and the class indefinite. The class definite is an enumeration of actual individuals, as the Peers of the Realm, the oceans of the globe, the known planets. . . . The class indefinite is unenumerated. Such classes are stars, planets, gold-bearing rocks, men, poets, virtuous. . . . In this last acceptation of the word, class name and general name are identical. The class name denotes an indefinite number of individuals and connotes the points of community or likeness."

The theory controverted in the text tacitly supposes all classes to be *definite*. I have assumed them to be indefinite, because, for the purposes of logic, definite classes, as such, are almost useless, though often serviceable as means of abridged expression. (*Vide infra*, book III, chap. 2.)

3. *What it really is*

Let the predicate be, as we have said, a connotative term, and, to take the simplest case first, let the subject be a proper name: "The summit of Chimborazo is white." The word "white" connotes an attribute which is possessed by the individual object designated by the words "summit of Chimborazo," which attribute consists in the physical fact of its exciting in human beings the sensation which we call a sensation of white. It will be admitted that, by asserting the proposition, we wish to communicate information of that physical fact and are not thinking of the names, except as the necessary means of making that communication. The meaning of the proposition, therefore, is that the individual thing denoted by the subject has the attributes connoted by the predicate.

If we now suppose the subject also to be a connotative name, the meaning expressed by the proposition has advanced a step further in complication. Let us first suppose the proposition to be universal, as well as affirmative: "All men are mortal." In this case, as in the last, what the proposition asserts (or expresses a belief of) is, of course, that the objects denoted by the subject (man) possess the attributes connoted by the predicate (mortal). But the characteristic of this case is that the objects are no longer *individually* designated. They are pointed out only by some of their attributes; they are the objects called men, that is, possessing the attributes connoted by the name man, and the only thing known of them may be those attributes; indeed, as the proposition is general, and the objects denoted by the subject are, therefore, indefinite in number, most of them are not known individually at all. The assertion, therefore, is not as before that the attributes which the predicate connotes are possessed by any given individual, or by any number of individuals previously known as John, Thomas, etc., but that those attributes are possessed by each and every individual possessing certain other attributes; that whatever has the attributes connoted by the subject, has also those connoted by the predicate; that the latter set of attributes *constantly accompany* the former set.[3] Whatever has the attributes of man has the

[3]To the preceding statement it has been objected that "we naturally construe the subject of a proposition in its extension, and the predicate (which

attribute of mortality; mortality constantly accompanies the attributes of man.

If it be remembered that every attribute is *grounded* on some fact or phenomenon, either of outward sense or of inward consciousness, and that to *possess* an attribute is another phrase for being the cause of, or forming part of, the fact or phenomenon upon which the attribute is grounded, we may add one more step to complete the analysis. The proposition which asserts that one attribute always accompanies another attribute really asserts thereby no other thing than this, that one phenomenon always accompanies another phenomenon; insomuch that where we find the latter, we have assurance of the existence of the former. Thus, in the proposition, "All men are mortal," the word "man" connotes the attributes which we ascribe to a certain kind of living creatures on the ground of certain phenomena which they exhibit, and which are partly physical phenomena, namely, the impressions made on our senses by their bodily form and structure, and partly mental phenomena, namely, the sentient and intellectual life which they have of their own. All this is understood when we utter the word man, by any one to whom the meaning of the word is known. Now, when we say, "Man is mortal," we mean that wherever these various physical and mental phenomena are all found, there we have assurance that the other physical and mental phenomenon, called death, will not fail to take place. The proposition does not affirm *when*, for the connotation of the word *mortal* goes no further

therefore may be an adjective) in its intension (connotation); and that consequently co-existence of attributes does not, any more than the opposite theory of equation of groups, correspond with the living processes of thought and language." I acknowledge the distinction here drawn, which, indeed, I had myself laid down and exemplified a few pages back. But though it is true that we naturally "construe the subject of a proposition in its extension," this extension, or in other words, the extent of the class denoted by the name, is not apprehended or indicated directly. It is both apprehended and indicated solely through the attributes. In the "living processes of thought and language" the extension, though in this case really thought of (which in the case of the predicate it is not), is thought of only through the medium of what my acute and courteous critic terms the "intension."

For further illustrations of this subject, see *Examination of Sir William Hamilton's Philosophy*, chap. XXII.

than to the occurrence of the phenomenon at some time or other,
leaving the particular time undecided.

4. *It asserts (or denies) a sequence, a co-existence, a simple existence,*
   a causation

We have already proceeded far enough, not only to demonstrate
the error of Hobbes, but to ascertain the real import of by far the
most numerous class of propositions. The object of belief in a
proposition, when it asserts anything more than the meaning of
words, is generally, as in the cases which we have examined, either
the co-existence or the sequence of two phenomena. At the very
commencement of our inquiry, we found that every act of belief
implied two things; we have now ascertained what, in the most
frequent case, these two things are, namely, two phenomena, in
other words, two states of consciousness, and what it is which the
proposition affirms (or denies) to subsist between them, namely,
either succession or co-existence. And this case includes innumerable instances which no one, previous to reflection, would think
of referring to it. Take the following example: "A generous person
is worthy of honor." Who would expect to recognize here a case
of co-existence between phenomena? But so it is. The attribute
which causes a person to be termed generous is ascribed to him
on the ground of states of his mind and particulars of his conduct;
both are phenomena: the former are facts of internal consciousness;
the latter, so far as distinct from the former, are physical facts, or
perceptions of the senses. "Worthy of honor" admits of a similar
analysis. Honor, as here used, means a state of approving and
admiring emotion, followed on occasion by corresponding outward
acts. "Worthy of honor" connotes all this, together with our
approval of the act of showing honor. All these are phenomena,
states of internal consciousness, accompanied or followed by physical facts. When we say, "A generous person is worthy of honor,"
we affirm co-existence between the two complicated phenomena
connoted by the two terms respectively. We affirm that wherever
and whenever the inward feelings and outward facts implied in
the word generosity have place, then and there the existence and

manifestation of an inward feeling, honor, would be followed in our minds by another inward feeling, approval.

. . . .

This, however, though the most common, is not the only meaning which propositions are ever intended to convey. In the first place, sequences and co-existences are not only asserted respecting phenomena; we make propositions also respecting those hidden causes of phenomena, which are named substances and attributes. A substance, however, being to us nothing but either that which causes, or that which is conscious of, phenomena; and the same being true, *mutatis mutandis*, of attributes; no assertion can be made, at least with a meaning, concerning these unknown and unknowable entities, except in virtue of the phenomena by which alone they manifest themselves to our faculties. When we say Socrates was contemporary with the Peloponnesian war, the foundation of this assertion, as of all assertions concerning substances, is an assertion concerning the phenomena which they exhibit, namely, that the series of facts by which Socrates manifested himself to mankind and the series of mental states which constituted his sentient existence went on simultaneously with the series of facts known by the name of the Peloponnesian war. Still, the proposition as commonly understood does not assert that alone; it asserts that the thing in itself, the *noumenon* Socrates, was existing and doing or experiencing those various facts during the same time. Co-existence and sequence, therefore, may be affirmed or denied not only between phenomena, but between noumena, or between a noumenon and phenomena. And both of noumena and of phenomena we may affirm simple existence. But what is a noumenon? An unknown cause. In affirming, therefore, the existence of a noumenon, we affirm causation. Here, therefore, are two additional kinds of fact, capable of being asserted in a proposition. Besides the propositions which assert sequence or co-existence, there are some which assert simple existence;[4] and others assert

[4]Professor Bain, in his *Logic* (i., 256), excludes Existence from the list, considering it as a mere name. All propositions, he says, which predicate mere existence "are more or less abbreviated, or elliptical; when fully expressed they fall under either co-existence or succession. When we say there *exists* a conspiracy for a particular purpose, we mean that at the present time a body of men have formed themselves into a society for a particular object; which is a

causation, which, subject to the explanations which will follow in the Third Book, must be considered provisionally as a distinct and peculiar kind of assertion.

complex affirmation, resolvable into propositions of co-existence and succession (as causation). The assertion that the dodo does not exist, points to the fact that this animal, once known in a certain place, has disappeared or become extinct, is no longer associated with the locality; all which may be better stated without the use of the verb 'exist.' There is a debated question — Does an ether exist? but the concrete form would be this — 'Are heat and light and other radiant influences propagated by an ethereal medium diffused in space,' which is a proposition of causation. In like manner the question of the Existence of a Deity cannot be discussed in that form. It is properly a question as to the First *Cause* of the Universe, and as to the continued exertion of that Cause in providential superintendence." (II, 407.)

Mr. Bain thinks it "fictitious and unmeaning language" to carry up the classification of Nature to one *summum genus*, Being, or that which Exists, since nothing can be perceived or apprehended but by way of contrast with something else (of which important truth, under the name of Law of Relativity, he has been in our time the principal expounder and champion), and we have no other class to oppose to Being, or fact to contrast with Existence.

I accept fully Mr. Bain's Law of Relativity, but I do not understand by it that to enable us to apprehend or be conscious of any fact, it is necessary that we should contrast it with some other positive fact. The antithesis necessary to consciousness need not, I conceive, be an antithesis between two positives; it may be between one positive and its negative. Hobbes was undoubtedly right when he said that a single sensation indefinitely prolonged would cease to be felt at all; but simple intermission, without other change, would restore it to consciousness. In order to be conscious of heat, it is not necessary that we should pass to it from cold; it suffices that we should pass to it from a state of no sensation, or from a sensation of some other kind. The relative opposite of Being, considered as a summum genus, is Nonentity, or Nothing; and we have, now and then, occasion to consider and discuss things merely in contrast with Nonentity.

I grant that the *decision* of questions of Existence usually if not always depends on a previous question of either Causation or Co-existence. But Existence is nevertheless a different thing from Causation or Co-existence and can be predicated apart from them. The meaning of the abstract name Existence, and the connotation of the concrete name Being, consist, like the meaning of all other names, in sensations or states of consciousness; their peculiarity is that to exist is to excite, or be capable of exciting, *any* sensations or states of consciousness; no matter what, but it is indispensable that there should be some. It was from overlooking this that Hegel, finding that Being is an abstraction reached by thinking away all particular attributes, arrived at the self-contradictory proposition on which he founded all his philosophy, that Being is the same as Nothing. It is really the name of Something, taken in the most comprehensive sense of the word.

5. — *or a resemblance*

To these four kinds of matter-of-fact or assertion must be added a fifth, resemblance. This was a species of attribute which we found it impossible to analyze; for which no *fundamentum* distinct from the objects themselves could be assigned. Besides propositions which assert a sequence or co-existence between two phenomena, there are, therefore, also propositions which assert resemblance between them, as, "This color is like that color," "The heat of today is *equal* to the heat of yesterday." It is true that such an assertion might with some plausibility be brought within the description of an affirmation of sequence by considering it as an assertion that the simultaneous contemplation of the two colors is *followed* by a specific feeling termed the feeling of resemblance. But there would be nothing gained by incumbering ourselves, especially in this place, with a generalization which may be looked upon as strained. Logic does not undertake to analyze mental facts into their ultimate elements. Resemblance between two phenomena is more intelligible in itself than any explanation could make it, and under any classification must remain specifically distinct from the ordinary cases of sequence and co-existence.

It is sometimes said that all propositions whatever of which the predicate is a general name do, in point of fact, affirm or deny resemblance. All such propositions affirm that a thing belongs to a class, but things being classed together according to their resemblance, every thing is, of course, classed with the things which it is supposed to resemble most; and thence, it may be said, when we affirm that gold is a metal, or that Socrates is a man, the affirmation intended is that gold resembles other metals, and Socrates other men, more nearly than they resemble the objects contained in any other of the classes co-ordinate with these.

There is some slight degree of foundation for this remark, but no more than a slight degree. The arrangement of things into classes, such as the class *metal*, or the class *man*, is grounded indeed on a resemblance among the things which are placed in the same class, but not on a mere general resemblance; the resemblance it is grounded on consists in the possession by all those things of certain common peculiarities; and those peculiarities it is which the terms connote, and which the propositions consequently assert, not the resemblance. For though when I say, "Gold is a metal," I say by implication that if there be any other metals it must resemble them, yet if there were no other metals I might still assert the proposition with the same meaning as at present, namely, that gold has the various properties implied in the word metal; just as it might be said, "Christians are men," even if there were no men who were not Christians. Propositions, therefore, in which objects are referred to a class because they possess the attributes constituting the class are so far from asserting nothing but resemblance, that they do not, properly speaking, assert resemblance at all.

But we remarked some time ago (and the reasons of the remark will be more fully entered into in a subsequent Book)[5] that there is sometimes a convenience in extending the boundaries of a class so as to include things which possess in a very inferior degree, if in any, some of the characteristic properties of the class — provided they resemble that class more than any other, insomuch that the general propositions which are true of the class will be nearer to being true of those things than any other equally general propositions. For instance, there are substances called metals which have very few of the properties by which metals are commonly recognized, and almost every great family of plants or animals has a few anomalous genera or species on its borders which are admitted into it by a sort of courtesy, and concerning which it has been matter of discussion to what family they properly belonged. Now, when the class-name is predicated of any object of this description, we do, by so predicating it, affirm resemblance and nothing more. And in order to be scrupulously correct it ought to be said that in every case in which we predicate a general name, we affirm, not absolutely that the object possesses the properties designated by the name, but that it *either* possesses those properties or, if it does not, at any rate resembles the things which do so more than it resembles any other things. In most cases, however, it is unnecessary to suppose any such alternative, the latter of the two grounds being very seldom that on which the assertion is made, and when it is, there is generally some slight difference in the form of the expression, as, This species (or genus) is *considered*, or *may be ranked*, as belonging to such and such a family; we should

[5] Book IV, Chapter VII [in this edition: Book IV, Chapter II].

hardly say positively that it does belong to it unless it possessed unequivocally the properties of which the class-name is scientifically significant.

There is still another exceptional case, in which, though the predicate is the name of a class, yet in predicating it we affirm nothing but resemblance, the class being founded not on resemblance in any given particular but on general unanalyzable resemblance. The classes in question are those into which our simple sensations, or other simple feelings, are divided. Sensations of white, for instance, are classed together, not because we can take them to pieces and say they are alike in this and not alike in that, but because we feel them to be alike altogether, though in different degrees. When, therefore, I say, "The color I saw yesterday was a white color," or, "The sensation I feel is one of tightness," in both cases the attribute I affirm of the color or of the other sensation is mere resemblance — simple *likeness* to sensations which I have had before and which have had those names bestowed upon them. The names of feelings, like other concrete general names, are connotative, but they connote a mere resemblance. When predicated of any individual feeling, the information they convey is that of its likeness to the other feelings which we have been accustomed to call by the same name. Thus much may suffice in illustration of the kind of propositions in which the matter-of-fact asserted (or denied) is simple resemblance.

Existence, co-existence, sequence, causation, resemblance: one or other of these is asserted (or denied) in every proposition which is not merely verbal. This five-fold division is an exhaustive classification of matters-of-fact, of all things that can be believed or tendered for belief, of all questions that can be propounded, and all answers that can be returned to them.

·   ·   ·   ·   ·   ·   ·   ·   ·   ·   ·   ·   ·   ·   ·   ·   ·   ·

6. *Propositions of which the terms are abstract*

In the foregoing inquiry into the import of propositions, we have thought it necessary to analyze directly those alone in which the terms of the proposition (or the predicate at least) are concrete terms. But, in doing so, we have indirectly analyzed those in which the terms are abstract. The distinction between an abstract term and its corresponding concrete does not turn upon any difference in what they are appointed to signify, for the real signification of a concrete general name is, as we have so often said, its connotation, and what the concrete term connotes forms the entire meaning of the abstract name. Since there is nothing in the import of an abstract name which is not in the import of the corresponding concrete, it is natural to suppose that neither can there be anything in the import of a proposition of which the terms are abstract but what there is in some proposition which can be framed of concrete terms.

And this presumption a closer examination will confirm. An abstract name is the name of an attribute or combination of attributes. The corresponding concrete is a name given to things because of, and in order to express, their possessing that attribute or that combination of attributes. When, therefore, we predicate of anything a concrete name, the attribute is what we in reality predicate of it. But it has now been shown that in all propositions of which the predicate is a concrete name, what is really predicated is one of five things: Existence, Co-existence, Causation, Sequence, or Resemblance. An attribute, therefore, is necessarily either an existence, a co-existence, a causation, a sequence, or a resemblance. When a proposition consists of a subject and predicate which are abstract terms, it consists of terms which must necessarily signify one or other of these things. When we predicate of anything an abstract name, we affirm of the thing that it is one or other of these five things, that it is a case of Existence, or of Co-existence, or of Causation, or of Sequence, or of Resemblance.

It is impossible to imagine any proposition expressed in abstract terms which cannot be transformed into a precisely equivalent proposition in which the terms are concrete; namely, either the concrete names which connote the attributes themselves, or th names of the *fundamenta* of those attributes, the facts or phenomena on which they are grounded. To illustrate the latter case, let us take this proposition, of which the subject only is an abstract name, "Thoughtlessness is dangerous." Thoughtlessness is an attribute, grounded on the facts which we call thoughtless actions; and the proposition is equivalent to this, "Thoughtless actions are dangerous." In the next example the predicate as well as the subject are abstract names: "Whiteness is a color;" or "The color of snow is a whiteness." These attributes being grounded on sensations, the equivalent propositions in the concrete would be, "The sensation of white is one of the sensations called those of color" — "The sensation of sight, caused by looking at snow, is one of the sensations called sensations of white." In these propositions, as we have before seen, the matter-of-fact asserted is a resemblance. In the following examples, the concrete terms are those which directly correspond to the abstract names, connoting the attribute which these denote. "Prudence is a virtue;" this may be rendered, "All prudent persons, *in so far as* prudent, are virtuous;" "Courage is deserving of honor," thus, "All courageous persons are deserving of honor *in so far* as they are courageous," which is equivalent to this, "All courageous persons deserve an addition to the honor, or a diminution of the disgrace, which would attach to them on other grounds."

In order to throw still further light upon the import of propositions of which the terms are abstract, we will subject one of the examples given above to a minuter analysis. The proposition we shall select is the following: "Prudence is a virtue." Let us substitute for the word virtue an equivalent but more definite expression, such as "a mental quality beneficial to society," or "a mental quality pleasing to God," or whatever else we adopt as the definition of virtue. What the proposition asserts is a sequence accompanied with causation, namely, that benefit to society, or that the approval of God, is consequent on, and caused by, prudence. Here is a sequence; but between what? We understand the consequent of the sequence, but we have yet to analyze the antecedent. Prudence is an attribute; and, in connection with it, two things besides itself are to be considered: prudent persons, who are the *subjects* of the attribute, and prudential conduct, which may be called the *foundation* of it. Now is either of these the antecedent; and, first, is it meant, that the approval of God, or benefit to society, is attendant upon all prudent *persons?* No; except *in so far* as they are prudent; for prudent persons who are scoundrels can seldom, on the whole, be beneficial to society, nor can they be acceptable to a good being. Is it upon prudential *conduct,* then, that divine approbation and benefit to mankind are supposed to be invariably consequent? Neither is this the assertion meant, when it is said that prudence is a virtue, except with the same reservation as before, and for the same reason, namely, that prudential conduct, although in *so far as* it is prudential it is beneficial to society, may yet, by reason of some other of its qualities, be productive of an injury outweighing the benefit, and deserve a displeasure exceeding the approbation which would be due to the prudence. Neither the substance, therefore (*viz.*, the person), nor the phenomenon (the conduct), is an antecedent on which the other term of the sequence is universally consequent. But the proposition, "Prudence is a virtue," is a universal proposition. What is it, then, upon which the proposition affirms the effects in question to be universally consequent? Upon that in the person and in the conduct which causes them to be called prudent, and which is equally in them when the action, though prudent, is wicked, namely, a correct foresight of consequences, a just estimation of their importance to the object in view, and repression of any unreflecting impulse at variance with the deliberate purpose. These, which are states of the person's mind, are the real antecedent in the sequence, the real cause in the causation, asserted by the proposition. But these are also the real ground, or foundation, of the attribute Prudence; since wherever these states of mind exist we may predicate prudence, even before we know whether any conduct has followed. And in this manner every assertion respecting an attribute may be transformed into an assertion exactly equivalent respecting the fact or phenomenon which is the ground of the attribute. And no case can be assigned where that which is predicated of the fact or phenomenon does not belong to one or other of the five species formerly enumerated: it is either simple existence, or it is some sequence, co-existence, causation, or resemblance.

And as these five are the only things which can be affirmed, so are they the only things which can be denied. "No horses are web-footed" denies that the attributes of a horse ever co-exist with web-feet. It is scarcely necessary to apply the same analysis to particular affirmations and negations. "Some birds are web-footed" affirms that, with the attributes connoted by *bird*, the phenomenon web-feet is sometimes co-existent; "Some birds are not web-footed" asserts that there are other instances in which this co-existence does not have place. Any further explanation of a thing which, if the previous exposition has been assented to, is so obvious, may here be spared.

CHAPTER V*

OF PROPOSITIONS MERELY VERBAL

1. *All essential propositions are identical propositions*

Almost all metaphysicians prior to Locke, as well as many since his time, have made a great mystery of essential predication, and of predicates which are said to be of the *essence* of the subject. The essence of a thing, they said, was that without which the thing could neither be nor be conceived to be. Thus, rationality was of the essence of man because without rationality man could not be conceived to exist. The different attributes which made up the essence of the thing were called its essential properties, and a proposition in which any of these were predicated of it was called an essential proposition and was considered to go deeper into the nature of the thing and to convey more important information respecting it than any other proposition could do. All properties not of the essence of the thing were called its accidents, were supposed to have nothing at all, or nothing comparatively, to do with its inmost nature, and the propositions in which any of these were predicated of it were called accidental propositions. A connection may be traced between this distinction, which originated with the schoolmen, and the well-known dogmas of *substantiae secundae* or general substances, and *substantial forms*, doctrines which under varieties of language pervaded alike the Aristotelian and the Platonic schools, and of which more of the spirit has come down

* [Chapter VI of the eighth edition.]

to modern times than might be conjectured from the disuse of the phraseology. The false views of the nature of classification and generalization which prevailed among the schoolmen and of which these dogmas were the technical expression afford the only explanation which can be given of their having misunderstood the real nature of those essences which held so conspicuous a place in their philosophy. They said, truly, that *man* cannot be conceived without rationality. But though *man* cannot, a being may be conceived exactly like a man in all points except that one quality and those others which are the conditions or consequences of it. All, therefore, which is really true in the assertion that man cannot be conceived without rationality is only that, if he had not rationality, he would not be reputed a man. There is no impossibility in conceiving the *thing*, nor, for aught we know, in its existing; the impossibility is in the conventions of language, which will not allow the thing, even if it exist, to be called by the name which is reserved for rational beings. Rationality, in short, is involved in the meaning of the word "man," is one of the attributes connoted by the name. The essence of man simply means the whole of the attributes connoted by the word; and any one of those attributes taken singly is an essential property of man.

But these reflections, so easy to us, would have been difficult to persons who thought, as most of the later Aristotelians did, that objects were made what they were called, that gold (for instance) was made gold not by the possession of certain properties to which mankind have chosen to attach that name, but by participation in the nature of a general substance, called gold in general, which substance, together with all the properties that belonged to it, *inhered* in every individual piece of gold.[1] As they did not consider these universal substances to be attached to all general names but only to some, they thought that an object borrowed only a part of its properties from a universal substance, and that the rest

[1] The doctrines which prevented the real meaning of Essences from being understood had not assumed so settled a shape in the time of Aristotle and his immediate followers as was afterward given to them by the Realists of the Middle Ages. Aristotle himself (in his Treatise on the Categories) expressly denies that the δεύτεραι οὐσίαι or *substantiae secundae*, inhere in a subject. They are only, he says, predicated of it.

belonged to it individually; the former they called its essence, and the latter its accidents. The scholastic doctrine of essences long survived the theory on which it rested, that of the existence of real entities corresponding to general terms, and it was reserved for Locke, at the end of the seventeenth century, to convince philosophers that the supposed essences of classes were merely the signification of their names; nor, among the signal services which his writings rendered to philosophy, was there one more needful or more valuable.

Now, as the most familiar of the general names by which an object is designated usually connotes not one only, but several attributes of the object, each of which attributes separately forms also the bond of union of some class and the meaning of some general name, we may predicate of a name which connotes a variety of attributes another name which connotes only one of these attributes, or some smaller number of them than all. In such cases, the universal affirmative proposition will be true, since whatever possesses the whole of any set of attributes must possess any part of that same set. A proposition of this sort, however, conveys no information to anyone who previously understood the whole meaning of the terms. The propositions, "Every man is a corporeal being," "Every man is a living creature," "Every man is rational," convey no knowledge to anyone who was already aware of the entire meaning of the word *man*, for the meaning of the word includes all this; and that every *man* has the attributes connoted by all these predicates is already asserted when he is called a man. Now, of this nature are all the propositions which have been called essential. They are, in fact, identical propositions.

It is true that a proposition which predicates any attribute, even though it be one implied in the name, is in most cases understood to involve a tacit assertion that there *exists* a thing corresponding to the name and possessing the attributes connoted by it, and this implied assertion may convey information, even to those who understood the meaning of the name. But all information of this sort, conveyed by all the essential propositions of which man can be made the subject, is included in the assertion, "Men exist." And this assumption of real existence is, after all, the result of an imperfection of language. It arises from the ambiguity of the copula, which, in addition to its proper office of a mark to show that an assertion is made, is also, as formerly remarked, a concrete word connoting existence. The actual existence of the subject of the proposition is therefore only apparently, not really, implied in the predication, if an essential one; we may say, "A ghost is a disembodied spirit," without believing in ghosts. But an accidental, or non-essential, affirmation, does imply the real existence of the subject, because in the case of a non-existent subject there is nothing for the proposition to assert. Such a proposition as, "The ghost of a murdered person haunts the couch of the murderer," can only have a meaning if understood as implying a belief in ghosts; for since the signification of the word *ghost* implies nothing of the kind, the speaker either means nothing, or means to assert a thing which he wishes to be believed to have really taken place.

It will be hereafter seen that, when any important consequences seem to follow, as in mathematics, from an essential proposition, or, in other words, from a proposition involved in the meaning of a name, what they really flow from is the tacit assumption of the real existence of the objects so named. Apart from this assumption of real existence, the class of propositions in which the predicate is of the essence of the subject (that is, in which the predicate connotes the whole or part of what the subject connotes, but nothing besides) answer no purpose but that of unfolding the whole or some part of the meaning of the name to those who did not previously know it. Accordingly, the most useful, and in strictness the only useful kind of essential propositions, are definitions, which, to be complete, should unfold the whole of what is involved in the meaning of the word defined, that is (when it is a connotative word), the whole of what it connotes. In defining a name, however, it is not usual to specify its entire connotation, but so much only as is sufficient to mark out the objects usually denoted by it from all other known objects. And sometimes a merely accidental property, not involved in the meaning of the name, answers this purpose equally well. The various kinds of definition which these distinctions give rise to and the purposes to which they are respectively subservient will be minutely considered in the proper place.

2. *Individuals have no essences*

According to the above view of essential propositions, no proposition can be reckoned such which relates to an individual by name, that is, in which the subject is a proper name. Individuals have no essences. When the schoolmen talked of the essence of an individual, they did not mean the properties implied in its name, for the names of individuals imply no properties. They regarded as of the essence of an individual whatever was of the essence of the species in which they were accustomed to place that individual, that is, of the class to which it was most familiarly referred, and to which, therefore, they conceived that it by nature belonged. Thus, because the proposition, "Man is a rational being," was an essential proposition, they affirmed the same thing of the proposition, "Julius Caesar is a rational being." This followed very naturally if genera and species were to be considered as entities, distinct from, but *inhering* in, the individuals composing them. If *man* was a substance inhering in each individual man, the *essence* of man (whatever that might mean) was naturally supposed to accompany it, to inhere in John Thompson, and to form the *common essence* of Thompson and Julius Caesar. It might then be fairly said that rationality, being of the essence of Man, was of the essence also of Thompson. But, if Man altogether be only the individual men and a name bestowed upon them in consequence of certain common properties, what becomes of John Thompson's essence?

A fundamental error is seldom expelled from philosophy by a single victory. It retreats slowly, defends every inch of ground, and often, after it has been driven from the open country, retains a footing in some remote fastness. The essences of individuals were an unmeaning figment arising from a misapprehension of the essences of classes, yet even Locke, when he extirpated the parent error, could not shake himself free from that which was its fruit. He distinguished two sorts of essences, real and nominal. His nominal essences were the essences of classes, explained nearly as we have now explained them. Nor is anything wanting to render the Third Book of Locke's *Essay* a nearly unexceptional treatise on the connotation of names except to free its language from the assumption of what are called abstract ideas, which unfortunately is involved in the phraseology though not necessarily connected with the thoughts contained in that immortal Third Book.[2] But besides nominal essences, he admitted real essences, or essences of individual objects, which he supposed to be the causes of the sensible properties of those objects. We know not (said he) what these are (and this acknowledgment rendered the fiction comparatively innocuous), but if we did, we could, from them alone, demonstrate the sensible properties of the object, as the properties of the triangle are demonstrated from the definition of the triangle. I shall have occasion to revert to this theory in treating of demonstration, and of the conditions under which one property of a thing admits of being demonstrated from another property. It is enough here to remark that, according to this definition, the real essence of an object has, in the progress of physics, come to be conceived as nearly equivalent, in the case of bodies, to their corpuscular structure; what it is now supposed to mean in the case of any other entities, I would not take upon myself to define.

3. *Real propositions, how distinguished from verbal*

An essential proposition, then, is one which is purely verbal, which asserts of a thing under a particular name only what is asserted of it in the fact of calling it by that name, and which, therefore, either gives no information, or gives it respecting the name, not the thing. Non-essential, or accidental propositions, on the contrary, may be called real propositions, in opposition to verbal. They predicate of a thing some fact not involved in the signification of the name by which the proposition speaks of it, some attribute not connoted by that name. Such are all propositions con-

[2]The always acute and often profound author of *An Outline of Sematology* (Mr. B. H. Smart) justly says, "Locke will be much more intelligible, if, in the majority of places, we substitute 'the knowledge of' for what he calls 'the idea of' " (p. 10). Among the many criticisms on Locke's use of the word Idea, this is the one which, as it appears to me, most nearly hits the mark; and I quote it for the additional reason that it precisely expresses the point of difference respecting the import of propositions between my view and what I have spoken of as the conceptualist view of them. Where a conceptualist says that a name or a proposition expresses our idea of a thing, I should generally say (instead of our idea) our knowledge, or belief, concerning the thing itself.

cerning things individually designated, and all general or particular propositions in which the predicate connotes any attribute not connoted by the subject. All these, if true, add to our knowledge; they convey information not already involved in the names employed. When I am told that all, or even that some objects, which have certain qualities or which stand in certain relations, have also certain other qualities or stand in certain other relations, I learn from this proposition a new fact, a fact not included in my knowledge of the meaning of the words, nor even of the existence of things answering to the signification of those words. It is this class of propositions only which are in themselves instructive, or from which any instructive propositions can be inferred.[3]

Nothing has probably contributed more to the opinion so long prevalent of the futility of the school logic than the circumstance that almost all the examples used in the common school books to illustrate the doctrine of predication and that of the syllogism consist of essential propositions. They were usually taken either from the branches or from the main trunk of the predicamental tree, which included nothing but what was of the *essence* of the species: *Omne corpus est substantia, Omne animal est corpus, Omnis homo est corpus, Omnis homo est animal, Omnis homo est rationalis*, and so forth. It is far from wonderful that the syllogistic art should have been thought to be of no use in assisting correct reasoning when almost the only propositions which, in the hands of its professed teachers, it was employed to prove were such as every one assented to without proof the moment he comprehended the meaning of the words, and stood exactly on a level, in point of evidence, with the premises from which they were drawn. I have, therefore, throughout this work, avoided the employment of essential propositions as examples, except where the nature of the principle to be illustrated specifically required them.

4. *Two modes of representing the import of a real proposition*

With respect to propositions which do convey information — which assert something of a thing, under a name that does not

[3]This distinction corresponds to that which is drawn by Kant and other metaphysicians between what they term *analytic* and *synthetic* judgments, the former being those which can be evolved from the meaning of the terms used.

already presuppose what is about to be asserted—there are two different aspects in which these, or, rather, such of them as are general propositions, may be considered: we may either look at them as portions of speculative truth, or as memoranda for practical use. According as we consider propositions in one or the other of these lights, their import may be conveniently expressed in one or in the other of two formulas.

According to the formula which we have hitherto employed and which is best adapted to express the import of the proposition as a portion of our theoretical knowledge, "All men are mortal," means that the attributes of man are always accompanied by the attribute mortality; "No men are gods," means that the attributes of man are never accompanied by the attributes, or at least never by all the attributes, signified by the word *god*. But when the proposition is considered as a memorandum for practical use, we shall find a different mode of expressing the same meaning better adapted to indicate the office which the proposition performs. The practical use of a proposition is to apprise or remind us what we have to expect in any individual case which comes within the assertion contained in the proposition. In reference to this purpose, the proposition, "All men are mortal," means that the attributes of man are *evidence of*, are a *mark* of, mortality, an indication by which the presence of that attribute is made manifest. "No men are gods," means that the attributes of man are a mark or evidence that some or all of the attributes understood to belong to a god are not there, that where the former are, we need not expect to find the latter.

These two forms of expression are at bottom equivalent; but the one points the attention more directly to what a proposition means, the latter to the manner in which it is to be used.

Now it is to be observed that reasoning (the subject to which we are next to proceed) is a process into which propositions enter not as ultimate results, but as means to the establishment of other propositions. We may expect, therefore, that the mode of exhibiting the import of a general proposition which shows it in its application to practical use will best express the function which propositions perform in reasoning. And, accordingly, in the theory of reasoning, the mode of viewing the subject which considers a proposition as asserting that one fact or phenomenon is a *mark* or *evidence* of another fact or phenomenon will be found almost indispensable. For the purposes of that theory, the best mode of defining the import of a proposition is not the mode which shows most clearly what it is in itself, but that which most distinctly suggests the manner in which it may be made available for advancing from it to other propositions.

CHAPTER VI*

OF THE NATURE OF CLASSIFICATION AND THE FIVE PREDICABLES

1. *Classification, how connected with naming*

.   .   .   .

Although . . . predication does not presuppose classification, and though the theory of names and of propositions is not cleared up but only encumbered by intruding the idea of classification into it, there is nevertheless a close connection between classification and the employment of general names. By every general name which we introduce, we create a class, if there be any things, real or imaginary, to compose it, that is, any things corresponding to the signification of the name. Classes, therefore, mostly owe their existence to general language. But general language, also, though that is not the most common case, sometimes owes its existence to classes. A general, which is as much as to say a significant, name is, indeed, mostly introduced because we have a signification to express by it, because we need a word by means of which to predicate the attributes which it connotes. But it is also true that a name is sometimes introduced because we have found it convenient to create a class, because we have thought it useful for the regulation of our mental operations that a certain group of objects should be thought of together. A naturalist, for purposes

* [Chapter VII of the eighth edition.]

connected with his particular science, sees reason to distribute the animal or vegetable creation into certain groups rather than into any others, and he requires a name to bind, as it were, each of his groups together. It must not, however, be supposed that such names, when introduced, differ in any respect, as to their mode of signification, from other connotative names. The classes which they denote are, as much as any other classes, constituted by certain common attributes, and their names are significant of those attributes and of nothing else. The names of Cuvier's classes and orders, *Plantigrades, Digitigrades*, and so forth, are as much the expression of attributes as if those names had preceded, instead of grown out of, his classification of animals. The only peculiarity of the case is that the convenience of classification was here the primary, motive for introducing the names, while, in other cases, the name is introduced as a means of predication, and the formation of a class denoted by it is only an indirect consequence.

.   .   .   .

2. *Kinds have a real existence in nature*

It is a fundamental principle in logic that the power of framing classes is unlimited, as long as there is any (even the smallest) difference to found a distinction upon. Take any attribute whatever, and, if some things have it and others have not, we may ground on the attribute a division of all things into two classes, and we actually do so the moment we create a name which connotes the attribute. The number of possible classes, therefore, is boundless; and there are as many actual classes (either of real or of imaginary things) as there are general names, positive and negative together.

But if we contemplate any one of the classes so formed, such as the class animal or plant, or the class sulphur or phosphorus, or the class white or red, and consider in what particulars the individuals included in the class differ from those which do not come within it, we find a very remarkable diversity in this respect between some classes and others. There are some classes, the things contained in which differ from other things only in certain particulars which may be numbered, while others differ in more than can be numbered, more even than we need ever expect to know. Some classes have little or nothing in common to characterize them by, except precisely what is connoted by the name; white things, for example, are not distinguished by any common properties except whiteness, or, if they are, it is only by such as are in some way dependent on, or connected with, whiteness. But a hundred generations have not exhausted the common properties of animals or of plants, of sulphur or of phosphorus; nor do we suppose them to be exhaustible, but proceed to new observations and experiments in the full confidence of discovering new properties which were by no means implied in those we previously knew. While, if any one were to propose for investigation the common properties of all things which are of the same color, the same shape, or the same specific gravity, the absurdity would be palpable. We have no ground to believe that any such common properties exist, except such as may be shown to be involved in the supposition itself or to be derivable from it by some law of causation. It appears, therefore, that the properties on which we ground our classes sometimes exhaust all that the class has in common or contain it all by some mode of implication; but, in other instances, we make a selection of a few properties from among not only a greater number, but a number inexhaustible by us, and to which, as we know no bounds, they may, so far as we are concerned, be regarded as infinite.

There is no impropriety in saying that, of these two classifications, the one answers to a much more radical distinction in the things themselves than the other does. And if anyone even chooses to say that the one classification is made by nature, the other by us for our convenience, he will be right, provided he means no more than this: where a certain apparent difference between things (though perhaps in itself of little moment) answers to we know not what number of other differences, pervading not only their known properties, but properties yet undiscovered, it is not optional but imperative to recognize this difference as the foundation of a specific distinction; while, on the contrary, differences that are merely finite and determinate, like those designated by the words *white, black, or red,* may be disregarded if the purpose for which the classification is made does not require attention to those particular properties. The differences, however, are made by nature, in both cases, while the recognition of those differences as grounds of classification and of naming is, equally in both cases, the act of man; only in the one case, the ends of language and of classification would be subverted if no notice were taken of the difference, while, in the other case, the necessity of taking notice of it depends on the importance or unimportance of the particular qualities in which the difference happens to consist.

Now, these classes, distinguished by unknown multitudes of properties and not solely by a few determinate ones — which are parted off from one another by an unfathomable chasm, instead of a mere ordinary ditch with a visible bottom — are the only classes which, by the Aristotelian logicians, were considered as genera or species. Differences which extended only to a certain property or properties and there terminated they considered as differences only in the *accidents* of things; but where any class differed from other things by an infinite series of differences, known and unknown, they considered the distinction as one of *kind* and spoke of it as being an *essential* difference, which is also one of the current meanings of that vague expression at the present day.

Conceiving the schoolmen to have been justified in drawing a broad line of separation between these two kinds of classes and of class-distinctions, I shall not only retain the division itself but continue to express it in their language. According to that language, the proximate (or lowest) kind to which any individual is referrible is called its species. Conformably to this, Isaac Newton would be said to be of the species man. There are indeed numerous sub-classes included in the class man to which Newton also belongs, for example, Christian, and Englishman, and Mathematician. But these, though distinct classes, are not, in our sense of the term, distinct kinds of men. A Christian, for example, differs from other human beings, but he differs only in the attribute which the word expresses, namely, belief in Christianity and whatever else that implies, either as involved in the fact itself, or connected with it through some law of cause and effect. We should never think of inquiring what properties, unconnected with Christianity, either as cause or effect, are common to all Christians and peculiar to them, while, in regard to all men, physiologists are perpetually carrying on such an inquiry; nor is the answer ever likely to be completed. Man, therefore, we may call a species; Christian, or Mathematician, we cannot.

Note here, that it is by no means intended to imply that there may not be different kinds, or logical species, of man. The various races and temperaments, the two sexes, and even the various ages, may be differences of kind, within our meaning of the term. I do not say that they are so. For in the progress of physiology it may almost be said to be made out that the differences which really exist between different races, sexes, etc. follow as consequences, under laws of nature, from a small number of primary differences which can be precisely determined, and which, as the phrase is, *account for* all the rest. If this be so, these are not distinctions in kind; no more than Christian, Jew, Mussulman, and Pagan, a difference which also carries many consequences along with it. And in this way classes are often mistaken for real kinds, which are afterward proved not to be so. But if it turned out that the differences were not capable of being thus accounted for, then Caucasian, Mongolian, Negro, etc. would be really different kinds of human beings and entitled to be ranked as species by the logician, though not by the naturalist. For (as already noticed) the word *species* is used in a different signification in logic and in natural history. By the naturalist, organized beings are not usually said to be of different species if it is supposed that they have descended from the same stock. That, however, is a sense artificially given to the word for the technical purposes of a particular science. To the logician, if a negro and a white man differ in the same manner (however less in degree) as a horse and a camel do, that is, if their differences are inexhaustible, and not referrible to any common cause, they are different species, whether they are descended from common ancestors or not. But if their differences can all be traced to climate and habits, or to some one or a few special differences in structure, they are not, in the logician's view, specifically distinct.

When the *infima species*, or proximate kind, to which an individual belongs has been ascertained, the properties common to that kind include necessarily the whole of the common properties of every other real kind to which the individual can be refer-rible. Let the individual, for example, be Socrates, and the proxi-mate kind, man. Animal, or living creature, is also a real kind, and includes Socrates, but, since it likewise includes man, or in other words, since all men are animals, the properties common to animals form a portion of the common properties of the sub-class, man. And if there be any class which includes Socrates without including man, that class is not a real kind. Let the class, for example, be *flat-nosed*, that being a class which includes Socrates without including all men. To determine whether it is a real kind, we must ask ourselves this question: Have all flat-nosed animals, in addition to whatever is implied in their flat noses, any common properties other than those which are common to all animals whatever? If they had, if a flat nose were a mark or index to an indefinite number of other peculiarities not deducible from the former by an ascertainable law, then out of the class man we might cut another class, flat-nosed man, which, according to our defi-nition, would be a kind. But if we could do this, man would not be, as it was assumed to be, the proximate kind. Therefore, the properties of the proximate kind do comprehend those (whether known or unknown) of all other kinds to which the individual belongs, which was the point we undertook to prove. And hence, every other kind which is predicable of the individual will be to the proximate kind in the relation of a genus, according to even the popular acceptation of the terms genus and species, that is, it will be a larger class, including it and more.

We are now able to fix the logical meaning of these terms. Every class which is a real kind, that is, which is distinguished from all other classes by an indeterminate multitude of properties not derivable from one another, is either a genus or a species. A kind which is not divisible into other kinds cannot be a genus, because it has no species under it; but it is itself a species, both with refer-ence to the individuals below and to the genera above (*Species Praedicabilis and Species Subjicibilis*). But every kind which admits of division into real kinds (as animal into mammal, bird, fish, etc., or bird into various species of birds) is a genus to all below it, a species to all genera in which it is itself included. . . ,

CHAPTER VII*

OF DEFINITION

1. *A definition, what*

. . . .

The simplest and most correct notion of a definition is, a proposition declaratory of the meaning of a word, namely, either the meaning which it bears in common acceptation, or that which the speaker or writer, for the particular purposes of his discourse, intends to annex to it.

The definition of a word being the proposition which enunciates its meaning, words which have no meaning are unsusceptible of definition. Proper names, therefore, cannot be defined. A proper name being a mere mark put upon an individual, and of which it is the characteristic property to be destitute of meaning, its meaning cannot, of course, be declared, though we may indicate by language, as we might indicate still more conveniently by pointing with the finger, upon what individual that particular mark has been, or is intended to be, put. It is no definition of "John Thomson" to say he is "the son of General Thomson," for the name John Thomson does not express this. Neither is it any definition of "John Thomson" to say he is "the man now crossing the street." These propositions may serve to make known who is the particular man to whom the name belongs, but that may be done still more unambiguously by pointing to him, which, however, has not been esteemed one of the modes of definition.

In the case of connotative names, the meaning, as has been so often observed, is the connotation, and the definition of a connotative name is the proposition which declares its connotation. This might be done either directly or indirectly. The direct mode would be by a proposition in this form: "Man" (or whatsoever the word may be) "is a name connoting such and such attributes," or "is a name which, when predicated of anything, signifies the possession of such and such attributes by that thing." Or thus: Man is everything which possesses such and such attributes: Man

* [Chapter VIII of the eighth edition.]

is everything which possesses corporeity, organization, life, rationality, and certain peculiarities of external form.

This form of definition is the most precise and least equivocal of any, but it is not brief enough and is besides too technical for common discourse. The more usual mode of declaring the connotation of a name is to predicate of it another name or names of known signification, which connote the same aggregation of attributes. This may be done either by predicating of the name intended to be defined another connotative name exactly synonymous, as, "Man is a human being," which is not commonly accounted a definition at all, or by predicating two or more connotative names, which make up among them the whole connotation of the name to be defined. In this last case, again, we may either compose our definition of as many connotative names as there are attributes, each attribute being connoted by one, as, "Man is a corporeal, organized, animated, rational being, shaped so and so," or we employ names which connote several of the attributes at once, as, "Man is a rational *animal*, shaped so and so."

The definition of a name, according to this view of it, is the sum total of all the *essential* propositions which can be framed with that name for their subject. All propositions the truth of which is implied in the name, all those which we are made aware of by merely hearing the name, are included in the definition, if complete, and may be evolved from it without the aid of any other premises, whether the definition expresses them in two or three words or in a larger number. It is, therefore, not without reason that Condillac and other writers have affirmed a definition to be an *analysis*. To resolve any complex whole into the elements of which it is compounded is the meaning of analysis; and this we do when we replace one word which connotes a set of attributes collectively by two or more which connote the same attributes singly or in smaller groups.

2. *Every name can be defined whose meaning is susceptible of analysis*

From this, however, the question naturally arises, in what manner are we to define a name which connotes only a single attribute, for instance, "white," which connotes nothing but whiteness, "rational," which connotes nothing but the possession of reason. It might seem that the meaning of such names could only be declared in two ways: by a synonymous term, if any such can be found, or in the direct way already alluded to, "White is a name connoting the attribute whiteness." Let us see, however, whether the analysis of the meaning of the name, that is, the breaking down of that meaning into several parts, admits of being carried farther. Without at present deciding this question as to the word *white*, it is obvious that in the case of *rational* some further explanation may be given of its meaning than is contained in the proposition, "Rational is that which possesses the attribute of reason," since the attribute reason itself admits of being defined. And here we must turn our attention to the definitions of attributes or, rather, of the names of attributes, that is, of abstract names.

In regard to such names of attributes as are connotative and express attributes of those attributes, there is no difficulty; like other connotative names, they are defined by declaring their connotation. Thus the word *fault* may be defined, "a quality productive of evil or inconvenience." Sometimes, again, the attribute to be defined is not one attribute but a union of several; we have only, therefore, to put together the names of all the attributes taken separately, and we obtain the definition of the name which belongs to them all taken together, a definition which will correspond exactly to that of the corresponding concrete name. For, as we define a concrete name by enumerating the attributes which it connotes, and as the attributes connoted by a concrete name form the entire signification of the corresponding abstract name, the same enumeration will serve for the definition of both. Thus, if the definition of *a human being* be this, "a being, corporeal, animated, rational, shaped so and so," the definition of *humanity* will be corporeity and animal life, combined with rationality, and with such and such a shape.

When, on the other hand, the abstract name does not express a complication of attributes but a single attribute, we must remember that every attribute is grounded on some fact or phenomenon from which, and which alone, it derives its meaning. To that fact or phenomenon, called in a former chapter the foundation of the attribute, we must, therefore, have recourse for its definition. Now, the foundation of the attribute may be a phenomenon of any degree of complexity, consisting of many different parts, either co-existent or in succession. To obtain a definition of the attribute, we must analyze the phenomenon into these parts. Eloquence, for example, is the name of one attribute only, but this attribute is grounded on external effects of a complicated nature, flowing from acts of the person to whom we ascribe the attribute; and, by resolving this phenomenon of causation into its two parts, the cause and the effect, we obtain a definition of eloquence, viz., the power of influencing the feelings by speech or writing.

A name, therefore, whether concrete or abstract, admits of definition, provided we are able to analyze, that is, to distinguish into parts, the attribute or set of attributes which constitute the meaning both of the concrete name and of the corresponding abstract: if a set of attributes, by enumerating them; if a single attribute, by dissecting the fact or phenomenon (whether of percep-tion or of internal consciousness) which is the foundation of the attribute. But, further, even when the fact is one of our simple feelings or states of consciousness, and therefore unsusceptible of analysis, the names both of the object and of the attribute still admit of definition, or, rather, would do so if all our simple feelings had names. Whiteness may be defined: the property or power of exciting the sensation of white. A white object may be defined: an object which excites the sensation of white. The only names which are unsusceptible of definition, because their meaning is unsus-ceptible of analysis, are the names of the simple feelings themselves. These are in the same condition as proper names. They are not, indeed, like proper names, unmeaning; for the words *sensation of white* signify that the sensation which I so denominate resembles other sensations which I remember to have had before and to have called by that name. But as we have no words by which to recall those former sensations, except the very word which we seek to define or some other which, being exactly synonymous with it, requires definition as much, words cannot unfold the signification of this class of names, and we are obliged to make a direct appeal to the personal experience of the individual whom we address.

3. *How distinguished from descriptions*

. . . .

What would otherwise be a mere description may be raised to the rank of a real definition by the peculiar purpose which the speaker or writer has in view. ... It may, for the ends of a particular art or science, or for the more convenient statement of an author's particular doctrines, be advisable to give to some general name, without altering its denotation, a special connotation, different from its ordinary one. When this is done, a definition of the name by means of the attributes which make up the special connotation, though in general a mere accidental definition or description, becomes on the particular occasion and for the particular purpose a complete and genuine definition. This actually occurs with respect to one of the preceding examples, "Man is a mammiferous animal having two hands," which is the scientific definition of man, considered as one of the species in Cuvier's distribution of the animal kingdom.

In cases of this sort, though the definition is still a declaration of the meaning which in the particular instance the name is appointed to convey, it cannot be said that to state the meaning of the word is the purpose of the definition. The purpose is not to expound a name, but a classification. The special meaning which Cuvier assigned to the word Man (quite foreign to its ordinary meaning, though involving no change in the denotation of the word) was incidental to a plan of arranging animals into classes on a certain principle, that is, according to a certain set of distinctions. And, since the definition of Man according to the ordinary connotation of the word, though it would have answered every other purpose of a definition, would not have pointed out the place which the species ought to occupy in that particular classification, he gave the word a special connotation, that he might be able to define it by the kind of attributes on which, for reasons of scientific convenience, he had resolved to found his division of animated nature.

Scientific definitions, whether they are definitions of scientific terms, or of common terms used in a scientific sense, are almost always of the kind last spoken of; their main purpose is to serve as the landmarks of scientific classification. And, since the classifications in any science are continually modified as scientific knowledge advances, the definitions in the sciences are also constantly varying. A striking instance is afforded by the words *acid* and *alkali*, especially the former. As experimental discovery advanced, the substances classed with acids have been constantly multiplying, and by a natural consequence the attributes connoted by the word have receded and become fewer. At first it connoted the attributes of combining with an alkali to form a neutral substance (called a salt), being compounded of a base and oxygen, causticity to the taste and touch, fluidity, etc. The true analysis of muriatic acid, into chlorine and hydrogen, caused the second property, composition from a base and oxygen, to be excluded from the connotation. The same discovery fixed the attention of chemists upon hydrogen as an important element in acids; and more recent discoveries having led to the recognition of its presence in sulphuric, nitric, and many other acids, where its existence was not previously suspected, there is now a tendency to include the presence of this element in the connotation of the word. But carbonic acid, silica, sulphurous acid, have no hydrogen in their composition; that property cannot, therefore, be connoted by the term, unless those substances are no longer to be considered acids. Causticity and fluidity have long since been excluded from the characteristics of the class, by the inclusion of silica and many other substances in it; and the formation of neutral bodies by combination with alkalis, together with such electro-chemical peculiarities as this is supposed to imply, are now the only *differentiae* which form the fixed connotation of the word acid as a term of chemical science.

. . . .

In the same manner in which a special or technical definition has for its object to expound the artificial classification out of which it grows, the Aristotelian logicians seem to have imagined that it was also the business of ordinary definition to expound the ordinary, and what they deemed the natural, classification of things, namely, the division of them into kinds, and to show the place which each kind occupies, as superior, collateral, or subordinate, among other kinds. This notion would account for the rule that all definition must necessarily be *per genus et differ-*

entiam and would also explain why a single differentia was deemed sufficient. But to expound or express in words a distinction of kind has already been shown to be an impossibility; the very meaning of a kind is that the properties which distinguish it do not grow out of one another, and cannot, therefore, be set forth in words, even by implication, otherwise than by enumerating them all; and all are not known, nor are ever likely to be so. It is idle, therefore, to look to this as one of the purposes of a definition; while, if it be only required that the definition of a kind should indicate what kinds include it or are included by it, any definitions which expound the connotation of the names will do this, for the name of each class must necessarily connote enough of its properties to fix the boundaries of the class. If the definition, therefore, be a full statement of the connotation, it is all that a definition can be required to be.

4. *What are called definitions of things are definitions of names with an implied assumption of the existence of things corresponding to them*

. . . We shall next examine an ancient doctrine, once generally prevalent and still by no means exploded, which I regard as the source of a great part of the obscurity hanging over some of the most important processes of the understanding in the pursuit of truth. According to this, the definitions of which we have now treated are only one of two sorts into which definitions may be divided, viz., definitions of names and definitions of things. The former are intended to explain the meaning of a term; the latter, the nature of a thing, the last being incomparably the most important.

This opinion was held by the ancient philosophers and by their followers, with the exception of the Nominalists; but as the spirit of modern metaphysics, until a recent period, has been, on the whole, a Nominalist spirit, the notion of definitions of things has been to a certain extent in abeyance, still continuing, however, to breed confusion in logic, by its consequences, indeed, rather than by itself. Yet the doctrine in its own proper form now and then breaks out and has appeared (among other places) where it was scarcely to be expected, in a justly admired work, Archbishop Whately's *Logic*. In a review of that work published by me in the *Westminster Review* for January, 1828, and containing some opinions which I no longer entertain, I find the following observations on the question now before us, observations with which my present view of that question is still sufficiently in accordance.

"The distinction between nominal and real definitions, between definitions of words and what are called definitions of things, though conformable to the ideas of most of the Aristotelian logicians, cannot, as it appears to us, be maintained. We apprehend that no definition is ever intended to 'explain and unfold the nature of a thing.' It is some confirmation of our opinion that none of those writers who have thought that there were definitions of things have ever succeeded in discovering any criterion by which the definition of a thing can be distinguished from any other proposition relating to the thing. The definition, they say, unfolds the nature of the thing; but no definition can unfold its whole nature; and every proposition in which any quality whatever is predicated of the thing unfolds some part of its nature. The true state of the case we take to be this. All definitions are of names, and of names only, but, in some definitions, it is clearly apparent that nothing is intended except to explain the meaning of the word, while, in others, besides explaining the meaning of the word, it is intended to be implied that there exists a thing corresponding to the word. Whether this be or be not implied in any given case cannot be collected from the mere form of the expression. 'A centaur is an animal with the upper parts of a man and the lower parts of a horse,' and 'A triangle is a rectilineal figure with three sides,' are, in form, expressions precisely similar; although in the former it is not implied that any *thing* conformable to the term really exists, while in the latter it is, as may be seen by substituting in both definitions the word *means* for *is*. In the first expression, 'A centaur means an animal,' etc., the sense would remain unchanged; in the second, 'A triangle means,' etc., the meaning would be altered, since it would be obviously impossible to deduce any of the truths of geometry from a proposition expressive only of the manner in which we intend to employ a particular sign.

"There are, therefore, expressions, commonly passing for

definitions, which include in themselves more than the mere explanation of the meaning of a term. But it is not correct to call an expression of this sort a peculiar kind of definition. Its difference from the other kind consists in this, that it is not a definition, but a definition and something more. The definition above given of a triangle, obviously comprises not one, but two propositions, perfectly distinguishable. The one is, 'There may exist a figure, bounded by three straight lines;' the other, 'And this figure may be termed a triangle.' The former of these propositions is not a definition at all; the latter is a mere nominal definition, or explanation of the use and application of a term. The first is susceptible of truth or falsehood and may, therefore, be made the foundation of a train of reasoning. The latter can neither be true nor false; the only character it is susceptible of is that of conformity or disconformity to the ordinary usage of language."

There is a real distinction, then, between definitions of names, and what are erroneously called definitions of things, but it is that the latter, along with the meaning of a name, covertly asserts a matter of fact. This covert assertion is not a definition but a postulate. The definition is a mere identical proposition which gives information only about the use of language, and from which no conclusions affecting matters of fact can possibly be drawn. The accompanying postulate, on the other hand, affirms a fact which may lead to consequences of every degree of importance. It affirms the actual or possible existence of things possessing the combination of attributes set forth in the definition, and this, if true, may be foundation sufficient on which to build a whole fabric of scientific truth.

.   .   .   .

To save the credit of the doctrine that definitions are the premises of scientific knowledge, the proviso is sometimes added that they are so only under a certain condition, namely, that they be framed conformably to the phenomena of nature; that is, that they ascribe such meanings to terms as shall suit objects actually existing. But this is only an instance of the attempt so often made to escape from the necessity of abandoning old language after the ideas which it expresses have been exchanged for contrary ones. From the meaning of a name (we are told) it is possible to infer physical facts, provided the name has corresponding to it an existing thing. But, if this proviso be necessary, from which of the two is the inference really drawn? From the existence of a thing having the properties, or from the existence of a name meaning them?

Take, for instance, any of the definitions laid down as premises in Euclid's *Elements*, the definition, let us say, of a circle. This, being analyzed, consists of two propositions, the one an assumption with respect to a matter of fact, the other a genuine definition. "A figure may exist having all the points in the line which bounds it equally distant from a single point within it;" "Any figure possessing this property is called a circle." Let us look at one of the demonstrations which are said to depend on this definition and observe to which of the two propositions contained in it the demonstration really appeals. "About the centre A, describe the circle B C D." Here is an assumption that a figure such as the definition expresses *may* be described, which is no other than the postulate, or covert assumption, involved in the so-called definition. But whether that figure be called a circle or not is quite immaterial. The purpose would be as well answered, in all respects except brevity, were we to say, "Through the point B, draw a line returning into itself, of which every point shall be at an equal distance from the point A." By this the definition of a circle would be got rid of and rendered needless, but not the postulate implied in it; without that the demonstration could not stand. The circle being now described, let us proceed to the consequence. "Since B C D is a circle, the radius B A is equal to the radius C A." B A is equal to C A, not because B C D is a circle, but because B C D is a figure with the radii equal. Our warrant for assuming that such a figure about the centre A, with the radius B A, may be made to exist is the postulate. Whether the admissibility of these postulates rests on intuition or on proof may be a matter of dispute, but, in either case, they are the premises on which the theorems depend, and while these are retained it would make no difference in the certainty of geometrical truths though every definition in Euclid and every technical term therein defined were laid aside.

5. *Definitions, though of names only, must be grounded on knowledge of the corresponding things*

Although, according to the opinion here presented, definitions are properly of names only and not of things, it does not follow from this that definitions are arbitrary. How to define a name may not only be an inquiry of considerable difficulty and intricacy, but may involve considerations going deep into the nature of the things which are denoted by the name. Such, for instance, are the inquiries which form the subjects of the most important of Plato's dialogues, as, "What is rhetoric?" the topic of the Gorgias, or, "What is justice?" that of the Republic. Such also is the question scornfully asked by Pilate, "What is truth?" and the fundamental question with speculative moralists in all ages, "What is virtue?"

.   .   .   .

Although the meaning of every concrete general name resides in the attributes which it connotes, the objects were named before the attributes, as appears from the fact that, in all languages, abstract names are mostly compounds or other derivatives of the concrete names which correspond to them. Connotative names, therefore, were, after proper names, the first which were used; and, in the simpler cases, no doubt, a distinct connotation was present to the minds of those who first used the name and was distinctly intended by them to be conveyed by it. The first person who used the word white, as applied to snow or to any other object, knew, no doubt, very well what quality he intended to predicate and had a perfectly distinct conception in his mind of the attribute signified by the name.

But where the resemblances and differences on which our classifications are founded are not of this palpable and easily determinable kind, especially where they consist not in any one quality but in a number of qualities, the effects of which, being blended together, are not very easily discriminated and referred each to its true source, it often happens that names are applied to namable objects with no distinct connotation present to the minds of those who apply them. They are only influenced by a general resemblance between the new object and all or some of the old familiar objects which they have been accustomed to call by that name. This, as we have seen, is the law which even the mind of the philosopher must follow in giving names to the simple elementary feelings of our nature; but, where the things to be named are complex wholes, a philosopher is not content with noticing a general resemblance; he examines what the resemblance consists in, and he only gives the same name to things which resemble one another in the same definite particulars. The philosopher, therefore, habitually employs his general names with a definite connotation. But language was not made and can only in some small degree be mended by philosophers. In the minds of the real arbiters of language, general names, especially where the classes they denote cannot be brought before the tribunal of the outward senses to be identified and discriminated, connote little more than a vague gross resemblance to the things which they were earliest, or have been most, accustomed to call by those names. When, for instance, ordinary persons predicate the words *just* or *unjust* of any action, *noble* or *mean* of any sentiment, expression, or demeanor, *statesman* or *charlatan* of any personage figuring in politics, do they mean to affirm of those various subjects any determinate attributes, of whatever kind? No; they merely recognize, as they think, some likeness, more or less vague and loose, between these and some other things which they have been accustomed to denominate or to hear denominated by those appellations.

. . . .

Whenever the inquiry into the definition of the name of any real object consists of anything else than a mere comparison of authorities, we tacitly assume that a meaning must be found for the name compatible with its continuing to denote, if possible, all, but, at any rate, the greater or the more important part, of the things of which it is commonly predicated. The inquiry, therefore, into the definition is an inquiry into the resemblances and differences among those things: whether there be any resemblance running through them all; if not, through what portion of them such a general resemblance can be traced; and, finally, what are the common attributes, the possession of which gives to them all, or to that portion of them, the character of resemblance which has led to their being classed together. When these common attributes have been ascertained and specified, the name which belongs in common to the resembling objects acquires a distinct instead of a vague connotation, and, by possessing this distinct connotation, becomes susceptible of definition.

BOOK II

Of Reasoning

Διωρισμένων δε τούτων λέγωμεν ἤδη, διὰ τίνων, καὶ πότε, καὶ πῶς γίνεται πᾶς συλλογισμός ὕστερον δὲ λεκτέον μερὶ ἀποδείξεως. Πρότερον γὰρ περὶ συλλογισμοῦ λεκτέον, ἢ περὶ ἀποδείξεως διὰ τὸ καθόλου μᾶλλον εἶναι τὸν συλλογισμόν. Ἡ μέν γὰρ ἀπόδειξις, συλλογισμός τις· ὁ συλλογισμός δὲ οὐ πᾶς, ἀπόδειξις. — ARIST., *Analyt. Prior.*, l. i., cap. 4.

CHAPTER I

OF INFERENCE, OR REASONING, IN GENERAL

1. *Retrospect of the preceding book*

.   .   .   .

We say of a fact or statement that it is proved when we believe its truth by reason of some other fact or statement from which it is said to *follow*. Most of the propositions, whether affirmative or negative, universal, particular, or singular, which we believe are not believed on their own evidence, but on the ground of something previously assented to, from which they are said to be *inferred*. To infer a proposition from a previous proposition or propositions, to give credence to it, or claim credence for it, as a conclusion from something else, is to *reason*, in the most extensive sense of the term. There is a narrower sense in which the name reasoning is confined to the form of inference which is termed ratiocination and of which the syllogism is the general type. The reasons for not conforming to this restricted use of the term were stated in an earlier stage of our inquiry, and additional motives will be suggested by the considerations on which we are now about to enter.

2. *Inferences improperly so called*

In proceeding to take into consideration the cases in which inferences can legitimately be drawn, we shall first mention some cases in which the inference is apparent, not real, and which require notice chiefly that they may not be confounded with cases of inference properly so called. This occurs when the proposition ostensibly inferred from another appears on analysis to be merely a repetition of the same, or part of the same, assertion which was contained in the first. All the cases mentioned in books of logic as examples of equipollency or equivalence of propositions are of this nature. Thus, if we were to argue, "No man is incapable of reason, for every man is rational," or, "All men are mortal, for no man is exempt from death," it would be plain that we were not proving the proposition but only appealing to another mode of wording it, which may or may not be more readily comprehensible by the hearer or better adapted to suggest the real proof, but which contains in itself no shadow of proof.

Another case is where, from a universal proposition, we affect to infer another which differs from it only in being particular: as "All A is B, therefore some A is B," "No A is B, therefore some A is not B." This, too, is not to conclude one proposition from another, but to repeat a second time something which had been asserted at first, with the difference that we do not here repeat the whole of the previous assertion, but only an indefinite part of it.

A third case is where, the antecedent having affirmed a predicate of a given subject, the consequent affirms of the same subject something already connoted by the former predicate, as, "Socrates is a man, therefore Socrates is a living creature," where all that is connoted by living creature was affirmed of Socrates when he was asserted to be a man. If the propositions are negative, we must invert their order, thus: "Socrates is not a living creature, therefore he is not a man," for if we deny the less, the greater, which includes it, is already denied by implication. These, therefore, are not really cases of inference, and yet the trivial examples by which, in manuals of logic, the rules of the syllogism are illustrated, are often of this ill-chosen kind: formal demonstrations of conclusions to which whoever understands the terms used in the statement of the data has already, and consciously, assented.[1]

. . . .

In all these cases there is not really any inference; there is in the conclusion no new truth, nothing but what was already asserted in the premises, and obvious to whoever apprehends them. The fact asserted in the conclusion is either the very same fact, or part of the fact, asserted in the original proposition. . . .

. . . . . : . . . .

CHAPTER II

OF RATIOCINATION, OR SYLLOGISM

1. *Analysis of the syllogism*

. . . .

All valid ratiocination, all reasoning by which, from general propositions previously admitted, other propositions equally or less general are inferred, may be exhibited in some of the above forms. The whole of Euclid, for example, might be thrown without diffi- culty into a series of syllogisms, regular in mood and figure.[2]

[1] The different cases of equipollency, or "equivalent propositional forms," are set forth with some fullness in Professor Bain's *Logic*. One of the common- est of these changes of expression, that from affirming a proposition to denying its negative, or vice versa, Mr. Bain designates, very happily, by the name Obversion.

[2] [A syllogism contains three propositions, the proposition to be proved being called the *conclusion*, the other two the *premises*. Moreover, a syllogism con- tains just three distinct *terms:* the subject and the predicate of the conclusion are called the *minor* and the *major* terms, respectively, and the term which appears in both premises is called the *middle term*. The premise containing the major term is the major premise, the one containing the minor term is the minor premise.

Syllogisms are divided into *figures*, according to the position of the middle

Though a syllogism framed according to any of these formulae is a valid argument, all correct ratiocination admits of being stated in syllogisms of the first figure alone. . . .

.   .   .   .

. . . We are therefore at liberty, in conformity with the general opinion of logicians, to consider the two elementary forms of the first figure as the universal types of all correct ratiocination, the one, when the conclusion to be proved is affirmative, the other, when it is negative; even though certain arguments may have a tendency to clothe themselves in the forms of the second, third, and fourth figures, which, however, cannot possibly happen with the only class of arguments which are of first-rate scientific importance, those in which the conclusion is a universal affirmative, such conclusions being susceptible of proof in the first figure alone.

2. *The* dictum de omni *not the foundation of reasoning, but a mere identical proposition*

On examining, then, these two general formulae, we find that in both of them one premise, the major, is a universal proposition, and according as this is affirmative or negative, the conclusion is so too. All ratiocination, therefore, starts from a *general* proposition, principle, or assumption, a proposition in which a predicate is affirmed or denied of an entire class, that is, in which some attribute, or the negation of some attribute, is asserted of an indefinite number of objects distinguished by a common characteristic and designated, in consequence, by a common name.

The other premise is always affirmative and asserts that something (which may be either an individual, a class, or part of a

term, which may either be the subject in both premises, the predicate in both, or the subject in one and the predicate in the other. A syllogism is said to be in the *first figure* if the middle term is the subject of the major premise and the predicate in the minor premise; it is in the *second figure*, if the middle term is the predicate in both premises; it is in the *third figure*, if the middle term is the subject in both premises; and it is in the *fourth figure*, if the middle term is the predicate of the major premise and the subject of the minor premise.

Each figure is divided into *moods*, according to the *quantity* and *quality* of the propositions, that is, according as the propositions are universal or particular, affirmative or negative. — ED.]

class) belongs to, or is included in, the class respecting which something was affirmed or denied in the major premise. It follows that the attribute affirmed or denied of the entire class may (if that affirmation or denial was correct) be affirmed or denied of the object or objects alleged to be included in the class; and this is precisely the assertion made in the conclusion.

Whether or not the foregoing is an adequate account of the constituent parts of the syllogism will be presently considered; but as far as it goes it is a true account. It has accordingly been generalized and erected into a logical maxim on which all ratiocination is said to be founded, insomuch that to reason and to apply the maxim are supposed to be one and the same thing. The maxim is, "That whatever can be affirmed (or denied) of a class, may be affirmed (or denied) of everything included in the class." This axiom, supposed to be the basis of the syllogistic theory, is termed by logicians the *dictum de omni et nullo*.

This maxim, however, when considered as a principle of reasoning, appears suited to a system of metaphysics once, indeed, generally received, but which for the last two centuries has been considered as finally abandoned, though there have not been wanting in our own day attempts at its revival. So long as what are termed "universals" were regarded as a peculiar kind of substances having an objective existence distinct from the individual objects classed under them, the *dictum de omni* conveyed an important meaning, because it expressed the intercommunity of nature which it was necessary on that theory that we should suppose to exist between those general substances and the particular substances which were subordinated to them. That every thing predicable of the universal was predicable of the various individuals contained under it was then no identical proposition, but a statement of what was conceived as a fundamental law of the universe. The assertion that the entire nature and properties of the *substantia secunda* formed part of the nature and properties of each of the individual substances called by the same name, that the properties of Man, for example, were properties of all men, was a proposition of real significance when man did not *mean* all men, but something inherent in men, and vastly superior to them in dignity. Now, however, when it is known that a class, a universal, a genus or species, is not an entity *per se*, but neither more nor less than the individual substances themselves which are placed in the class, and that there is nothing real in the matter except those objects, a common name given to them, and common attributes indicated by the name, what, I should be glad to know, do we learn by being told that whatever can be affirmed of a class may be affirmed of every object contained in the class? The class *is* nothing but the objects contained in it; and the *dictum de omni* merely amounts to the identical proposition that whatever is true of certain objects is true of each of those objects. If all ratiocination were no more than the application of this maxim to particular cases, the syllogism would indeed be, what it has so often been declared to be, solemn trifling. The *dictum de omni* is on a par with another truth, which in its time was also reckoned of great importance, "Whatever is, is." To give any real meaning to the *dictum de omni*, we must consider it not as an axiom, but as a definition; we must look upon it as intended to explain, in a circuitous and paraphrastic manner, the meaning of the word *class*.

An error which seemed finally refuted and dislodged from thought often needs only put on a new suit of phrases to be welcomed back to its old quarters and allowed to repose unquestioned for another cycle of ages. Modern philosophers have not been sparing in their contempt for the scholastic dogma that genera and species are a peculiar kind of substances, which general substances being the only permanent things, while the individual substances comprehended under them are in a perpetual flux, knowledge, which necessarily imports stability, can only have relation to those general substances or universals and not to the facts or particulars included under them. Yet, though nominally rejected, this very doctrine, whether disguised under the "abstract ideas" of Locke (whose speculations, however, it has less vitiated than those of perhaps any other writer who has been infected with it), under the ultra-nominalism of Hobbes and Condillac, or the ontology of the later German schools, has never ceased to poison philosophy. Once accustomed to consider scientific investigation as essentially consisting in the study of universals, men did not drop this habit of thought when they ceased to regard universals as possessing an independent existence; and even those who went the length of considering them as mere names could not free themselves from the notion that the investigation of truth consisted entirely or partly in some kind of conjuration or juggle with those names. When a philosopher adopted fully the Nominalist view of the signification of general language, retaining along with it the *dictum de omni* as the foundation of all reasoning, two such premises fairly put together were likely, if he was a consistent thinker, to land him in rather startling conclusions. Accordingly it has been seriously held, by writers of deserved celebrity, that the process of arriving at new truths by reasoning consists in the mere substitution of one set of arbitrary signs for another, a doctrine which they suppose to derive irresistible confirmation from the example of algebra. If there were any process in sorcery or necromancy more preternatural than this, I should be much surprised. The culminating point of this philosophy is the noted aphorism of Condillac that a science is nothing, or scarcely anything, but *une langue bien faite;* in other words, that the one sufficient rule for discovering the nature and properties of objects is to name them properly, as if the reverse were not the truth, that it is impossible to name them properly except in proportion as we are already acquainted with their nature and properties. Can it be necessary to say that none, not even the most trivial knowledge with respect to things, ever was or could be originally got at by any conceivable manipulation of mere names, as such, and that what can be learned from names is only what somebody who used the names knew before? Philosophical analysis confirms the indication of common sense that the function of names is but that of enabling us to *remember* and to *communicate* our thoughts. That they also strengthen, even to an incalculable extent, the power of thought itself, is most true; but they do this by no intrinsic and peculiar virtue; they do it by the power inherent in an artificial memory, an instrument of which few have adequately considered the immense potency. As an artificial memory, language truly is, what it has so often been called, an instrument of thought; but it is one thing to be the instrument, and another to be the exclusive subject upon which the instrument is exercised. We think, indeed, to a considerable extent, by means of names, but what we think of are the things called by those names, and there cannot be a greater error than to imagine that thought can be carried on with nothing in our mind but names, or that we can make the names think for us.

3. *What is the really fundamental axiom of ratiocination?*

Those who considered the *dictum de omni* as the foundation of the syllogism looked upon arguments in a manner corresponding to the erroneous view which Hobbes took of propositions. Because there are some propositions which are merely verbal, Hobbes, in order apparently that his definition might be rigorously universal, defined a proposition as if no propositions declared anything except the meaning of words. If Hobbes was right, if no further account than this could be given of the import of propositions, no theory could be given but the commonly received one of the combination of propositions in a syllogism. If the minor premise asserted nothing more than that something belongs to a class, and if the major premise asserted nothing of that class except that it is included in another class, the conclusion would only be that what was included in the lower class is included in the higher, and the result, therefore, nothing except that the classification is consistent with itself. But we have seen that it is no sufficient account of the meaning of a proposition to say that it refers something to, or excludes something from, a class. Every proposition which conveys real information asserts a matter of fact, dependent on the laws of nature, and not on classification. It asserts that a given object does or does not possess a given attribute, or it asserts that two attributes, or sets of attributes, do or do not (constantly or occasionally) co-exist. Since such is the purport of all propositions which convey any real knowledge, and since ratiocination is a mode of acquiring real knowledge, any theory of ratiocination which does not recognize this import of propositions cannot, we may be sure, be the true one.

Applying this view of propositions to the two premises of a syllogism, we obtain the following results. The major premise, which, as already remarked, is always universal, asserts that all things which have a certain attribute (or attributes) have or have not along with it a certain other attribute (or attributes). The minor premise asserts that the thing or set of things which are the subject of that premise have the first-mentioned attribute; and the conclusion is that they have (or that they have not), the second. Thus in our former example,

> All men are mortal,
> Socrates is a man,
> therefore
> Socrates is mortal,

the subject and predicate of the major premise are connotative terms, denoting objects and connoting attributes. The assertion in the major premise is that, along with one of the two sets of attributes, we always find the other; that the attributes connoted by "man" never exist unless conjoined with the attribute called mortality. The assertion in the minor premise is that the individual named Socrates possesses the former attributes; and it is concluded that he possesses also the attribute mortality. Or, if both the premises are general propositions, as

> All men are mortal,
> All kings are men,
> therefore
> All kings are mortal,

the minor premise asserts that the attributes denoted by kingship only exist in conjunction with those signified by the word man. The major asserts, as before, that the last-mentioned attributes are never found without the attribute of mortality. The conclusion is that wherever the attributes of kingship are found, that of mortality is found also.

If the major premise were negative, as, "No men are omnipotent," it would assert, not that the attributes connoted by "man" never exist without, but that they never exist with, those connoted by "omnipotent;" from which, together with the minor premise, it is concluded, that the same incompatibility exists between the attribute omnipotence and those constituting a king. In a similar manner we might analyze any other example of the syllogism.

If we generalize this process and look out for the principle or law involved in every such inference and presupposed in every syllogism the propositions of which are anything more than merely verbal, we find, not the unmeaning *dictum de omni et nullo*, but a fundamental principle, or rather two principles, strikingly resembling the axioms of mathematics. The first, which is the principle of affirmative syllogisms, is that things which co-exist with the same thing, co-exist with one another; or (still more precisely) a thing which co-exists with another thing, which other co-exists with a third thing, also co-exists with that third thing. The second is the principle of negative syllogisms and is to this effect: that a thing which co-exists with another thing, with which other a third thing does not co-exist, is not co-existent with that third thing. These axioms manifestly relate to facts and not to conventions, and one or other of them is the ground of the legitimacy of every argument in which facts and not conventions are the matter treated of.

4. *The other form of the axiom*

It remains to translate this exposition of the syllogism from the one into the other of the two languages in which we formerly remarked[1] that all propositions, and of course therefore all combinations of propositions, might be expressed. We observed that a proposition might be considered in two different lights, as a portion of our knowledge of nature or as a memorandum for our guidance. Under the former or speculative aspect an affirmative general proposition is an assertion of a speculative truth, *viz.*, that whatever has a certain attribute has a certain other attribute. Under the other aspect it is to be regarded not as a part of our knowledge, but as an aid for our practical exigencies, by enabling us when we see or learn that an object possesses one of the two attributes to infer that it possesses the other, thus employing the first attribute as a mark or evidence of the second. Thus regarded, every syllogism comes within the following general formula:

Attribute A is a mark of attribute B,
The given object has the mark A,
                    therefore
The given object has the attribute B.

Referred to this type, the arguments which we have lately cited

[1]*Supra*, page 89.

as specimens of the syllogism will express themselves in the
following manner:

> The attributes of man are a mark of the attribute mortality,
> Socrates has the attributes of man,
>
> > therefore
>
> Socrates has the attribute mortality.

And again,

> The attributes of man are a mark of the attribute mortality,
> The attributes of a king are a mark of the attributes of man,
>
> > therefore
>
> The attributes of a king are a mark of the attribute mortality.

And lastly,

> The attributes of man are a mark of the absence of the
> > attribute omnipotence,
> The attributes of a king are a mark of the attributes of man,
> > therefore
> The attributes of a king are a mark of the absence of the
> > attribute signified by the word omnipotent (or are
> > evidence of the absence of that attribute).

To correspond with this alteration in the form of the syllogisms,
the axioms on which the syllogistic process is founded must undergo
a corresponding transformation. In this altered phraseology, both
these axioms may be brought under one general expression, namely,
that whatever has any mark has that which it is a mark of. Or,
when the minor premise as well as the major is universal, we may
state it thus, Whatever is a mark of any mark is a mark of that
which this last is a mark of. . . .

CHAPTER III

OF THE FUNCTIONS AND LOGICAL VALUE OF THE SYLLOGISM

1. *Is the syllogism a* petitio principii?

We have shown what is the real nature of the truths with which the syllogism is conversant, in contradistinction to the more superficial manner in which their import is conceived in the common theory, and what are the fundamental axioms on which its probative force or conclusiveness depends. We have now to inquire whether the syllogistic process, that of reasoning from generals to particulars, is or is not a process of inference, a progress from the known to the unknown, a means of coming to a knowledge of something which we did not know before.

Logicians have been remarkably unanimous in their mode of answering this question. It is universally allowed that a syllogism is vicious if there be anything more in the conclusion than was assumed in the premises. But this is, in fact, to say that nothing ever was or can be proved by syllogism which was not known or assumed to be known before. Is ratiocination, then, not a process of inference? And is the syllogism, to which the word reasoning has so often been represented to be exclusively appropriate, not really entitled to be called reasoning at all? This seems an inevitable consequence of the doctrine, admitted by all writers on the subject, that a syllogism can prove no more than is involved in the premises. Yet the acknowledgment so explicitly made has not prevented one set of writers from continuing to represent the syllogism as the correct analysis of what the mind actually performs in discovering and proving the larger half of the truths whether of science or of daily life which we believe, while those who have avoided this inconsistency and followed out the general theorem respecting the logical value of the syllogism to its legitimate corollary have been led to impute uselessness and frivolity to the syllogistic theory itself, on the ground of the *petitio principii* which they allege to be inherent in every syllogism. As I believe both these opinions to be fundamentally erroneous, I must request the attention of the reader to certain considerations without which any just appreciation of the true character of the syllogism and the functions it performs in philosophy appears to me impossible, but which seem to have been either overlooked or insufficiently adverted to both by the defenders of the syllogistic theory and by its assailants.

2. *Insufficiency of the common theory*

It must be granted that in every syllogism, considered as an argument to prove the conclusion, there is a *petitio principii.* When we say,

> All men are mortal,
> Socrates is a man,
> therefore
> Socrates is mortal;

it is unanswerably urged by the adversaries of the syllogistic theory that the proposition, "Socrates is mortal," is presupposed in the more general assumption, "All men are mortal"; that we cannot be assured of the mortality of all men unless we are already certain of the mortality of every individual man; that if it be still doubtful whether Socrates, or any other individual we choose to name, be mortal or not, the same degree of uncertainty must hang over the assertion, "All men are mortal"; that the general principle, instead of being given as evidence of the particular case, cannot itself be taken for true without exception until every shadow of doubt which could affect any case comprised with it is dispelled by evidence *aliundè;* and then what remains for the syllogism to prove? That, in short, no reasoning from generals to particulars can, as such, prove anything, since from a general principle we cannot infer any particulars but those which the principle itself assumes as known.

This doctrine appears to me irrefragable, and if logicians, though unable to dispute it, have usually exhibited a strong disposition to explain it away, this was not because they could discover any flaw in the argument itself, but because the contrary opinion seemed to rest on arguments equally indisputable. In the syllogism last referred to, for example, or in any of those which we previously constructed, is it not evident that the conclusion may, to the person to whom the syllogism is presented, be actually and *bona fide* a new truth? Is it not matter of daily experience that truths previously unthought of, facts which have not been, and cannot be, directly observed, are arrived at by way of general reasoning? We believe that the Duke of Wellington is mortal. We do not know this by direct observation, so long as he is not yet dead. If we were asked how, this being the case, we know the duke to be mortal, we should probably answer, "Because all men are so." Here, therefore, we arrive at the knowledge of a truth not (as yet) susceptible of observation by a reasoning which admits of being exhibited in the following syllogism:

> All men are mortal,
> The Duke of Wellington is a man,
> therefore
> The Duke of Wellington is mortal.

And since a large portion of our knowledge is thus acquired, logicians have persisted in representing the syllogism as a process of inference or proof, though none of them has cleared up the difficulty which arises from the inconsistency between that assertion and the principle that, if there be anything in the conclusion which was not already asserted in the premises, the argument is vicious. For it is impossible to attach any serious scientific value to such a mere salvo as the distinction drawn between being involved *by implication* in the premises and being directly asserted in them. When Archbishop Whately says[1] that the object of reasoning is "merely to expand and unfold the assertions wrapped up, as it were, and implied in those with which we set out, and to bring a person to perceive and acknowledge the full force of that which he has admitted," he does not, I think, meet the real difficulty requiring to be explained, namely, how it happens that a science, like geometry, *can* be all "wrapped up" in a few definitions and axioms. Nor does this defense of the syllogism differ much from what its assailants urge against it as an accusation, when they charge it with being of no use except to those who seek to press the con-

[1] *Logic*, p. 239 (9th ed.).

sequences of an admission into which a person has been entrapped without having considered and understood its full force. When you admitted the major premise, you asserted the conclusion, but, says Archbishop Whately, you asserted it by implication merely; this, however, can here only mean that you asserted it unconsciously, that you did not know you were asserting it; but, if so, the difficulty revives in this shape — Ought you not to have known? Were you warranted in asserting the general proposition without having satisfied yourself of the truth of everything which it fairly includes? And if not, is not the syllogistic art *prima facie* what its assailants affirm it to be, a contrivance for catching you in a trap, and holding you fast in it?[2]

3. *All inference is from particulars to particulars*

From this difficulty there appears to be but one issue. The proposition that the Duke of Wellington is mortal is evidently an inference; it is got at as a conclusion from something else; but do we, in reality, conclude it from the proposition, "All men are mortal"? I answer, no.

The error committed is, I conceive, that of overlooking the distinction between two parts of the process of philosophizing, the inferring part, and the registering part, and ascribing to the latter the functions of the former. The mistake is that of referring a person to his own notes for the origin of his knowledge. If a person is asked a question and is at the moment unable to answer

[2]It is hardly necessary to say that I am not contending for any such absurdity as that we *actually* "ought to have known" and considered the case of every individual man, past, present, and future, before affirming that all men are mortal, although this interpretation has been, strangely enough, put upon the preceding observations. There is no difference between me and Archbishop Whately or any other defender of the syllogism on the practical part of the matter; I am only pointing out an inconsistency in the logical theory of it, as conceived by almost all writers. I do not say that a person who affirmed, before the Duke of Wellington was born, that all men are mortal, *knew* that the Duke of Wellington was mortal; but I do say that he *asserted* it; and I ask for an explanation of the apparent logical fallacy of adducing in proof of the Duke of Wellington's mortality a general statement which presupposes it. Finding no sufficient resolution of this difficulty in any of the writers on logic, I have attempted to supply one.

it, he may refresh his memory by turning to a memorandum which he carries about with him. But if he were asked how the fact came to his knowledge, he would scarcely answer because it was set down in his note-book, unless the book was written, like the Koran, with a quill from the wing of the angel Gabriel.

Assuming that the proposition, "The Duke of Wellington is mortal," is immediately an inference from the proposition, "All men are mortal," whence do we derive our knowledge of that general truth? Of course from observation. Now, all which man can observe are individual cases. From these all general truths must be drawn, and into these they may be again resolved, for a general truth is but an aggregate of particular truths, a comprehensive expression by which an indefinite number of individual facts are affirmed or denied at once. But a general proposition is not merely a compendious form for recording and preserving in the memory a number of particular facts, all of which have been observed. Generalization is not a process of mere naming; it is also a process of inference. From instances which we have observed, we feel warranted in concluding that what we found true in those instances holds in all similar ones, past, present, and future, however numerous they may be. We then, by that valuable contrivance of language which enables us to speak of many as if they were one, record all that we have observed together with all that we infer from our observations in one concise expression, and have thus only one proposition, instead of an endless number, to remember or to communicate. The results of many observations and inferences and instructions for making innumerable inferences in unforeseen cases are compressed into one short sentence.

When, therefore, we conclude from the death of John and Thomas, and every other person we ever heard of in whose case the experiment had been fairly tried, that the Duke of Wellington is mortal like the rest, we may, indeed, pass through the generalization, "All men are mortal," as an intermediate stage, but it is not in the latter half of the process, the descent from all men to the Duke of Wellington, that the *inference* resides. The inference is finished when we have asserted that all men are mortal. What remains to be performed afterward is merely deciphering our own notes.

Archbishop Whately has contended that syllogizing, or reasoning from generals to particulars, is not, agreeably to the vulgar idea, a peculiar *mode* of reasoning, but the philosophical analysis of *the* mode in which all men reason and must do so if they reason at all. With the deference due to so high an authority, I cannot help thinking that the vulgar notion is, in this case, the more correct. If, from our experience of John, Thomas, etc., who once were living, but are now dead, we are entitled to conclude that all human beings are mortal, we might surely without any logical inconsequence have concluded at once from those instances that the Duke of Wellington is mortal. The mortality of John, Thomas, and others is, after all, the whole evidence we have for the mortality of the Duke of Wellington. Not one iota is added to the proof by interpolating a general proposition. Since the individual cases are all the evidence we can possess, evidence which no logical form into which we choose to throw it can make greater than it is, and since that evidence is either sufficient in itself, or, if insufficient for the one purpose, cannot be sufficient for the other, I am unable to see why we should be forbidden to take the shortest cut from these sufficient premises to the conclusion and constrained to travel the "high priori road" by the arbitrary fiat of logicians. I cannot perceive why it should be impossible to journey from one place to another unless we "march up a hill, and then march down again." It may be the safest road, and there may be a resting-place at the top of the hill, affording a commanding view of the surrounding country, but, for the mere purpose of arriving at our journey's end, our taking that road is perfectly optional; it is a question of time, trouble, and danger.

Not only *may* we reason from particulars to particulars without passing through generals, but we perpetually do so reason. All our earliest inferences are of this nature. From the first dawn of intelligence we draw inferences, but years elapse before we learn the use of general language. The child, who, having burned his fingers, avoids to thrust them again into the fire, has reasoned or inferred, though he has never thought of the general maxim, "Fire burns." He knows from memory that he has been burned, and on this evidence believes, when he sees a candle, that if he puts his finger into the flame of it, he will be burned again. He believes this in every case which happens to arise, but without looking, in each instance, beyond the present case. He is not generalizing; he is inferring a particular from particulars. In the same way, also, brutes reason. There is no ground for attributing to any of the lower animals the use of signs of such a nature as to render general propositions possible. But those animals profit by experience and avoid what they have found to cause them pain in the same manner, though not always with the same skill, as a human creature. Not only the burned child, but the burned dog, dreads the fire.

I believe that, in point of fact, when drawing inferences from our personal experience and not from maxims handed down to us by books or tradition, we much oftener conclude from particulars to particulars directly than through the intermediate agency of any general proposition. We are constantly reasoning from ourselves to other people, or from one person to another, without giving ourselves the trouble to erect our observations into general maxims of human or external nature. When we conclude that some person will, on some given occasion, feel or act so and so, we sometimes judge from an enlarged consideration of the manner in which human beings in general, or persons of some particular character, are accustomed to feel and act, but much oftener from merely recollecting the feelings and conduct of the same person in some previous instance, or from considering how we should feel or act ourselves. It is not only the village matron who, when called to a consultation upon the case of a neighbor's child, pronounces on the evil and its remedy simply on the recollection and authority of what she accounts the similar case of her Lucy. We all, where we have no definite maxims to steer by, guide ourselves in the same way; and if we have an extensive experience and retain its impressions strongly, we may acquire in this manner a very considerable power of accurate judgment, which we may be utterly incapable of justifying or of communicating to others. Among the higher order of practical intellects there have been many of whom it was remarked how admirably they suited their means to their ends, without being able to give any sufficient reasons for what they did, and applied, or seemed to apply, recondite principles which they were wholly unable to state. This is a natural consequence of having a mind stored with appropriate particulars and having been long accustomed to reason at once from these to fresh particulars, without practicing the habit of stating to one's self or to others the corresponding general propositions. An old warrior, on a rapid glance at the outlines of the ground, is able at once to give the necessary orders for a skillful arrangement of his troops, though, if he has received little theoretical instruction and has seldom been called upon to answer to other people for his conduct, he may never have had in his mind a single general theorem respecting the relation between ground and array. But his experience of encampments, in circumstances more or less similar, has left a number of vivid, unexpressed, ungeneralized analogies in his mind, the most appropriate of which, instantly suggesting itself, determines him to a judicious arrangement.

.   .   .   .

4. *General propositions are a record of such inferences, and the rules of the syllogism are rules for the interpretation of the record*

From the considerations now adduced, the following conclusions seem to be established: All inference is from particulars to particulars; general propositions are merely registers of such inferences already made, and short formulae for making more; the major premise of a syllogism, consequently, is a formula of this description, and the conclusion is not an inference drawn *from* the formula, but an inference drawn *according* to the formula, the real logical antecedent, or premise, being the particular facts from which the general proposition was collected by induction. Those facts, and the individual instances which supplied them, may have been forgotten; but a record remains, not indeed descriptive of the facts themselves, but showing how those cases may be distinguished, respecting which, the facts, when known, were considered to warrant a given inference. According to the indications of this record we draw our conclusion, which is, to all intents and purposes, a conclusion from the forgotten facts. For this it is essential that we should read the record correctly, and the rules of the syllogism are a set of precautions to insure our doing so.

This view of the functions of the syllogism is confirmed by the

consideration of precisely those cases which might be expected to
be least favorable to it, namely, those in which ratiocination is
independent of any previous induction. We have already observed
that the syllogism, in the ordinary course of our reasoning, is only
the latter half of the process of traveling from premises to a conclusion. There are, however, some peculiar cases in which it is
the whole process. Particulars alone are capable of being subjected
to observation; and all knowledge which is derived from observation begins, therefore, of necessity, in particulars; but our knowledge may, in cases of certain descriptions, be conceived as coming
to us from other sources than observation. It may present itself
as coming from testimony which, on the occasion and for the purpose in hand, is accepted as of an authoritative character; and the
information thus communicated may be conceived to comprise not
only particular facts but general propositions, as when a scientific
doctrine is accepted without examination on the authority of
writers or a theological doctrine on that of Scripture. Or the
generalization may not be, in the ordinary sense, an assertion at
all but a command, a law, not in the philosophical, but in the
moral and political sense of the term, an expression of the desire
of a superior that we, or any number of other persons, shall conform our conduct to certain general instructions. So far as this
asserts a fact, namely, a volition of the legislator, that fact is an
individual fact, and the proposition, therefore, is not a general
proposition. But the description therein contained of the conduct
which it is the will of the legislator that his subjects should observe
is general. The proposition asserts, not that all men *are* anything,
but that all men *shall* do something.

In both these cases the generalities are the original data, and the
particulars are elicited from them by a process which correctly
resolves itself into a series of syllogisms. The real nature, however,
of the supposed deductive process is evident enough. The only
point to be determined is whether the authority which declared
the general proposition intended to include this case in it, and
whether the legislator intended his command to apply to the present
case among others or not. This is ascertained by examining
whether the case possesses the marks by which, as those authorities
have signified, the cases which they meant to certify or to influence

may be known. The object of the inquiry is to make out the witness's or the legislator's intention, through the indication given by their words. This is a question, as the Germans express it, of hermeneutics. The operation is not a process of inference, but a process of interpretation.

In this last phrase we have obtained an expression which appears to me to characterize, more aptly than any other, the functions of the syllogism in all cases. When the premises are given by authority, the function of reasoning is to ascertain the testimony of a witness or the will of a legislator by interpreting the signs in which the one has intimated his assertion and the other his command. In like manner, when the premises are derived from observation, the function of reasoning is to ascertain what we (or our predecessors) formerly thought might be inferred from the observed facts, and to do this by interpreting a memorandum of ours or of theirs. The memorandum reminds us that from evidence, more or less carefully weighed, it formerly appeared that a certain attribute might be inferred wherever we perceive a certain mark. The proposition, "All men are mortal" (for instance) shows that we have had experience from which we thought it followed that the attributes connoted by the term man are a mark of mortality. But when we conclude that the Duke of Wellington is mortal, we do not infer this from the memorandum but from the former experience. All that we infer from the memorandum is our own previous belief (or that of those who transmitted to us the proposition) concerning the inferences which that former experience would warrant.

This view of the nature of the syllogism renders consistent and intelligible what otherwise remains obscure and confused in the theory of Archbishop Whately and other enlightened defenders of the syllogistic doctrine respecting the limits to which its functions are confined. They affirm, in as explicit terms as can be used, that the sole office of general reasoning is to prevent inconsistency in our opinions, to prevent us from assenting to anything the truth of which would contradict something to which we had previously on good grounds given our assent. And they tell us that the sole ground which a syllogism affords for assenting to the conclusion is that the supposition of its being false, combined with the supposition that the premises are true, would lead to a contradiction in terms. Now this would be but a lame account of the real grounds which we have for believing the facts which we learn from reasoning, in contradistinction to observation. The true reason why we believe that the Duke of Wellington will die is that his fathers, and our fathers, and all other persons who were contemporary with them, have died. Those facts are the real premises of the reasoning. But we are not led to infer the conclusion from those premises by the necessity of avoiding any verbal inconsistency. There is no contradiction in supposing that all those persons have died and that the Duke of Wellington may, notwithstanding, live forever. But there would be a contradiction if we first, on the ground of those same premises, made a general assertion including and covering the case of the Duke of Wellington, and then refused to stand to it in the individual case. There is an inconsistency to be avoided between the memorandum we make of the inferences which may be justly drawn in future cases and the inferences we actually draw in those cases when they arise. With this view we interpret our own formula, precisely as a judge interprets a law, in order that we may avoid drawing any inferences not conformable to our former intention, as a judge avoids giving any decision not conformable to the legislator's intention. The rules for this interpretation are the rules of the syllogism, and its sole purpose is to maintain consistency between the conclusions we draw in every particular case and the previous general directions for drawing them, whether those general directions were framed by ourselves as the result of induction or were received by us from an authority competent to give them.

5. *The syllogism not the type of reasoning but a test of it*

In the above observations it has, I think, been shown that, though there is always a process of reasoning or inference where a syllogism is used, the syllogism is not a correct analysis of that process of reasoning or inference; which is, on the contrary (when not a mere inference from testimony), an inference from particulars to particulars, authorized by a previous inference from particulars to generals, and substantially the same with it, of the nature, therefore, of induction. But while these conclusions appear to me undeniable, I must yet enter a protest, as strong as that of Archbishop Whately himself, against the doctrine that the syllogistic art is useless for the purposes of reasoning. The reasoning lies in the act of generalization, not in interpreting the record of that act; but the syllogistic form is an indispensable collateral security for the correctness of the generalization itself.

It has already been seen that if we have a collection of particulars sufficient for grounding an induction we need not frame a general proposition; we may reason at once from those particulars to other particulars. But it is to be remarked withal that whenever, from a set of particular cases, we can legitimately draw any inference, we may legitimately make our inference a general one. If, from observation and experiment, we can conclude to one new case, so may we to an indefinite number. If that which has held true in our past experience will, therefore, hold in time to come, it will hold not merely in some individual case, but in all cases of some given description. Every induction, therefore, which suffices to prove one fact proves an indefinite multitude of facts; the experience which justifies a single prediction must be such as will suffice to bear out a general theorem. This theorem it is extremely important to ascertain and declare, in its broadest form of generality, and thus to place before our minds, in its full extent, the whole of what our evidence must prove if it proves anything.

This throwing of the whole body of possible inferences from a given set of particulars into one general expression operates as a security for their being just inferences, in more ways than one. First, the general principle presents a larger object to the imagination than any of the singular propositions which it contains. A process of thought which leads to a comprehensive generality is felt as of greater importance than one which terminates in an insulated fact; and the mind is, even unconsciously, led to bestow greater attention upon the process, and to weigh more carefully the sufficiency of the experience appealed to for supporting the inference grounded upon it. There is another, and a more important, advantage. In reasoning from a course of individual observations to some new and unobserved case which we are but imperfectly acquainted with (or we should not be inquiring into it) and in which, since we are inquiring into it, we probably feel a peculiar interest, there is very little to prevent us from giving way to negligence, or to any bias which may affect our wishes or our imagination and, under that influence, accepting insufficient evidence as sufficient. But if, instead of concluding straight to the particular case, we place before ourselves an entire class of facts — the whole contents of a general proposition, every tittle of which is legitimately inferable from our premises, if that one particular conclusion is so—there is then a considerable likelihood that if the premises are insufficient, and the general inference, therefore, groundless, it will comprise within it some fact or facts the reverse of which we already know to be true, and we shall thus discover the error in our generalization by a *reductio ad impossibile*.

. . . .

The value, therefore, of the syllogistic form and of the rules for using it correctly does not consist in their being the form and the rules according to which our reasonings are necessarily, or even usually, made, but in their furnishing us with a mode in which those reasonings may always be represented and which is admirably calculated, if they are inconclusive, to bring their inconclusiveness to light. An induction from particulars to generals, followed by a syllogistic process from those generals to other particulars, is a form in which we may always state our reasonings if we please. It is not a form in which we *must* reason, but it is a form in which we *may* reason and into which it is indispensable to throw our reasoning when there is any doubt of its validity; though when the case is familiar and little complicated, and there is no suspicion of error, we may and do reason at once from the known particular cases to unknown ones.[3]

These are the uses of syllogism as a mode of verifying any given

[3]The language of ratiocination would, I think, be brought into closer agreement with the real nature of the process if the general propositions employed in reasoning, instead of being in the form "All men are mortal," or "Every man is mortal," were expressed in the form "Any man is mortal." This mode of expression, exhibiting as the type of all reasoning from experience, "The men A, B, C, etc., are so and so, therefore *any* man is so and so," would much better manifest the true idea — that inductive reasoning is always, at bottom, inference from particulars to particulars, and that the whole function of general propositions in reasoning is to vouch for the legitimacy of such inferences.

argument. Its ulterior uses, as respects the general course of our intellectual operations, hardly require illustration, being in fact the acknowledged uses of general language. They amount substantially to this, that the inductions may be made once for all; a single careful interrogation of experience may suffice, and the result may be registered in the form of a general proposition which is committed to memory or to writing and from which afterward we have only to syllogize. The particulars of our experiments may then be dismissed from the memory, in which it would be impossible to retain so great a multitude of details, while the knowledge which those details afforded for future use, and which would otherwise be lost as soon as the observations were forgotten or as their record became too bulky for reference, is retained in a commodious and immediately available shape by means of general language.

.   .   .   .

6. *The true type, what*

To complete the series of considerations connected with the philosophical character of the syllogism, it is requisite to consider, since the syllogism is not the universal type of the reasoning process, what is the real type. This resolves itself into the question, what is the nature of the minor premise, and in what manner it contributes to establish the conclusion; for, as to the major, we now fully understand that the place which it nominally occupies in our reasonings properly belongs to the individual facts or observations of which it expresses the general result, the major itself being no real part of the argument, but an intermediate halting-place for the mind, interposed by an artifice of language between the real premises and the conclusion, by way of a security, which it is in a most material degree, for the correctness of the process. The minor, however, being an indispensable part of the syllogistic expression of an argument, without doubt either is, or corresponds to, an equally indispensable part of the argument itself, and we have only to inquire what part.

.   .   .   .

In the argument, then, which proves that Socrates is mortal, one indispensable part of the premises will be as follows: "My father, and my father's father, A, B, C, and an indefinite number of other persons, were mortal," which is only an expression in different words of the observed fact that they have died. This is the major premise divested of the *petitio principii*, and cut down to as much as is really known by direct evidence.

In order to connect this proposition with the conclusion Socrates is mortal, the additional link necessary is such a proposition as the following: "Socrates resembles my father, and my father's father, and the other individuals specified." This proposition we assert when we say that Socrates is a man. By saying so, we likewise assert in what respect he resembles them, namely, in the attributes connoted by the word man. And we conclude that he further resembles them in the attribute mortality.

7. *Relation between induction and deduction*

We have thus obtained what we were seeking, a universal type of the reasoning process. We find it resolvable in all cases into the following elements: Certain individuals have a given attribute; an individual or individuals resemble the former in certain other attributes; therefore they resemble them also in the given attribute. This type of ratiocination does not claim, like the syllogism, to be conclusive from the mere form of the expression, nor can it possibly be so. That one proposition does or does not assert the very fact which was already asserted in another may appear from the form of the expression, that is, from a comparison of the language; but when the two propositions assert facts which are *bona fide* different, whether the one fact proves the other or not can never appear from the language, but must depend on other considerations. Whether, from the attributes in which Socrates resembles those men who have heretofore died, it is allowable to infer that he resembles them also in being mortal, is a question of induction, and is to be decided by the principles or canons which we shall hereafter recognize as tests of the correct performance of that great mental operation.

Meanwhile, however, it is certain, as before remarked, that if this inference can be drawn as to Socrates, it can be drawn as to all others who resemble the observed individuals in the same attributes in which he resembles them, that is (to express the thing concisely), of all mankind. If, therefore, the argument be admissible in the case of Socrates, we are at liberty, once for all, to treat the possession of the attributes of man as a mark, or satisfactory evidence, of the attribute of mortality. This we do by laying down the universal proposition, "All men are mortal," and interpreting this, as occasion arises, in its application to Socrates and others. By this means we establish a very convenient division of the entire logical operation into two steps: first, that of ascertaining what attributes are marks of mortality; and, secondly, whether any given individuals possess those marks. And it will generally be advisable, in our speculations on the reasoning process, to consider this double operation as in fact taking place, and all reasoning as carried on in the form into which it must necessarily be thrown to enable us to apply to it any test of its correct performance.

Although, therefore, all processes of thought in which the ultimate premises are particulars, whether we conclude from particulars to a general formula, or from particulars to other particulars according to that formula, are equally induction, we shall yet, conformably to usage, consider the name induction as more peculiarly belonging to the process of establishing the general proposition, and the remaining operation, which is substantially that of interpreting the general proposition, we shall call by its usual name, deduction. And we shall consider every process by which anything is inferred respecting an unobserved case as consisting of an induction followed by a deduction; because, although the process needs not necessarily be carried on in this form, it is always susceptible of the form and must be thrown into it when assurance of scientific accuracy is needed and desired.

CHAPTER IV

OF TRAINS OF REASONING AND DEDUCTIVE SCIENCES

1. *For what purpose trains of reasoning exist*

In our analysis of the syllogism, it appeared that the minor premise always affirms a resemblance between a new case and some cases previously known, while the major premise asserts something which, having been found true of those known cases, we consider ourselves warranted in holding true of any other case resembling the former in certain given particulars.

If all ratiocinations resembled, as to the minor premise, the examples which were exclusively employed in the preceding chapter, if the resemblance which that premise asserts were obvious to the senses, as in the proposition "Socrates is a man," or were at once ascertainable by direct observation, there would be no necessity for trains of reasoning, and deductive or ratiocinative sciences would not exist. Trains of reasoning exist only for the sake of extending an induction, founded, as all inductions must be, on observed cases, to other cases in which we not only cannot directly observe the fact which is to be proved, but cannot directly observe even the mark which is to prove it.

2. *A train of reasoning is a series of inductive inferences*

Suppose the syllogism to be, "All cows ruminate, the animal which is before me is a cow, therefore it ruminates." The minor, if true at all, is obviously so; the only premise the establishment of which requires any anterior process of inquiry is the major, and, provided the induction of which that premise is the expression was correctly performed, the conclusion respecting the animal now present will be instantly drawn; because, as soon as she is compared with the formula, she will be identified as being included in it. But suppose the syllogism to be the following: "All arsenic is poisonous, the substance which is before me is arsenic, therefore it is poisonous." The truth of the minor may not here be obvious at first sight; it may not be intuitively evident, but may itself be known only by inference. It may be the conclusion of another argument, which, thrown into the syllogistic form, would stand thus: "Whatever when lighted produces a dark spot on a piece of white porcelain held in the flame, which spot is soluble in hypochloride of calcium, is arsenic; the substance before me conforms to this condition; therefore it is arsenic." To establish, therefore, the ultimate conclusion, "The substance before me is poisonous," requires a process which, in order to be syllogistically expressed stands in need of two syllogisms, and we have a train of reasoning.

When, however, we thus add syllogism to syllogism, we are really adding induction to induction. Two separate inductions must have taken place to render this chain of inference possible; inductions founded, probably, on different sets of individual instances, but which converge in their results so that the instance which is the subject of inquiry comes within the range of them both. The record of these inductions is contained in the majors of the two syllogisms. First, we, or others for us, have examined various objects which yielded under the given circumstances a dark spot with the given property and found that they possessed the properties connoted by the word arsenic: they were metallic, volatile, their vapor had a smell of garlic, and so forth. Next, we, or others for us, have examined various specimens which possessed this metallic and volatile character, whose vapor had this smell, etc., and have invariably found that they were poisonous. The first observation we judge that we may extend to all substances whatever which yield that particular kind of dark spot; the second, to all metallic and volatile substances resembling those we examined; and, consequently, not to those only which are seen to be such, but to those which are concluded to be such by the prior induction. The substance before us is only seen to come within one of these inductions, but, by means of this one, it is brought within the other. We are still, as before, concluding from particulars to particulars; but we are now concluding from particulars observed to other particulars which are not, as in the simple case, *seen* to resemble them in material points, but *inferred* to do so because resembling them in something else, which we have been led by quite a different set of instances to consider as a mark of the former resemblance.

. . . .

3. — *from particulars to particulars through marks of marks*

Notwithstanding the superior complication of these examples compared with those by which in the preceding chapter we illustrated the general theory of reasoning, every doctrine which we then laid down holds equally true in these more intricate cases. The successive general propositions are not steps in the reasoning, are not intermediate links in the chain of inference, between the particulars observed and those to which we apply the observation. If we had sufficiently capacious memories and a sufficient power of maintaining order among a huge mass of details, the reasoning could go on without any general propositions; they are mere formulae for inferring particulars from particulars. The principle of general reasoning is (as before explained) that if, from observation of certain known particulars, what was seen to be true of them can be inferred to be true of any others, it may be inferred of all others which are of a certain description. And in order that we may never fail to draw this conclusion in a new case when it can be drawn correctly and may avoid drawing it when it cannot, we determine once for all what are the distinguishing marks by which such cases may be recognized. The subsequent process is merely that of identifying an object and ascertaining it to have those marks, whether we identify it by the very marks themselves or by others which we have ascertained (through another and a similar process) to be marks of those marks. The real inference is always from particulars to particulars, from the observed instances to an unobserved one, but in drawing this inference, we conform to a formula which we have adopted for our guidance in such operations and which is a record of the criteria by which we thought we had ascertained that we might distinguish when the inference could, and when it could not, be drawn. The real premises are the individual observations, even though they may have been forgotten, or, being the observations of others and not of ourselves, may, to us, never have been known; but we have before us proof that we or others once thought them sufficient for an induction, and we have marks to show whether any new case is one of those to which, if then known, the induction would have been deemed to extend. These marks we either recognize at once, or by the aid of other marks which by another previous induction we collected to be marks of the first. Even these marks of marks may only be recognized through a third set of marks; and we may have a train of reasoning, of any length, to bring a new case within the scope of an induction grounded on particulars its similarity to which is only ascertained in this indirect manner.

.   .   .   .

In the more complex branches of knowledge, the deductions seldom consist, as in the examples hitherto exhibited, of a single chain, a a mark of b, b of c, c of d, therefore a a mark of d. They consist (to carry on the same metaphor) of several chains united at the extremity, as thus: a a mark of d, b of e, c of f, $d\ e\ f$ of n, therefore $a\ b\ c$ a mark of n. Suppose, for example, the following combination of circumstances: 1st, rays of light impinging on a reflecting surface; 2d, that surface parabolic; 3d, those rays parallel to each other and to the axis of the surface. It is to be proved that the concourse of these three circumstances is a mark that the reflected rays will pass through the focus of the parabolic surface. Now each of the three circumstances is singly a mark of something material to the case. Rays of light impinging on a reflecting surface are a mark that those rays will be reflected at an angle equal to the angle of incidence. The parabolic form of the surface is a mark that, from any point of it, a line drawn to the focus and a line parallel to the axis will make equal angles with the surface. And, finally, the parallelism of the rays to the axis is a mark that their angle of incidence coincides with one of these equal angles. The three marks taken together are, therefore, a mark of all these three things united. But the three united are evidently a mark that the angle of reflection must coincide with the other of the two equal angles, that formed by a line drawn to the focus; and this again, by the fundamental axiom concerning straight lines, is a mark that the reflected rays pass through the focus. Most chains of physical deduction are of this more complicated type, and even in mathematics such are abundant, as in all propositions where the hypothesis includes numerous conditions: "*If* a circle be taken, and *if* within that circle a point be taken, not the centre, and *if* straight lines be drawn from that point to the circumference, then," etc.

4. *Why there are deductive sciences*

The considerations now stated remove a serious difficulty from the view we have taken of reasoning, which view might otherwise have seemed not easily reconcilable with the fact that there are deductive or ratiocinative sciences. It might seem to follow, if all reasoning be induction, that the difficulties of philosophical investigation must lie in the inductions exclusively, and that when these were easy, and susceptible of no doubt or hesitation, there could be no science or, at least, no difficulties in science. The existence, for example, of an extensive science of mathematics, requiring the highest scientific genius in those who contributed to its creation and calling for a most continued and vigorous exertion of intellect in order to appropriate it when created, may seem hard to be accounted for on the foregoing theory. But the considerations more recently adduced remove the mystery, by showing that, even when the inductions themselves are obvious, there may be much difficulty in finding whether the particular case which is the subject of inquiry comes within them, and ample room for scientific ingenuity in so combining various inductions as, by means of one within which the case evidently falls, to bring it within others in which it cannot be directly seen to be included.

When the more obvious of the inductions which can be made in any science from direct observations have been made, and general formulas have been framed, determining the limits within which these inductions are applicable, as often as a new case can be at once seen to come within one of the formulas, the induction is applied to the new case, and the business is ended. But new cases are continually arising which do not obviously come within any formula whereby the question we want solved in respect of them could be answered. Let us take an instance from geometry, and, as it is taken only for illustration, let the reader concede to us for the present what we shall endeavor to prove in the next chapter, that the first principles of geometry are results of induction. Our example shall be the fifth proposition of the first book of Euclid. The inquiry is, Are the angles at the base of an isosceles triangle equal or unequal? The first thing to be considered is what inductions we have, from which we can infer equality or inequality. For inferring equality we have the following formulae: things which, being applied to each other, coincide are equals. Things which are equal to the same thing are equals. A whole and the sum of its parts are equals. The sums of equal things are equals. The differences of equal things are equals. There are no other original formulae to prove equality. For inferring inequality we have the following: A whole and its parts are unequals. The sums of equal things and unequal things are unequals. The differences of equal things and unequal things are unequals. In all, eight formulae. The angles at the base of an isosceles triangle do not obviously come within any of these. The formulae specify certain marks of equality and of inequality, but the angles cannot be perceived intuitively to have any of those marks. On examination it appears that they have; and we ultimately succeed in bringing them within the formula, "The differences of equal things are equal." Whence comes the difficulty of recognizing these angles as the differences of equal things? Because each of them is the difference not of one pair only, but of innumerable pairs of angles; and out of these we had to imagine and select two, which could either be intuitively perceived to be equals, or possessed some of the marks of equality set down in the various formulae. By an exercise of ingenuity, which, on the part of the first inventor, deserves to be regarded as considerable, two pairs of angles were hit upon which united these requisites. First, it could be perceived intuitively that their differences were the angles at the base; and, secondly, they possessed one of the marks of equality, namely, coincidence when applied to one another. This coincidence, however, was not perceived intuitively, but inferred, in conformity to another formula.

.   .   .   .

5. *Why other sciences still remain experimental*

It will be seen hereafter[1] that there are weighty scientific reasons for giving to every science as much of the character of a deductive science as possible, for endeavoring to construct the science from the fewest and the simplest possible inductions, and to make these, by any combinations however complicated, suffice for proving even such truths relating to complex cases, as could be proved, if we chose, by inductions from specific experience. Every branch of natural philosophy was originally experimental; each generalization rested on a special induction and was derived from its own distinct set of observations and experiments. From being sciences of pure experiment, as the phrase is, or, to speak more correctly, sciences in which the reasonings mostly consist of no more than one step and are expressed by single syllogisms, all these sciences have become to some extent, and some of them in nearly the whole of their extent, sciences of pure reasoning, whereby multitudes of truths, already known by induction from as many different sets of experiments, have come to be exhibited as deductions or corollaries from inductive propositions of a simpler and more universal character. Thus mechanics, hydrostatics, optics, acoustics, thermology have successively been rendered mathematical, and astronomy was brought by Newton within the laws of general mechanics. Why it is that the substitution of this circuitous mode of proceeding for a process apparently much easier and more natural is held, and justly, to be the greatest triumph of the investigation of nature, we are not, in this stage of our inquiry, prepared to examine. But it is necessary to remark that, although, by this progressive transformation, all sciences tend to become more and more deductive, they are not, therefore, the less inductive; every step in the deduction is still an induction. The opposition is not between the terms deductive and inductive, but between deductive and experimental. A science is experimental in proportion as every new case which presents any peculiar features stands in need of a new set of observations and experiments — a fresh induction. It is deductive in proportion as it can draw conclusions respecting cases of a new kind by processes which bring those cases under old inductions, by

---

[1] *Infra*, Book III, Ch. IV, § 3, and elsewhere.

ascertaining that cases which cannot be observed to have the requisite marks have, however, marks of those marks.

We can now, therefore, perceive what is the generic distinction between sciences which can be made deductive and those which must as yet remain experimental. The difference consists in our having been able, or not yet able, to discover marks of marks. If by our various inductions we have been able to proceed no further than to such propositions as these: *a* a mark of *b*, or *a* and *b* marks of one another, *c* a mark of *d*, or *c* and *d* marks of one another, without anything to connect *a* or *b* with *c* or *d*, we have a science of detached and mutually independent generalizations, such as these: that acids redden vegetable blues, and that alkalies color them green, from neither of which propositions could we, directly or indirectly, infer the other; and a science, so far as it is composed of such propositions, is purely experimental. Chemistry, in the present state of our knowledge, has not yet thrown off this character. There are other sciences, however, of which the propositions are of this kind: *a* a mark of *b*, *b* a mark of *c*, *c* of *d*, *d* of *e*, etc. In these sciences we can mount the ladder from *a* to *e* by a process of ratiocination; we can conclude that *a* is a mark of *e*, and that every object which has the mark *a* has the property *e*, although, perhaps, we never were able to observe *a* and *e* together, and although even *d*, our only direct mark of *e*, may not be perceptible in those objects, but only inferable. Or, varying the first metaphor, we may be said to get from *a* to *e* underground; the marks *b*, *c*, *d*, which indicate the route, must all be possessed somewhere by the objects concerning which we are inquiring, but they are below the surface; *a* is the only mark that is visible, and by it we are able to trace in succession all the rest.

6. *Experimental sciences may become deductive by the progress of experiment*

We can now understand how an experimental may transform itself into a deductive science by the mere progress of experiment. In an experimental science the inductions, as we have said, lie detached, as, *a* a mark of *b*, *c* a mark of *d*, *e* a mark of *f*, and so on; now, a new set of instances and a consequent new induction may

at any time bridge over the interval between two of these unconnected arches; *b*, for example, may be ascertained to be a mark of *c*,
which enables us thenceforth to prove deductively that *a* is a mark
of *c*. Or, as sometimes happens, some comprehensive induction
may raise an arch high in the air which bridges over hosts of them
at once, *b*, *d*, *f*, and all the rest turning out to be marks of some
one thing or of things between which a connection has already
been traced. As when Newton discovered that the motions,
whether regular or apparently anomalous, of all the bodies of the
solar system (each of which motions had been inferred by a separate logical operation, from separate marks) were all marks of
moving round a common center, with a centripetal force varying
directly as the mass, and inversely as the square of the distance
from that center. This is the greatest example which has yet
occurred of the transformation, at one stroke, of a science which
was still to a great degree merely experimental into a deductive
science.

. . . .

CHAPTER V

OF DEMONSTRATION AND NECESSARY TRUTHS

1. *The theorems of geometry are necessary truths only in the sense of
necessarily following from hypotheses*

If, as laid down in the two preceding chapters, the foundation
of all sciences, even deductive or demonstrative sciences, is induction, if every step in the ratiocinations even of geometry is an act
of induction, and if a train of reasoning is but bringing many
inductions to bear upon the same subject of inquiry and drawing
a case within one induction by means of another, wherein lies the
peculiar certainty always ascribed to the sciences which are entirely,

or almost entirely, deductive? Why are they called the exact sciences? Why are mathematical certainty and the evidence of demonstration common phrases to express the very highest degree of assurance attainable by reason? Why are mathematics by almost all philosophers, and (by some) even those branches of natural philosophy which, through the medium of mathematics, have been converted into deductive sciences, considered to be independent of the evidence of experience and observation and characterized as systems of necessary truth?

The answer I conceive to be that this character of necessity ascribed to the truths of mathematics and (even with some reservations to be hereafter made) the peculiar certainty attributed to them is an illusion, in order to sustain which, it is necessary to suppose that those truths relate to, and express the properties of, purely imaginary objects. It is acknowledged that the conclusions of geometry are deduced, partly at least, from the so-called definitions, and that those definitions are assumed to be correct representations, as far as they go, of the objects with which geometry is conversant. Now we have pointed out that from a definition as such no proposition, unless it be one concerning the meaning of a word, can ever follow, and that what apparently follows from a definition follows in reality from an implied assumption that there exists a real thing conformable thereto. This assumption, in the case of the definitions of geometry, is not strictly true; there exist no real things exactly conformable to the definitions. There exist no points without magnitude; no lines without breadth, nor perfectly straight; no circles with all their radii exactly equal, nor squares with all their angles perfectly right. It will perhaps be said that the assumption does not extend to the actual, but only to the possible, existence of such things. I answer that, according to any test we have of possibility, they are not even possible. Their existence, so far as we can form any judgment, would seem to be inconsistent with the physical constitution of our planet at least, if not of the universe. To get rid of this difficulty and at the same time to save the credit of the supposed system of necessary truth, it is customary to say that the points, lines, circles, and squares which are the subject of geometry exist in our conceptions merely and are part of our minds, which minds, by working on their own materials, construct an *a priori* science, the evidence of which is purely mental and has nothing whatever to do with outward experience. By howsoever high authorities this doctrine may have been sanctioned, it appears to me psychologically incorrect. The points, lines, circles, and squares which anyone has in his mind are (I apprehend) simply copies of the points, lines, circles, and squares which he has known in his experience. Our idea of a point I apprehend to be simply our idea of the *minimum visibile*, the smallest portion of surface which we can see. A line, as defined by geometers, is wholly inconceivable. We can reason about a line as if it had no breadth, because we have a power, which is the foundation of all the control we can exercise over the operations of our minds, the power, when a perception is present to our senses or a conception to our intellects, of *attending* to a part only of that perception or conception instead of the whole. But we cannot *conceive* a line without breadth; we can form no mental picture of such a line; all the lines which we have in our minds are lines possessing breadth. If anyone doubts this, we may refer him to his own experience. I much question if anyone who fancies that he can conceive what is called a mathematical line thinks so from the evidence of his consciousness; I suspect it is rather because he supposes that, unless such a conception were possible, mathematics could not exist as a science, a supposition which there will be no difficulty in showing to be entirely groundless.

Since, then, neither in nature nor in the human mind do there exist any objects exactly corresponding to the definitions of geometry, while yet that science cannot be supposed to be conversant about nonentities, nothing remains but to consider geometry as conversant with such lines, angles, and figures as really exist, and the definitions, as they are called, must be regarded as some of our first and most obvious generalizations concerning those natural objects. The correctness of those generalizations, *as* generalizations, is without a flaw; the equality of all the radii of a circle is true of all circles, so far as it is true of any one, but it is not exactly true of any circle; it is only nearly true, so nearly that no error of any importance in practice will be incurred by feigning it to be exactly true. When we have occasion to extend these inductions or their consequences to cases in which the error would be appreciable — to lines of perceptible breadth or thickness, parallels which deviate sensibly from equidistance, and the like — we correct our conclusions by combining with them a fresh set of propositions relating to the aberration, just as we also take in propositions relating to the physical or chemical properties of the material if those properties happen to introduce any modification into the result, which they easily may, even with respect to figure and magnitude, as in the case, for instance, of expansion by heat. So long, however, as there exists no practical necessity for attending to any of the properties of the object except its geometrical properties or to any of the natural irregularities in those, it is convenient to neglect the consideration of the other properties and of the irregularities and to reason as if these did not exist; accordingly, we formally announce in the definitions that we intend to proceed on this plan. But it is an error to suppose, because we resolve to confine our attention to a certain number of the properties of an object, that we therefore conceive, or have an idea of, the object denuded of its other properties. We are thinking, all the time, of precisely such objects as we have seen and touched and with all the properties which naturally belong to them, but, for scientific convenience, we feign them to be divested of all properties except those which are material to our purpose and in regard to which we design to consider them.

The peculiar accuracy supposed to be characteristic of the first principles of geometry thus appears to be fictitious. The assertions on which the reasonings of the science are founded do not, any more than in other sciences, exactly correspond with the fact, but we suppose that they do so, for the sake of tracing the consequences which follow from the supposition. The opinion of Dugald Stewart respecting the foundations of geometry is, I conceive, substantially correct: that it is built on hypotheses; that it owes to this alone the peculiar certainty supposed to distinguish it; and that in any science whatever, by reasoning from a set of hypotheses, we may obtain a body of conclusions as certain as those of geometry, that is, as strictly in accordance with the hypotheses and as irresistibly compelling assent, *on condition* that those hypotheses are true.[1]

[1]It is justly remarked by Professor Bain (*Logic*, II, 134) that the word Hypothesis is here used in a somewhat peculiar sense. An hypothesis, in

When, therefore, it is affirmed that the conclusions of geometry are necessary truths, the necessity consists in reality only in this, that they correctly follow from the suppositions from which they are deduced. Those suppositions are so far from being necessary that they are not even true; they purposely depart, more or less widely, from the truth. The only sense in which necessity can be ascribed to the conclusions of any scientific investigation is that of legitimately following from some assumption which, by the conditions of the inquiry, is not to be questioned. In this relation, of course, the derivative truths of every deductive science must stand to the inductions or assumptions on which the science is founded, and which, whether true or untrue, certain or doubtful in themselves, are always supposed certain for the purposes of the particular science. . . .

2. *Some of the first principles of geometry are axioms, and these are not hypothetical*

. . . Some of the axioms of Euclid might, no doubt, be exhibited in the form of definitions or might be deduced, by reasoning, from propositions similar to what are so called. Thus, if instead of the axiom, "magnitudes which can be made to coincide are equal," we introduce a definition, "equal magnitudes are those which may be so applied to one another as to coincide," the three axioms which follow (magnitudes which are equal to the same are equal to one another — if equals are added to equals, the sums are equal — if

science, usually means a supposition not proved to be true, but surmised to be so, because if true it would account for certain known facts, and the final result of the speculation may be to prove its truth. The hypotheses spoken of in the text are of a different character; they are known not to be literally true, while as much of them as is true is not hypothetical, but certain. The two cases, however, resemble in the circumstance that in both we reason, not from a truth, but from an assumption, and the truth, therefore, of the conclusions is conditional, not categorical. This suffices to justify, in point of logical propriety, Stewart's use of the term. It is, of course, needful to bear in mind that the hypothetical element in the definitions of geometry is the assumption that what is very nearly true is exactly so. This unreal exactitude might be called a fiction as properly as an hypothesis, but that appellation, still more than the other, would fail to point out the close relation which exists between the fictitious point or line and the points and lines of which we have experience.

equals are taken from equals, the remainders are equal) may be proved by an imaginary superposition, resembling that by which the fourth proposition of the first book of Euclid is demonstrated. But though these and several others may be struck out of the list of first principles because, though not requiring demonstration, they are susceptible of it, there will be found in the list of axioms two or three fundamental truths not capable of being demonstrated, among which must be reckoned the proposition that two straight lines cannot inclose a space (or its equivalent, straight lines which coincide in two points coincide altogether) and some property of parallel lines other than that which constitutes their definition, one of the most suitable for the purpose being that selected by Professor Playfair: "Two straight lines which intersect each other cannot both of them be parallel to a third straight line."[2]

The axioms, as well those which are indemonstrable as those which admit of being demonstrated, differ from that other class of fundamental principles which are involved in the definitions in this, that they are true without any mixture of hypothesis. That things which are equal to the same thing are equal to one another is as true of the lines and figures in nature as it would be of the imaginary ones assumed in the definitions. In this respect, however, mathematics are only on a par with most other sciences. In almost all sciences there are some general propositions which are exactly true, while the greater part are only more or less distant approximations to the truth. Thus, in mechanics, the first law of motion (the continuance of a movement once impressed, until stopped or slackened by some resisting force) is true without qualification or error. The rotation of the earth in twenty-four hours, of the same

[2]We might, it is true, insert this property into the definition of parallel lines, framing the definition so as to require both that when produced indefinitely they shall never meet and also that any straight line which intersects one of them shall, if prolonged, meet the other. But by doing this we by no means get rid of the assumption; we are still obliged to take for granted the geometrical truth that all straight lines in the same plane which have the former of these properties have also the latter. For if it were possible that they should not, that is, if any straight lines in the same plane, other than those which are parallel according to the definition, had the property of never meeting although indefinitely produced, the demonstrations of the subsequent portions of the theory of parallels could not be maintained.

length as in our time, has gone on since the first accurate observations, without the increase or diminution of one second in all that period. These are inductions which require no fiction to make them be received as accurately true; but along with them there are others, as for instance the propositions respecting the figure of the earth, which are but approximations to the truth, and in order to use them for the further advancement of our knowledge, we must feign that they are exactly true, though they really want something of being so.

3. — but are experimental truths

It remains to inquire what is the ground of our belief in axioms — what is the evidence on which they rest? I answer, they are experimental truths, generalizations from observation. The proposition, "Two straight lines cannot inclose a space" — or, in other words, "Two straight lines which have once met, do not meet again, but continue to diverge" — is an induction from the evidence of our senses.

This opinion runs counter to a scientific prejudice of long standing and great strength, and there is probably no proposition enunciated in this work for which a more unfavorable reception is to be expected. It is, however, no new opinion, and, even if it were so, would be entitled to be judged not by its novelty, but by the strength of the arguments by which it can be supported. I consider it very fortunate that so eminent a champion of the contrary opinion as Dr. Whewell has found occasion for a most elaborate treatment of the whole theory of axioms in attempting to construct the philosophy of the mathematical and physical sciences on the basis of the doctrine against which I now contend. Whoever is anxious that a discussion should go to the bottom of the subject must rejoice to see the opposite side of the question worthily represented. If what is said by Dr. Whewell, in support of an opinion which he has made the foundation of a systematic work, can be shown not to be conclusive, enough will have been done, without going elsewhere in quest of stronger arguments and a more powerful adversary.

It is not necessary to show that the truths which we call axioms are originally *suggested* by observation and that we should never have known that two straight lines cannot inclose a space if we had never seen a straight line, thus much being admitted by

Dr. Whewell and by all, in recent times, who have taken his view of the subject. But they contend that it is not experience which *proves* the axiom, but that its truth is perceived *a priori*, by the constitution of the mind itself, from the first moment when the meaning of the proposition is apprehended, and without any necessity for verifying it by repeated trials, as is requisite in the case of truths really ascertained by observation.

They cannot, however, but allow that the truth of the axiom, "Two straight lines cannot inclose a space," even if evident independently of experience, is also evident from experience. Whether the axiom needs confirmation or not, it receives confirmation in almost every instant of our lives, since we cannot look at any two straight lines which intersect one another without seeing that from that point they continue to diverge more and more. Experimental proof crowds in upon us in such endless profusion, and without one instance in which there can be even a suspicion of an exception to the rule, that we should soon have stronger ground for believing the axiom, even as an experimental truth, than we have for almost any of the general truths which we confessedly learn from the evidence of our senses. Independently of *a priori* evidence, we should certainly believe it with an intensity of conviction far greater than we accord to any ordinary physical truth, and this, too, at a time of life much earlier than that from which we date almost any part of our acquired knowledge, and much too early to admit of our retaining any recollection of the history of our intellectual operations at that period. Where, then, is the necessity for assuming that our recognition of these truths has a different origin from the rest of our knowledge when its existence is perfectly accounted for by supposing its origin to be the same? when the causes which produce belief in all other instances exist in this instance, and in a degree of strength as much superior to what exists in other cases as the intensity of the belief itself is superior? The burden of proof lies on the advocates of the contrary opinion; it is for them to point out some fact inconsistent with the supposition that this part of our knowledge of nature is derived from the same sources as every other part.[3]

[3] Some persons find themselves prevented from believing that the axiom, "Two straight lines cannot inclose a space," could ever become known to us through experience, by a difficulty which may be stated as follows: If the

This, for instance, they would be able to do, if they could prove chronologically that we had the conviction (at least practically) so early in infancy as to be anterior to those impressions on the senses upon which, on the other theory, the conviction is founded. This, however, cannot be proved, the point being too far back to be within the reach of memory and too obscure for external observation. The advocates of the *a priori* theory are obliged to have recourse to other arguments. These are reducible to two, which I shall endeavor to state as clearly and as forcibly as possible.

4. *An objection answered*

In the first place it is said that if our assent to the proposition that two straight lines cannot inclose a space were derived from the senses, we could only be convinced of its truth by actual trial, that is, by seeing or feeling the straight lines, whereas, in fact, it is seen to be true by merely thinking of them. That a stone thrown into water goes to the bottom may be perceived by our senses, but

---

straight lines spoken of are those contemplated in the definition — lines absolutely without breadth and absolutely straight — that such are incapable of inclosing a space is not proved by experience, for lines such as these do not present themselves in our experience. If, on the other hand, the lines meant are such straight lines as we do meet with in experience, lines straight enough for practical purposes, but in reality slightly zigzag, and with some, however trifling, breadth; as applied to these lines the axiom is not true, for two of them may, and sometimes do, inclose a small portion of space. In neither case, therefore, does experience prove the axiom.

Those who employ this argument to show that geometrical axioms cannot be proved by induction show themselves unfamiliar with a common and perfectly valid mode of inductive proof: proof by approximation. Though experience furnishes us with no lines so unimpeachably straight that two of them are incapable of inclosing the smallest space, it presents us with gradations of lines possessing less and less either of breadth or of flexure, of which series the straight line of the definition is the ideal limit. And observation shows that just as much and as nearly as the straight lines of experience approximate to having no breadth or flexure, so much and so nearly does the space-inclosing power of any two of them approach to zero. The inference that if they had no breadth or flexure at all they would inclose no space at all, is a correct inductive inference from these facts, conformable to one of the four Inductive Methods hereinafter characterized, the Method of Concomitant Variations, of which the mathematical Doctrine of Limits presents the extreme case.

mere thinking of a stone thrown into the water would never have led us to that conclusion; not so, however, with the axioms relating to straight lines: if I could be made to conceive what a straight line is, without having seen one, I should at once recognize that two such lines cannot inclose a space. Intuition is "imaginary looking,"[4] but experience must be real looking; if we see a property of straight lines to be true by merely fancying ourselves to be looking at them, the ground of our belief cannot be the senses, or experience; it must be something mental.

To this argument it might be added in the case of this particular axiom (for the assertion would not be true of all axioms) that the evidence of it from actual ocular inspection is not only unnecessary but unattainable. What says the axiom? That two straight lines *cannot* inclose a space; that, after having once intersected, if they are prolonged to infinity they do not meet, but continue to diverge from one another. How can this, in any single case, be proved by actual observation? We may follow the lines to any distance we please, but we cannot follow them to infinity; for aught our senses can testify, they may, immediately beyond the farthest point to which we have traced them, begin to approach, and at last meet. Unless, therefore, we had some other proof of the impossibility than observation affords us, we should have no ground for believing the axiom at all.

To these arguments, which I trust I cannot be accused of understating, a satisfactory answer will, I conceive, be found, if we advert to one of the characteristic properties of geometrical forms — their capacity of being painted in the imagination with a distinctness equal to reality; in other words, the exact resemblance of our ideas of form to the sensations which suggest them. This, in the first place, enables us to make (at least with a little practice) mental pictures of all possible combinations of lines and angles which resemble the realities quite as well as any which we could make on paper; and, in the next place, make those pictures just as fit subjects of geometrical experimentation as the realities themselves, inasmuch as pictures, if sufficiently accurate, exhibit, of course, all the properties which would be manifested by the realities at one given instant and on simple inspection; and in geometry we

[4] Whewell's *History of Scientific Ideas*, I, 140.

are concerned only with such properties, and not with that which pictures could not exhibit, the mutual action of bodies one upon another. The foundations of geometry would, therefore, be laid in direct experience, even if the experiments (which in this case consist merely in attentive contemplation) were practiced solely upon what we call our ideas, that is, upon the diagrams in our minds, and not upon outward objects. For in all systems of experimentation we take some objects to serve as representatives of all which resemble them, and in the present case the conditions which qualify a real object to be the representative of its class are completely fulfilled by an object existing only in our fancy. Without denying, therefore, the possibility of satisfying ourselves that two straight lines cannot inclose a space by merely thinking of straight lines without actually looking at them, I contend that we do not believe this truth on the ground of the imaginary intuition simply, but because we know that the imaginary lines exactly resemble real ones and that we may conclude from them to real ones with quite as much certainty as we could conclude from one real line to another. The conclusion, therefore, is still an induction from observation. And we should not be authorized to substitute observation of the image in our mind for observation of the reality, if we had not learned by long continued experience that the properties of the reality are faithfully represented in the image, just as we should be scientifically warranted in describing an animal which we have never seen from a picture made of it with a daguerreotype, but not until we had learned by ample experience that observation of such a picture is precisely equivalent to observation of the original.

These considerations also remove the objection arising from the impossibility of ocularly following the lines in their prolongation to infinity. For though, in order actually to see that two given lines never meet, it would be necessary to follow them to infinity, yet without doing so we may know that if they ever do meet, or if, after diverging from one another, they begin again to approach, this must take place not at an infinite, but at a finite distance. Supposing, therefore, such to be the case, we can transport ourselves thither in imagination and can frame a mental image of the appearance which one or both of the lines must present at that point, which we may rely on as being precisely similar to the reality. Now, whether we fix our contemplation upon this imaginary picture or call to mind the generalizations we have had occasion to make from former ocular observation, we learn by the evidence of experience that a line which, after diverging from another straight line, begins to approach to it produces the impression on our senses which we describe by the expression, "a bent line," not by the expression, "a straight line."[5]

. . . .

[5] Dr. Whewell (*Philosophy of Discovery*, p. 289) thinks it unreasonable to contend that we know by experience that our idea of a line exactly resembles a real line. "It does not appear," he says, "how we can compare our ideas with the realities, since we know the realities only by our ideas." We know the realities by our sensations. Dr. Whewell surely does not hold the "doctrine of perception by means of ideas," which Reid gave himself so much trouble to refute.

If Dr. Whewell doubts whether we compare our ideas with the corresponding sensations and assume that they resemble, let me ask on what evidence do we judge that a portrait of a person not present is like the original. Surely because it is like our idea, or mental image of the person, and because our idea is like the man himself.

Dr. Whewell also says, that it does not appear why this resemblance of ideas to the sensations of which they are copies should be spoken of as if it were a peculiarity of one class of ideas, those of space. My reply is that I do not so speak of it. The peculiarity I contend for is only one of degree. All our ideas of sensation, of course, resemble the corresponding sensations, but they do so with very different degrees of exactness and of reliability. No one, I presume, can recall in imagination a color or an odor with the same distinctness and accuracy with which almost everyone can mentally reproduce an image of a straight line or a triangle. To the extent, however, of their capabilities of accuracy, our recollections of colors or of odors may serve as subjects of experimentation, as well as those of lines and spaces, and may yield conclusions which will be true of their external prototypes. A person in whom, either from natural gift or from cultivation, the impressions of color were peculiarly vivid and distinct, if asked which of two blue flowers was of the darkest tinge, though he might never have compared the two, or even looked at them together, might be able to give a confident answer on the faith of his distinct recollection of the colors, that is, he might examine his mental pictures and find there a property of the outward objects. But in hardly any case except that of simple geometrical forms could this be done by mankind generally, with a degree of assurance equal to that which is given by a contemplation of the objects themselves. Persons differ most widely in the precision of their recollection, even of forms; one person, when he has looked anyone in the face for half a minute, can draw

5. *Dr. Whewell's opinions on axioms examined*

The first of the two arguments in support of the theory that axioms are *a priori* truths having, I think, been sufficiently answered, I proceed to the second, which is usually the most relied on. Axioms (it is asserted) are conceived by us not only as true, but as universally and necessarily true. Now, experience cannot possibly give to any proposition this character. I may have seen snow a hundred times and may have seen that it was white, but this cannot give me entire assurance even that all snow is white, much less that snow *must* be white. "However many instances we may have observed of the truth of a proposition, there is nothing to assure us that the next case shall not be an exception to the rule. If it be strictly true that every ruminant animal yet known has cloven hoofs, we still cannot be sure that some creature will not hereafter be discovered which has the first of these attributes, without having the other. . . . . Experience must always consist of a limited number of observations; and, however numerous these may be, they can show nothing with regard to the infinite number of cases in which the experiment has not been made." Besides, axioms are not only universal, they are also necessary. Now "experience cannot offer the smallest ground for the necessity of a proposition. She can observe and record what has happened; but she cannot find, in any case, or in any accumulation of cases, any reason for what *must* happen. She may see objects side by side; but she cannot see a reason why they must ever be side by side. She finds certain events to occur in succession; but the succession supplies, in its occurrence, no reason for its recurrence. She contemplates external objects; but she cannot detect any internal bond, which indissolubly connects the future with the past, the possible with the real. To learn a proposition by experience, and to see it to be necessarily true, are two altogether different processes of

an accurate likeness of him from memory; another may have seen him every day for six months, and hardly know whether his nose is long or short. But everybody has a perfectly distinct mental image of a straight line, a circle, or a rectangle. And everyone concludes confidently from these mental images to the corresponding outward things. The truth is that we may, and continually do, study nature in our recollections, when the objects themselves are absent; and in the case of geometrical forms we can perfectly, but in most other cases only imperfectly, trust our recollections.

thought."[6] And Dr. Whewell adds, "If anyone does not clearly comprehend this distinction of necessary and contingent truths, he will not be able to go along with us in our researches into the foundations of human knowledge; nor, indeed, to pursue with success any speculation on the subject."[7]

.   .   .   .

Although Dr. Whewell has naturally and properly employed a variety of phrases to bring his meaning more forcibly home, he would, I presume, allow that they are all equivalent, and that what he means by a necessary truth would be sufficiently defined, a proposition the negation of which is not only false but inconceivable. I am unable to find in any of his expressions, turn them what way you will, a meaning beyond this, and I do not believe he would contend that they mean anything more.

This, therefore, is the principle asserted: that propositions, the negation of which is inconceivable, or, in other words, which we cannot figure to ourselves as being false, must rest on evidence of a higher and more cogent description than any which experience can afford.

Now I cannot but wonder that so much stress should be laid on the circumstance of inconceivableness when there is such ample experience to show that our capacity or incapacity of conceiving a thing has very little to do with the possibility of the thing in itself, but is, in truth, very much an affair of accident, and depends on the past history and habits of our own minds. There is no more generally acknowledged fact in human nature than the extreme difficulty at first felt in conceiving anything as possible, which is in contradiction to long established and familiar experience, or even to old familiar habits of thought. And this difficulty is a necessary result of the fundamental laws of the human mind. When we have often seen and thought of two things together and have never in any one instance either seen or thought of them separately, there is by the primary law of association an increasing difficulty, which may in the end become insuperable, of conceiving the two things apart. This is most of all conspicuous in uneducated persons who are, in general, utterly unable to separate any two ideas which

[6]*History of Scientific Ideas*, I, 65–67.
[7]*Ibid.*, I, 60.

have once become firmly associated in their minds; and if persons of cultivated intellect have any advantage on the point, it is only because, having seen and heard and read more, and being more accustomed to exercise their imagination, they have experienced their sensations and thoughts in more varied combinations and have been prevented from forming many of these inseparable associations. But this advantage has necessarily its limits. The most practiced intellect is not exempt from the universal laws of our conceptive faculty. If daily habit presents to anyone for a long period two facts in combination, and if he is not led during that period either by accident or by his voluntary mental operations to think of them apart, he will probably in time become incapable of doing so even by the strongest effort, and the supposition that the two facts can be separated in nature will at last present itself to his mind with all the characters of an inconceivable phenomenon.[8] There are remarkable instances of this in the history of science, instances in which the most instructed men rejected as impossible, because inconceivable, things which their posterity, by earlier practice and longer perseverance in the attempt, found it quite easy to conceive, and which everybody now knows to be true. There was a time when men of the most cultivated intellects and the most emancipated from the dominion of early prejudice could not credit the existence of antipodes, were unable to conceive, in opposition to old association, the force of gravity acting upward instead of downward. The Cartesians long rejected the Newtonian doctrine of the gravitation of all bodies toward one another, on the faith of a general proposition, the reverse of which seemed to them to be inconceivable — the proposition that a body cannot act where it is not. All the cumbrous machinery of imaginary vortices, assumed without the smallest particle of evidence, appeared to these philosophers a more rational mode of explaining the heavenly motions than one which involved

---

[8]"If all mankind had spoken one language, we cannot doubt that there would have been a powerful, perhaps a universal, school of philosophers, who would have believed in the inherent connection between names and things, who would have taken the sound *man* to be the mode of agitating the air which is essentially communicative of the ideas of reason, cookery, bipedality, etc." — De Morgan, *Formal Logic*, p. 246.

what seemed to them so great an absurdity.[9] And they no doubt
found it as impossible to conceive that a body should act upon the
earth from the distance of the sun or moon as we find it to conceive
an end to space or time, or two straight lines inclosing a space.
Newton himself had not been able to realize the conception or we
should not have had his hypothesis of a subtle ether, the occult
cause of gravitation, and his writings prove that though he deemed
the particular nature of the intermediate agency a matter of
conjecture, the necessity of *some* such agency appeared to him
indubitable.

If, then, it be so natural to the human mind, even in a high state
of culture, to be incapable of conceiving and on that ground to
believe impossible what is afterward not only found to be conceivable but proved to be true, what wonder if in cases where the
association is still older, more confirmed, and more familiar, and
in which nothing ever occurs to shake our conviction or even
suggest to us any conception at variance with the association, the
acquired incapacity should continue and be mistaken for a natural
incapacity? It is true, our experience of the varieties in nature
enables us, within certain limits, to conceive other varieties analogous to them. We can conceive the sun or moon falling, for
though we never saw them fall, nor ever, perhaps, imagined them
falling, we have seen so many other things fall, that we have
innumerable familiar analogies to assist the conception, which,
after all, we should probably have some difficulty in framing, were
we not well accustomed to see the sun and moon move (or appear

[9]It would be difficult to name a man more remarkable at once for the great-
ness and the wide range of his mental accomplishments than Leibnitz. Yet
this eminent man gave as a reason for rejecting Newton's scheme of the solar
system that God *could not* make a body revolve round a distant centre, unless
either by some impelling mechanism or by miracle: "Tout ce qui n'est pas
explicable," says he in a letter to the Abbé Conti, "par la nature des créatures,
est miraculeux. Il ne suffit pas de dire: Dieu a fait une telle loi de nature; donc
la chose est naturelle. Il faut que la loi soit exécutable par les natures des
créatures. *Si* Dieu donnait cette loi, par exemple, à un corps libre, de tourner
à l'entour d'un certain centre, *il faudrait ou qu'il y joignît d'autres corps qui par
leur impulsion l'obligeassent de rester toujours dans son orbite circulaire, ou qu'il
mit un ange à ses trousses, ou enfin il faudrait qu'il y concourût extraordinaire-
ment;* car naturellement il s'écartera par la tangente." — *Works of Leibniz*, ed.
Dutens, III, 446.

to move) so that we are only called upon to conceive a slight change
in the direction of motion, a circumstance familiar to our experience. But when experience affords no model on which to shape
the new conception, how is it possible for us to form it? How, for
example, can we imagine an end to space or time? We never saw
any object without something beyond it, nor experienced any
feeling without something following it. When, therefore, we
attempt to conceive the last point of space, we have the idea
irresistibly raised of other points beyond it. When we try to
imagine the last instant of time, we cannot help conceiving another
instant after it. Nor is there any necessity to assume, as is done
by a modern school of metaphysicians, a peculiar fundamental law
of the mind to account for the feeling of infinity inherent in our
conceptions of space and time; that apparent infinity is sufficiently
accounted for by simpler and universally acknowledged laws.

Now, in the case of a geometrical axiom, such, for example, as
that two straight lines cannot inclose a space — a truth which is
testified to us by our very earliest impressions of the external world
— how is it possible (whether those external impressions be or be
not the ground of our belief) that the reverse of the proposition
could be otherwise than inconceivable to us? What analogy have
we, what similar order of facts in any other branch of our experience, to facilitate to us the conception of two straight lines inclosing
a space? Nor is even this all. I have already called attention to
the peculiar property of our impressions of form, that the ideas or
mental images exactly resemble their prototypes and adequately
represent them for the purposes of scientific observation. From
this and from the intuitive character of the observation, which in
this case reduces itself to simple inspection, we cannot so much as
call up in our imagination two straight lines, in order to attempt
to conceive them inclosing a space, without by that very act
repeating the scientific experiment which establishes the contrary.
Will it really be contended that the inconceivableness of the thing,
in such circumstances, proves anything against the experimental
origin of the conviction? Is it not clear that in whichever mode
our belief in the proposition may have originated, the impossibility
of our conceiving the negative of it must, on either hypothesis, be
the same? As, then, Dr. Whewell exhorts those who have any

difficulty in recognizing the distinction held by him between necessary and contingent truths to study geometry — a condition which I can assure him I have conscientiously fulfilled — I, in return, with equal confidence, exhort those who agree with him to study the general laws of association, being convinced that nothing more is requisite than a moderate familiarity with those laws to dispel the illusion which ascribes a peculiar necessity to our earliest inductions from experience and measures the possibility of things in themselves by the human capacity of conceiving them.

.   .   .   .

CHAPTER VI

THE SAME SUBJECT CONTINUED

1. *All deductive sciences are inductive*

.   .   .   .

From these considerations it would appear that deductive or demonstrative sciences are all, without exception, inductive sciences, that their evidence is that of experience, but that they are also, in virtue of the peculiar character of one indispensable portion of the general formulae according to which their inductions are made, hypothetical sciences. Their conclusions are only true on certain suppositions which are, or ought to be, approximations to the truth, but are seldom, if ever, exactly true, and to this hypothetical character is to be ascribed the peculiar certainty which is supposed to be inherent in demonstration.

What we have now asserted, however, cannot be received as universally true of deductive or demonstrative sciences until verified by being applied to the most remarkable of all those sciences, that of Numbers, the theory of the Calculus, Arithmetic and Algebra. It is harder to believe of the doctrines of this science than of any other, either that they are not truths *a priori* but experimental truths, or that their peculiar certainty is owing to their being not absolute but only conditional truths. This, therefore, is a case which merits examination apart, and the more so because on this subject we have a double set of doctrines to contend with: that of the *a priori* philosophers on one side; and, on the other, a theory the most opposite to theirs which was at one time very generally received and is still far from being altogether exploded among metaphysicians.

2. *The propositions of the science of number are not verbal, but generalizations from experience*

This theory attempts to solve the difficulty apparently inherent in the case by representing the propositions of the science of numbers as merely verbal and its processes as simple transformations of language, substitutions of one expression for another. The proposition, "Two and one is equal to three," according to these writers, is not a truth, is not the assertion of a really existing fact, but a definition of the word three, a statement that mankind have agreed to use the name three as a sign exactly equivalent to two and one, to call by the former name whatever is called by the other more clumsy phrase. According to this doctrine, the longest process in algebra is but a succession of changes in terminology by which equivalent expressions are substituted one for another, a series of translations of the same fact from one into another language; though how, after such a series of translations, the fact itself comes out changed (as when we demonstrate a new geometrical theorem by algebra) they have not explained, and it is a difficulty which is fatal to their theory.

It must be acknowledged that there are peculiarities in the processes of arithmetic and algebra which render the theory in question very plausible, and have not unnaturally made those sciences the stronghold of Nominalism. The doctrine that we can discover facts, detect the hidden processes of nature, by an artful manipulation of language is so contrary to common sense that a person must have made some advances in philosophy to believe it: men fly to so paradoxical a belief to avoid, as they think, some even greater difficulty which the vulgar do not see. What has led many to believe that reasoning is a mere verbal process is that no other theory seemed reconcilable with the nature of the science of numbers.   For we do not carry any ideas along with us when we use the symbols of arithmetic or of algebra.   In a geometrical demonstration we have a mental diagram, if not one on paper; AB, AC, are present to our imagination as lines, intersecting other lines, forming an angle with one another, and the like; but not so *a* and *b*.   These may represent lines or any other magnitudes, but those magnitudes are never thought of; nothing is realized in our imagination but *a* and *b*.   The ideas which, on the particular occasion, they happen to represent are banished from the mind during every intermediate part of the process between the beginning, when the premises are translated from things into signs, and the end, when the conclusion is translated back from signs into things. Nothing, then, being in the reasoner's mind but the symbols, what can seem more inadmissible than to contend that the reasoning process has to do with anything more?   We seem to have come to one of Bacon's prerogative instances, an *experimentum crucis* on the nature of reasoning itself.

Nevertheless, it will appear on consideration that this apparently so decisive instance is no instance at all; that there is in every step of an arithmetical or algebraical calculation a real induction, a real inference of facts from facts; and that what disguises the induction is simply its comprehensive nature and the consequent extreme generality of the language.   All numbers must be numbers of something; there are no such things as numbers in the abstract.   *Ten* must mean ten bodies, or ten sounds, or ten beatings of the pulse. But though numbers must be numbers of something, they may be numbers of anything.   Propositions, therefore, concerning numbers have the remarkable peculiarity that they are propositions concerning all things whatever, all objects, all existences of every kind known to our experience.   All things possess quantity, consist of parts which can be numbered, and in that character possess all the properties which are called properties of numbers.   That half of four is two must be true whatever the word four represents, whether four hours, four miles, or four pounds weight.   We need only conceive a thing divided into four equal parts (and all things may be conceived as so divided) to be able to predicate of it every property of the number four, that is, every arithmetical proposition in which the number four stands on one side of the equation. Algebra extends the generalization still farther; every number represents that particular number of all things without distinction, but every algebraical symbol does more; it represents all numbers without distinction. As soon as we conceive a thing divided into equal parts, without knowing into what number of parts, we may call it a or x, and apply to it, without danger of error, every algebraical formula in the books. The proposition, $2(a + b) = 2a + 2b$, is a truth coextensive with all nature. Since, then, algebraical truths are true of all things whatever, and not, like those of geometry, true of lines only or of angles only, it is no wonder that the symbols should not excite in our minds ideas of any things in particular. When we demonstrate the forty-seventh proposition of Euclid, it is not necessary that the words should raise in us an image of all right-angled triangles, but only of some one right-angled triangle; so in algebra we need not, under the symbol a, picture to ourselves all things whatever, but only some one thing; why not, then, the letter itself? The mere written characters, a, b, x, y, z, serve as well for representatives of things in general as any more complex and apparently more concrete conception. That we are conscious of them, however, in their character of things and not of mere signs is evident from the fact that our whole process of reasoning is carried on by predicating of them the properties of things. In resolving an algebraic equation, by what rules do we proceed? By applying at each step to a, b, and x the proposition that equals added to equals make equals, that equals taken from equals leave equals, and other propositions founded on these two. These are not properties of language or of signs as such, but of magnitudes, which is as much as to say of all things. The inferences, therefore, which are successively drawn are inferences concerning things, not symbols; though as any things whatever will serve the turn, there is no necessity for keeping the idea of the thing at all distinct, and consequently the process of thought may, in this case, be allowed without danger to do what all processes of thought, when they have been performed often, will do if permitted, namely, to become entirely mechanical. Hence the general language of algebra comes to be used familiarly without exciting ideas, as all other general language is prone to do from mere habit, though in no other case than this can it be done with complete safety. But when we look back to see from whence the probative force of the process is derived, we find that at every single step, unless we suppose ourselves to be thinking and talking of the things and not the mere symbols, the evidence fails.

There is another circumstance which, still more than that which we have now mentioned, gives plausibility to the notion that the propositions of arithmetic and algebra are merely verbal. That is that when considered as propositions respecting things, they all have the appearance of being identical propositions. The assertion, "two and one is equal to three," considered as an assertion respecting objects, as for instance, "two pebbles and one pebble are equal to three pebbles," does not affirm equality between two collections of pebbles, but absolute identity. It affirms that if we put one pebble to two pebbles, those very pebbles are three. The objects, therefore, being the very same, and the mere assertion that "objects are themselves being insignificant, it seems but natural to consider the proposition, "two and one is equal to three," as asserting mere identity of signification between the two names.

This, however, though it looks so plausible, will not bear examination. The expression "two pebbles and one pebble" and the expression "three pebbles" stand, indeed, for the same aggregation of objects, but they by no means stand for the same physical fact. They are names of the same objects, but of those objects in two different states; though they *de*note the same things, their *con*notation is different. Three pebbles in two separate parcels, and three pebbles in one parcel, do not make the same impression on our senses; and the assertion that the very same pebbles may by an alteration of place and arrangement be made to produce either the one set of sensations or the other, though a very familiar proposition, is not an identical one. It is a truth known to us by early and constant experience, an inductive truth, and such truths are the foundation of the science of number. The fundamental truths of that science all rest on the evidence of sense; they are proved by showing to our eyes and our fingers that any given number of objects — ten balls, for example — may by separation and rearrangement exhibit to our senses all the different sets of numbers the sums of which is equal to ten. All the improved methods of teaching arithmetic to children proceed on a knowledge of this fact. All who wish to carry the child's *mind* along with them in learning arithmetic, all who wish to teach numbers, and not mere ciphers — now teach it through the evidence of the senses, in the manner we have described.

We may, if we please, call the proposition, "Three is two and one," a definition of the number three and assert that arithmetic, as it has been asserted that geometry, is a science founded on definitions. But they are definitions in the geometrical sense, not the logical; asserting not the meaning of a term only, but along with it an observed matter of fact. The proposition, "A circle is a figure bounded by a line which has all its points equally distant from a point within it," is called the definition of a circle; but the proposition from which so many consequences follow and which is really a first principle in geometry is that figures answering to this description exist. And thus we may call "three is two and one" a definition of three; but the calculations which depend on that proposition do not follow from the definition itself, but from an arithmetical theorem presupposed in it, namely, that collections of objects exist which, while they impress the senses thus, °₀°, may be separated into two parts, thus, ∞ ₀. This proposition being granted, we term all such parcels threes, after which the enuncia- tion of the above-mentioned physical fact will serve also for a definition of the word *three*.

The science of number is thus no exception to the conclusion we previously arrived at that the processes even of deductive sciences are altogether inductive and that their first principles are generali- zations from experience. It remains to be examined whether this science resembles geometry in the further circumstance that some of its inductions are not exactly true, and that the peculiar cer- tainty ascribed to it, on account of which its propositions are called "necessary truths," is fictitious and hypothetical, being true in no other sense than that those propositions legitimately follow from the hypothesis of the truth of premises which are avowedly mere approximations to truth.

3. *In what sense hypothetical*

The inductions of arithmetic are of two sorts: first, those which we have just expounded, such as "one and one are two," "two and one are three," etc., which may be called the definitions of the various numbers, in the improper or geometrical sense of the word *definition;* and secondly, the two following axioms: "The sums of equals are equal," "The differences of equals are equal." These two are sufficient, for the corresponding propositions respecting unequals may be proved from these by a *reductio ad absurdum.*

These axioms, and likewise the so-called definitions, are, as has already been said, results of induction, true of all objects whatever and, as it may seem, exactly true without the hypothetical assumption of unqualified truth where an approximation to it is all that exists. The conclusions, therefore, it will naturally be inferred, are exactly true, and the science of number is an exception to other demonstrative sciences in this, that the categorical certainty which is predicable of its demonstrations is independent of all hypothesis.

On more accurate investigation, however, it will be found that, even in this case, there is one hypothetical element in the ratiocination. In all propositions concerning numbers, a condition is implied without which none of them would be true, and that condition is an assumption which may be false. The condition is that $1 = 1$, that all the numbers are numbers of the same or of equal units. Let this be doubtful, and not one of the propositions of arithmetic will hold true. How can we know that one pound and one pound make two pounds, if one of the pounds may be troy and the other avoirdupois? They may not make two pounds of either, or of any weight. How can we know that a forty horse power is always equal to itself, unless we assume that all horses are of equal strength? It is certain that 1 is always equal in *number* to 1, and, where the mere number of objects, or of the parts of an object, without supposing them to be equivalent in any other respect, is all that is material, the conclusions of arithmetic, so far as they go to that alone, are true without mixture of hypothesis. There are such cases in statistics, as, for instance, an inquiry into the amount of the population of any country. It is indifferent to that inquiry whether they are grown people or children, strong or weak, tall or short; the only thing we want to ascertain is their number. But whenever, from equality or inequality of number, equality or inequality in any other respect is to be inferred, arithmetic carried into such inquiries becomes as hypothetical a science as geometry. All units must be assumed to be equal in that other respect, and this is never accurately true, for one actual pound weight is not exactly equal to another, nor one measured mile's length to another; a nicer balance or more accurate measuring instruments would always detect some difference.

What is commonly called mathematical certainty, therefore, which comprises the twofold conception of unconditional truth and perfect accuracy, is not an attribute of all mathematical truths, but of those only which relate to pure number, as distinguished from quantity in the more enlarged sense, and only so long as we abstain from supposing that the numbers are a precise index to actual quantities. The certainty usually ascribed to the conclusions of geometry and even to those of mechanics is nothing whatever but certainty of inference. We can have full assurance of particular results under particular suppositions, but we cannot have the same assurance that these suppositions are accurately true, nor that they include all the data which may exercise an influence over the result in any given instance.

4. *Definition of demonstrative evidence*

It has . . . been held by some writers that all ratiocination rests in the last resort on a *reductio ad absurdum*, since the way to enforce assent to it, in case of obscurity, would be to show that if the conclusion be denied we must deny some one at least of the premises, which, as they are all supposed true, would be a contradiction. And, in accordance with this, many have thought that the peculiar nature of the evidence of ratiocination consisted in the impossibility of admitting the premises and rejecting the conclusion without a contradiction in terms. This theory, however, is inadmissible as an explanation of the grounds on which ratiocination itself rests. If anyone denies the conclusion notwithstanding his admission of the premises, he is not involved in any direct and express contradiction until he is compelled to deny some premise, and he can only be forced to do this by a *reductio ad absurdum*, that is, by another ratiocination; now, if he denies the validity of the reasoning process itself, he can no more be forced to assent to the second syllogism than to the first. In truth, therefore, no one is ever forced to a contradiction in terms; he can only be forced to a contradiction (or rather an infringement) of the fundamental maxim of ratiocination, namely, that whatever has a mark has what it is a mark of, or (in the case of universal propositions) that whatever is a mark of anything is a mark of whatever else that thing is a mark of. For in the case of every correct argument, as soon as thrown into the syllogistic form, it is evident without the aid of any other syllogism that he who, admitting the premises, fails to draw the conclusion does not conform to the above axiom.

We have now proceeded as far in the theory of deduction as we can advance in the present stage of our inquiry. Any further insight into the subject requires that the foundation shall have been laid of the philosophic theory of induction itself, in which theory that of deduction, as a mode of induction, which we have now shown it to be, will assume spontaneously the place which belongs to it and will receive its share of whatever light may be thrown upon the great intellectual operation of which it forms so important a part.

BOOK III

Of Induction

"According to the doctrine now stated, the highest, or rather the only proper object of physics, is to ascertain those established conjunctions of successive events, which constitute the order of the universe; to record the phenomena which it exhibits to our observations, or which it discloses to our experiments; and to refer these phenomena to their general laws."
— D. Stewart, *Elements of the Philosophy of the Human Mind*, Vol. I, Ch. IV, sect. 1.

"In such cases the inductive and deductive methods of inquiry may be said to go hand in hand, the one verifying the conclusions deduced by the other; and the combination of experiment and theory, which may thus be brought to bear in such cases, forms an engine of discovery infinitely more powerful than either taken separately. This state of any department of science is perhaps of all others the most interesting, and that which promises the most to research." — Sir J. Herschel, *Discourse on the Study of Natural Philosophy.*

CHAPTER I

PRELIMINARY OBSERVATIONS ON INDUCTION IN GENERAL

1. *Importance of an inductive logic*

The portion of the present inquiry upon which we are now about to enter may be considered as the principal, both from its surpassing in intricacy all the other branches, and because it relates to a process which has been shown in the preceding book to be that in which the investigation of nature essentially consists. We have found that all inference, consequently all proof, and all discovery of truths not self-evident, consists of inductions and the interpretation of inductions; that all our knowledge, not intuitive, comes to us exclusively from that source. What induction is, therefore, and what conditions render it legitimate cannot but be deemed the main question of the science of logic — the question which includes all others. . . .

2. *The logic of science is also that of business and life*

For the purposes of the present inquiry, induction may be defined: the operation of discovering and proving general propositions. It is true that (as already shown) the process of indirectly ascertaining individual facts is as truly inductive as that by which we establish general truths. But it is not a different kind of induction; it is a form of the very same process, since, on the one hand, generals are but collections of particulars, definite in kind but indefinite in number, and, on the other hand, whenever the evidence which we derive from observation of known cases justifies us in drawing an inference respecting even one unknown case, we should on the same evidence be justified in drawing a similar inference with respect to a whole class of cases. The inference either does not hold at all or it holds in all cases of a certain description, in all cases which, in certain definable respects, resemble those we have observed.

If these remarks are just, if the principles and rules of inference are the same whether we infer general propositions or individual facts, it follows that a complete logic of the sciences would be also a complete logic of practical business and common life. Since there is no case of legitimate inference from experience in which the conclusion may not legitimately be a general proposition, an analysis of the process by which general truths are arrived at is virtually an analysis of all induction whatever. Whether we are inquiring into a scientific principle or into an individual fact, and whether we proceed by experiment or by ratiocination, every step in the train of inferences is essentially inductive, and the legitimacy of the induction depends in both cases on the same conditions.

True it is that in the case of the practical inquirer who is endeavoring to ascertain facts not for the purposes of science but for those of business, such, for instance, as the advocate or the judge, the chief difficulty is one in which the principles of induction will afford him no assistance. It lies not in making his inductions, but in the selection of them; in choosing from among all general propositions ascertained to be true, those which furnish marks by which he may trace whether the given subject possesses or not the predicate in question. In arguing a doubtful question of fact before a jury, the general propositions or principles to which the advocate appeals are mostly, in themselves, sufficiently trite and assented to as soon as stated; his skill lies in bringing his case under those propositions or principles, in calling to mind such of the known or received maxims of probability as admit of application to the case in hand, and selecting from among them those best adapted to his object. Success is here dependent on natural or acquired sagacity, aided by knowledge of the particular subject and of subjects allied with it. Invention, though it can be cultivated, cannot be reduced to rule; there is no science which will enable a man to bethink himself of that which will suit his purpose.

But when he *has* thought of something, science can tell him whether that which he has thought of will suit his purpose or not. The inquirer or arguer must be guided by his own knowledge and sagacity in the choice of the inductions out of which he will construct his argument. But the validity of the argument when constructed depends on principles and must be tried by tests which are the same for all descriptions of inquiries, whether the result be to give A an estate or to enrich science with a new general truth. In the one case and in the other, the senses, or testimony, must decide on the individual facts; the rules of the syllogism will determine whether, those facts being supposed correct, the case really falls within the formulae of the different inductions under which it has been successively brought; and, finally, the legitimacy of the inductions themselves must be decided by other rules, and these it is now our purpose to investigate. If this third part of the operation be, in many of the questions of practical life, not the most, but the least arduous portion of it, we have seen that this is also the case in some great departments of the field of science, in all those which are principally deductive, and most of all in mathematics, where the inductions themselves are few in number, and so obvious and elementary that they seem to stand in no need of the evidence of experience, while to combine them so as to prove

a given theorem or solve a problem may call for the utmost powers
of invention and contrivance with which our species is gifted.

.   .   .   .

CHAPTER II

OF INDUCTIONS IMPROPERLY SO CALLED

1. *Inductions distinguished from verbal transformations*

.   .   .   .

Induction, as above defined, is a process of inference; it proceeds
from the known to the unknown; and any operation involving no
inference, any process in which what seems the conclusion is no
wider than the premises from which it is drawn, does not fall within
the meaning of the term.   Yet in the common books of logic we
find this laid down as the most perfect, indeed the only quite
perfect, form of induction.   In those books, every process which
sets out from a less general and terminates in a more general
expression — which admits of being stated in the form, "This
and that A are B, therefore every A is B" — is called an induction,
whether anything be really concluded or not; and the induction
is asserted not to be perfect unless every single individual of the
class A is included in the antecedent, or premise, that is, unless
what we affirm of the class has already been ascertained to be
true of every individual in it, so that the nominal conclusion is
not really a conclusion, but a mere reassertion of the premises.
If we were to say, "All the planets shine by the sun's light," from
observation of each separate planet, or "All the Apostles were
Jews," because this is true of Peter, Paul, John, and every other
apostle — these, and such as these, would, in the phraseology in
question, be called perfect, and the only perfect inductions.   This,
however, is a totally different kind of induction from ours; it is not
an inference from facts known to facts unknown, but a mere short-

hand registration of facts known. The two simulated arguments which we have quoted are not generalizations; the propositions purporting to be conclusions from them are not really general propositions. A general proposition is one in which the predicate is affirmed or denied of an unlimited number of individuals, namely, all, whether few or many, existing or capable of existing, which possess the properties connoted by the subject of the proposition. "All men are mortal" does not mean all now living, but all men past, present, and to come. When the signification of the term is limited so as to render it a name not for any and every individual falling under a certain general description, but only for each of a number of individuals, designated as such, and as it were, counted off individually, the proposition, though it may be general in its language, is no general proposition, but merely that number of singular propositions, written in an abridged character. The operation may be very useful, as most forms of abridged notation are, but it is no part of the investigation of truth, though often bearing an important part in the preparation of the materials for that investigation.

As we may sum up a definite number of singular propositions in one proposition which will be apparently, but not really, general, so we may sum up a definite number of general propositions in one proposition which will be apparently, but not really, more general. If, by a separate induction applied to every distinct species of animals, it has been established that each possesses a nervous system, and we affirm thereupon that all animals have a nervous system, this looks like a generalization; though, as the conclusion merely affirms of all what has already been affirmed of each, it seems to tell us nothing but what we knew before. A distinction, however, must be made. If in concluding that all animals have a nervous system we mean the same thing and no more as if we had said "all known animals," the proposition is not general, and the process by which it is arrived at is not induction. But if our meaning is that the observations made of the various species of animals have discovered to us a law of animal nature, and that we are in a condition to say that a nervous system will be found even in animals yet undiscovered, this indeed is an induction; but in this case the general proposition contains more than the sum of the special propositions from which it is inferred. The distinction is still more forcibly brought out when we consider that, if this real generalization be legitimate at all, its legitimacy probably does not require that we should have examined without exception every known species. It is the number and nature of the instances, and not their being the whole of those which happen to be known, that makes them sufficient evidence to prove a general law; while the more limited assertion, which stops at all known animals, cannot be made unless we have rigorously verified it in every species. In like manner (to return to a former example) we might have inferred not that all *the* planets, but that all *planets*, shine by reflected light; the former is no induction, the latter is an induction, and a bad one, being disproved by the case of double stars — self-luminous bodies which are properly planets, since they revolve round a centre.

2. — *and from descriptions*

There remains [another] improper use of the term induction which it is of real importance to clear up, because the theory of induction has been, in no ordinary degree, confused by it and because the confusion is exemplified in the most recent and elaborate treatise on the inductive philosophy which exists in our language. The error in question is that of confounding a mere description, by general terms, of a set of observed phenomena with an induction from them.

Suppose that a phenomenon consists of parts, and that these parts are only capable of being observed separately and, as it were, piecemeal. When the observations have been made, there is a convenience (amounting for many purposes to a necessity) in obtaining a representation of the phenomenon as a whole by combining or, as we may say, piecing these detached fragments together. A navigator sailing in the midst of the ocean discovers land; he cannot at first, or by any one observation, determine whether it is a continent or an island, but he coasts along it, and after a few days finds himself to have sailed completely round it; he then pronounces it an island. Now there was no particular time or place of observation at which he could perceive that this land was entirely surrounded by water; he ascertained the fact by a succession of partial observations and then selected a general expression which summed up in two or three words the whole of what he so observed. But is there anything of the nature of an induction in this process? Did he infer anything that had not been observed from something else which had? Certainly not. He had observed the whole of what the proposition asserts. That the land in question is an island is not an inference from the partial facts which the navigator saw in the course of his circumnavigation; it is the facts themselves; it is a summary of those facts, the description of a complex fact, to which those simpler ones are as the parts of a whole.

Now there is, I conceive, no difference in kind between this simple operation and that by which Kepler ascertained the nature of the planetary orbits; and Kepler's operation, all at least that was characteristic in it, was not more an inductive act than that of our supposed navigator.

The object of Kepler was to determine the real path described by each of the planets, or, let us say, by the planet Mars (since it was of that body that he first established the two of his three laws which did not require a comparison of planets). To do this there was no other mode than that of direct observation, and all which observation could do was to ascertain a great number of the successive places of the planet, or, rather, of its apparent places. That the planet occupied successively all these positions, or, at all events, positions which produced the same impressions on the eye, and that it passed from one of these to another insensibly, and without any apparent breach of continuity, thus much the senses, with the aid of the proper instruments, could ascertain. What Kepler did more than this was to find what sort of a curve these different points would make, supposing them to be all joined together. He expressed the whole series of the observed places of Mars by what Dr. Whewell calls the general conception of an ellipse. This operation was far from being as easy as that of the navigator who expressed the series of his observations on successive points of the coast by the general conception of an island. But it is the very same sort of operation, and if the one is not an induction but a description, this must also be true of the other.

The only real induction concerned in the case consisted in inferring that because the observed places of Mars were correctly represented by points in an imaginary ellipse, therefore Mars would continue to revolve in that same ellipse, and in concluding (before the gap had been filled up by further observations) that the positions of the planet during the time which intervened between two observations must have coincided with the intermediate points of the curve. For these were facts which had not been directly observed. They were inferences from the observations, facts inferred, as distinguished from facts seen. But these inferences were so far from being a part of Kepler's philosophical operation that they had been drawn long before he was born. Astronomers had long known that the planets periodically returned to the same places. When this had been ascertained, there was no induction left for Kepler to make, nor did he make any further induction. He merely applied his new conception to the facts inferred, as he did to the facts observed. Knowing already that the planets continued to move in the same paths, when he found that an ellipse correctly represented the past path, he knew that it would represent the future path. In finding a compendious expression for the one set of facts, he found one for the other; but he found the expression only, not the inference, nor did he (which is the true test of a general truth) add anything to the power of prediction already possessed.

3. *Examination of Dr. Whewell's theory of induction*

The descriptive operation which enables a number of details to be summed up in a single proposition, Dr. Whewell, by an aptly chosen expression, has termed the "colligation of facts." In most of his observations concerning that mental process I fully agree and would gladly transfer all that portion of his book into my own pages. I only think him mistaken in setting up this kind of operation, which according to the old and received meaning of the term is not induction at all, as the type of induction generally, and laying down, throughout his work, as principles of induction, the principles of mere colligation.

Dr. Whewell maintains that the general proposition which binds together the particular facts and makes them, as it were, one fact, is not the mere sum of those facts, but something more, since there is introduced a conception of the mind, which did not exist in the facts themselves. "The particular facts," says he, "are not merely brought together, but there is a new element added to the combination by the very act of thought by which they are combined. ... When the Greeks, after long observing the motions of the planets, saw that these motions might be rightly considered as produced by the motion of one wheel revolving in the inside of another wheel, these wheels were creations of their minds, added to the facts which they perceived by sense. And even if the wheels were no longer supposed to be material, but were reduced to mere geometrical spheres or circles, they were not the less products of the mind alone — something additional to the facts observed. The same is the case in all other discoveries. The facts are known, but they are insulated and unconnected, till the discoverer supplies from his own store a principle of connection. The pearls are there, but they will not hang together till someone provides the string."[1]

Let me first remark that Dr. Whewell, in this passage, blends together, indiscriminately, examples of both the processes which I am endeavoring to distinguish from one another. When the Greeks abandoned the supposition that the planetary motions were produced by the revolution of material wheels and fell back upon the idea of "mere geometrical spheres or circles," there was more in this change of opinion than the mere substitution of an ideal curve for a physical one. There was the abandonment of a theory, and the replacement of it by a mere description. No one would think of calling the doctrine of material wheels a mere description. That doctrine was an attempt to point out the force by which the planets were acted upon and compelled to move in their orbits. But when, by a great step in philosophy, the materiality of the wheels was discarded and the geometrical forms alone retained, the attempt to account for the motions was given up, and what was left of the theory was a mere description of the orbits. The assertion that the planets were carried round by wheels revolving in the inside of other wheels gave place to the proposition that they moved in the same lines which would be

[1] *Novum Organum Renovatum*, pp. 72, 73.

traced by bodies so carried, which was a mere mode of representing the sum of the observed facts, as Kepler's was another and a better mode of representing the same observations.

It is true that for these simply descriptive operations, as well as for the erroneous inductive one, a conception of the mind was required. The conception of an ellipse must have presented itself to Kepler's mind before he could identify the planetary orbits with it. According to Dr. Whewell, the conception was something added to the facts. He expresses himself as if Kepler had put something into the facts by his mode of conceiving them. But Kepler did no such thing. The ellipse was in the facts before Kepler recognized it, just as the island was an island before it had been sailed round. Kepler did not *put* what he had conceived into the facts, but *saw* it in them. A conception implies and corresponds to something conceived; and though the conception itself is not in the facts but in our mind, yet if it is to convey any knowledge relating to them, it must be a conception *of* something which really is in the facts, some property which they actually possess, and which they would manifest to our senses if our senses were able to take cognizance of it. If, for instance, the planet left behind it in space a visible track, and if the observer were in a fixed position at such a distance from the plane of the orbit as would enable him to see the whole of it at once, he would see it to be an ellipse; and if gifted with appropriate instruments and powers of locomotion, he could prove it to be such by measuring its different dimensions. Nay, further, if the track were visible, and he were so placed that he could see all parts of it in succession, but not all of them at once, he might be able, by piecing together his successive observations, to discover both that it was an ellipse and that the planet moved in it. The case would then exactly resemble that of the navigator who discovers the land to be an island by sailing round it. If the path was visible, no one, I think, would dispute that to identify it with an ellipse is to describe it; and I cannot see why any difference should be made by its not being directly an object of sense, when every point in it is as exactly ascertained as if it were so.

Subject to the indispensable condition which has just been stated, I do not conceive that the part which conceptions have in the operation of studying facts has ever been overlooked or under-valued. No one ever disputed that in order to reason about any-thing we must have a conception of it, or that, when we include a multitude of things under a general expression, there is implied in the expression a conception of something common to those things. But it by no means follows that the conception is neces-sarily pre-existent, or constructed by the mind out of its own materials. If the facts are rightly classed under the conception, it is because there is in the facts themselves something of which the conception is itself a copy, and which if we cannot directly perceive, it is because of the limited power of our organs and not because the thing itself is not there. The conception itself is often obtained by abstraction from the very facts which, in Dr. Whew-ell's language, it is afterward called in to connect. This he him-self admits, when he observes (which he does on several occasions) how great a service would be rendered to the science of physiology by the philosopher "who should establish a precise, tenable, and consistent conception of life."[2] Such a conception can only be abstracted from the phenomena of life itself, from the very facts which it is put in requisition to connect. In other cases, no doubt, instead of collecting the conception from the very phenomena which we are attempting to colligate, we select it from among those which have been previously collected by abstraction from other facts. In the instance of Kepler's laws, the latter was the case. The facts being out of the reach of being observed in any such manner as would have enabled the senses to identify directly the path of the planet, the conception requisite for framing a general description of that path could not be collected by abstrac-tion from the observations themselves; the mind had to supply hypothetically, from among the conceptions it had obtained from other portions of its experience, some one which would correctly represent the series of the observed facts. It had to frame a supposition respecting the general course of the phenomenon and ask itself, "If this be the general description, what will the details be?" and then compare these with the details actually observed. If they agreed, the hypothesis would serve for a description of the phenomenon; if not, it was necessarily abandoned, and another

[2] *Ibid.*, p. 32.

tried. It is such a case as this which gives rise to the doctrine that the mind, in framing the descriptions, adds something of its own which it does not find in the facts.

Yet it is a fact surely that the planet does describe an ellipse, and a fact which we could see if we had adequate visual organs and a suitable position. Not having these advantages, but possessing the conception of an ellipse, or (to express the meaning in less technical language) knowing what an ellipse was, Kepler tried whether the observed places of the planet were consistent with such a path. He found they were so, and he, consequently, asserted as a fact that the planet moved in an ellipse. But this fact, which Kepler did not add to, but found in, the motions of the planet, namely, that it occupied in succession the various points in the circumference of a given ellipse, was the very fact the separate parts of which had been separately observed; it was the sum of the different observations.

. . . .

CHAPTER III

OF THE GROUND OF INDUCTION

1. *Axiom of the uniformity of the course of nature*

Induction properly so called, as distinguished from those mental operations, sometimes, though improperly, designated by the name, which I have attempted in the preceding chapter to characterize, may, then, be summarily defined as generalization from experience. It consists in inferring from some individual instances in which a phenomenon is observed to occur that it occurs in all instances of a certain class, namely, in all which *resemble* the former in what are regarded as the material circumstances.

In what way the material circumstances are to be distinguished from those which are immaterial, or why some of the circumstances are material and others not so, we are not yet ready to point out. We must first observe that there is a principle implied in the very statement of what induction is; an assumption with regard to the course of nature and the order of the universe, namely, that there are such things in nature as parallel cases; that what happens once will, under a sufficient degree of similarity of circumstances, happen again, and not only again, but as often as the same circumstances recur. This, I say, is an assumption involved in every case of induction. And, if we consult the actual course of nature, we find that the assumption is warranted. The universe, so far as known to us, is so constituted that whatever is true in any one case is true in all cases of a certain description; the only difficulty is to find what description.

This universal fact, which is our warrant for all inferences from experience, has been described by different philosophers in different forms of language: that the course of nature is uniform; that the universe is governed by general laws; and the like. . . .

Whatever be the most proper mode of expressing it, the proposition that the course of nature is uniform is the fundamental principle or general axiom of induction. It would yet be a great error to offer this large generalization as any explanation of the inductive process. On the contrary, I hold it to be itself an instance of induction, and induction by no means of the most obvious kind. Far from being the first induction we make, it is one of the last or, at all events, one of those which are latest in attaining strict philosophical accuracy. As a general maxim, indeed, it has scarcely entered into the minds of any but philosophers; nor even by them, as we shall have many opportunities of remarking, have its extent and limits been always very justly conceived. The truth is that this great generalization is itself founded on prior generalizations. The obscurer laws of nature were discovered by means of it, but the more obvious ones must have been understood and assented to as general truths before it was ever heard of. We should never have thought of affirming that all phenomena take place according to general laws if we had not first arrived, in the case of a great multitude of phenomena, at some knowledge of the laws themselves, which could be done no otherwise than by induction. In what sense, then, can a principle which is so far from being our earliest induction be regarded as our warrant for all the others? In the only sense in which (as we have already seen) the general propositions which we place at the head of our reasonings when we throw them into syllogisms ever really contribute to their validity. As Archbishop Whately remarks, every induction is a syllogism with the major premise suppressed; or (as I prefer expressing it) every induction may be thrown into the form of a syllogism by supplying a major premise. If this be actually done, the principle which we are now considering, that of the uniformity of the course of nature, will appear as the ultimate major premise of all inductions and will, therefore, stand to all inductions in the relation in which, as has been shown at so much length, the major proposition of a syllogism always stands to the conclusion, not contributing at all to prove it, but being a necessary condition of its being proved; since no conclusion is proved for which there cannot be found a true major premise.

The statement that the uniformity of the course of nature is the ultimate major premise in all cases of induction may be thought to require some explanation. The immediate major premise in every inductive argument it certainly is not. Of that, Archbishop Whately's must be held to be the correct account. The induction, "John, Peter, etc., are mortal, therefore all mankind are mortal," may, as he justly says, be thrown into a syllogism by prefixing as a major premise (what is at any rate a necessary condition of the validity of the argument), namely, that what is true of John, Peter, etc., is true of all mankind. But how came we by this major premise? It is not self-evident; nay, in all cases of unwarranted generalization, it is not true. How, then, is it arrived at? Necessarily either by induction or ratiocination; and if by induction, the process, like all other inductive arguments, may be thrown into the form of a syllogism. This previous syllogism it is, therefore, necessary to construct. There is, in the long run, only one possible construction. The real proof that what is true of John, Peter, etc., is true of all mankind can only be that a different supposition would be inconsistent with the uniformity which we know to exist in the course of nature. Whether there would be this inconsistency or not may be a matter of long and delicate inquiry, but unless there would, we have no sufficient ground for the major of the inductive syllogism. It hence appears that, if we throw the whole course of any inductive argument into a series of syllogisms, we shall arrive by more or fewer steps at an ultimate syllogism which will have for its major premise the principle or axiom of the uniformity of the course of nature.[1]

.   .   .   .

2. *The question of inductive logic stated*

In order to a better understanding of the problem which the logician must solve if he would establish a scientific theory of induction, let us compare a few cases of incorrect inductions with others which are acknowledged to be legitimate. Some, we know, which were believed for centuries to be correct were nevertheless incorrect. That all swans are white cannot have been a good induction, since the conclusion has turned out erroneous. The experience, however, on which the conclusion rested was genuine. From the earliest records, the testimony of the inhabitants of the known world was unanimous on the point. The uniform experience, therefore, of the inhabitants of the known world, agreeing in a common result, without one known instance of deviation from that result, is not always sufficient to establish a general conclusion.

[1]But though it is a condition of the validity of every induction that theer be uniformity in the course of nature, it is not a necessary condition that the uniformity should pervade all nature. It is enough that it pervades the particular class of phenomena to which the induction relates. An induction concerning the motions of the planets or the properties of the magnet would not be vitiated though we were to suppose that wind and weather are the sport of chance, provided it be assumed that astronomical and magnetic phenomena are under the dominion of general laws. Otherwise the early experience of mankind would have rested on a very weak foundation, for in the infancy of science it could not be known that *all* phenomena are regular in their course.

Neither would it be correct to say that every induction by which we infer any truth implies the general fact of uniformity *as foreknown*, even in reference to the kind of phenomena concerned. It implies *either* that this general fact is already known, *or* that we may now know it; as the conclusion, the Duke of Wellington is mortal, drawn from the instances A, B, and C, implies either that we have already concluded all men to be mortal, or that we are now entitled to do so from the same evidence. A vast amount of confusion and paralogism respecting the grounds of induction would be dispelled by keeping in view these simple considerations.

But let us now turn to an instance apparently not very dissimilar to this. Mankind were wrong, it seems, in concluding that all swans were white; are we also wrong when we conclude that all men's heads grow above their shoulders and never below, in spite of the conflicting testimony of the naturalist Pliny? As there were black swans, though civilized people had existed for three thousand years on the earth without meeting with them, may there not also be "men whose heads do grow beneath their shoulders," notwithstanding a rather less perfect unanimity of negative testimony from observers? Most persons would answer, No; it was more credible that a bird should vary in its color than that men should vary in the relative position of their principal organs. And there is no doubt that in so saying they would be right; but to say why they are right would be impossible without entering more deeply than is usually done into the true theory of induction.

Again, there are cases in which we reckon with the most unfailing confidence upon uniformity, and other cases in which we do not count upon it at all. In some we feel complete assurance that the future will resemble the past, the unknown be precisely similar to the known. In others, however invariable may be the result obtained from the instances which have been observed, we draw from them no more than a very feeble presumption that the like result will hold in all other cases. That a straight line is the shortest distance between two points we do not doubt to be true even in the region of the fixed stars.[2] When a chemist announces the existence and properties of a newly-discovered substance, if we confide in his accuracy, we feel assured that the conclusions he has arrived at will hold universally, though the induction be founded but on a single instance. We do not withhold our assent, waiting for a repetition of the experiment; or if we do, it is from a doubt whether the one experiment was properly made, not whether if properly made it would be conclusive. Here, then, is a general law of nature inferred without hesitation from a single instance, a universal proposition from a singular one. Now mark another case, and contrast it with this. Not all the instances which have been observed since the beginning of the world in support of the

---

[2] In strictness, wherever the present constitution of space exists, which we have ample reason to believe that it does in the region of the fixed stars.

general proposition that all crows are black would be deemed a sufficient presumption of the truth of the proposition to outweigh the testimony of one unexceptionable witness who should affirm that, in some region of the earth not fully explored, he had caught and examined a crow and had found it to be gray.

Why is a single instance, in some cases, sufficient for a complete induction, while, in others, myriads of concurring instances, without a single exception known or presumed, go such a very little way toward establishing a universal proposition? Whoever can answer this question knows more of the philosophy of logic than the wisest of the ancients and has solved the problem of induction.

CHAPTER IV

OF LAWS OF NATURE

1. *The general regularity in nature is a tissue of partial regularities called laws*

In the contemplation of that uniformity in the course of nature which is assumed in every inference from experience, one of the first observations that present themselves is that the uniformity in question is not properly uniformity, but uniformities. The general regularity results from the co-existence of partial regularities. The course of nature in general is constant because the course of each of the various phenomena that compose it is so. A certain fact invariably occurs whenever certain circumstances are present and does not occur when they are absent; the like is true of another fact; and so on. From these separate threads of connection between parts of the great whole which we term nature, a general tissue of connection unavoidably weaves itself by which the whole is held together. If A is always accompanied by D, B by E, and C by F, it follows that A B is accompanied by D E, A C by D F, B C by E F, and finally A B C by D E F; and thus the general character of regularity is produced which, along with and in the midst of infinite diversity, pervades all nature.

The first point, therefore, to be noted in regard to what is called the uniformity of the course of nature is that it is itself a complex fact, compounded of all the separate uniformities which exist in respect to single phenomena. These various uniformities, when ascertained by what is regarded as a sufficient induction, we call, in common parlance, laws of nature. Scientifically speaking, that title is employed in a more restricted sense to designate the uniformities when reduced to their most simple expression. Thus in the illustration already employed, there were seven uniformities, all of which, if considered sufficiently certain, would, in the more lax application of the term, be called laws of nature. But of the seven, three alone are properly distinct and independent; these being presupposed, the others follow of course. The first three, therefore, according to the stricter acceptation, are called laws of nature, the remainder not, because they are in truth mere *cases* of the first three, virtually included in them, said, therefore, to *result* from them; whoever affirms those three has already affirmed all the rest.

To substitute real examples for symbolical ones, the following are three uniformities, or call them laws of nature: the law that air has weight, the law that pressure on a fluid is propagated equally in all directions, and the law that pressure in one direction, not opposed by equal pressure in the contrary direction, produces motion which does not cease until equilibrium is restored. From these three uniformities we should be able to predict another uniformity, namely, the rise of the mercury in the Torricellian tube. This, in the stricter use of the phrase, is not a law of nature. It is the result of laws of nature. It is a *case* of each and every one of the three laws, and is the only occurrence by which they could all be fulfilled. If the mercury were not sustained in the barometer, and sustained at such a height that the column of mercury were equal in weight to a column of the atmosphere of the same diameter, here would be a case, either of the air not pressing upon the surface of the mercury with the force which is called its weight, or of the downward pressure on the mercury not being propagated equally in an upward direction, or of a body pressed in one direction and not in the direction opposite, either not moving in the direction in which it is pressed, or stopping before it had attained equilibrium. If we knew, therefore, the three simple laws but had never tried the Torricellian experiment, we might *deduce* its result from those laws. The known weight of the air, combined with the position of the apparatus, would bring the mercury within the first of the three inductions; the first induction would bring it within the second, and the second within the third, in the manner which we characterized in treating of ratiocination. We should thus come to know the more complex uniformity, independently of specific experience, through our knowledge of the simpler ones from which it results, though, for reasons which will appear hereafter, *verification* by specific experience would still be desirable and might possibly be indispensable.

Complex uniformities which, like this, are mere cases of simpler ones and have, therefore, been virtually affirmed in affirming those may with propriety be called *laws*, but can scarcely, in the strictness of scientific speech, be termed "laws of nature." It is the custom in science, wherever regularity of any kind can be traced, to call the general proposition which expresses the nature of that regularity a law; as when, in mathematics, we speak of the law of decrease of the successive terms of a converging series. But the expression *law of nature* has generally been employed with a sort of tacit reference to the original sense of the word law, namely, the expression of the will of a superior. When, therefore, it appeared that any of the uniformities which were observed in nature would result spontaneously from certain other uniformities, no separate act of creative will being supposed necessary for the production of the derivative uniformities, these have not usually been spoken of as laws of nature. According to one mode of expression, the question, "What are the laws of nature?" may be stated thus: "What are the fewest and simplest assumptions, which being granted, the whole existing order of nature would result?" Another mode of stating it would be thus: "What are the fewest general propositions from which all the uniformities which exist in the universe might be deductively inferred?"

2. *Scientific induction must be grounded on previous spontaneous inductions*

In thus attempting to ascertain the general order of nature by ascertaining the particular order of the occurrence of each one of the phenomena of nature, the most scientific proceeding can be no more than an improved form of that which was primitively pursued by the human understanding, while undirected by science. . . . No science was needed to teach that food nourishes, that water drowns or quenches thirst, that the sun gives light and heat, that bodies fall to the ground. The first scientific inquirers assumed these and the like as known truths and set out from them to discover others which were unknown; nor were they wrong in so doing, subject, however, as they afterward began to see, to an ulterior revision of these spontaneous generalizations themselves when the progress of knowledge pointed out limits to them or showed their truth to be contingent on some circumstance not originally attended to. It will appear, I think, from the subsequent part of our inquiry that there is no logical fallacy in this mode of proceeding; but we may see already that any other mode is rigorously impracticable, since it is impossible to frame any scientific method of induction, or test of the correctness of inductions, unless on the hypothesis that some inductions deserving of reliance have been already made.

Let us revert, for instance, to one of our former illustrations and consider why it is that, with exactly the same amount of evidence, both negative and positive, we did not reject the assertion that there are black swans while we should refuse credence to any testimony which asserted that there were men wearing their heads underneath their shoulders. The first assertion was more credible than the latter. But why more credible? So long as neither phenomenon had been actually witnessed, what reason was there for finding the one harder to be believed than the other? Apparently because there is less constancy in the colors of animals than in the general structure of their anatomy. But how do we know this? Doubtless, from experience. It appears, then, that we need experience to inform us in what degree and in what cases, or sorts of cases, experience is to be relied on. Experience must be consulted in order to learn from it under what circumstances arguments from it will be valid. We have no ulterior test to which we subject experience in general, but we make experience its own test. Experience testifies that, among the uniformities which it exhibits or seems to exhibit, some are more to be relied on than others; and uniformity, therefore, may be presumed, from any given number of instances, with a greater degree of assurance, in proportion as the case belongs to a class in which the uniformities have hitherto been found more uniform.

This mode of correcting one generalization by means of another, a narrower generalization by a wider, which common sense suggests and adopts in practice, is the real type of scientific induction. All that art can do is but to give accuracy and precision to this process and adapt it to all varieties of cases without any essential alteration in its principle.

. . . .

3. Are there any inductions fitted to be a test of all others?

. . . .

It may be affirmed as a general principle that all inductions, whether strong or weak, which can be connected by ratiocination are confirmatory of one another, while any which lead deductively to consequences that are incompatible become mutually each other's test, showing that one or other must be given up, or at least more guardedly expressed. In the case of inductions which confirm each other, the one which becomes a conclusion from ratiocination rises to at least the level of certainty of the weakest of those from which it is deduced, while in general all are more or less increased in certainty. Thus the Torricellian experiment, though a mere case of three more general laws, not only strengthened greatly the evidence on which those laws rested, but converted one of them (the weight of the atmosphere) from a still doubtful generalization into a completely established doctrine.

If, then, a survey of the uniformities which have been ascertained to exist in nature should point out some which, as far as any human purpose requires certainty, may be considered quite certain and quite universal, then by means of these uniformities we may be able to raise multitudes of other inductions to the same point in the scale. For if we can show, with respect to any inductive inference, that either it must be true or one of these certain and universal inductions must admit of an exception, the former generalization will attain the same certainty and indefeasibleness within the bounds assigned to it which are the attributes of the latter. It will be proved to be a law, and, if not a result of other and simpler laws, it will be a law of nature.

There are such certain and universal inductions, and it is because there are such that a Logic of Induction is possible.

CHAPTER V

OF THE LAW OF UNIVERSAL CAUSATION

1. *The universal law of successive phenomena is the Law of Causation*

The phenomena of nature exist in two distinct relations to one another: that of simultaneity, and that of succession. Every phenomenon is related, in a uniform manner, to some phenomena that co-exist with it and to some that have preceded and will follow it.

Of the uniformities which exist among synchronous phenomena, the most important, on every account, are the laws of number; and next to them those of space, or, in other words, of extension and figure. The laws of number are common to synchronous and successive phenomena. That two and two make four is equally true whether the second two follow the first two or accompany them. It is as true of days and years as of feet and inches. The laws of extension and figure (in other words, the theorems of geometry, from its lowest to its highest branches) are, on the contrary, laws of simultaneous phenomena only. The various parts of space and of the objects which are said to fill space co-exist, and the unvarying laws which are the subject of the science of geometry are an expression of the mode of their co-existence.

This is a class of laws, or, in other words, of uniformities, for the comprehension and proof of which it is not necessary to suppose any lapse of time, any variety of facts or events succeeding one another. The propositions of geometry are independent of the succession of events. All things which possess extension, or, in other words, which fill space, are subject to geometrical laws. Possessing extension, they possess figure; possessing figure, they must possess some figure in particular and have all the properties which geometry assigns to that figure. If one body be a sphere and another a cylinder of equal height and diameter, the one will be exactly two thirds of the other, let nature and quality of the material be what it will. Again, each body and each point of a body must occupy some place or position among other bodies, and the position of two bodies relatively to each other, of whatever nature the bodies be, may be unerringly inferred from the position of each of them relatively to any third body.

In the laws of number, then, and in those of space, we recognize in the most unqualified manner the rigorous universality of which we are in quest. Those laws have been in all ages the type of certainty, the standard of comparison for all inferior degrees of evidence. Their invariability is so perfect that it renders us unable even to conceive any exception to them; and philosophers have been led, though (as I have endeavored to show) erroneously, to consider their evidence as lying not in experience but in the original constitution of the intellect. If, therefore, from the laws of space and number we were able to deduce uniformities of any other description, this would be conclusive evidence to us that those other uniformities possessed the same rigorous certainty. But this we cannot do. From laws of space and number alone, nothing can be deduced but laws of space and number.

Of all truths relating to phenomena, the most valuable to us are those which relate to the order of their succession. On a knowledge of these is founded every reasonable anticipation of future facts and whatever power we possess of influencing those facts to our advantage. Even the laws of geometry are chiefly of practical importance to us as being a portion of the premises from which the order of the succession of phenomena may be inferred. Inasmuch as the motion of bodies, the action of forces, and the propagation of influences of all sorts take place in certain lines and over definite spaces, the properties of those lines and spaces are an important part of the laws to which those phenomena are themselves subject. Again, motions, forces, or other influences, and times are numerable quantities, and the properties of number are applicable to them as to all other things. But though the laws of number and space are important elements in the ascertainment of uniformities of succession, they can do nothing toward it when taken by themselves. They can only be made instrumental to that purpose when we combine with them additional premises, expressive of uniformities of succession already known. By taking, for instance, as premises these propositions: that bodies acted upon by an instantaneous force move with uniform velocity in straight lines; that bodies acted upon by a continuous force move with accelerated velocity in straight lines; and that bodies acted upon by two forces in different directions move in the diagonal of a parallelogram, whose sides represent the direction and quantity of those forces, we may, by combining these truths with propositions relating to the properties of straight lines and of parallelograms (as that a triangle is half a parallelogram of the same base and altitude, deduce another important uniformity of succession, viz., that a body moving round a center of force describes areas proportional to the times. But unless there had been laws of succession in our premises, there could have been no truths of succession in our conclusions. A similar remark might be extended to every other class of phenomena really peculiar, and, had it been attended to, would have prevented many chimerical attempts at demonstrations of the indemonstrable and explanations which do not explain.

It is not, therefore, enough for us that the laws of space, which are only laws of simultaneous phenomena, and the laws of number, which though true of successive phenomena do not relate to their succession, possess the rigorous certainty and universality of which we are in search. We must endeavor to find some law of succession which has those same attributes and is therefore fit to be made the foundation of processes for discovering and of a test for verifying all other uniformities of succession. This fundamental law must

resemble the truths of geometry in their most remarkable peculiarity, that of never being, in any instance whatever, defeated or
suspended by any change of circumstances.

Now among all those uniformities in the succession of phenomena
which common observation is sufficient to bring to light, there are
very few which have any, even apparent, pretension to this rigorous
indefeasibility; and, of those few, one only has been found capable
of completely sustaining it. In that one, however, we recognize a
law which is universal also in another sense: it is co-extensive with
the entire field of successive phenomena, all instances whatever of
succession being examples of it. This law is the law of causation.
The truth that every fact which has a beginning has a cause is
co-extensive with human experience.

This generalization may appear to some minds not to amount
to much, since, after all, it asserts only this: "It is a law, that every
event depends on some law"; "It is a law, that there is a law for
everything." We must not, however, conclude that the generality
of the principle is merely verbal; it will be found on inspection to
be no vague or unmeaning assertion, but a most important and
really fundamental truth.

2. — *that is, the law that every consequent has an invariable
      antecedent*

The notion of cause being the root of the whole theory of
induction, it is indispensable that this idea should, at the very
outset of our inquiry, be, with the utmost practicable degree of
precision, fixed and determined. . . .

I premise, then, that, when in the course of this inquiry I speak
of the cause of any phenomenon, I do not mean a cause which is
not itself a phenomenon; I make no research into the ultimate or
ontological cause of anything. To adopt a distinction familiar in
the writings of the Scotch metaphysicians and especially of Reid,
the causes with which I concern myself are not *efficient* but *physical*
causes. They are causes in that sense alone in which one physical
fact is said to be the cause of another. Of the efficient causes of
phenomena, or whether any such causes exist at all, I am not
called upon to give an opinion. The notion of causation is deemed,

by the schools of metaphysics most in vogue at the present moment, to imply a mysterious and most powerful tie, such as cannot, or at least does not, exist between any physical fact and that other physical fact on which it is invariably consequent and which is popularly termed its cause; and thence is deduced the supposed necessity of ascending higher, into the essences and inherent constitution of things, to find the true cause, the cause which is not only followed by, but actually produces, the effect. No such necessity exists for the purposes of the present inquiry, nor will any such doctrine be found in the following pages. The only notion of a cause which the theory of induction requires is such a notion as can be gained from experience. The law of causation, the recognition of which is the main pillar of inductive science, is but the familiar truth that invariability of succession is found by observation to obtain between every fact in nature and some other fact which has preceded it, independently of all considerations respecting the ultimate mode of production of phenomena and of every other question regarding the nature of "things in themselves."

. . . .

3. *The cause of a phenomenon is the assemblage of its conditions*

It is seldom, if ever, between a consequent and a single antecedent, that this invariable sequence subsists. It is usually between a consequent and the sum of several antecedents; the concurrence of all of them being requisite to produce, that is, to be certain of being followed by, the consequent. In such cases it is very common to single out one only of the antecedents under the denomination of cause, calling the others merely conditions. Thus, if a person eats of a particular dish and dies in consequence, that is, would not have died if he had not eaten of it, people would be apt to say that eating of that dish was the cause of his death. There needs not, however, be any invariable connection between eating of the dish and death; but there certainly is, among the circumstances which took place, some combination or other on which death is invariably consequent, as, for instance, the act of eating of the dish, combined with a particular bodily constitution, a particular state of present health, and perhaps even a certain state of the atmosphere; the whole of which circumstances perhaps constituted in this particular case the *conditions* of the phenomenon, or, in other words, the set of antecedents which determined it and but for which it would not have happened. The real cause is the whole of these antecedents, and we have, philosophically speaking, no right to give the name of cause to one of them, exclusively of the others. What, in the case we have supposed, disguises the incorrectness of the expression is this: that the various conditions, except the single one of eating the food, were not *events* (that is, instantaneous changes or successions of instantaneous changes) but *states*, possessing more or less of permanency, and might, therefore, have preceded the effect by an indefinite length of duration for want of the event which was requisite to complete the required concurrence of conditions, while as soon as that event, eating the food, occurs, no other cause is waited for, but the effect begins immediately to take place; and hence the appearance is presented of a more immediate and close connection between the effect and that one antecedent than between the effect and the remaining conditions. But though we may think proper to give the name of cause to that one condition the fulfillment of which completes the tale and brings about the effect without further delay, this condition has really no closer relation to the effect than any of the other conditions has. All the conditions were equally indispensable to the production of the consequent, and the statement of the cause is incomplete unless in some shape or other we introduce them all. A man takes mercury, goes out-of-doors, and catches cold. We say, perhaps, that the cause of his taking cold was exposure to the air. It is clear, however, that his having taken mercury may have been a necessary condition of his catching cold; and though it might consist with usage to say that the cause of his attack was exposure to the air, to be accurate we ought to say that the cause was exposure to the air while under the effect of mercury.

If we do not, when aiming at accuracy, enumerate all the conditions, it is only because some of them will in most cases be understood without being expressed, or because for the purpose in view they may without detriment be overlooked. For example, when we say the cause of a man's death was that his foot slipped in climbing a ladder, we omit as a thing unnecessary to be stated the circumstance of his weight, though quite as indispensable a condition of the effect which took place. When we say that the assent of the crown to a bill makes it law, we mean that the assent, being never given until all the other conditions are fulfilled, makes up the sum of the conditions, though no one now regards it as the principal one. When the decision of a legislative assembly has been determined by the casting vote of the chairman, we sometimes say that this one person was the cause of all the effects which resulted from the enactment. Yet we do not really suppose that his single vote contributed more to the result than that of any other person who voted in the affirmative; but, for the purpose we have in view, which is to insist on his individual responsibility, the part which any other person had in the transaction is not material.

. . . .

Thus we see that each and every condition of the phenomenon may be taken in its turn and, with equal propriety in common parlance, but with equal impropriety in scientific discourse, may be spoken of as if it were the entire cause. And, in practice, that particular condition is usually styled the cause whose share in the matter is superficially the most conspicuous, or whose requisiteness to the production of the effect we happen to be insisting on at the moment. . . .

There is, no doubt, a tendency (which our first example, that of death from taking a particular food, sufficiently illustrates) to associate the idea of causation with the proximate antecedent *event*, rather than with any of the antecedent *states*, or permanent facts, which may happen also to be conditions of the phenomenon, the reason being that the event not only exists, but begins to exist immediately previous, while the other conditions may have pre-existed for an indefinite time. . . . But even this peculiarity of being in closer proximity to the effect than any other of its conditions is, as we have already seen, far from being necessary to the common notion of a cause, with which notion, on the contrary, any one of the conditions, either positive or negative, is found, on occasion, completely to accord.

The cause, then, philosophically speaking, is the sum total of the conditions, positive and negative taken together, the whole of the contingencies of every description, which being realized, the consequent invariably follows. . . .

4. *The cause is not the invariable antecedent, but the* unconditional *invariable antecedent*

It now remains to advert to a distinction which is of first-rate importance both for clearing up the notion of cause and for obviating a very specious objection often made against the view which we have taken of the subject.

When we define the cause of anything (in the only sense in which the present inquiry has any concern with causes) to be "the antecedent which it invariably follows," we do not use this phrase as exactly synonymous with "the antecedent which it invariably *has* followed in our past experience." Such a mode of conceiving causation would be liable to the objection very plausibly urged by Dr. Reid, namely, that according to this doctrine night must be the cause of day and day the cause of night, since these phenomena have invariably succeeded one another from the beginning of the world. But it is necessary to our using the word cause that we should believe not only that the antecedent always *has* been followed by the consequent, but that, as long as the present constitution of things[1] endures, it always *will* be so. And this would not be true of day and night. We do not believe that night will be followed by day under all imaginable circumstances, but only that it will be so *provided* the sun rises above the horizon. If the sun ceased to rise, which, for aught we know, may be perfectly compatible with the general laws of matter, night would be, or might be, eternal. On the other hand, if the sun is above the horizon, his light not extinct, and no opaque body between us and him, we believe firmly that, unless a change takes place in the properties of matter, this combination of antecedents will be

---

[1] I mean by this expression the ultimate laws of nature (whatever they may be) as distinguished from the derivative laws and from the collocations. The diurnal revolution of the earth (for example) is not a part of the constitution of things, because nothing can be so called which might possibly be terminated or altered by natural causes.

followed by the consequent, day; that, if the combination of antecedents could be indefinitely prolonged, it would be always day;
and that, if the same combination had always existed, it would
always have been day, quite independently of night as a previous
condition. Therefore is it that we do not call night the cause, nor
even a condition, of day. The existence of the sun (or some such
luminous body) and there being no opaque medium in a straight
line[2] between that body and the part of the earth where we are
situated are the sole conditions, and the union of these, without
the addition of any superfluous circumstance, constitutes the cause.
This is what writers mean when they say that the notion of cause
involves the idea of necessity. If there be any meaning which
confessedly belongs to the term necessity, it is *unconditionalness*.
That which is necessary, that which *must* be, means that which
will be whatever supposition we may make in regard to all other
things. The succession of day and night evidently is not necessary
in this sense. It is conditional on the occurrence of other antecedents. That which will be followed by a given consequent when,
and only when, some third circumstance also exists is not the cause,
even though no case should ever have occurred in which the phenomenon took place without it.

Invariable sequence, therefore, is not synonymous with causation,
unless the sequence, besides being invariable, is unconditional.
There are sequences, as uniform in past experience as any others
whatever, which yet we do not regard as cases of causation, but
as conjunctions in some sort accidental. Such, to an accurate
thinker, is that of day and night. The one might have existed for
any length of time, and the other not have followed the sooner for
its existence; it follows only if certain other antecedents exist, and,
where those antecedents existed, it would follow in any case. No
one, probably, ever called night the cause of day; mankind must
so soon have arrived at the very obvious generalization that the

---

[2] I use the words "straight line" for brevity and simplicity. In reality the
line in question is not exactly straight, for, from the effect of refraction, we
actually see the sun for a short interval during which the opaque mass of the
earth is interposed in a direct line between the sun and our eyes, thus realizing,
though but to a limited extent, the coveted desideratum of seeing round a
corner.

state of general illumination which we call day would follow from
the presence of a sufficiently luminous body, whether darkness had
preceded or not.

We may define, therefore, the cause of a phenomenon to be the
antecedent, or the concurrence of antecedents, on which it is
invariably and *unconditionally* consequent. Or if we adopt the
convenient modification of the meaning of the word cause which
confines it to the assemblage of positive conditions without the
negative, then instead of "unconditionally," we must say, "subject
to no other than negative conditions."

To some it may appear that, the sequence between night and day
being invariable in our experience, we have as much ground in this
case as experience can give in any case for recognizing the two
phenomena as cause and effect, and that to say that more is
necessary — to require a belief that the succession is unconditional,
or, in other words, that it would be invariable under all changes
of circumstances — is to acknowledge in causation an element of
belief not derived from experience. The answer to this is that it
is experience itself which teaches us that one uniformity of sequence
is conditional and another unconditional. When we judge that the
succession of night and day is a derivative sequence, depending on
something else, we proceed on grounds of experience. It is the
evidence of experience which convinces us that day could equally
exist without being followed by night and that night could equally
exist without being followed by day. To say that these beliefs are
"not generated by our mere observation of sequence"[3] is to forget
that twice in every twenty-four hours, when the sky is clear, we
have an *experimentum crucis* that the cause of day is the sun. We
have an experimental knowledge of the sun which justifies us on
experimental grounds in concluding that if the sun were always
above the horizon there would be day though there had been no
night, and that if the sun were always below the horizon there
would be night though there had been no day. We thus know from
experience that the succession of night and day is not unconditional.
Let me add that the antecedent which is only conditionally invariable is not the invariable antecedent. Though a fact may, in
experience, have always been followed by another fact, yet if the

[3] *Second Burnett Prize Essay*, by Principal Tulloch, p. 25.

remainder of our experience teaches us that it might not always be so followed, or if the experience itself is such as leaves room for a possibility that the known cases may not correctly represent all possible cases, the hitherto invariable antecedent is not accounted the cause; but why? Because we are not sure that it *is* the invariable antecedent.

. . . .

5. *Idea of a permanent cause, or original natural agent*

It continually happens that several different phenomena, which are not in the slightest degree dependent or conditional on one another, are found all to depend, as the phrase is, on one and the same agent; in other words, one and the same phenomenon is seen to be followed by several sorts of effects quite heterogeneous, but which go on simultaneously one with another, provided, of course, that all other conditions requisite for each of them also exist. Thus, the sun produces the celestial motions, it produces daylight, and it produces heat. The earth causes the fall of heavy bodies, and it also, in its capacity of a great magnet, causes the phenomena of the magnetic needle. A crystal of galena causes the sensations of hardness, of weight, of cubical form, of gray color, and many others between which we can trace no interdependence. The purpose to which the phraseology of properties and powers is specially adapted is the expression of this sort of cases. When the same phenomenon is followed (either subject or not to the presence of other conditions) by effects of different and dissimilar orders, it is usual to say that each different sort of effect is produced by a different property of the cause. Thus we distinguish the attractive or gravitative property of the earth and its magnetic property; the gravitative, luminiferous, and calorific properties of the sun; the color, shape, weight, and hardness of a crystal. These are mere phrases which explain nothing and add nothing to our knowledge of the subject, but, considered as abstract names denoting the connection between the different effects produced and the object which produces them, they are a very powerful instrument of abridgment and of that acceleration of the process of thought which abridgment accomplishes.

This class of considerations leads to a conception which we shall find to be of great importance, that of a permanent cause, or original natural agent. There exist in nature a number of permanent causes which have subsisted ever since the human race has been in existence and for an indefinite and probably an enormous length of time previous. The sun, the earth, and planets, with their various constituents, air, water, and other distinguishable substances, whether simple or compound, of which nature is made up, are such permanent causes. These have existed, and the effects or consequences which they were fitted to produce have taken place (as often as the other conditions of the production met) from the very beginning of our experience. But we can give no account of the origin of the permanent causes themselves. Why these particular natural agents existed originally and no others, or why they are commingled in such and such proportions, and distributed in such and such a manner throughout space is a question we cannot answer. More than this: we can discover nothing regular in the distribution itself; we can reduce it to no uniformity, to no law. There are no means by which, from the distribution of these causes or agents in one part of space, we could conjecture whether a similar distribution prevails in another. The coexistence, therefore, of primeval causes ranks, to us, among merely casual concurrences, and all those sequences or coexistences among the effects of several such causes, which, though invariable while those causes coexist would, if the coexistence terminated, terminate along with it, we do not class as cases of causation or laws of nature; we can only calculate on finding these sequences or coexistences where we know by direct evidence that the natural agents on the properties of which they ultimately depend are distributed in the requisite manner. These permanent causes are not always objects; they are sometimes events, that is to say, periodical cycles of events, that being the only mode in which events can possess the property of permanence. Not only, for instance, is the earth itself a permanent cause, or primitive natural agent, but the earth's rotation is so too; it is a cause which has produced, from the earliest period (by the aid of other necessary conditions), the succession of day and night, the ebb and flow of the sea, and many other effects, while, as we can assign no cause (except conjecturally) for the rotation itself, it is entitled to be ranked as a primeval cause. It is, however, only the *origin* of the rotation which is mysterious to us; once begun, its continuance is accounted for by the first law of motion (that of the permanence of rectilinear motion once impressed) combined with the gravitation of the parts of the earth toward one another.

All phenomena without exception which begin to exist, that is, all except the primeval causes, are effects either immediate or remote of those primitive facts or of some combination of them. There is no thing produced, no event happening, in the known universe which is not connected by a uniformity, or invariable sequence, with some one or more of the phenomena which preceded it; insomuch that it will happen again as often as those phenomena occur again, and as no other phenomenon having the character of a counteracting cause shall coexist. These antecedent phenomena, again, were connected in a similar manner with some that preceded them; and so on, until we reach, as the ultimate step attainable by us, either the properties of some one primeval cause or the conjunction of several. The whole of the phenomena of nature were therefore the necessary, or, in other words, the unconditional, consequences of some former collocation of the permanent causes.

The state of the whole universe at any instant we believe to be the consequence of its state at the previous instant; insomuch that one who knew all the agents which exist at the present moment, their collocation in space, and all their properties, in other words, the laws of their agency, could predict the whole subsequent history of the universe, at least unless some new volition of a power capable of controlling the universe should supervene. . . .

CHAPTER VI

OF THE COMPOSITION OF CAUSES

1. *Two modes of the conjunct action of causes, the mechanical and the chemical*

The preceding discussions have rendered us familiar with the case in which several agents, or causes, concur as conditions to the production of an effect; a case, in truth, almost universal, there being very few effects to the production of which no more than one agent contributes. Suppose, then, that two different agents, operating jointly, are followed, under a certain set of collateral conditions, by a given effect. If either of these agents, instead of being joined with the other, had operated alone, under the same set of conditions in all other respects, some effect would probably have followed which would have been different from the joint effect of the two and more or less dissimilar to it. Now, if we happen to know what would be the effect of each cause when acting separately from the other, we are often able to arrive deductively, or *a priori*, at a correct prediction of what will arise from their conjunct agency. To render this possible, it is only necessary that the same law which expresses the effect of each cause acting by itself shall also correctly express the part due to that cause of the effect which follows from the two together. This condition is realized in the extensive and important class of phenomena commonly called mechanical, namely, the phenomena of the communication of motion (or of pressure, which is tendency to motion) from one body to another. In this important class of cases of causation, one cause never, properly speaking, defeats or frustrates another; both have their full effect. If a body is propelled in two directions by two forces, one tending to drive it to the north and the other to the east, it is caused to move in a given time exactly as far in both directions as the two forces would separately have carried it, and is left precisely where it would have arrived if it had been acted upon first by one of the two forces and afterward by the other. This law of nature is called, in dynamics, the principle of the composition of forces, and, in imitation of that well-chosen expression, I shall give the name of the composition of causes to the principle which is exemplified in all cases in which the joint effect of several causes is identical with the sum of their separate effects.

This principle, however, by no means prevails in all departments of the field of nature. The chemical combination of two substances produces, as is well known, a third substance, with properties different from those of either of the two substances separately or of both of them taken together. Not a trace of the properties of hydrogen or of oxygen is observable in those of their compound, water. The taste of sugar of lead is not the sum of the tastes of its component elements, acetic acid and lead or its oxide, nor is the color of blue vitriol a mixture of the colors of sulphuric acid and copper. This explains why mechanics is a deductive or demonstrative science, and chemistry not. In the one, we can compute the effects of combinations of causes, whether real or hypothetical, from the laws which we know to govern those causes when acting separately, because they continue to observe the same laws when in combination which they observe when separate; whatever would have happened in consequence of each cause taken by itself, happens when they are together, and we have only to cast up the results. Not so in the phenomena which are the peculiar subject of the science of chemistry. There most of the uniformities to which the causes conform when separate cease altogether when they are conjoined, and we are not, at least in the present state of our knowledge, able to foresee what result will follow from any new combination until we have tried the specific experiment.

If this be true of chemical combinations, it is still more true of those far more complex combinations of elements which constitute organized bodies, and in which those extraordinary new uniformities arise which are called the laws of life. All organized bodies are composed of parts similar to those composing inorganic nature, and which have even themselves existed in an inorganic state, but the phenomena of life, which result from the juxtaposition of those parts in a certain manner, bear no analogy to any of the effects which would be produced by the action of the component substances considered as mere physical agents. To whatever degree we might imagine our knowledge of the properties of the several ingredients of a living body to be extended and perfected, it is certain that no mere summing up of the separate actions of those elements will ever amount to the action of the living body itself. The tongue, for instance, is, like all other parts of the animal frame, composed of gelatine, fibrine, and other products of the chemistry of digestion, but from no knowledge of the properties of those substances could we ever predict that it could taste, unless gelatine or fibrine could themselves taste; for no elementary fact can be in the conclusion which was not in the premises.

There are thus two different modes of the conjunct action of causes, from which arise two modes of conflict, or mutual inter- ference, between laws of nature. Suppose, at a given point of time and space, two or more causes, which, if they acted separately, would produce effects contrary, or at least conflicting with each other, one of them tending to undo, wholly or partially, what the other tends to do. Thus the expansive force of the gases generated by the ignition of gunpowder tends to project a bullet toward the sky, while its gravity tends to make it fall to the ground. A stream running into a reservoir at one end tends to fill it higher and higher, while a drain at the other extremity tends to empty it. Now, in such cases as these, even if the two causes which are in joint action exactly annul one another, still the laws of both are fulfilled; the effect is the same as if the drain had been open for half an hour first, and the stream had flowed in for as long after- ward. Each agent produces the same amount of effect as if it had acted separately, though the contrary effect which was taking place during the same time obliterated it as fast as it was produced. Here, then, are two causes, producing by their joint operations an effect which at first seems quite dissimilar to those which they produce separately, but which on examination proves to be really the sum of those separate effects. It will be noticed that we here enlarge the idea of the sum of two effects so as to include what is commonly called their difference but which is in reality the result of the addition of opposites, a conception to which mankind are indebted for that admirable extension of the algebraical calculus, which has so vastly increased its powers as an instrument of discov- ery by introducing into its reasonings (with the sign of subtraction prefixed, and under the name of negative quantities) every description whatever of positive phenomena, provided they are of such a quality in reference to those previously introduced that to add the one is equivalent to subtracting an equal quantity of the other.

There is, then, one mode of the mutual interference of laws of nature in which, even when the concurrent causes annihilate each other's effects, each exerts its full efficacy according to its own law — its law as a separate agent. But in the other description of cases, the agencies which are brought together cease entirely, and a totally different set of phenomena arise, as in the experiment of two liquids which, when mixed in certain proportions, instantly become not a larger amount of liquid, but a solid mass.

2. *The composition of causes the general rule, the other case exceptional*

This difference between the case in which the joint effect of causes is the sum of their separate effects and the case in which it is heterogeneous to them — between laws which work together without alteration, and laws which, when called upon to work together, cease and give place to others — is one of the fundamental distinctions in nature. The former case, that of the composition of causes, is the general one; the other is always special and exceptional. There are no objects which do not, as to some of their phenomena, obey the principle of the composition of causes, none that have not some laws which are rigidly fulfilled in every combination into which the objects enter. . . .

Again, laws which were themselves generated in the second mode may generate others in the first. Though there are laws which, like those of chemistry and physiology, owe their existence to a breach of the principle of composition of causes, it does not follow that these peculiar, or, as they might be termed, *heteropathic*, laws are not capable of composition with one another. The causes which by one combination have had their laws altered may carry their new laws with them unaltered into their ulterior combinations. And hence there is no reason to despair of ultimately raising chemistry and physiology to the condition of deductive sciences, for, though it is impossible to deduce all chemical and physiological truths from the laws or properties of simple substances or elementary agents, they may possibly be deducible from laws which commence when these elementary agents are brought together into some moderate number of not very complex combinations. The laws of life will never be deducible from the mere laws of the ingredients, but the prodigiously complex facts of life may all be deducible from comparatively simple laws of life, which laws (depending indeed on combinations, but on comparatively simple combinations, of antecedents) may, in more complex circumstances, be strictly compounded with one another and with the physical and chemical laws of the ingredients. The details of the vital phenomena, even now, afford innumerable exemplifications of the composition of causes, and, in proportion as these phenomena are more accurately studied, there appears more reason to believe that the same laws which operate in the simpler combinations of circumstances do, in fact, continue to be observed in the more complex. This will be found equally true in the phenomena of mind and even in social and political phenomena, the results of the laws of mind. . . .

CHAPTER VII

OF OBSERVATION AND EXPERIMENT

1. *The first step of inductive inquiry is a mental analysis of complex phenomena into their elements*

It results from the preceding exposition that the process of ascertaining what consequents, in nature, are invariably connected with what antecedents, or, in other words, what phenomena are related to each other as causes and effects, is in some sort a process of analysis. . . . If the whole prior state of the entire universe could again recur, it would again be followed by the present state. The question is how to resolve this complex uniformity into the simpler uniformities which compose it and assign to each portion of the vast antecedent the portion of the consequent which is attendant on it.

This operation, which we have called analytical inasmuch as it is the resolution of a complex whole into the component elements, is more than a merely mental analysis. No mere contemplation of the phenomena and partition of them by the intellect alone will of itself accomplish the end we have now in view. Nevertheless, such a mental partition is an indispensable first step. The order of nature, as perceived at a first glance, presents at every instant a chaos followed by another chaos. We must decompose each chaos into single facts. We must learn to see in the chaotic antecedent a multitude of distinct antecedents, in the chaotic consequent a multitude of distinct consequents. This, supposing it done, will not of itself tell us on which of the antecedents each consequent is invariably attendant. To determine that point, we must endeavor to effect a separation of the facts from one another not in our minds only, but in nature. The mental analysis, however, must take place first. And everyone knows that in the mode of performing it one intellect differs immensely from another. It is the essence of the act of observing, for the observer is not he who merely sees the thing which is before his eyes, but he who sees what parts that thing is composed of. . . .

The extent and minuteness of observation which may be requisite and the degree of decomposition to which it may be necessary to carry the mental analysis depend on the particular purpose in view. To ascertain the state of the whole universe at any particular moment is impossible, but would also be useless. In making chemical experiments, we do not think it necessary to note the position of the planets, because experience has shown, as a very superficial experience is sufficient to show, that in such cases that circumstance is not material to the result; and accordingly, in the ages when men believed in the occult influences of the heavenly bodies, it might have been unphilosophical to omit ascertaining the precise condition of those bodies at the moment of the experiment. As to the degree of minuteness of the mental subdivision, if we were obliged to break down what we observe into its very simplest elements, that is, literally into single facts, it would be difficult to say where we should find them; we can hardly ever affirm that our divisions of any kind have reached the ultimate unit. But this, too, is fortunately unnecessary. The only object of the mental separation is to suggest the requisite physical separation, so that we may either accomplish it ourselves or seek for it in nature, and we have done enough when we have carried the subdivision as far as the point at which we are able to see what observations or experiments we require. It is only essential, at whatever point our mental decomposition of facts may for the present have stopped, that we should hold ourselves ready and able to carry it further as occasion requires and should not allow the freedom of our discriminating faculty to be imprisoned by the swathes and bands of ordinary classification, as was the case with all early speculative inquirers, not excepting the Greeks, to whom it seldom occurred that what was called by one abstract name might, in reality, be several phenomena, or that there was a possibility of decomposing the facts of the universe into any elements but those which ordinary language already recognized.

2. *The next is an actual separation of those elements*

The different antecedents and consequents being, then, supposed to be, so far as the case requires, ascertained and discriminated from one another, we are to inquire which is connected with which. In every instance which comes under our observation, there are many antecedents and many consequents. If those antecedents could not be severed from one another except in thought or if those consequents never were found apart, it would be impossible for us to distinguish (*a posteriori*, at least) the real laws, or to assign to any cause its effect, or to any effect its cause. To do so, we must be able to meet with some of the antecedents apart from the rest and observe what follows from them, or some of the consequents and observe by what they are preceded. We must, in short, follow the Baconian rule of *varying the circumstances*. This is, indeed, only the first rule of physical inquiry and not, as some have thought, the sole rule, but it is the foundation of all the rest.

For the purpose of varying the circumstances, we may have recourse (according to a distinction commonly made) either to observation or to experiment; we may either *find* an instance in nature suited to our purposes or, by an artificial arrangement of circumstances, *make* one. The value of the instance depends on what it is in itself, not on the mode in which it is obtained; its employment for the purposes of induction depends on the same principles in the one case and in the other, as the uses of money are the same whether it is inherited or acquired. There is, in short, no difference in kind, no real logical distinction, between the two processes of investigation. There are, however, practical distinctions to which it is of considerable importance to advert.

CHAPTER VIII

OF THE FOUR METHODS OF EXPERIMENTAL INQUIRY

1. *Method of agreement*

The simplest and most obvious modes of singling out from among the circumstances which precede or follow a phenomenon those with which it is really connected by an invariable law are two in number. One is by comparing together different instances in which the phenomenon occurs. The other is by comparing instances in which the phenomenon does occur with instances in other respects similar in which it does not. These two methods may be respectively denominated the method of agreement and the method of difference.

In illustrating these methods, it will be necessary to bear in mind the twofold character of inquiries into the laws of phenomena, which may be either inquiries into the cause of a given effect or into the effects or properties of a given cause. We shall consider the methods in their application to either order of investigation and shall draw our examples equally from both.

We shall denote antecedents by the large letters of the alphabet and the consequents corresponding to them by the small. Let A, then, be an agent or cause, and let the object of our inquiry be to ascertain what are the effects of this cause. If we can either find or produce the agent A in such varieties of circumstances that the different cases have no circumstance in common except A, then whatever effect we find to be produced in all our trials is indicated as the effect of A. Suppose, for example, that A is tried along with B and C and that the effect is *a b c;* and suppose that A is next tried with D and E, but without B and C, and that the effect is *a d e.* Then we may reason thus: *b* and *c* are not effects of A, for they were not produced by it in the second experiment; nor are *d* and *e,* for they were not produced in the first. Whatever is really the effect of A must have been produced in both instances; now this condition is fulfilled by no circumstance except *a.* The phenomenon *a* cannot have been the effect of B or C, since it was produced where they were not; nor of D or E, since it was produced where they were not. Therefore, it is the effect of A.

For example, let the antecedent A be the contact of an alkaline substance and an oil. This combination being tried under several varieties of circumstances, resembling each other in nothing else, the results agree in the production of a greasy and detersive or saponaceous substance; it is, therefore, concluded that the combination of an oil and an alkali causes the production of a soap. It is thus we inquire by the method of agreement into the effect of a given cause.

In a similar manner we may inquire into the cause of a given effect. Let *a* be the effect. Here, as shown in the last chapter, we have only the resource of observation without experiment; we cannot take a phenomenon of which we know not the origin and try to find its mode of production by producing it; if we succeeded in such a random trial, it could only be by accident. But if we can observe *a* in two different combinations, *a b c* and *a d e,* and if we know or can discover that the antecedent circumstances in these cases respectively were A B C and A D E, we may conclude, by a reasoning similar to that in the preceding example, that A is the antecedent connected with the consequent *a* by a law of causation. B and C, we may say, cannot be causes of *a,* since on its second occurrence they were not present; nor are D and E, for they were not present on its first occurrence. A, alone of the five circumstances, was found among the antecedents of a in both instances.

For example, let the effect a be crystallization. We compare instances in which bodies are known to assume crystalline structure but which have no other point of agreement, and we find them to have one and, as far as we can observe, only one, antecedent in common: the deposition of a solid matter from a liquid state, either a state of fusion or of solution. We conclude, therefore, that the solidification of a substance from a liquid state is an invariable antecedent of its crystallization.

In this example we may go further and say it is not only the invariable antecedent but the cause, or, at least, the proximate event which completes the cause. For in this case we are able, after detecting the antecedent A, to produce it artificially and, by finding that a follows it, verify the result of our induction. The importance of thus reversing the proof was strikingly manifested when, by keeping a phial of water charged with siliceous particles undisturbed for years, a chemist (I believe Dr. Wollaston) succeeded in obtaining crystals of quartz, and in the equally interesting experiment in which Sir James Hall produced artificial marble by the cooling of its materials from fusion under immense pressure; two admirable examples of the light which may be thrown upon the most secret processes of Nature by well-contrived interrogation of her.

But if we cannot artificially produce the phenomenon A, the conclusion that it is the cause of a remains subject to very considerable doubt. Though an invariable, it may not be the unconditional antecedent of a, but may precede it as day precedes night or night day. This uncertainty arises from the impossibility of assuring ourselves that A is the *only* immediate antecedent common to both the instances. If we could be certain of having ascertained all the invariable antecedents, we might be sure that the unconditional invariable antecedent, or cause, must be found somewhere among them. Unfortunately, it is hardly ever possible to ascertain all the antecedents unless the phenomenon is one which we can produce artificially. Even then, the difficulty is merely lightened, not removed; men knew how to raise water in pumps long before they adverted to what was really the operating circumstance in the means they employed, namely, the pressure of the atmosphere on the open surface of the water. It is, however, much easier to analyze completely a set of arrangements made by ourselves than the whole complex mass of the agencies which nature happens to be exerting at the moment of the production of a given phenomenon. We may overlook some of the material circumstances in an experiment with an electrical machine, but we shall, at the worst, be better acquainted with them than with those of a thunderstorm.

The mode of discovering and proving laws of nature which we have now examined proceeds on the following axiom: whatever circumstances can be excluded without prejudice to the phenomenon, or can be absent notwithstanding its presence, is not connected with it in the way of causation. The casual circumstances being thus eliminated, if only one remains, that one is the cause which we are in search of; if more than one, they either are, or contain among them, the cause; and so, *mutatis mutandis*, of the effect. As this method proceeds by comparing different instances to ascertain in what they agree, I have termed it the method of agreement, and we may adopt as its regulating principal the following canon:

First Canon

If two or more instances of the phenomenon under investigation have only one circumstance in common, the circumstance in which alone all the instances agree is the cause (or effect) of the given phenomenon.

Quitting for the present the method of agreement, to which we shall almost immediately return, we proceed to a still more potent instrument of the investigation of nature, the method of difference.

2. *Method of difference*

In the method of agreement, we endeavored to obtain instances which agreed in the given circumstance but differed in every other;

in the present method we require, on the contrary, two instances resembling one another in every other respect, but differing in the presence or absence of the phenomenon we wish to study. If our object be to discover the effects of an agent A, we must procure A in some set of ascertained circumstances, as A B C, and having noted the effects produced, compare them with the effect of the remaining circumstances B C, when A is absent. If the effect of A B C is *a b c*, and the effect of B C *b c*, it is evident that the effect of A is *a*. So again, if we begin at the other end and desire to investigate the cause of an effect *a*, we must select an instance, as *a b c*, in which the effect occurs, and in which the antecedents were A B C, and we must look out for another instance in which the remaining circumstances, *b c*, occur without *a*. If the antecedents, in that instance, are B C, we know that the cause of *a* must be A—either A alone, or A in conjunction with some of the other circumstances present.

It is scarcely necessary to give examples of a logical process to which we owe almost all the inductive conclusions we draw in daily life. When a man is shot through the heart, it is by this method we know that it was the gunshot which killed him, for he was in the fullness of life immediately before, all circumstances being the same except the wound.

The axioms implied in this method are evidently the following: whatever antecedent cannot be excluded without preventing the phenomenon is the cause, or a condition, of that phenomenon; whatever consequent can be excluded, with no other difference in the antecedents than the absence of a particular one, is the effect of that one. Instead of comparing different instances of a phenomenon to discover in what they agree, this method compares an instance of its occurrence with an instance of its non-occurrence to discover in what they differ. The canon which is the regulating principle of the method of difference may be expressed as follows:

SECOND CANON

If an instance in which the phenomenon under investigation occurs and an instance in which it does not occur have every circumstance in common save one, that one occurring only in the former, the circum-

stance in which alone the two instances differ is the effect, or the cause, or an indispensable part of the cause, of the phenomenon.

3. *Mutual relation of these two methods*

The two methods which we have now stated have many features of resemblance, but there are also many distinctions between them. Both are methods of *elimination*. This term (employed in the theory of equations to denote the process by which one after another of the elements of a question is excluded, and the solution made to depend on the relation between the remaining elements only) is well suited to express the operation, analogous to this, which has been understood since the time of Bacon to be the foundation of experimental inquiry, namely, the successive exclusion of the various circumstances which are found to accompany a phenomenon in a given instance, in order to ascertain what are those among them which can be absent consistently with the existence of the phenomenon. The method of agreement stands on the ground that whatever can be eliminated is not connected with the phenomenon by any law. The method of difference has for its foundation that whatever cannot be eliminated is connected with the phenomenon by a law.

Of these methods, that of difference is more particularly a method of artificial experiment, while that of agreement is more especially the resource employed where experimentation is impossible. A few reflections will prove the fact and point out the reason of it.

It is inherent in the peculiar character of the method of difference that the nature of the combinations which it requires is much more strictly defined than in the method of agreement. The two instances which are to be compared with one another must be exactly similar in all circumstances except the one which we are attempting to investigate; they must be in the relation of A B C and B C, or of *a b c* and *b c*. It is true that this similarity of circumstances needs not extend to such as are already known to be immaterial to the result. And in the case of most phenomena we learn at once, from the commonest experience, that most of the co-existent phenomena of the universe may be either present or absent without affecting the given phenomenon, or, if present, are present indifferently when the phenomenon does not happen and when it does. Still, even limiting the identity which is required between the two instances, A B C and B C, to such circumstances as are not already known to be indifferent, it is very seldom that nature affords two instances, of which we can be assured that they stand in this precise relation to one another. In the spontaneous operations of nature there is generally such complication and such obscurity, they are mostly either on so overwhelmingly large or on so inaccessibly minute a scale, we are so ignorant of a great part of the facts which really take place, and even those of which we are not ignorant are so multitudinous, and therefore so seldom exactly alike in any two cases, that a spontaneous experiment of the kind required by the method of difference is commonly not to be found. When, on the contrary, we obtain a phenomenon by an artificial experiment, a pair of instances such as the method requires is obtained almost as a matter of course, provided the process does not last a long time. A certain state of surrounding circumstances existed before we commenced the experiment; this is B C. We then introduce A, say, for instance, by merely bringing an object from another part of the room before there has been time for any change in the other elements. It is, in short (as M. Comte observes), the very nature of an experiment to introduce into the pre-existing state of circumstances a change perfectly definite. We choose a previous state of things with which we are well acquainted so that no unforeseen alteration in that state is likely to pass unobserved, and into this we introduce, as rapidly as possible, the phenomenon which we wish to study; so that, in general, we are entitled to feel complete assurance that the pre-existing state and the state which we have produced differ in nothing except the presence or absence of that phenomenon. If a bird is taken from a cage and instantly plunged into carbonic acid gas, the experimentalist may be fully assured (at all events after one or two repetitions) that no circumstance capable of causing suffocation had supervened in the interim except the change from immersion in the atmosphere to immersion in carbonic acid gas. There is one doubt, indeed, which may remain in some cases of this description; the effect may have been produced not by the change, but by the means employed to produce the change.

The possibility, however, of this last supposition generally admits of being conclusively tested by other experiments. It thus appears that in the study of the various kinds of phenomena which we can, by our voluntary agency, modify or control, we can, in general, satisfy the requisitions of the method of difference, but that by the spontaneous operations of nature those requisitions are seldom fulfilled.

The reverse of this is the case with the method of agreement. We do not here require instances of so special and determinate a kind. Any instances whatever in which nature presents us with a phenomenon may be examined for the purposes of this method, and, if all such instances agree in anything, a conclusion of considerable value is already attained. We can seldom, indeed, be sure that the one point of agreement is the only one; but this ignorance does not, as in the method of difference, vitiate the conclusion; the certainty of the result, as far as it goes, is not affected. We have ascertained one invariable antecedent or consequent, however many other invariable antecedents or consequents may still remain unascertained. If A B C, A D E, A F G, are all equally followed by a, then a is an invariable consequent of A. If $a\,b\,c$, $a\,d\,e$, $a\,f\,g$, all number A among their antecedents, then A is connected as an antecedent, by some invariable law, with a. But to determine whether this invariable antecedent is a cause or this invariable consequent an effect, we must be able, in addition, to produce the one by means of the other, or, at least, to obtain that which alone constitutes our assurance of having produced anything, namely, an instance in which the effect, a, has come into existence with no other change in the pre-existing circumstances than the addition of A. And this, if we can do it, is an application of the method of difference, not of the method of agreement.

It thus appears to be by the method of difference alone that we can ever, in the way of direct experience, arrive with certainty at causes. The method of agreement leads only to laws of phenomena (as some writers call them, but improperly, since laws of causation are also laws of phenomena), that is, to uniformities which either are not laws of causation or in which the question of causation must for the present remain undecided. The method of agreement is chiefly to be resorted to as a means of suggesting applications of the method of difference (as in the last example the comparison of A B C, A D E, A F G, suggested that A was the antecedent on which to try the experiment whether it could produce *a*), or as an inferior resource, in case the method of difference is impracticable, which, as we before showed, generally arises from the impossibility of artificially producing the phenomena. And hence it is that the method of agreement, though applicable in principle to either case, is more emphatically the method of investigation on those subjects where artificial experimentation is impossible, because on those it is, generally, our only resource of a directly inductive nature, while, in the phenomena which we can produce at pleasure, the method of difference generally affords a more efficacious process which will ascertain causes as well as mere laws.

4. *Joint method of agreement and difference*

There are, however, many cases in which, though our power of producing the phenomenon is complete, the method of difference either cannot be made available at all, or not without a previous employment of the method of agreement. This occurs when the agency by which we can produce the phenomenon is not that of one single antecedent, but a combination of antecedents which we have no power of separating from each other and exhibiting apart. For instance, suppose the subject of inquiry to be the cause of the double refraction of light. We can produce this phenomenon at pleasure by employing any one of the many substances which are known to refract light in that peculiar manner. But if, taking one of those substances, as Iceland spar, for example, we wish to determine on which of the properties of Iceland spar this remarkable phenomenon depends, we can make no use, for that purpose, of the method of difference, for we cannot find another substance precisely resembling Iceland spar except in some one property. The only mode, therefore, of prosecuting this inquiry is that afforded by the method of agreement, by which, in fact, through a comparison of all the known substances which have the property of doubly refracting light, it was ascertained that they agree in the circumstance of being crystalline substances, and though the converse does not hold, though all crystalline substances have not the property of double refraction, it was concluded, with reason, that there is a real connection between these two properties, that either crystalline structure or the cause which gives rise to that structure is one of the conditions of double refraction.

Out of this employment of the method of agreement arises a peculiar modification of that method which is sometimes of great avail in the investigation of nature. In cases similar to the above, in which it is not possible to obtain the precise pair of instances which our second canon requires — instances agreeing in every antecedent except A or in every consequent except a — we may yet be able, by a double employment of the method of agreement, to discover in what the instances which contain A or a differ from those which do not.

If we compare various instances in which a occurs and find that they all have in common the circumstance A, and (as far as can be observed) no other circumstance, the method of agreement, so far, bears testimony to a connection between A and a. In order to convert this evidence of connection into proof of causation by the direct method of difference, we ought to be able, in some one of these instances, as for example, A B C, to leave out A, and observe whether by doing so, a is prevented. Now supposing (what is often the case) that we are not able to try this decisive experiment; yet, provided we can by any means discover what would be its result if we could try it, the advantage will be the same. Suppose, then, that as we previously examined a variety of instances in which a occurred and found them to agree in containing A, so we now observe a variety of instances in which a does not occur and find them agree in not containing A, which establishes, by the method of agreement, the same connection between the absence of A and the absence of a which was before established between their presence. As, then, it had been shown that whenever A is present a is present, so, it being now shown that when A is taken away a is removed along with it, we have by the one proposition A B C, $a\, b\, c$, by the other B C, $b\, c$, the positive and negative instances which the method of difference requires.

This method may be called the indirect method of difference, or the joint method of agreement and difference, and consists in a double employment of the method of agreement, each proof being independent of the other and corroborating it.   But it is not equivalent to a proof by the direct method of difference.   For the requisitions of the method of difference are not satisfied unless we can be quite sure either that the instances affirmative of *a* agree in no antecedent whatever but A, or that the instances negative of *a* agree in nothing but the negation of A.   Now, if it were possible, which it never is, to have this assurance, we should not need the joint method, for either of the two sets of instances separately would then be sufficient to prove causation.   This indirect method, therefore, can only be regarded as a great extension and improvement of the method of agreement, but not as participating in the more cogent nature of the method of difference. The following may be stated as its canon:

THIRD CANON

If two or more instances in which the phenomenon occurs have only one circumstance in common, while two or more instances in which it does not occur have nothing in common save the absence of that circumstance, the circumstance in which alone the two sets of instances differ is the effect, or the cause, or an indispensable part of the cause, of the phenomenon.

We shall presently see that the joint method of agreement and difference constitutes, in another respect not yet adverted to, an improvement upon the common method of agreement, namely, in being unaffected by a characteristic imperfection of that method, the nature of which still remains to be pointed out.   But as we cannot enter into this exposition without introducing a new element of complexity into this long and intricate discussion, I shall postpone it to a subsequent chapter and shall at once proceed to a statement of two other methods, which will complete the enumeration of the means which mankind possess for exploring the laws of nature by specific observation and experience.

5. *Method of residues*

The first of these has been aptly denominated the method of residues.   Its principle is very simple.   Subducting from any given phenomenon all the portions which, by virtue of preceding inductions, can be assigned to known causes, the remainder will be the effect of the antecedents which had been overlooked or of which the effect was as yet an unknown quantity.

Suppose, as before, that we have the antecedents A B C, followed by the consequents a b c, and that by previous inductions (founded, we will suppose, on the method of difference) we have ascertained the causes of some of these effects or the effects of some of these causes, and are thence apprised that the effect of A is a, and that the effect of B is b. Subtracting the sum of these effects from the total phenomenon, there remains c, which now, without any fresh experiments, we may know to be the effect of C. This method of residues is in truth a peculiar modification of the method of difference. If the instance A B C, a b c, could have been compared with a single instance A B, a b, we should have proved C to be the cause of c by the common process of the method of difference. In the present case, however, instead of a single instance A B, we have had to study separately the causes A and B, and to infer from the effects which they produce separately what effect they must produce in the case A B C, where they act together. Of the two instances, therefore, which the method of difference requires — the one positive, the other negative — the negative one, or that in which the given phenomenon is absent, is not the direct result of observation and experiment, but has been arrived at by deduction. As one of the forms of the method of difference, the method of residues partakes of its rigorous certainty, provided the previous inductions, those which gave the effects of A and B, were obtained by the same infallible method, and provided we are certain that C is the *only* antecedent to which the residual phenomenon c can be referred, the only agent of which we had not already calculated and subducted the effect. But, as we can never be quite certain of this, the evidence derived from the method of residues is not complete unless we can obtain C artificially and try it separately, or unless its agency, when once suggested, can be accounted for and proved deductively from known laws.

Even with these reservations, the method of residues is one of the most important among our instruments of discovery. Of all the methods of investigating laws of nature, this is the most fertile in unexpected results, often informing us of sequences in which neither the cause nor the effect were sufficiently conspicuous to attract of themselves the attention of observers. The agent C may be an obscure circumstance, not likely to have been perceived unless sought for, nor likely to have been sought for until attention had been awakened by the insufficiency of the obvious causes to account for the whole of the effect. And c may be so disguised by its intermixture with a and b, that it would scarcely have presented itself spontaneously as a subject of separate study. Of these uses of the method, we shall presently cite some remarkable examples. The canon of the method of residues is as follows:

Fourth Canon

Subduct from any phenomenon such part as is known by previous inductions to be the effect of certain antecedents, and the residue of the phenomenon is the effect of the remaining antecedents.

6. *Method of concomitant variations*

There remains a class of laws which it is impracticable to ascertain by any of the three methods which I have attempted to characterize, namely, the laws of those permanent causes, or indestructible natural agents which it is impossible either to exclude or to isolate, which we can neither hinder from being present, nor contrive that they shall be present alone. It would appear at first sight that we could by no means separate the effects of these agents from the effects of those other phenomena with which they cannot be prevented from co-existing. In respect, indeed, to most of the permanent causes, no such difficulty exists, since, though we cannot eliminate them as co-existing facts, we can eliminate them as influencing agents by simply trying our experiment in a local situation beyond the limits of their influence. The pendulum, for example, has its oscillations disturbed by the vicinity of a mountain; we remove the pendulum to a sufficient distance from the mountain, and the disturbance ceases; from these data we can determine by the method of difference the amount of effect due to the mountain, and beyond a certain distance every-thing goes on precisely as it would do if the mountain exercised no influence whatever, which, accordingly, we, with sufficient reason, conclude to be the fact.

The difficulty, therefore, in applying the methods already treated of to determine the effects of permanent causes is confined to the cases in which it is impossible for us to get out of the local limits of their influence. The pendulum can be removed from the influence of the mountain, but it cannot be removed from the influence of the earth; we cannot take away the earth from the pendulum nor the pendulum from the earth, to ascertain whether it would continue to vibrate if the action which the earth exerts upon it were withdrawn. On what evidence, then, do we ascribe its vibrations to the earth's influence? Not on any sanctioned by the method of difference, for one of the two instances, the negative instance, is wanting. Nor by the method of agreement, for, though all pendulums agree in this, that during their oscillations the earth is always present, why may we not as well ascribe the phenomenon to the sun, which is equally a co-existent fact in all the experiments? It is evident that to establish even so simple a fact of causation as this, there was required some method over and above those which we have yet examined.

As another example, let us take the phenomenon heat. Independently of all hypothesis as to the real nature of the agency so called, this fact is certain, that we are unable to exhaust any body of the whole of its heat. It is equally certain that no one ever perceived heat not emanating from a body. Being unable, then, to separate body and heat, we cannot effect such a variation of circumstances as the foregoing three methods require; we cannot ascertain by those methods what portion of the phenomena exhibited by any body is due to the heat contained in it. If we could observe a body with its heat and the same body entirely divested of heat, the method of difference would show the effect due to the heat, apart from that due to the body. If we could observe heat under circumstances agreeing in nothing but heat and, therefore, not characterized also by the presence of a body, we could ascertain the effects of heat, from an instance of heat with a body and an instance of heat without a body, by the method of agreement; or we could determine by the method of difference what effect was due to the body, when the remainder which was due to the heat would be given by the method of residues. But we can do none of these things, and without them the application of any of the three methods to the solution of this problem would be illusory. It would be idle, for instance, to attempt to ascertain the effect of heat by subtracting from the phenomena exhibited by a body all that is due to its other properties, for, as we have never been able to observe any bodies without a portion of heat in them, effects due to that heat might form a part of the very results which we were affecting to subtract in order that the effect of heat might be shown by the residue.

If, therefore, there were no other methods of experimental investigation than these three, we should be unable to determine the effects due to heat as a cause. But we have still a resource. Though we cannot exclude an antecedent altogether, we may be able to produce, or nature may produce for us, some modification in it. By a modification is here meant a change in it not amounting to its total removal. If some modification in the antecedent A is always followed by a change in the consequent *a*, the other consequents *b* and *c* remaining the same, or vice versa, if every change in *a* is found to have been preceded by some modification in A, none being observable in any of the other antecedents, we may safely conclude that *a* is, wholly or in part, an effect traceable to A, or at least in some way connected with it through causation. For example, in the case of heat, though we cannot expel it altogether from any body, we can modify it in quantity, we can increase or diminish it, and, doing so, we find by the various methods of experimentation or observation already treated of that such increase or diminution of heat is followed by expansion or contraction of the body. In this manner we arrive at the conclusion, otherwise unattainable by us, that one of the effects of heat is to enlarge the dimensions of bodies, or, what is the same thing in other words, to widen the distances between their particles.

A change in a thing not amounting to its total removal, that is, a change which leaves it still the same thing it was, must be a change either in its quantity or in some of its variable relations to other things, of which variable relations the principal is its position in space. In the previous example, the modification which was produced in the antecedent was an alteration in its quantity. Let us now suppose the question to be, what influence the moon exerts on the surface of the earth. We cannot try an experiment in the absence of the moon, so as to observe what terrestrial phenomena her annihilation would put an end to, but, when we find that all the variations in the *position* of the moon are followed by corresponding variations in the time and place of high water, the place being always either the part of the earth which is nearest to or that which is most remote from, the moon, we have ample evidence that the moon is, wholly or partially, the cause which determines the tides. It very commonly happens, as it does in this instance, that the variations of an effect are correspondent or analogous to those of its cause; as the moon moves farther toward the east, the high-water point does the same; but this is not an indispensable condition, as may be seen in the same example, for along with that high-water point there is at the same instant another high-water point diametrically opposite to it, and which, therefore, of necessity, moves toward the west, as the moon, followed by the nearer of the tide waves, advances toward the east, and yet both these motions are equally effects of the moon's motion.

That the oscillations of the pendulum are caused by the earth is proved by similar evidence. Those oscillations take place between equidistant points on the two sides of a line, which, being perpendicular to the earth, varies with every variation in the earth's position, either in space or relatively to the object. Speaking accurately, we only know by the method now characterized, that all terrestrial bodies tend to the earth, and not to some unknown fixed point lying in the same direction. In every twenty-four hours, by the earth's rotation, the line drawn from the body at right angles to the earth coincides successively with all the radii of a circle, and in the course of six months the place of that circle varies by nearly two hundred millions of miles; yet, in all these changes of the earth's position, the line in which bodies tend to fall continues to be directed toward it, which proves that terrestrial gravity is directed to the earth and not, as was once fancied by some, to a fixed point of space.

The method by which these results were obtained may be termed the method of concomitant variations; it is regulated by the following canon:

FIFTH CANON

Whatever phenomenon varies in any manner whenever another phenomenon varies in some particular manner is either a cause or an effect of that phenomenon, or is connected with it through some fact of causation.

The last clause is subjoined because it by no means follows, when two phenomena accompany each other in their variations, that the one is cause and the other effect. The same thing may and indeed must happen supposing them to be two different effects of a common cause; and by this method alone it would never be possible to ascertain which of the suppositions is the true one. The only way to solve the doubt would be that which we have so often adverted to, viz., by endeavoring to ascertain whether we can produce the one set of variations by means of the other. In the case of heat, for example, by increasing the temperature of a body we increase its bulk, but by increasing its bulk we do not increase its temperature; on the contrary (as in the rarefaction of air under the receiver of an air-pump), we generally diminish it; therefore heat is not an effect, but a cause, of increase of bulk. If we cannot ourselves produce the variations, we must endeavor, though it is an attempt which is seldom successful, to find them produced by nature in some case in which the pre-existing circumstances are perfectly known to us.

It is scarcely necessary to say that, in order to ascertain the uniform concomitance of variations in the effect with variations in the cause, the same precautions must be used as in any other case of the determination of an invariable sequence. We must endeavor to retain all the other antecedents unchanged, while that particular one is subjected to the requisite series of variations; or, in other words, that we may be warranted in inferring causation from concomitance of variations, the concomitance itself must be proved by the method of difference.

It might at first appear that the method of concomitant variations assumes a new axiom, or law of causation in general, namely, that every modification of the cause is followed by a change in the effect. And it does usually happen that when a phenomenon A causes a phenomenon *a*, any variation in the quantity or in the various relations of A is uniformly followed by a variation in the quantity or relations of *a*. To take a familiar instance, that of gravitation: The sun causes a certain tendency to motion in the earth; here we have cause and effect; but that tendency is *toward* the sun and, therefore, varies in direction as the sun varies in the relation of position; and, moreover, the tendency varies in intensity in a certain numerical correspondence to the sun's distance from the earth, that is, according to another relation of the sun. Thus we see that there is not only an invariable connection between the sun and the earth's gravitation, but that two of the relations of the sun, its position with respect to the earth and its distance from the earth, are invariably connected as antecedents with the quantity and direction of the earth's gravitation. The cause of the earth's gravitating at all is simply the sun, but the cause of its gravitating with a given intensity and in a given direction is the existence of the sun in a given direction and at a given distance. It is not strange that a modified cause, which is in truth a different cause, should produce a different effect.

Although it is for the most part true that a modification of the cause is followed by a modification of the effect, the method of concomitant variations does not, however, presuppose this as an axiom. It only requires the converse proposition, that anything on whose modifications modifications of an effect are invariably consequent must be the cause (or connected with the cause) of that effect; a proposition the truth of which is evident, for, if the thing itself had no influence on the effect, neither could the modifications of the thing have any influence. If the stars have no power over the fortunes of mankind, it is implied in the very terms that the conjunctions or oppositions of different stars can have no such power.

Although the most striking applications of the method of concomitant variations take place in the cases in which the method of difference, strictly so called, is impossible, its use is not confined to those cases; it may often usefully follow after the method of difference, to give additional precision to a solution which that has found. When by the method of difference it has first been ascertained that a certain object produces a certain effect, the method of concomitant variations may be usefully called in to determine according to what law the quantity or the different relations of the effect follow those of the cause.

7. *Limitations of this last method*

The case in which this method admits of the most extensive employment is that in which the variations of the cause are variations of quantity. Of such variations we may in general affirm with safety that they will be attended not only with variations but with similar variations of the effect; the proposition that more of the cause is followed by more of the effect being a corollary from the principle of the composition of causes, which, as we have seen, is the general rule of causation; cases of the opposite description, in which causes change their properties on being conjoined with one another, being, on the contrary, special and exceptional. Suppose, then, that when A changes in quantity, *a* also changes in quantity, and in such a manner that we can trace the numerical relation which the changes of the one bear to such changes of the other as take place within our limits of observation. We may then, with certain precautions, safely conclude that the same numerical relation will hold beyond those limits. If, for instance, we find that when A is double, *a* is double, that when A is treble or quadruple, *a* is treble or quadruple, we may conclude that if A were a half or a third, *a* would be a half or a third, and, finally, that if A were annihilated, *a* would be annihilated, and that *a* is wholly the effect of A, or wholly the effect of the same cause with A. And so with any other numerical relation according to which A and *a* would vanish simultaneously, as, for instance, if *a* were proportional to the square of A. If, on the other hand, *a* is not wholly the effect of A, but yet varies when A varies, it is probably a mathematical function not of A alone but of A and something else; its changes, for example, may be such as would occur if part of it remained constant or varied on some other principle, and the remainder varied in some numerical relations to the variations of A. In that case, when A diminishes, *a* will be seen to approach not toward zero, but toward some other limit; and when the series of variations is such as to indicate what that limit is, if constant, or the law of its variation, if variable, the limit will exactly measure how much of *a* is the effect of some other and independent cause, and the remainder will be the effect of A (or of the cause of A).

These conclusions, however, must not be drawn without certain precautions. In the first place, the possibility of drawing them at all manifestly supposes that we are acquainted not only with the variations but with the absolute quantities both of A and *a*. If we do not know the total quantities, we cannot, of course, determine the real numerical relation according to which those quantities vary. It is, therefore, an error to conclude, as some have concluded, that because increase of heat expands bodies, that is, increases the distance between their particles, therefore the distance is wholly the effect of heat, and that if we could entirely exhaust the body of its heat, the particles would be in complete contact. This is no more than a guess, and of the most hazardous sort, not a legitimate induction, for, since we neither know how much heat there is in any body nor what is the real distance between any two of its particles, we cannot judge whether the contraction of the distance does or does not follow the diminution of the quantity of heat according to such a numerical relation that the two quantities would vanish simultaneously.

In contrast with this, let us consider a case in which the absolute quantities are known, the case contemplated in the first law of motion, viz., that all bodies in motion continue to move in a straight line with uniform velocity until acted upon by some new force. This assertion is in open opposition to first appearances; all terrestrial objects, when in motion, gradually abate their velocity and at last stop, which, accordingly, the ancients, with their *inductio per enumerationem simplicem*, imagined to be the law. Every moving body, however, encounters various obstacles, as friction, the resistance of the atmosphere, etc., which we know by daily experience to be causes capable of destroying motion. It was suggested that the whole of the retardation might be owing to these causes. How was this inquired into? If the obstacles could have been entirely removed, the case would have been amenable to the method of difference. They could not be removed; they could only be diminished; and the case, therefore, admitted only of the method of concomitant variations. This, accordingly, being employed, it was found that every diminution of the obstacles diminished the retardation of the motion; and, inasmuch as in this case (unlike the case of heat) the total quantities both of the antecedent and of the consequent were known, it was practicable to estimate, with an approach to accuracy, both the amount of the retardation and the amount of the retarding causes, or resistances, and to judge how near they both were to being exhausted, and it appeared that the effect dwindled as rapidly and at each step was as far on the road toward annihilation as the cause was. The simple oscillation of a weight suspended from a fixed point and moved a little out of the perpendicular, which in ordinary circumstances lasts but a few minutes, was prolonged in Borda's experiments to more than thirty hours by diminishing as much as possible the friction at the point of suspension and by making the body oscillate in a space exhausted as nearly as possible of its air. There could, therefore, be no hesitation in assigning the whole of the retardation of motion to the influence of the obstacles, and since, after subducting this retardation from the total phenomenon, the remainder was a uniform velocity, the result was the proposition known as the first law of motion.

There is also another characteristic uncertainty affecting the inference that the law of variation which the quantities observe within our limits of observation will hold beyond those limits. There is, of course, in the first instance, the possibility that beyond the limits, and in circumstances, therefore, of which we have no direct experience, some counteracting cause might develop itself; either a new agent or a new property of the agents concerned, which lies dormant in the circumstances we are able to observe. This is an element of uncertainty which enters largely into all our predictions of effects, but it is not peculiarly applicable to the method of concomitant variations. The uncertainty, however, of which I am about to speak is characteristic of that method, especially in the cases in which the extreme limits of our observation are very narrow in comparison with the possible variations in the quantities of the phenomena. Anyone who has the slightest acquaintance with mathematics is aware that very different laws of variation may produce numerical results which differ but slightly from one another within narrow limits; and it is often only when the absolute amounts of variation are considerable that the differ-

ence between the results given by one law and by another becomes
appreciable. When, therefore, such variations in the quantity of
the antecedents as we have the means of observing are small in
comparison with the total quantities, there is much danger lest we
should mistake the numerical law and be led to miscalculate the
variations which would take place beyond the limits, a miscalcula-
tion which would vitiate any conclusion respecting the dependence
of the effect upon the cause that could be founded on those variations. Examples are not wanting of such mistakes. "The formulae,"
says Sir John Herschel,[1] "which have been empirically deduced for
the elasticity of steam (till very recently), and those for the resistance of fluids, and other similar subjects," when relied on beyond
the limits of the observations from which they were deduced,
"have almost invariably failed to support the theoretical structures
which have been erected on them."

In this uncertainty, the conclusion we may draw from the
concomitant variations of a and A to the existence of an invariable
and exclusive connection between them, or to the permanency of
the same numerical relation between their variations when the
quantities are much greater or smaller than those which we have
had the means of observing, cannot be considered to rest on a
complete induction. All that in such a case can be regarded as
proved on the subject of causation is that there is some connection
between the two phenomena: that A, or something which can
influence A, must be *one* of the causes which collectively determine
a. We may, however, feel assured that the relation which we have
observed to exist between the variations of A and a will hold true
in all cases which fall between the same extreme limits; that is,
wherever the utmost increase or diminution in which the result has
been found by observation to coincide with the law is not exceeded.

The four methods which it has now been attempted to describe
are the only possible modes of experimental inquiry — of direct
induction *a posteriori*, as distinguished from deduction; at least, I
know not, nor am able to imagine any others. And even of these,
the method of residues, as we have seen, is not independent of
deduction, though, as it also requires specific experience, it may,

[1] *Discourse on the Study of Natural Philosophy*, p. 179.

without impropriety, be included among methods of direct observation and experiment.

These, then, with such assistance as can be obtained from deduction, compose the available resources of the human mind for ascertaining the laws of the succession of phenomena. Before proceeding to point out certain circumstances by which the employment of these methods is subjected to an immense increase of complication and of difficulty, it is expedient to illustrate the use of the methods by suitable examples drawn from actual physical investigations. These, accordingly, will form the subject of the succeeding chapter.

CHAPTER IX

MISCELLANEOUS EXAMPLES OF THE FOUR METHODS

1. *Dr. Whewell's objections to the four methods*

Dr. Whewell has expressed a very unfavorable opinion of the utility of the four methods, as well as of the aptness of the examples by which I have attempted to illustrate them. His words are these:[1]

Upon these methods, the obvious thing to remark is, that they take for granted the very thing which is most difficult to discover, the reduction of the phenomena to formulae such as are here presented to us. When we have any set of complex facts offered to us; for instance, those which were offered in the cases of discovery which I have mentioned — the facts of the planetary paths, of falling bodies, of refracted rays, of cosmical motions, of chemical analysis; and when, in any of these cases, we would discover the law of nature which governs them, or, if anyone chooses so to term it, the feature in which all the cases agree, where are we to look

[1]*Philosophy of Discovery*, pp. 263, 264.

for our A, B, C, and *a*, *b*, *c?* Nature does not present to us the cases in this form; and how are we to reduce them to this form? You say *when* we find the combination of A B C with *a b c* and A B D with *a b d*, then we may draw our inference. Granted; but when and where are we to find such combinations? Even now that the discoveries are made, who will point out to us what are the A, B, C, and *a*, *b*, *c*, elements of the cases which have just been enumerated? Who will tell us which of the methods of inquiry those historically real and successful inquiries exemplify? Who will carry these formulae through the history of the sciences, as they have really grown up, and show us that these four methods have been operative in their formation; or that any light is thrown upon the steps of their progress by reference to these formulae?

He adds that, in this work, the methods have not been applied "to a large body of conspicuous and undoubted examples of discovery, extending along the whole history of science," which ought to have been done in order that the methods might be shown to possess the "advantage" (which he claims as belonging to his own) of being those "by which all great discoveries in science have really been made" (p. 277).

There is a striking similarity between the objections here made against canons of induction and what was alleged, in the last century, by as able men as Dr. Whewell, against the acknowledged canon of ratiocination. Those who protested against the Aristotelian logic said of the syllogism what Dr. Whewell says of the inductive methods, that it "takes for granted the very thing which is most difficult to discover, the reduction of the argument to formulae such as are here presented to us." The grand difficulty, they said, is to obtain your syllogism, not to judge of its correctness when obtained. On the matter of fact, both they and Dr. Whewell are right. The greatest difficulty in both cases is, first, that of obtaining the evidence and, next, of reducing it to the form which tests its conclusiveness. But if we try to reduce it without knowing what it is to be reduced to, we are not likely to make much progress. It is a more difficult thing to solve a geometrical problem than to judge whether a proposed solution is correct, but if people were not able to judge of the solution when found, they would have little chance of finding it. And it cannot be pretended that to judge of an induction when found is perfectly easy, is a thing for which aids and instruments are superfluous, for erroneous inductions, false inferences from experience, are quite as common, on some subjects much commoner than true ones. The business of inductive logic is to provide rules and models (such as the syllogism and its rules are for ratiocination) to which if inductive arguments conform, those arguments are conclusive, and not otherwise. This is what the four methods profess to be, and what I believe they are universally considered to be by experimental philosophers, who had practiced all of them long before anyone sought to reduce the practice to theory.

The assailants of the syllogism had also anticipated Dr. Whewell in the other branch of his argument. They said that no discoveries were ever made by syllogism, and Dr. Whewell says, or seems to say, that none were ever made by the four methods of induction. To the former objectors, Archbishop Whately very pertinently answered that their argument, if good at all, was good against the reasoning process altogether, for whatever cannot be reduced to syllogism is not reasoning. And Dr. Whewell's argument, if good at all, is good against all inferences from experience. In saying that no discoveries were ever made by the four methods, he affirms that none were ever made by observation and experiment, for, assuredly, if any were, it was by processes reducible to one or other of those methods.

This difference between us accounts for the dissatisfaction which my examples give him, for I did not select them with a view to satisfy anyone who required to be convinced that observation and experiment are modes of acquiring knowledge; I confess that in the choice of them I thought only of illustration and of facilitating the *conception* of the methods by concrete instances. If it had been my object to justify the processes themselves as means of investigation, there would have been no need to look far off or make use of recondite or complicated instances. As a specimen of a truth ascertained by the method of agreement, I might have chosen the proposition, "Dogs bark." This dog, and that dog, and the other dog, answer to A B C, A D E, A F G. The circumstance of being a dog answers to A. Barking answers to *a*. As a truth made known by the method of difference, "Fire burns" might have sufficed. Before I touch the fire I am not burned; this is B C; I touch it, and am burned; this is A B C, *a b c.*

Such familiar experimental processes are not regarded as inductions by Dr. Whewell, but they are perfectly homogeneous with those by which, even on his own showing, the pyramid of science is supplied with its base. In vain he attempts to escape from this conclusion by laying the most arbitrary restrictions on the choice of examples admissible as instances of induction; they must neither be such as are still matter of discussion (p. 265), nor must any of them be drawn from mental and social subjects (p. 269), nor from ordinary observation and practical life (pp. 241–247). They must be taken exclusively from the generalizations by which scientific thinkers have ascended to great and comprehensive laws of natural phenomena. Now it is seldom possible, in these complicated inquiries, to go much beyond the initial steps without calling in the instrument of deduction and the temporary aid of hypothesis, as I myself, in common with Dr. Whewell, have maintained against the purely empirical school. Since, therefore, such cases could not conveniently be selected to illustrate the principles of mere observation and experiment, Dr. Whewell is misled by their absence into representing the experimental methods as serving no purpose in scientific investigation, forgetting that if those methods had not supplied the first generalizations, there would have been no materials for his own conception of induction to work upon.

His challenge, however, to point out which of the four methods are exemplified in certain important cases of scientific inquiry, is easily answered. "The planetary paths," as far as they are a case of induction at all,[2] fall under the method of agreement. The law of "falling bodies," namely, that they describe spaces proportional to the squares of the times, was historically a deduction from the first law of motion, but the experiments by which it was verified and by which it might have been discovered were examples of the method of agreement, and the apparent variation from the true law caused by the resistance of the air was cleared up by experiments *in vacuo*, constituting an application of the method of difference. The law of "refracted rays" (the constancy of the ratio between the sines of incidence and of refraction for each refracting substance) was ascertained by direct measurement and, therefore,

[2]See, on this point, the second chapter of the present book.

by the method of agreement. The "cosmical motions" were determined by highly complex processes of thought in which deduction was predominant, but the methods of agreement and of concomitant variations had a large part in establishing the empirical laws. Every case without exception of "chemical analysis" constitutes a well-marked example of the method of difference. To anyone acquainted with the subjects—to Dr. Whewell himself—there would not be the smallest difficulty in setting out "the A B C and *a b c* elements" of these cases.

If discoveries are ever made by observation and experiment without deduction, the four methods are methods of discovery; but even if they were not methods of discovery, it would not be the less true that they are the sole methods of proof, and, in that character, even the results of deduction are amenable to them. The great generalizations which begin as hypotheses must end by being proved and are, in reality (as will be shown hereafter), proved by the four methods. Now it is with proof, as such, that logic is principally concerned. This distinction has indeed no chance of finding favor with Dr. Whewell, for it is the peculiarity of his system not to recognize, in cases of induction, any necessity for proof. If, after assuming an hypothesis and carefully collating it with facts, nothing is brought to light inconsistent with it, that is, if experience does not *dis*prove it, he is content; at least until a simpler hypothesis, equally consistent with experience, presents itself. If this be induction, doubtless there is no necessity for the four methods. But to suppose that it is so appears to me a radical misconception of the nature of the evidence of physical truths.

So real and practical is the need of a test for induction similar to the syllogistic test of ratiocination, that inferences which bid defiance to the most elementary notions of inductive logic are put forth without misgiving by persons eminent in physical science as soon as they are off the ground on which they are conversant with the facts and not reduced to judge only by the arguments; and, as for educated persons in general, it may be doubted if they are better judges of a good or a bad induction than they were before Bacon wrote. The improvement in the results of thinking has seldom extended to the processes, or has reached, if any process, that of investigation only, not that of proof. A knowledge of many laws of nature has doubtless been arrived at by framing hypotheses and finding that the facts corresponded to them, and many errors have been got rid of by coming to a knowledge of facts which were inconsistent with them, but not by discovering that the mode of thought which led to the errors was itself faulty and might have been known to be such independently of the facts which disproved the specific conclusion. Hence it is that while the thoughts of mankind have on many subjects worked themselves practically right, the thinking power remains as weak as ever; and on all subjects on which the facts which would check the result are not accessible, as in what relates to the invisible world, and even, as has been seen lately, to the visible world of the planetary regions, men of the greatest scientific acquirements argue as pitiably as the merest ignoramus. For though they have made many sound inductions, they have not learned from them (and Dr. Whewell thinks there is no necessity that they should learn) the principles of inductive *evidence*.

CHAPTER X

OF PLURALITY OF CAUSES AND OF THE INTERMIXTURE OF EFFECTS

1. *One effect may have several causes*

In the preceding exposition of the four methods of observation and experiment by which we contrive to distinguish among a mass of co-existent phenomena the particular effect due to a given cause or the particular cause which gave birth to a given effect, it has been necessary to suppose, in the first instance, for the sake of simplification, that this analytical operation is encumbered by no other difficulties than what are essentially inherent in its nature, and to represent to ourselves, therefore, every effect, on the one hand as connected exclusively with a single cause, and on the other hand as incapable of being mixed and confounded with any other co-existent effect. We have regarded *a b c d e*, the aggregate of the phenomena existing at any moment, as consisting of dissimilar facts, *a*, *b*, *c*, *d*, and *e*, for each of which one, and only one, cause needs be sought, the difficulty being only that of singling out this one cause from the multitude of antecedent circumstances, A, B, C, D, and E. The cause, indeed, may not be simple; it may consist of an assemblage of conditions; but we have supposed that there was only one possible assemblage of conditions from which the given effect could result.

If such were the fact, it would be comparatively an easy task to investigate the laws of nature. But the supposition does not hold in either of its parts. In the first place, it is not true that the same phenomenon is always produced by the same cause; the effect *a* may sometimes arise from A, sometimes from B. And, secondly, the effects of different causes are often not dissimilar but homogeneous, and marked out by no assignable boundaries from one another; A and B may produce not *a* and *b* but different portions of an effect *a*. The obscurity and difficulty of the investigation of the laws of phenomena is singularly increased by the necessity of adverting to these two circumstances, intermixture of effects and plurality of causes. To the latter, being the simpler of the two considerations, we shall first direct our attention.

It is not true, then, that one effect must be connected with only one cause or assemblage of conditions, that each phenomenon can be produced only in one way. There are often several independent modes in which the same phenomenon could have originated. One fact may be the consequent in several invariable sequences; it may follow, with equal uniformity, any one of several antecedents or collections of antecedents. Many causes may produce mechanical motion; many causes may produce some kinds of sensation; many causes may produce death. A given effect may really be produced by a certain cause and yet be perfectly capable of being produced without it.

2. — *which is the source of a characteristic imperfection of the method of agreement*

One of the principal consequences of this fact of plurality of causes is to render the first of the inductive methods, that of agreement, uncertain. To illustrate that method, we supposed two instances, A B C followed by *a b c*, and A D E followed by *a d e*. From these instances it might apparently be concluded that A is an invariable antecedent of *a*, and even that it is the unconditional invariable antecedent, or cause, if we could be sure that there is no other antecedent common to the two cases. That this difficulty may not stand in the way, let us suppose the two cases positively ascertained to have no antecedent in common except A. The moment, however, that we let in the possibility of a plurality of causes, the conclusion fails. For it involves a tacit supposition that *a* must have been produced in both instances by the same cause. If there can possibly have been two causes, those two may, for example, be C and E; the one may have been the cause of *a* in the former of the instances, the other in the latter, A having no influence in either case.

Suppose, for example, that two great artists or great philosophers, that two extremely selfish or extremely generous characters, were compared together as to the circumstances of their education and history, and the two cases were found to agree only in one circumstance; would it follow that this one circumstance was the cause of the quality which characterized both those individuals? Not at all; for the causes which may produce any type of character are very numerous, and the two persons might equally have agreed in their character though there had been no manner of resemblance in their previous history.

This, therefore, is a characteristic imperfection of the method of agreement, from which imperfection the method of difference is free. For if we have two instances, A B C and B C, of which B C gives *b c*, and A being added converts it into *a b c*, it is certain that in this instance at least A was either the cause of *a* or an indispensable portion of its cause, even though the cause which produces it in other instances may be altogether different. Plurality of causes, therefore, not only does not diminish the reliance due to the method of difference, but does not even render a greater number of observations or experiments necessary; two instances, the one positive and the other negative, are still sufficient for the most complete and rigorous induction. Not so, however, with the method of agreement. The conclusions which that yields, when the number of instances compared is small, are of no real value, except as, in the character of suggestions, they may lead either to experiments bringing them to the test of the method of difference or to reasonings which may explain and verify them deductively.

It is only when the instances, being indefinitely multiplied and varied, continue to suggest the same result that this result acquires any high degree of independent value. If there are but two instances, A B C and A D E, though these instances have no antecedent in common except A, yet, as the effect may possibly have been produced in the two cases by different causes, the result is at most only a slight probability in favor of A; there may be causation, but it is almost equally probable that there was only a coincidence. But the oftener we repeat the observation, varying the circumstances, the more we advance toward a solution of this doubt. For if we try A F G, A H K, etc., all unlike one another except in containing the circumstance A, and if we find the effect a entering into the result in all these cases, we must suppose one of two things, either that it is caused by A or that it has as many different causes as there are instances. With each addition, therefore, to the number of instances, the presumption is strengthened in favor of A. The inquirer, of course, will not neglect, if an opportunity present itself, to exclude A from some one of these combinations, from A H K for instance, and by trying H K separately appeal to the method of difference in aid of the method of agreement. By the method of difference alone can it be ascertained that A is the cause of a,. but that it is either the cause or another effect of the same cause may be placed beyond any reasonable doubt by the method of agreement, provided the instances are very numerous as well as sufficiently various.

After how great a multiplication, then, of varied instances, all agreeing in no other antecedent except A, is the supposition of a plurality of causes sufficiently rebutted, and the conclusion that a is connected with A divested of the characteristic imperfection and reduced to a virtual certainty? This is a question which we cannot be exempted from answering, but the consideration of it belongs to what is called the theory of probability, which will form the subject of a chapter hereafter. It is seen, however, at once, that the conclusion does amount to a practical certainty after a sufficient number of instances and that the method, therefore, is not radically vitiated by the characteristic imperfection. The result of these considerations is only, in the first place, to point out a new source of inferiority in the method of agreement as compared with other modes of investigation, and new reasons for never resting contented with the results obtained by it without attempting to confirm them either by the method of difference or by connecting them deductively with some law or laws already ascertained by that superior method. And, in the second place, we learn from this the true theory of the value of mere *number* of instances in inductive inquiry. The plurality of causes is the only reason why mere number is of any importance. The tendency of unscientific inquirers is to rely too much on number without analyzing the instances, without looking closely enough into their nature to ascertain what circumstances are or are not eliminated by means of them. Most people hold their conclusions with a degree of assurance proportioned to the mere *mass* of the experience on which they appear to rest, not considering that by the addition of instances to instances, all of the same kind, that is, differing from one another only in points already recognized as immaterial, nothing whatever is added to the evidence of the conclusion. A single instance eliminating some antecedent which existed in all the other cases is of more value than the greatest multitude of instances which are reckoned by their number alone. It is necessary, no doubt, to assure ourselves, by repetition of the observation or experiment, that no error has been committed concerning the individual facts observed; and, until we have assured ourselves of this, instead of varying the circumstances, we cannot too scrupulously repeat the same experiment or observation without any change. But, when once this assurance has been obtained, the multiplication of instances which do not exclude any more circumstances is entirely useless, provided there have been already enough to exclude the supposition of plurality of causes.

3. *Concurrence of causes which do not compound their effects*

A concurrence of two or more causes, not separately producing each its own effect, but interfering with or modifying the effects of one another, takes place, as has already been explained, in two different ways. In the one, which is exemplified by the joint operation of different forces in mechanics, the separate effects of all the causes continue to be produced but are compounded with one another and disappear in one total. In the other, illustrated by the case of chemical action, the separate effects cease entirely and are succeeded by phenomena altogether different and governed by different laws.

Of these cases the former is by far the more frequent, and this case it is which, for the most part, eludes the grasp of our experimental methods. The other and exceptional case is essentially amenable to them. When the laws of the original agents cease entirely, and a phenomenon makes its appearance which, with reference to those laws, is quite heterogeneous, when, for example, two gaseous substances, hydrogen and oxygen, on being brought together, throw off their peculiar properties and produce the substance called water, in such cases the new fact may be subjected to experimental inquiry, like any other phenomenon, and the elements which are said to compose it may be considered as the mere agents of its production — the conditions on which it depends, the facts which make up its cause.

The *effects* of the new phenomenon, the *properties* of water, for instance, are as easily found by experiment as the effects of any other cause. But to discover the *cause* of it, that is, the particular conjunction of agents from which it results, is often difficult enough. In the first place, the origin and actual production of the phenomenon are most frequently inaccessible to our observation. If we could not have learned the composition of water until we found instances in which it was actually produced from oxygen and hydrogen, we should have been forced to wait until the casual thought struck some one of passing an electric spark through a mixture of the two gases, or inserting a lighted taper into it, merely to try what would happen. Besides, many substances, though they can be analyzed, cannot by any known artificial means be recompounded. Further, even if we could have ascertained by the method of agreement that oxygen and hydrogen were both present when water is produced, no experimentation on oxygen and hydrogen separately, no knowledge of their laws, could have enabled us deductively to infer that they would produce water. We require a specific experiment on the two combined.

Under these difficulties, we should generally have been indebted for our knowledge of the causes of this class of effects not to any inquiry directed specifically toward that end, but either to accident, or to the gradual progress of experimentation on the different combinations of which the producing agents are susceptible, if it were not for a peculiarity belonging to effects of this description, that they often, under some particular combination of circumstances, reproduce their causes. If water results from the juxtaposition of hydrogen and oxygen whenever this can be made sufficiently close and intimate, so, on the other hand, if water itself be placed in certain situations, hydrogen and oxygen are reproduced from it; an abrupt termination is put to the new laws, and the agents re-appear separately with their own properties as at first. What is called chemical analysis is the process of searching for the causes of a phenomenon among its effects, or, rather, among the effects produced by the action of some other causes upon it.

. . . .

Where two phenomena between the laws or properties of which, considered in themselves, no connection can be traced are thus reciprocally cause and effect, each capable in its turn of being produced from the other, and each, when it produces the other, ceasing itself to exist (as water is produced from oxygen and hydrogen, and oxygen and hydrogen are reproduced from water), this causation of the two phenomena by one another, each being generated by the other's destruction, is properly transformation. The idea of chemical composition is an idea of transformation but of a transformation which is incomplete, since we consider the oxygen and hydrogen to be present in the water *as* oxygen and hydrogen, and capable of being discovered in it if our senses were sufficiently keen; a supposition (for it is no more) grounded solely on the fact that the weight of the water is the sum of the separate weights of the two ingredients. If there had not been this exception to the entire disappearance, in the compound, of the laws of the separate ingredients, if the combined agents had not, in this one particular of weight, preserved their own laws and produced a joint result equal to the sum of their separate results, we should never, probably, have had the notion now implied by the words chemical composition, and in the facts of water produced from hydrogen and oxygen and hydrogen and oxygen produced from water, as the transformation would have been complete, we should have seen only a transformation.

In these cases, where the heteropathic effect (as we called it in a former chapter)[1] is but a transformation of its cause, or, in other words, where the effect and its cause are reciprocally such and mutually convertible into each other, the problem of finding the cause resolves itself into the far easier one of finding an effect, which is the kind of inquiry that admits of being prosecuted by direct experiment. But there are other cases of heteropathic effects to which this mode of investigation is not applicable. Take, for instance, the heteropathic laws of mind, that portion of the phenomena of our mental nature which are analogous to chemical rather than to dynamical phenomena, as when a complex passion is formed by the coalition of several elementary impulses, or a complex emotion by several simple pleasures or pains of which it is the result without being the aggregate or in any respect homogeneous with them. The product, in these cases, is generated by its various factors, but the factors cannot be reproduced from the product; just as a youth can grow into an old man, but an old man cannot grow into a youth. We cannot ascertain from what simple feelings any of our complex states of mind are generated, as we ascertain the ingredients of a chemical compound, by making it, in its turn, generate them. We can only, therefore, discover these laws by the slow process of studying the simple feelings themselves and ascertaining synthetically, by experimenting on the various combinations of which they are susceptible, what they, by their mutual action upon one another, are capable of generating.

4. *Difficulties of the investigation when causes compound their effects*

It might have been supposed that the other, and apparently simpler variety of the mutual interference of causes, where each cause continues to produce its own proper effect according to the

[1]*Ante*, Chap. VII, § 1 [of the eighth edition].

same laws to which it conforms in its separate state, would have presented fewer difficulties to the inductive inquirer than that of which we have just finished the consideration. It presents, however, so far as direct induction apart from deduction is concerned, infinitely greater difficulties. When a concurrence of causes gives rise to a new effect, bearing no relation to the separate effects of those causes, the resulting phenomenon stands forth undisguised, inviting attention to its peculiarity and presenting no obstacle to our recognizing its presence or absence among any number of surrounding phenomena. It admits, therefore, of being easily brought under the canons of induction, provided instances can be obtained such as those canons require, and the non-occurrence of such instances or the want of means to produce them artificially is the real and only difficulty in such investigations; a difficulty not lógical but in some sort physical. It is otherwise with cases of what, in a preceding chapter, has been denominated the composition of causes. There, the effects of the separate causes do not terminate and give place to others, thereby ceasing to form any part of the phenomenon to be investigated; on the contrary, they still take place, but are intermingled with, and disguised by, the homogeneous and closely allied effects of other causes. They are no longer a, b, c, d, e, existing side by side and continuing to be separately discernible; they are $+ a$, $- a$, $\frac{1}{2} b$, $- b$, $2 b$, etc.; some of which cancel one another, while many others do not appear distinguishably but merge in one sum, forming altogether a result between which and the causes whereby it was produced there is often an insurmountable difficulty in tracing by observation any fixed relation whatever.

The general idea of the composition of causes has been seen to be that, though two or more laws interfere with one another and apparently frustrate or modify one another's operation, yet in reality all are fulfilled, the collective effect being the exact sum of the effects of the causes taken separately. A familiar instance is that of a body kept in equilibrium by two equal and contrary forces. One of the forces if acting alone would carry the body in a given time a certain distance to the west, the other if acting alone would carry it exactly as far toward the east, and the result is the same as if it had been first carried to the west as far as the one force would carry it, and then back toward the east as far as the other would carry it — that is, precisely the same distance, being ultimately left where it was found at first.

All laws of causation are liable to be in this manner counteracted and seemingly frustrated by coming into conflict with other laws, the separate result of which is opposite to theirs or more or less inconsistent with it. And, hence, with almost every law, many instances in which it really is entirely fulfilled do not, at first sight, appear to be cases of its operation at all. It is so in the example just adduced; a force in mechanics means neither more nor less than a cause of motion, yet the sum of the effects of two causes of motion may be rest. Again, a body solicited by two forces in directions making an angle with one another, moves in the diagonal; and it seems a paradox to say that motion in the diagonal is the sum of two motions in two other lines. Motion, however, is but change of place, and at every instant the body is in the exact place it would have been in if the forces had acted during alternate instants instead of acting in the same instant (saving that if we suppose two forces to act successively which are in truth simultaneous we must, of course, allow them double the time). It is evident, therefore, that each force has had, during each instant, all the effect which belonged to it, and that the modifying influence which one of two concurrent causes is said to exercise with respect to the other may be considered as exerted not over the action of the cause itself but over the effect after it is completed. For all purposes of predicting, calculating, or explaining their joint result, causes which compound their effects may be treated as if they produced simultaneously each of them its own effect, and all these effects co-existed visibly.

Since the laws of causes are as really fulfilled when the causes are said to be counteracted by opposing causes as when they are left to their own undisturbed action, we must be cautious not to express the laws in such terms as would render the assertion of their being fulfilled in those cases a contradiction. If, for instance, it were stated as a law of nature that a body to which a force is applied moves in the direction of the force with a velocity proportioned to the force directly and to its own mass inversely, when, in point of fact, some bodies to which a force is applied do not

move at all, and those which do move (at least in the region of
our earth) are, from the very first, retarded by the action of gravity
and other resisting forces and at last stopped altogether, it is clear
that the general proposition, though it would be true under a
certain hypothesis, would not express the facts as they actually
occur. To accommodate the expression of the law to the real
phenomena, we must say not that the object moves, but that it
tends to move, in the direction and with the velocity specified.
We might, indeed, guard our expression in a different mode by
saying that the body moves in that manner unless prevented, or
except in so far as prevented, by some counteracting cause. But
the body does not only move in that manner unless counteracted;
it *tends* to move in that manner even when counteracted; it still
exerts, in the original direction, the same energy of movement as
if its first impulse had been undisturbed and produces, by that
energy, an exactly equivalent quantity of effect. This is true even
when the force leaves the body as it found it, in a state of absolute
rest, as when we attempt to raise a body of three tons' weight with
a force equal to one ton. For if, while we are applying this force,
wind or water or any other agent supplies an additional force just
exceeding two tons, the body will be raised, thus proving that the
force we applied exerted its full effect, by neutralizing an equivalent
portion of the weight which it was insufficient altogether to overcome. And if, while we are exerting this force of one ton upon the
object in a direction contrary to that of gravity, it be put into a
scale and weighed, it will be found to have lost a ton of its weight,
or, in other words, to press downward with a force only equal to
the difference of the two forces.

These facts are correctly indicated by the expression *tendency*.
All laws of causation, in consequence of their liability to be counteracted, require to be stated in words affirmative of tendencies only,
and not of actual results. In those sciences of causation which
have an accurate nomenclature, there are special words which
signify a tendency to the particular effect with which the science
is conversant; thus *pressure*, in mechanics, is synonymous with
tendency to motion, and forces are not reasoned on as causing
actual motion, but as exerting pressure. A similar improvement

in terminology would be very salutary in many other branches of science.

.   .   .   .

5. *Three modes of investigating the laws of complex effects*

We have now to consider according to what method these complex effects, compounded of the effects of many causes, are to be studied; how we are enabled to trace each effect to the concurrence of causes in which it originated and ascertain the conditions of its recurrence — the circumstances in which it may be expected again to occur. The conditions of a phenomenon which arises from a composition of causes may be investigated either deductively or experimentally.

The case, it is evident, is naturally susceptible of the deductive mode of investigation. The law of an effect of this description is a result of the laws of the separate causes on the combination of which it depends and is, therefore, in itself capable of being deduced from these laws. This is called the method *a priori*. The other, or *a posteriori* method, professes to proceed according to the canons of experimental inquiry. Considering the whole assemblage of concurrent causes which produced the phenomenon as one single cause, it attempts to ascertain the cause in the ordinary manner by a comparison of instances. This second method subdivides itself into two different varieties. If it merely collates instances of the effect, it is a method of pure observation. If it operates upon the causes and tries different combinations of them in hopes of ultimately hitting the precise combination which will produce the given total effect, it is a method of experiment.

In order more completely to clear up the nature of each of these three methods and determine which of them deserves the preference, it will be expedient (conformably to a favorite maxim of Lord Chancellor Eldon, to which, though it has often incurred philosophical ridicule, a deeper philosophy will not refuse its sanction) to "clothe them in circumstances." We shall select for this purpose a case which as yet furnishes no very brilliant example of the success of any of the three methods, but which is all the more suited to illustrate the difficulties inherent in them. Let the subject of inquiry be the conditions of health and disease in the human body, or (for greater simplicity) the conditions of recovery from a given disease; and, in order to narrow the question still more, let it be limited, in the first instance, to this one inquiry: Is, or is not, some particular medicament (mercury, for instance) a remedy for the given disease.

Now, the deductive method would set out from known properties of mercury and known laws of the human body, and by reasoning from these would attempt to discover whether mercury will act upon the body when in the morbid condition supposed in such a manner as would tend to restore health. The experimental method would simply administer mercury in as many cases as possible, noting the age, sex, temperament, and other peculiarities of bodily constitution, the particular form or variety of the disease, the particular stage of its progress, etc., remarking in which of these cases it was attended with a salutary effect, and with what circumstances it was on those occasions combined. The method of simple observation would compare instances of recovery to find whether they agreed in having been preceded by the administration of mercury, or would compare instances of recovery with instances of failure to find cases which, agreeing in all other respects, differed only in the fact that mercury had been administered or that it had not.

6. *The method of simple observation inapplicable*

That the last of these three modes of investigation is applicable to the case no one has ever seriously contended. No conclusions of value on a subject of such intricacy ever were obtained in that way.... The reason is that which we have spoken of as constituting the characteristic imperfection of the method of agreement, plurality of causes. Supposing even that mercury does tend to cure the disease, so many other causes, both natural and artificial, also tend to cure it, that there are sure to be abundant instances of recovery in which mercury has not been administered, unless, indeed, the practice be to administer it in all cases, on which supposition it will equally be found in the cases of failure.

. . . .

7. *The purely experimental method inapplicable*

The inapplicability of the method of simple observation to ascertain the conditions of effects dependent on many concurring causes being thus recognized, we shall next inquire whether any greater benefit can be expected from the other branch of the *a posteriori* method, that which proceeds by directly trying different combinations of causes, either artificially produced or found in nature, and taking notice what is their effect, as, for example, by actually trying the effect of mercury in as many different circumstances as possible. . . .

The method now under consideration is called the empirical method, and, in order to estimate it fairly, we must suppose it to be completely, not incompletely, empirical. We must exclude from it everything which partakes of the nature not of an experimental, but of a deductive operation. . . .

Let us see, therefore, how far the case admits of the observance of those rules of experimentation which it is found necessary to observe in other cases. When we devise an experiment to ascertain the effect of a given agent, there are certain precautions which we never, if we can help it, omit. In the first place, we introduce the agent into the midst of a set of circumstances which we have exactly ascertained. It needs hardly be remarked how far this condition is from being realized in any case connected with the phenomena of life; how far we are from knowing what are all the circumstances which pre-exist in any instance in which mercury is administered to a living being. This difficulty, however, though insuperable in most cases, may not be so in all; there are sometimes concurrences of many causes in which we yet know accurately what the causes are. Moreover, the difficulty may be attenuated by sufficient multiplication öf experiments, in circumstances rendering it improbable that any of the unknown causes should exist in them all. But when we have got clear of this obstacle, we encounter another still more serious. In other cases, when we intend to try an experiment, we do not reckon it enough that there be no circumstance in the case the presence of which is unknown to us. We require, also, that none of the circumstances which we do know shall have effects susceptible of being confounded with those of the agents whose properties we wish to study. We take the utmost pains to exclude all causes capable of composition with the given cause, or, if forced to let in any such causes, we take care to make them such that we can compute and allow for their influence, so that the effect of the given cause may, after the subduction of those other effects, be apparent as a residual phenomenon.

These precautions are inapplicable to such cases as we are now considering. The mercury of our experiment being tried with an unknown multitude (or even let it be a known multitude) of other influencing circumstances, the mere fact of their being influencing circumstances implies that they disguise the effect of the mercury and preclude us from knowing whether it has any effect or not. Unless we already knew what and how much is owing to every other circumstance (that is, unless we suppose the very problem solved which we are considering the means of solving), we cannot tell that those other circumstances may not have produced the whole of the effect, independently or even in spite of the mercury. . .

Anything like a scientific use of the method of experiment in these complicated cases is, therefore, out of the question. . . .

CHAPTER XI

OF THE DEDUCTIVE METHOD

1. *First stage: ascertainment of the laws of the separate causes by direct induction*

The mode of investigation which, from the proved inapplicability of direct methods of observation and experiment, remains to us as the main source of the knowledge we possess or can acquire respecting the conditions and laws of recurrence of the more complex phenomena is called, in its most general expression, the deductive method, and consists of three operations: the first, one of direct induction; the second, of ratiocination; the third, of verification.

I call the first step in the process an inductive operation because there must be a direct induction as the basis of the whole, though in many particular investigations the place of the induction may be supplied by a prior deduction; but the premises of this prior deduction must have been derived from induction.

The problem of the deductive method is to find the law of an effect from the laws of the different tendencies of which it is the joint result. The first requisite, therefore, is to know the laws of those tendencies, the law of each of the concurrent causes, and this supposes a previous process of observation or experiment upon each cause separately, or else a previous deduction which also must depend for its ultimate premises on observation or experiment. Thus if the subject be social or historical phenomena, the premises of the deductive method must be the laws of the causes which determine that class of phenomena, and those causes are human actions, together with the general outward circumstances under the influence of which mankind are placed and which constitute man's position on the earth. The deductive method, applied to social phenomena, must begin, therefore, by investigating, or must suppose to have been already investigated, the laws of human action and those properties of outward things by which the actions of human beings in society are determined. Some of these general truths will naturally be obtained by observation and experiment, others by deduction; the more complex laws of human action, for example, may be deduced from the simpler ones, but the simple or elementary laws will always, and necessarily, have been obtained by a directly inductive process.

To ascertain, then, the laws of each separate cause which takes a share in producing the effect is the first desideratum of the deductive method. To know what the causes are which must be subjected to this process of study may or may not be difficult. In the case last mentioned, this first condition is of easy fulfillment. That social phenomena depend on the acts and mental impressions of human beings never could have been a matter of any doubt, however imperfectly it may have been known either by what laws those impressions and actions are governed or to what social consequences their laws naturally lead. Neither, again, after physical science had attained a certain development, could there be any real doubt

where to look for the laws on which the phenomena of life depend,
since they must be the mechanical and chemical laws of the solid
and fluid substances composing the organized body and the medium
in which it subsists, together with the peculiar vital laws of the
different tissues constituting the organic structure. In other cases,
really far more simple than these, it was much less obvious in what
quarter the causes were to be looked for, as in the case of the
celestial phenomena. Until, by combining the laws of certain
causes, it was found that those laws explained all the facts which
experience had proved concerning the heavenly motions and led to
predictions which it always verified, mankind never knew that
those *were* the causes. But whether we are able to put the question
before, or not until after we have become capable of answering it,
in either case it must be answered; the laws of the different causes
must be ascertained before we can proceed to deduce from them
the conditions of the effect.

The mode of ascertaining those laws neither is nor can be any
other than the fourfold method of experimental inquiry, already
discussed. . . .

.   .   .   .

2. *Second stage: ratiocination from the simple laws of the complex cases*

When the laws of the causes have been ascertained, and the first
stage of the great logical operation now under discussion satisfactorily accomplished, the second part follows, that of determining
from the laws of the causes what effect any given combination of
those causes will produce. This is a process of calculation, in the
wider sense of the term, and very often involves processes of calculation in the narrowest sense. It is a ratiocination; and when our
knowledge of the causes is so perfect as to extend to the exact
numerical laws which they observe in producing their effects, the
ratiocination may reckon among its premises the theorems of the
science of number, in the whole immense extent of that science.
Not only are the most advanced truths of mathematics often
required to enable us to compute an effect, the numerical law of
which we already know, but, even by the aid of those most ad-

vanced truths, we can go but a little way. In so simple a case as the common problem of three bodies gravitating toward one another with a force directly as their mass and inversely as the square of the distance, all the resources of the calculus have not hitherto sufficed to obtain any general solution but an approximate one. In a case a little more complex, but still one of the simplest which arise in practice, that of the motion of a projectile, the causes which affect the velocity and range (for example) of a cannon-ball may be all known and estimated: the force of the gunpowder, the angle of elevation, the density of the air, the strength and direction of the wind; but it is one of the most difficult of mathematical problems to combine all these so as to determine the effect resulting from their collective action.

. . . .

3. *Third stage: verification by specific experience*

But (it may here be asked) are not the same arguments by which the methods of direct observation and experiment were set aside as illusory, when applied to the laws of complex phenomena, applicable with equal force against the method of deduction? When in every single instance a multitude, often an unknown multitude, of agencies are clashing and combining, what security have we that in our computation *a priori* we have taken all these into our reckoning? How many must we not generally be ignorant of? Among those which we know, how probable that some have been overlooked; and, even were all included, how vain the pretense of summing up the effects of many causes, unless we know accurately the numerical law of each — a condition in most cases not to be fulfilled; and, even when it is fulfilled, to make the calculation transcends, in any but very simple cases, the utmost power of mathematical science with all its most modern improvements.

These objections have real weight and would be altogether unanswerable if there were no test by which, when we employ the deductive method, we might judge whether an error of any of the above descriptions had been committed or not. Such a test, however, there is; and its application forms, under the name of verification, the third essential component part of the deductive method, without which all the results it can give have little other value than that of conjecture. To warrant reliance on the general conclusions arrived at by deduction, these conclusions must be found, on careful comparison, to accord with the results of direct observation wherever it can be had. If, when we have experience to compare with them, this experience confirms them, we may safely trust to them in other cases of which our specific experience is yet to come. But if our deductions have led to the conclusion that from a particular combination of causes a given effect would result, then in all known cases where that combination can be shown to have existed and where the effect has not followed, we must be able to show (or at least to make a probable surmise) what frustrated it; if we cannot, the theory is imperfect, and not yet to be relied upon. Nor is the verification complete unless some of the cases in which the theory is borne out by the observed result are of at least equal complexity with any other cases in which its application could be called for.

. . . .

In order, therefore, to facilitate the verification of theories obtained by deduction, it is important that as many as possible of the empirical laws of the phenomena should be ascertained by a comparison of instances, conformably to the method of agreement; as well as (it must be added) that the phenomena themselves should be described in the most comprehensive as well as accurate manner possible, by collecting from the observation of parts the simplest possible correct expressions for the corresponding wholes, as when the series of the observed places of a planet was first expressed by a circle, then by a system of epicycles, and subsequently by an ellipse.

It is worth remarking that complex instances which would have been of no use for the discovery of the simple laws into which we ultimately analyze their phenomena, nevertheless, when they have served to verify the analysis, become additional evidence of the laws themselves. Although we could not have got at the law from complex cases, still when the law, got at otherwise, is found to be in accordance with the result of a complex case, that case becomes a new experiment on the law and helps to confirm what it did not assist to discover. It is a new trial of the principle in a different set of circumstances, and occasionally serves to eliminate some circumstance not previously excluded, and the exclusion of which might require an experiment impossible to be executed. . . .

To the deductive method, thus characterized in its three constituent parts, induction, ratiocination, and verification, the human mind is indebted for its most conspicuous triumphs in the investigation of nature. To it we owe all the theories by which vast and complicated phenomena are embraced under a few simple laws, which, considered as the laws of those great phenomena, could nèver have been detected by their direct study. . . .

CHAPTER XII*

OF THE LIMITS TO THE EXPLANATION OF LAWS OF NATURE, AND OF HYPOTHESES

1. *Can all the sequences of nature be resolvable into one law?*

The preceding considerations have led us to recognize a distinction between two kinds of laws, or observed uniformities in nature: ultimate laws, and what may be termed derivative laws. Derivative laws are such as are deducible from, and may, in any of the modes which we have pointed out, be resolved into, other and more general ones. Ultimate laws are those which cannot. We are not sure that any of the uniformities with which we are yet acquainted are ultimate laws; but we know that there must be ultimate laws, and that every resolution of a derivative law into more general laws brings us nearer to them.

Since we are continually discovering that uniformities, not previously known to be other than ultimate, are derivative and resolvable into more general laws, since (in other words) we are continually discovering the explanation of some sequence which was previously known only as a fact, it becomes an interesting

* Chapter XIV of the eighth. edition.

question whether there are any necessary limits to this philosophical operation, or whether it may proceed until all the uniform sequences in nature are resolved into some one universal law. For this seems, at first sight, to be the ultimatum toward which the progress of induction by the deductive method, resting on a basis of observation and experiment, is tending. . . .

2. *Ultimate laws cannot be less numerous than the distinguishable feelings of our nature*

It is, therefore, useful to remark that the ultimate laws of nature cannot possibly be less numerous than the distinguishable sensations or other feelings of our nature, those, I mean, which are distinguishable from one another in quality and not merely in quantity or degree. For example, since there is a phenomenon *sui generis*, called color, which our consciousness testifies to be not a particular degree of some other phenomenon, as heat or odor or motion, but intrinsically unlike all others, it follows that there are ultimate laws of color, that, though the facts of color may admit of explanation, they never can be explained from laws of heat or odor alone, or of motion alone, but that, however far the explanation may be carried, there will always remain in it a law of color. I do not mean that it might not possibly be shown that some other phenomenon, some chemical or mechanical action, for example, invariably precedes and is the cause of every phenomenon of color. But though this, if proved, would be an important extension of our knowledge of nature, it would not explain how or why a motion or a chemical action can produce a sensation of color, and, however diligent might be our scrutiny of the phenomena, whatever number of hidden links we might detect in the chain of causation terminating in the color, the last link would still be a law of color, not a law of motion, nor of any other phenomenon whatever. Nor does this observation apply only to color as compared with any other of the great classes of sensations; it applies to every particular color as compared with others. White color can in no manner be explained exclusively by the laws of the production of red color. In any attempt to explain it, we cannot but introduce, as one element of the explanation, the proposition that some antecedent or other produces the sensation of white.

The ideal limit, therefore, of the explanation of natural phenomena (toward which, as toward other ideal limits, we are constantly tending, without the prospect of ever completely attaining it) would be to show that each distinguishable variety of our sensations or other states of consciousness has only one sort of cause, that, for example, whenever we perceive a white color, there is some one condition or set of conditions which is always present, and the presence of which always produces in us that sensation. As long as there are several known modes of production of a phenomenon (several different substances, for instance, which have the property of whiteness, and between which we cannot trace any other resemblance), so long it is not impossible that one of these modes of production may be resolved into another, or that all of them may be resolved into some more general mode of production not hitherto recognized. But when the modes of production are reduced to one, we cannot, in point of simplification, go any further. This one may not, after all, be the ultimate mode; there may be other links to be discovered between the supposed cause and the effect; but we can only further resolve the known law by introducing some other law hitherto unknown, which will not diminish the number of ultimate laws.

.   .   .   .

3. *In what sense ultimate facts can be explained*

As, however, there is scarcely any one of the principles of a true method of philosophizing which does not require to be guarded against errors on both sides, I must enter a caveat against another misapprehension, of a kind directly contrary to the preceding. M. Comte, among other occasions on which he has condemned, with some asperity, any attempt to explain phenomena which are "evidently primordial" (meaning, apparently, no more than that every peculiar phenomenon must have at least one peculiar and, therefore, inexplicable law), has spoken of the attempt to furnish any explanation of the color belonging to each substance, *"la*

couleur élémentaire propre à chaque substance," as essentially illusory.
"No one," says he, "in our time attempts to explain the particular
specific gravity of each substance or of each structure. Why
should it be otherwise as to the specific color, the notion of which
is undoubtedly no less primordial?"[1]

Now although, as he elsewhere observes, a color must always
remain a different thing from a weight or a sound, varieties of color
might nevertheless follow or correspond to given varieties of
weight, or sound, or some other phenomenon as different as these
are from color itself. It is one question what a thing is, and
another what it depends on; and though to ascertain the conditions
of an elementary phenomenon is not to obtain any new insight into
the nature of the phenomenon itself, that is no reason against
attempting to discover the conditions. The interdict against endeavoring to reduce distinctions of color to any common principle
would have held equally good against a like attempt on the subject
of distinctions of sound, which nevertheless have been found to be
immediately preceded and caused by distinguishable varieties in
the vibrations of elastic bodies; though a sound, no doubt, is quite
as different as a color is from any motion of particles, vibratory or
otherwise. We might add that, in the case of colors, there are
strong positive indications that they are not ultimate properties of
the different kinds of substances but depend on conditions capable
of being superinduced upon all substances, since there is no substance which cannot, according to the kind of light thrown upon it,
be made to assume almost any color, and since almost every change
in the mode of aggregation of the particles of the same substance
is attended with alterations in its color and in its optical properties
generally.

The really weak point in the attempts which have been made to
account for colors by the vibrations of a fluid is not that the attempt
itself is unphilosophical, but that the existence of the fluid and the
fact of its vibratory motion are not proved, but are assumed, on no
other ground than the facility they are supposed to afford of
explaining the phenomena. And this consideration leads to the
important question of the proper use of scientific hypotheses, the
connection of which with the subject of the explanation of the

[1] *Cours de Philosophie Positive* II, 656.

phenomena of nature and of the necessary limits to that explanation need not be pointed out.

4. *The proper use of scientific hypotheses*

An hypothesis is any supposition which we make (either without actual evidence, or on evidence avowedly insufficient) in order to endeavor to deduce from it conclusions in accordance with facts which are known to be real, under the idea that, if the conclusions to which the hypothesis leads are known truths, the hypothesis itself either must be, or, at least, is likely to be, true. If the hypothesis relates to the cause or mode of production of a phenomenon, it will serve, if admitted, to explain such facts as are found capable of being deduced from it. And this explanation is the purpose of many, if not most hypotheses. Since explaining, in the scientific sense, means resolving a uniformity which is not a law of causation into the laws of causation from which it results, or a complex law of causation into simpler and more general ones from which it is capable of being deductively inferred, if there do not exist any known laws which fulfill this requirement, we may feign or imagine some which would fulfill it, and this is making an hypothesis.

An hypothesis being a mere supposition, there are no other limits to hypotheses than those of the human imagination; we may, if we please, imagine, by way of accounting for an effect, some cause of a kind utterly unknown and acting according to a law altogether fictitious. But as hypotheses of this sort would not have any of the plausibility belonging to those which ally themselves by analogy with known laws of nature, and besides would not supply the want which arbitrary hypotheses are generally invented to satisfy by enabling the imagination to represent to itself an obscure phenomenon in a familiar light, there is probably no hypothesis in the history of science in which both the agent itself and the law of its operation were fictitious. Either the phenomenon assigned as the cause is real, but the law according to which it acts merely supposed, or the cause is fictitious, but is supposed to produce its effects according to laws similar to those of some known class of phenomena. An instance of the first kind is afforded by the different suppositions made respecting the law of the planetary central force, anterior to the discovery of the true law, that the force varies as the inverse square of the distance, which also suggested itself to Newton, in the first instance, as an hypothesis and was verified by proving that it led deductively to Kepler's laws. Hypotheses of the second kind are such as the vortices of Descartes, which were fictitious, but were supposed to obey the known laws of rotatory motion; or the two rival hypotheses respecting the nature of light, the one ascribing the phenomena to a fluid emitted from all luminous bodies, the other (now generally received) attributing them to vibratory motions among the particles of an ether pervading all space. Of the existence of either fluid there is no evidence save the explanation they are calculated to afford of some of the phenomena, but they are supposed to produce their effects according to known laws: the ordinary laws of continued locomotion in the one case, and, in the other, those of the propagation of undulatory movements among the particles of an elastic fluid.

According to the foregoing remarks, hypotheses are invented to enable the deductive method to be earlier applied to phenomena. But in order to discover the cause of any phenomenon by the deductive method, the process must consist of three parts: induction, ratiocination, and verification. . . .

Now, the hypothetical method suppresses the first of the three steps, the induction to ascertain the law, and contents itself with the other two operations, ratiocination and verification, the law which is reasoned from being assumed instead of proved.

This process may evidently be legitimate on one supposition, namely, if the nature of the case be such that the final step, the verification, shall amount to, and fulfill the conditions of, a complete induction. We want to be assured that the law we have hypothetically assumed is a true one, and its leading deductively to true results will afford this assurance, provided the case be such that a false law cannot lead to a true result, provided no law except the very one which we have assumed can lead deductively to the same conclusions which that leads to. And this proviso is often realized. . . .

. . . .

It appears, then, to be a condition of the most genuinely scientific hypothesis that it be not destined always to remain an hypothesis, but be of such a nature as to be either proved or disproved by comparison with observed facts. This condition is fulfilled when the effect is already known to depend on the very cause supposed, and the hypothesis relates only to the precise mode of dependence; the law of the variation of the effect according to the variations in the quantity or in the relations of the cause. With these may be classed the hypotheses which do not make any supposition with regard to causation, but only with regard to the law of correspondence between facts which accompany each other in their variations, though there may be no relation of cause and effect between them. Such were the different false hypotheses which Kepler made respecting the law of the refraction of light. It was known that the direction of the line of refraction varied with every variation in the direction of the line of incidence, but it was not known how, that is, what changes of the one corresponded to the different changes of the other. In this case any law different from the true one must have led to false results. And, lastly, we must add to these all hypothetical modes of merely representing or *describing* phenomena, such as the hypothesis of the ancient astronomers that the heavenly bodies moved in circles; the various hypotheses of eccentrics, deferents, and epicycles which were added to that original hypothesis; the nineteen false hypotheses which Kepler made and abandoned respecting the form of the planetary orbits; and even the doctrine in which he finally rested, that those orbits are ellipses, which was but an hypothesis like the rest until verified by facts.

In all these cases, verification is proof; if the supposition accords with the phenomena, there needs no other evidence of it. But in order that this may be the case, I conceive it to be necessary, when the hypothesis relates to causation, that the supposed cause should not only be a real phenomenon, something actually existing in nature, but should be already known to exercise, or, at least, to be capable of exercising, an influence of some sort over the effect. In any other case, it is no sufficient evidence of the truth of the hypothesis that we are able to deduce the real phenomena from it.

Is it, then, never allowable in a scientific hypothesis to assume a cause, but only to ascribe an assumed law to a known cause? I do not assert this. I only say that in the latter case alone can the hypothesis be received as true merely because it explains the phenomena. In the former case it may be very useful by suggesting a line of investigation which may possibly terminate in obtaining real proof. But for this purpose, as is justly remarked by M. Comte, it is indispensable that the cause suggested by the hypothesis should be in its own nature susceptible of being proved by other evidence. This seems to be the philosophical import of Newton's maxim (so often cited with approbation by subsequent writers) that the cause assigned for any phenomenon must not only be such as if admitted would explain the phenomenon, but also must be a *vera causa*. What he meant by a *vera causa* Newton did not indeed very explicitly define; and Dr. Whewell, who dissents from the propriety of any such restriction upon the latitude of framing hypotheses, has had little difficulty in showing[2] that his conception of it was neither precise nor consistent with itself; accordingly his optical theory was a signal instance of the violation of his own rule. It is certainly not necessary that the cause assigned should be a cause already known, otherwise we should sacrifice our best opportunities of becoming acquainted with new causes. But what is true in the maxim is that the cause, though not known previously, should be capable of being known thereafter, that its existence should be capable of being detected, and its connection with the effect ascribed to it should be susceptible of being proved, by independent evidence. The hypothesis, by suggesting observations and experiments, puts us on the road to that independent evidence, if it be really attainable, and, till it be attained, the hypothesis ought only to count for a more or less plausible conjecture.

5. *Their indispensableness*

This function, however, of hypotheses is one which must be reckoned absolutely indispensable in science. When Newton said, "Hypotheses non fingo," he did not mean that he deprived himself of the facilities of investigation afforded by assuming in the first instance what he hoped ultimately to be able to prove. Without

[2] *Philosophy of Discovery*, p. 185 *et seq.*

such assumptions, science could never have attained its present state; they are necessary steps in the progress to something more certain; and nearly everything which is now theory was once hypothesis. Even in purely experimental science, some inducement is necessary for trying one experiment rather than another, and, though it is abstractedly possible that all the experiments which have been tried might have been produced by the mere desire to ascertain what would happen in certain circumstances, without any previous conjecture as to the result; yet, in point of fact, those unobvious, delicate, and often cumbrous and tedious processes of experiment which have thrown most light upon the general constitution of nature would hardly ever have been undertaken by the persons or at the time they were unless it had seemed to depend on them whether some general doctrine or theory which had been suggested, but not yet proved, should be admitted or not. If this be true even of merely experimental inquiry, the conversion of experimental into deductive truths could still less have been effected without large temporary assistance from hypotheses. The process of tracing regularity in any complicated and, at first sight, confused set of appearances is necessarily tentative; we begin by making any supposition, even a false one, to see what consequences will follow from it, and, by observing how these differ from the real phenomena, we learn what corrections to make in our assumption. The simplest supposition which accords with the more obvious facts is the best to begin with, because its consequences are the most easily traced. This rude hypothesis is then rudely corrected, and the operation repeated; and the comparison of the consequences deducible from the corrected hypothesis with the observed facts suggests still further correction, until the deductive results are at last made to tally with the phenomena. "Some fact is as yet little understood, or some law is unknown; we frame on the subject an hypothesis as accordant as possible with the whole of the data already possessed; and the science, being thus enabled to move forward freely, always ends by leading to new consequences capable of observation, which either confirm or refute, unequivocally, the first supposition." Neither induction nor deduction would enable us to understand even the simplest phenomena, "if we did not often commence by anticipating on the results; by making a provisional supposition, at first essentially conjectural, as to some of the very notions which constitute the final object of the inquiry."[3] Let anyone watch the manner in which he himself unravels a complicated mass of evidence; let him observe how, for instance, he elicits the true history of any occurrence from the involved statements of one or of many witnesses; he will find that he does not take all the items of evidence into his mind at once and attempt to weave them together; he extemporizes, from a few of the particulars, a first rude theory of the mode in which the facts took place, and then looks at the other statements one by one to try whether they can be reconciled with that provisional theory, or what alterations or additions it requires to make it square with them. In this way, which has been justly compared to the methods of approximation of mathematicians, we arrive by means of hypotheses at conclusions not hypothetical.[4]

[3]Comte, *Philosophie Positive*, II, 434–37.

[4]As an example of legitimate hypothesis according to the test here laid down has been justly cited that of Broussais, who, proceeding on the very rational principle that every disease must originate in some definite part or other of the organism, boldly assumed that certain fevers, which not being known to be local were called constitutional, had their origin in the mucous membrane of the alimentary canal. The supposition was, indeed, as is now generally admitted, erroneous; but he was justified in making it since, by deducing the consequences of the supposition and comparing them with the facts of those maladies, he might be certain of disproving his hypothesis if it was ill founded and might expect that the comparison would materially aid him in framing another more conformable to the phenomena.

The doctrine now universally received that the earth is a natural magnet was originally an hypothesis of the celebrated Gilbert.

Another hypothesis, to the legitimacy of which no objection can lie, and which is well calculated to light the path of scientific inquiry, is that suggested by several recent writers that the brain is a voltaic pile, and that each of its pulsations is a discharge of electricity through the system. It has been remarked that the sensation felt by the hand from the beating of a brain bears a strong resemblance to a voltaic shock. And the hypothesis, if followed to its consequences, might afford a plausible explanation of many physiological facts, while there is nothing to discourage the hope that we may in time sufficiently understand the conditions of voltaic phenomena to render the truth of the hypothesis amenable to observation and experiment.

The attempt to localize in different regions of the brain the physical organs of our different mental faculties and propensities was, on the part of its original author, a legitimate example of a scientific hypothesis; and we ought not,

6. *The two degrees of legitimacy in hypotheses*

It is perfectly consistent with the spirit of the method to assume in this provisional manner not only an hypothesis respecting the law of what we already know to be the cause, but an hypothesis respecting the cause itself. It is allowable, useful, and often even necessary to begin by asking ourselves what cause *may* have produced the effect, in order that we may know in what direction to look out for evidence to determine whether it actually *did*. . . .

The prevailing hypothesis of a luminiferous ether, in other respects not without analogy to that of Descartes, is not in its own nature entirely cut off from the possibility of direct evidence in its favor. It is well known that the difference between the calculated and the observed times of the periodical return of Encke's comet has led to a conjecture that a medium capable of opposing resistance to motion is diffused through space. If this surmise should be confirmed, in the course of ages, by the gradual accumulation of a

therefore, to blame him for the extremely slight grounds on which he often proceeded in an operation which could only be tentative, though we may regret that materials barely sufficient for a first rude hypothesis should have been hastily worked up into the vain semblance of a science. If there be really a connection between the scale of mental endowments and the various degrees of complication in the cerebral system, the nature of that connection was in no other way so likely to be brought to light as by framing, in the first instance, an hypothesis similar to that of Gall. But the verification of any such hypothesis is attended, from the peculiar nature of the phenomena, with difficulties which phrenologists have not shown themselves even competent to appreciate, much less to overcome.

Mr. Darwin's remarkable speculation on the origin of species is another unimpeachable example of a legitimate hypothesis. What he terms "natural selection" is not only a *vera causa*, but one proved to be capable of producing effects of the same kind with those which the hypothesis ascribes to it; the question of possibility is entirely one of degree. It is unreasonable to accuse Mr. Darwin (as has been done) of violating the rules of induction. The rules of induction are concerned with the conditions of proof. Mr. Darwin has never pretended that his doctrine was proved. He was not bound by the rules of induction, but by those of hypothesis. And these last have seldom been more ⌐⌐⌐⌐letely fulfilled. He has opened a path of inquiry full of promise, the results of which none can foresee. And is it not a wonderful feat of scientific knowledge and ingenuity to have rendered so bold a suggestion, which the first impulse of everyone was to reject at once, admissible and discussible, even as a conjecture?

similar variance in the case of the other bodies of the solar system, the luminiferous ether would have made a considerable advance toward the character of a *vera causa*, since the existence would have been ascertained of a great cosmical agent possessing some of the attributes which the hypothesis assumes, though there would still remain many difficulties, and the identification of the ether with the resisting medium would even, I imagine, give rise to the new ones. At present, however, this supposition cannot be looked upon as more than a conjecture; the existence of the ether still rests on the possibility of deducing from its assumed laws a considerable number of actual phenomena, and this evidence I cannot regard as conclusive because we cannot have, in the case of such an hypothesis, the assurance that if the hypothesis be false it must lead to results at variance with the true facts.

Accordingly, most thinkers of any degree of sobriety allow that an hypothesis of this kind is not to be received as probably true because it accounts for all the known phenomena, since this is a condition sometimes fulfilled tolerably well by two conflicting hypotheses, while there are probably many others which are equally possible but which, for want of anything analogous in our experience, our minds are unfitted to conceive. But it seems to be thought that an hypothesis of the sort in question is entitled to a more favorable reception if, besides accounting for all the facts previously known, it has led to the anticipation and prediction of others which experience afterward verified, as the undulatory theory of light led to the prediction, subsequently realized by experiment, that two luminous rays might meet each other in such a manner as to produce darkness. Such predictions and their fulfillment are, indeed, well calculated to impress the uninformed, whose faith in science rests solely on similar coincidences between its prophecies and what comes to pass. But it is strange that any considerable stress should be laid upon such a coincidence by persons of scientific attainments. If the laws of the propagation of light accord with those of the vibrations of an elastic fluid in as many respects as is necessary to make the hypothesis afford a correct expression of all or most of the phenomena known at the time, it is nothing strange that they should accord with each other in one respect more. Though twenty such coincidences should occur, they would not prove the reality of the undulatory ether: it would not follow that the phenomena of light were results of the laws of elastic fluids, but, at most, that they are governed by laws partially identical with these, which, we may observe, is already certain from the fact that the hypothesis in question could be for a moment tenable.[5] Cases may be cited, even in our imperfect acquaintance with nature, where agencies that we have good reason to consider as radically distinct produce their effects, or some of their effects, according to laws which are identical. The law, for example, of the inverse square of the distance is the measure of the intensity not only of gravitation, but (it is believed) of illumination, and of heat diffused from a center. Yet no one looks upon this identity as proving similarity in the mechanism by which the three kinds of phenomena are produced.

. . . .

CHAPTER XIII*

OF EMPIRICAL LAWS

1. *Definition of an empirical law*

Scientific inquirers give the name of empirical laws to those uniformities which observation or experiment has shown to exist, but on which they hesitate to rely in cases varying much from those which have been actually observed for want of seeing any

[5]What has most contributed to accredit the hypothesis of a physical medium for the conveyance of light is the certain fact that light *travels* (which cannot be proved of gravitation), that its communication is not instantaneous, but requires time, and that it is intercepted (which gravitation is not) by intervening objects. These are analogies between its phenomena and those of the mechanical motion of a solid or fluid substance. But we are not entitled to assume that mechanical motion is the only power in nature capable of exhibiting those attributes.

*[Chapter XVI of the eighth edition.]

reason *why* such a law should exist. It is implied, therefore, in the notion of an empirical law that it is not an ultimate law, that, if true at all, its truth is capable of being and requires to be accounted for. It is a derivative law, the derivation of which is not yet known. To state the explanation, the *why*, of the empirical law would be to state the laws from which it is derived — the ultimate causes on which it is contingent. And if we knew these, we should also know what are its limits, under what conditions it would cease to be fulfilled.

. . . .

An empirical law, then, is an observed uniformity, presumed to be resolvable into simpler laws, but not yet resolved into them. The ascertainment of the empirical laws of phenomena often precedes by a long interval the explanation of those laws by the deductive method, and the verification of a deduction usually consists in the comparison of its results with empirical laws previously ascertained.

2. *Derivative laws commonly depend on collocations*

From a limited number of ultimate laws of causation there are necessarily generated a vast number of derivative uniformities, both of succession and co-existence. Some are laws of succession or of co-existence between different effects of the same cause; of these we had examples in the last chapter. Some are laws of succession between effects and their remote causes, resolvable into the laws which connect each with the intermediate link. Thirdly, when causes act together and compound their effects, the laws of those causes generate the fundamental law of the effect, namely, that it depends on the co-existence of those causes. And, finally, the order of succession or of co-existence which obtains among effects necessarily depends on their causes. If they are effects of the same cause, it depends on the laws of that cause; if on different causes, it depends on the laws of those causes severally, and on the circumstances which determine their co-existence. If we inquire further when and how the causes will co-exist, that, again, depends on *their* causes, and we may thus trace back the phenomena higher and higher, until the different series of effects meet in a point, and the whole is shown to have depended ultimately on some common cause, or until, instead of converging to one point, they terminate in different points, and the order of the effects is proved to have arisen from the collocation of some of the primeval causes or natural agents. For example, the order of succession and of co-existence among the heavenly motions which is expressed by Kepler's laws is derived from the co-existence of two primeval causes, the sun, and the original impulse or projectile force belonging to each planet.[1] Kepler's laws are resolved into the laws of these causes and the fact of their co-existence.

Derivative laws, therefore, do not depend solely on the ultimate laws into which they are resolvable; they mostly depend on those ultimate laws and an ultimate fact, namely, the mode of co-existence of some of the component elements of the universe. The ultimate laws of causation might be the same as at present and yet the derivative laws completely different, if the causes co-existed in different proportions or with any difference in those of their relations by which the effects are influenced. If, for example, the sun's attraction and the original projectile force had existed in some other ratio to one another than they did (and we know of no reason why this should not have been the case), the derivative laws of the heavenly motions might have been quite different from what they are. The proportions which exist happen to be such as to produce regular elliptical motions; any other proportions would have produced different ellipses, or circular, or parabolic, or hyperbolic motions, but still regular ones, because the effects of each of the agents accumulate according to a uniform law; and two regular series of quantities, when their corresponding terms are added, must produce a regular series of some sort, whatever the quantities themselves are.

3. *The collocations of the permanent causes are not reducible to any law*

Now this last-mentioned element in the resolution of a derivative law, the element which is not a law of causation but a collocation of causes, cannot itself be reduced to any law. There is, as formerly

[1] Or, according to Laplace's theory, the sun and the sun's rotation.

remarked,[2] no uniformity, no *norma*, principle, or rule, perceivable in the distribution of the primeval natural agents through the universe. The different substances composing the earth, the powers that pervade the universe, stand in no constant relation to one another. One substance is more abundant than others, one power acts through a larger extent of space than others, without any pervading analogy that we can discover. We not only do not know of any reason why the sun's attraction and the force in the direction of the tangent co-exist in the exact proportion they do, but we can trace no coincidence between it and the proportions in which any other elementary powers in the universe are intermingled. The utmost disorder is apparent in the combination of the causes, which is consistent with the most regular order in their effects, for, when each agent carries on its own operations according to a uniform law, even the most capricious combination of agencies will generate a regularity of some sort, as we see in the kaleidoscope, where any casual arrangement of colored bits of glass produces by the laws of reflection a beautiful regularity in the effect.

4. *Hence empirical laws cannot be relied on beyond the limits of actual experience*

In the above considerations lies the justification of the limited degree of reliance which scientific inquirers are accustomed to place in empirical laws.

A derivative law which results wholly from the operation of some one cause will be as universally true as the laws of the cause itself; that is, it will always be true except where some one of those effects of the cause on which the derivative law depends is defeated by a counteracting cause. But when the derivative law results not from different effects of one cause, but from effects of several causes, we cannot be certain that it will be true under any variation in the mode of co-existence of those causes or of the primitive natural agents on which the causes ultimately depend. The proposition that coal-beds rest on certain descriptions of strata exclusively, though true on the earth, so far as our observation has reached,

---

[2]*Supra*, Book III, Chap. V, § 7 [of the eighth edition].

cannot be extended to the moon or the other planets, supposing coal to exist there, because we cannot be assured that the original constitution of any other planet was such as to produce the different depositions in the same order as in our globe. The derivative law in this case depends not solely on laws, but on a collocation, and collocations cannot be reduced to any law.

Now it is the very nature of a derivative law which has not yet been resolved into its elements, in other words, an empirical law, that we do not know whether it results from the different effects of one cause or from effects of different causes. We cannot tell whether it depends wholly on laws, or partly on laws and partly on a collocation. If it depends on a collocation, it will be true in all the cases in which that particular collocation exists. But, since we are entirely ignorant, in case of its depending on a collocation, what the collocation is, we are not safe in extending the law beyond the limits of time and place in which we have actual experience of its truth. Since within those limits the law has always been found true, we have evidence that the collocations, whatever they are, on which it depends do really exist within those limits. But, knowing of no rule or principle to which the collocations themselves conform, we cannot conclude that because a collocation is proved to exist within certain limits of place or time it will exist beyond those limits. Empirical laws, therefore, can only be received as true within the limits of time and place in which they have been found true by observation, and not merely the limits of time and place, but of time, place, and circumstance, for, since it is the very meaning of an empirical law that we do not know the ultimate laws of causation on which it is dependent, we cannot foresee, without actual trial, in what manner or to what extent the introduction of any new circumstance may affect it.

CHAPTER XIV*

OF CHANCE AND ITS ELIMINATION

1. *The proof of empirical laws depends on the theory of chance*

. . . .

We found that the method of agreement has the defect of not proving causation, and can therefore only be employed for the ascertainment of empirical laws. But we also found that besides this deficiency it labors under a characteristic imperfection, tending to render uncertain even such conclusions as it is in itself adapted to prove. This imperfection arises from plurality of causes. Although two or more cases in which the phenomenon *a* has been met with may have no common antecedent except A, this does not prove that there is any connection between *a* and A, since *a* may have many causes, and may have been produced in these different instances not by anything which the instances had in common, but by some of those elements in them which were different. We nevertheless observed that in proportion to the multiplication of instances pointing to A as the antecedent, the characteristic uncertainty of the method diminishes, and the existence of a law of connection between A and *a* more nearly approaches to certainty. It is now to be determined after what amount of experience this certainty may be deemed to be practically attained, and the connection between A and *a* may be received as an empirical law.

This question may be otherwise stated in more familiar terms: After how many and what sort of instances may it be concluded that an observed coincidence between two phenomena is not the effect of chance?

It is of the utmost importance for understanding the logic of induction that we should form a distinct conception of what is meant by chance and how the phenomena which common language ascribes to that abstraction are really produced.

*[Chapter XVII of the eighth edition.]

2. Chance defined and characterized

Chance is usually spoken of in direct antithesis to law; whatever, it is supposed, cannot be ascribed to any law is attributed to chance. It is, however, certain that whatever happens is the result of some law, is an effect of causes, and could have been predicted from a knowledge of the existence of those causes, and from their laws. If I turn up a particular card, that is a consequence of its place in the pack. Its place in the pack was a consequence of the manner in which the cards were shuffled or of the order in which they were played in the last game, which, again, were effects of prior causes. At every stage, if we had possessed an accurate knowledge of the causes in existence, it would have been abstractedly possible to foretell the effect.

An event occurring by chance may be better described as a coincidence from which we have no ground to infer a uniformity — the occurrence of a phenomenon in certain circumstances without our having reason on that account to infer that it will happen again in those circumstances. This, however, when looked closely into, implies that the enumeration of the circumstances is not complete. Whatever the fact be, since it has occurred once, we may be sure that if *all* the same circumstances were repeated it would occur again; and not only if all, but there is some particular portion of those circumstances on which the phenomenon is invariably consequent. With most of them, however, it is not connected in any permanent manner; its conjunction with those is said to be the effect of chance, to be merely casual. Facts casually conjoined are separately the effects of causes and, therefore, of laws, but of different causes, and causes not connected by any law.

It is incorrect, then, to say that any phenomenon is produced by chance; but we may say that two or more phenomena are conjoined by chance, that they co-exist or succeed one another only by chance, meaning that they are in no way related through causation, that they are neither cause and effect, nor effects of the same cause, nor effects of causes between which there subsists any law of co-existence, nor even effects of the same collocation of primeval causes.

If the same casual coincidence never occurred a second time, we should have an easy test for distinguishing such from the coincidences which are the results of a law. As long as the phenomena had been found together only once, so long, unless we knew some more general laws from which the coincidence might have resulted, we could not distinguish it from a casual one, but if it occurred twice we should know that the phenomena so conjoined must be in some way connected through their causes.

There is, however, no such test. A coincidence may occur again and again and yet be only casual. Nay, it would be inconsistent with what we know of the order of nature to doubt that every casual coincidence will sooner or later be repeated, as long as the phenomena between which it occurred do not cease to exist or to be reproduced. The recurrence, therefore, of the same coincidence more than once, or even its frequent recurrence, does not prove that it is an instance of any law, does not prove that it is not casual, or, in common language, the effect of chance.

And yet, when a coincidence cannot be deduced from known laws nor proved by experiment to be itself a case of causation, the frequency of its occurrence is the only evidence from which we can infer that it is the result of a law. Not, however, its absolute frequency. The question is not whether the coincidence occurs often or seldom, in the ordinary sense of those terms, but whether it occurs more often than chance will account for, more often than might rationally be expected if the coincidence were casual. We have to decide, therefore, what degree of frequency in a coincidence chance will account for, and to this there can be no general answer. We can only state the principle by which the answer must be determined; the answer itself will be different in every different case.

Suppose that one of the phenomena, A, exists always, and the other phenomenon, B, only occasionally; it follows that every instance of B will be an instance of its coincidence with A, and yet the coincidence will be merely casual, not the result of any connection between them. . . . The uniformity, great though it be, is no greater than would occur on the supposition that no such connection exists.

On the other hand, suppose that we were inquiring whether there be any connection between rain and any particular wind. Rain, we know, occasionally occurs with every wind; therefore, the connection, if it exists, cannot be an actual law; but still rain may be connected with some particular wind through causation, that is, though they cannot be always effects of the same cause (for if so they would regularly co-exist), there may be some causes common to the two, so that in so far as either is produced by those common causes, they will, from the laws of the causes, be found to co-exist. How, then, shall we ascertain this? The obvious answer is by observing whether rain occurs with one wind more frequently than with any other. That, however, is not enough; for perhaps that one wind blows more frequently than any other; so that its blowing more frequently in rainy weather is no more than would happen although it had no connection with the causes of rain, provided it were not connected with causes adverse to rain. In England, westerly winds blow during about twice as great a portion of the year as easterly. If, therefore, it rains only twice as often with a westerly as with an easterly wind, we have no reason to infer that any law of nature is concerned in the coincidence. If it rains more than twice as often, we may be sure that some law is concerned; either there is some cause in nature which, in this climate, tends to produce both rain and a westerly wind, or a westerly wind has itself some tendency to produce rain. But if it rains less than twice as often, we may draw a directly opposite inference; the one, instead of being a cause or connected with causes of the other, must be connected with causes adverse to it or with the absence of some cause which produces it; and though it may still rain much oftener with a westerly wind than with an easterly, so far would this be from proving any connection between the phenomena that the connection proved would be between rain and an easterly wind to which, in mere frequency of coincidence, it is less allied.

Here, then, are two examples; in one, the greatest possible frequency of coincidence, with no instance whatever to the contrary, does not prove that there is any law; in the other, a much less frequency of coincidence, even when non-coincidence is still more frequent, does prove that there is a law. In both cases the principle is the same. In both we consider the positive frequency of the phenomena themselves and how great frequency of coincidence that must of itself bring about without supposing any connection between them, provided there be no repugnance, provided neither be connected with any cause tending to frustrate the other. If we find a greater frequency of coincidence than this, we conclude that there is some connection; if a less frequency, that there is some repugnance. In the former case, we conclude that one of the phenomena can under some circumstances cause the other or that there exists something capable of causing them both; in the latter, that one of them or some cause which produces one of them is capable of counteracting the production of the other. We have thus to deduct from the observed frequency of coincidence as much as may be the effect of chance, that is, of the mere frequency of the phenomena themselves, and, if anything remains, what does remain is the residual fact which proves the existence of a law.

The frequency of the phenomena can only be ascertained within definite limits of space and time, depending as it does on the quantity and distribution of the primeval natural agents of which we can know nothing beyond the boundaries of human observation, since no law, no regularity, can be traced in it enabling us to infer the unknown from the known. But for the present purpose this is no disadvantage, the question being confined within the same limits as the data. The coincidences occurred in certain places and times, and within those we can estimate the frequency with which such coincidences would be produced by chance. If, then, we find from observation that A exists in one case out of every two and B in one case out of every three, then, if there be neither connection nor repugnance between them or between any of their causes, the instances in which A and B will both exist, that is to say, will co-exist, will be one case in every six. For A exists in three cases out of six; and B, existing in one case out of every three without regard to the presence or absence of A, will exist in one case out of those three. There will, therefore, be, of the whole number of cases, two in which A exists without B, one case of B without A, two in which neither B nor A exists, and one case out of six in which they both exist. If, then, in point of fact, they are found to co-exist oftener than in one case out of six, and, consequently, A does not exist without B so often as twice in three times, nor B without A so often as once in every twice, there is some cause in existence which tends to produce a conjunction between A and B.

Generalizing the result, we may say that, if A occurs in a larger proportion of the cases where B is than of the cases where B is not, then will B also occur in a larger proportion of the cases where A is than of the cases where A is not, and there is some connection, through causation, between A and B. If we could ascend to the causes of the two phenomena, we should find, at some stage, either proximate or remote, some cause or causes common to both, and, if we could ascertain what these are, we could frame a generalization which would be true without restriction of place or time; but, until we can do so, the fact of a connection between the two phenomena remains an empirical law.

CHAPTER XV*

OF THE CALCULATION OF CHANCES

1. *Foundation of the doctrine of chances, as taught by mathematics*

"Probability," says Laplace,[1] "has reference partly to our ignorance, partly to our knowledge. We know that among three or more events, one, and only one, must happen; but there is nothing leading us to believe that any one of them will happen rather than the others. In this state of indecision, it is impossible for us to pronounce with certainty on their occurrence. It is, however, probable that any one of these events, selected at pleasure, will not take place; because we perceive several cases, all equally possible, which exclude its occurrence, and only one which favors it.

"The theory of chances consists in reducing all events of the

---

*[Chapter XVIII of the eighth edition.]

[1] *Essai philosophique sur les probabilités*, fifth Paris edition, p. 7

same kind to a certain number of cases equally possible, that is, such that we are *equally undecided* as to their existence; and in determining the number of these cases which are favorable to the event of which the probability is sought. The ratio of that number to the number of all the possible cases is the measure of the probability; which is thus a fraction, having for its numerator the number of cases favorable to the event, and for its denominator the number of all the cases which are possible."

To a calculation of chances, then, according to Laplace, two things are necessary: we must know that of several events some one will certainly happen, and no more than one; and we must not know, nor have any reason to expect, that it will be one of these events rather than another. It has been contended that these are not the only requisites, and that Laplace has overlooked, in the general theoretical statement, a necessary part of the foundation of the doctrine of chances. To be able (it has been said) to pronounce two events equally probable, it is not enough that we should know that one or the other must happen and should have no grounds for conjecturing which. Experience must have shown that the two events are of equally frequent occurrence. Why, in tossing up a half-penny, do we reckon it equally probable that we shall throw cross or pile? Because we know that in any great number of throws, cross and pile are thrown about equally often, and that the more throws we make, the more nearly the equality is perfect. We may know this, if we please, by actual experiment, or by the daily experience which life affords of events of the same general character, or, deductively, from the effect of mechanical laws on a symmetrical body acted upon by forces varying indefinitely in quantity and direction. We may know it, in short, either by specific experience or on the evidence of our general knowledge of nature. But, in one way or the other, we must know it to justify us in calling the two events equally probable, and, if we knew it not, we should proceed as much at haphazard in staking equal sums on the result, as in laying odds.

This view of the subject was taken in the first edition of the present work, but I have since become convinced that the theory of chances, as conceived by Laplace and by mathematicians generally, has not the fundamental fallacy which I had ascribed to it.

We must remember that the probability of an event is not a quality of the event itself, but a mere name for the degree of ground which we or someone else have for expecting it. The probability of an event to one person is a different thing from the probability of the same event to another, or to the same person after he has acquired additional evidence. The probability to me that an individual of whom I know nothing but his name will die within the year is totally altered by my being told the next minute that he is in the last stage of a consumption. Yet this makes no difference in the event itself nor in any of the causes on which it depends. Every event is in itself certain, not probable; if we knew all, we should either know positively that it will happen or positively that it will not. But its probability to us means the degree of expectation of its occurrence which we are warranted in entertaining by our present evidence.

Bearing this in mind, I think it must be admitted that even when we have no knowledge whatever to guide our expectations, except the knowledge that what happens must be some one of a certain number of possibilities, we may still reasonably judge that one supposition is more probable *to us* than another supposition, and, if we have any interest at stake, we shall best provide for it by acting conformably to that judgment.

2. *The doctrine tenable*

. . . .

The common theory, therefore, of the calculation of chances appears to be tenable. Even when we know nothing except the number of the possible and mutually excluding contingencies and are entirely ignorant of their comparative frequency, we may have grounds, and grounds numerically appreciable, for acting on one supposition rather than on another, and this is the meaning of probability.

3. *On what foundation it really rests*

The principle, however, on which the reasoning proceeds is sufficiently evident. It is the obvious one that, when the cases

which exist are shared among several kinds, it is impossible that
each of those kinds should be a majority of the whole; on the
contrary, there must be a majority against each kind, except one
at most; and, if any kind has more than its share in proportion to
the total number, the others collectively must have less. Granting
this axiom and assuming that we have no ground for selecting any
one kind as more likely than the rest to surpass the average proportion, it follows that we cannot rationally presume this of any,
which we should do if we were to bet in favor of it, receiving less
odds than in the ratio of the number of the other kinds. Even,
therefore, in this extreme case of the calculation of probabilities,
which does not rest on special experience at all, the logical ground
of the process is our knowledge — such knowledge as we then have
— of the laws governing the frequency of occurrence of the different
cases; but in this case the knowledge is limited to that which, being
universal and axiomatic, does not require reference to specific
experience or to any considerations arising out of the special nature
of the problem under discussion.

Except, however, in such cases as games of chance, where the
very purpose in view requires ignorance instead of knowledge, I can
conceive no case in which we ought to be satisfied with such an
estimate of chances as this — an estimate founded on the absolute
minimum of knowledge respecting the subject. It is plain that, in
the case of the colored balls, a very slight ground of surmise that
the white balls were really more numerous than either of the other
colors would suffice to vitiate the whole of the calculations made
in our previous state of indifference. It would place us in that
position of more advanced knowledge in which the probabilities, to
us, would be different from what they were before; and in estimating these new probabilities we should have to proceed on a totally
different set of data, furnished no longer by mere counting of
possible suppositions but by specific knowledge of facts. Such
data it should always be our endeavor to obtain; and in all inquiries, unless on subjects equally beyond the range of our means of
knowledge and our practical uses, they may be obtained, if not
good, at least better than none at all.[2]

[2]It even appears to me that the calculation of chances, where there are no
data grounded either on special experience or on special inference, must, in an

It is obvious, too, that even when the probabilities are derived from observation and experiment a very slight improvement in the data, by better observations, or by taking into fuller consideration the special circumstances of the case, is of more use than the most elaborate application of the calculus to probabilities founded on the data in their previous state of inferiority. The neglect of this obvious reflection has given rise to misapplications of the calculus of probabilities which have made it the real opprobrium of mathematics. It is sufficient to refer to the applications made of it to the credibility of witnesses and to the correctness of the verdicts of juries. In regard to the first, common sense would dictate that it is impossible to strike a general average of the veracity and other qualifications for true testimony of mankind, or of any class of them, and, even if it were possible, the employment of it for such a purpose implies a misapprehension of the use of averages, which serve, indeed, to protect those whose interest is at stake against mistaking the general result of large masses of instances, but are of extremely small value as grounds of expectation in any one individual instance unless the case be one of those in which the great majority of individual instances do not differ much from the average. In the case of a witness, persons of common sense would draw their conclusions from the degree of consistency of his statements, his conduct under cross-examination, and the relation of the case itself to his interests, his partialities, and his mental capacity, instead of applying so rude a standard (even if it were

immense majority of cases, break down, from sheer impossibility of assigning any principle by which to be guided in setting out the list of possibilities. In the case of the colored balls we have no difficulty in making the enumeration because we ourselves determine what the possibilities shall be. But suppose a case more analogous to those which occur in nature: instead of three colors, let there be in the box all possible colors, we being supposed ignorant of the comparative frequency with which different colors occur in nature or in the productions of art. How is the list of cases to be made out? Is every distinct shade to count as a color? If so, is the test to be a common eye, or an educated eye — a painter's, for instance? On the answer to these questions would depend whether the chances against some particular color would be estimated at ten, twenty, or perhaps five hundred to one. While, if we knew from experience that the particular color occurs on an average a certain number of times in every hundred or thousand, we should not require to know anything either of the frequency or of the number of the other possibilities.

capable of being verified) as the ratio between the number of true and the number of erroneous statements which he may be supposed to make in the course of his life.

. . . .

. . . Before applying the doctrine of chances to any scientific purpose, the foundation must be laid for an evaluation of the chances by possessing ourselves of the utmost attainable amount of positive knowledge. The knowledge required is that of the comparative frequency with which the different events in fact occur. For the purposes, therefore, of the present work, it is allowable to suppose that conclusions respecting the probability of a fact of a particular kind rest on our knowledge of the proportion between the cases in which facts of that kind occur and those in which they do not occur, this knowledge being either derived from specific experiment, or deduced from our knowledge of the causes in operation which tend to produce, compared with those which tend to prevent, the fact in question.

Such calculation of chances is grounded on an induction, and, to render the calculation legitimate, the induction must be a valid one. It is not less an induction though it does not prove that the event occurs in all cases of a given description, but only that out of a given number of such cases it occurs in about so many. The fraction which mathematicians use to designate the probability of an event is the ratio of these two numbers, the ascertained proportion between the number of cases in which the event occurs and the sum of all the cases, those in which it occurs and in which it does not occur, taken together. In playing at cross and pile, the description of cases concerned are throws, and the probability of cross is one-half because if we throw often enough cross is thrown about once in every two throws. In the cast of a die, the probability of ace is one-sixth; not simply because there are six possible throws of which ace is one, and because we do not know any reason why one should turn up rather than another — though I have admitted the validity of this ground in default of a better — but because we do actually know, either by reasoning or by experience, that in a hundred or a million of throws ace is thrown in about onesixth of that number, or once in six times.

4. *Its ultimate dependence on causation*

I say, "either by reasoning or by experience," meaning specific experience. But in estimating probabilities, it is not a matter of indifference from which of these two sources we derive our assurance. The probability of events, as calculated from their mere frequency in past experience, affords a less secure basis for practical guidance than their probability as deduced from an equally accurate knowledge of the frequency of occurrence of their causes.

The generalization that an event occurs in ten out of every hundred cases of a given description is as real an induction as if the generalization were that it occurs in all cases. But when we arrive at the conclusion by merely counting instances in actual experience and comparing the number of cases in which A has been present with the number in which it has been absent, the evidence is only that of the method of agreement, and the conclusion amounts only to an empirical law. We can make a step beyond this when we can ascend to the causes on which the occurrence of A or its non-occurrence will depend and form an estimate of the comparative frequency of the causes favorable and of those unfavorable to the occurrence. These are data of a higher order by which the empirical law derived from a mere numerical comparison of affirmative and negative instances will be either corrected or confirmed, and in either case we shall obtain a more correct measure of probability than is given by that numerical comparison. It has been well remarked that in the kind of examples by which the doctrine of chances is usually illustrated, that of balls in a box, the estimate of probabilities is supported by reasons of causation stronger than specific experience. "What is the reason that in a box where there are nine black balls and one white, we expect to draw a black ball nine times as much (in other words, nine times as often, frequency being the gauge of intensity in expectation) as a white? Obviously because the local conditions are nine times as favorable; because the hand may alight in nine places and get a black ball, while it can only alight in one place and find a white ball; just for the same reason that we do not expect to succeed in finding a friend in a crowd, the conditions in order that we and he should come together being many and difficult. This of course would not hold to the same extent were the white balls of smaller size than the black, neither would the probability remain the same; the larger ball would be much more likely to meet the hand."[3]

. . . .

Notwithstanding, however, the abstract superiority of an estimate of probability grounded on causes, it is a fact that, in almost all cases in which chances admit of estimation sufficiently precise to render their numerical appreciation of any practical value, the numerical data are not drawn from knowledge of the causes but from experience of the events themselves. The probabilities of life at different ages or in different climates, the probabilities of recovery from a particular disease, the chances of the birth of male or female offspring, the chances of the destruction of houses or other property by fire, the chances of the loss of a ship in a particular voyage are deduced from bills of mortality, returns from hospitals, registers of births, of shipwrecks, etc., that is, from the observed frequency not of the causes but of the effects. The reason is that in all these classes of facts the causes are either not amenable to direct observation at all or not with the requisite precision, and we have no means of judging of their frequency except from the empirical law afforded by the frequency of the effects. The inference does not the less depend on causation alone. We reason from an effect to a similar effect by passing through the cause. If the actuary of an insurance office infers from his tables that among a hundred persons now living of a particular age five on the average will attain the age of seventy, his inference is legitimate not for the simple reason that this is the proportion who have lived till seventy in times past, but because the fact of their having so lived shows that this is the proportion existing, at that place and time, between the causes which prolong life to the age of seventy and those tending to bring it to an earlier close.[4]

[3] *Prospective Review* for February, 1850.

[4] The writer last quoted says that the valuation of chances by comparing the number of cases in which the event occurs with the number in which it does not occur, "would generally be wholly erroneous," and "is not the true theory of probability." It is at least that which forms the foundation of insurance and of all those calculations of chances in the business of life which experience so abundantly verifies. The reason which the reviewer gives for rejecting the theory is that it "would regard an event as certain which had hitherto never failed; which is exceedingly far from the truth, even for a very large number of

CHAPTER XVI

OF THE EVIDENCE OF THE LAW OF UNIVERSAL CAUSATION

1. *The law of causality does not rest on an instinct*

We have now completed our review of the logical processes by which the laws or uniformities of the sequence of phenomena and those uniformities in their co-existence which depend on the laws of their sequence are ascertained or tested. As we recognized in the commencement and have been enabled to see more clearly in the progress of the investigation, the basis of all these logical operations is the law of causation. The validity of all the inductive methods depends on the assumption that every event, or the beginning of every phenomenon, must have some cause, some antecedent, on the existence of which it is invariably and unconditionally consequent. In the method of agreement this is obvious, that method avowedly proceeding on the supposition that we have found the true cause as soon as we have negatived every other. The assertion is equally true of the method of difference. That method authorizes us to infer a general law from two instances: one, in which A exists together with a multitude of other circumstances, and B follows; another, in which, A being removed and all other circumstances remaining the same, B is prevented. What, however, does this prove? It proves that B, in the particular instance, cannot have had any other cause than A; but to conclude from this that A was the cause or that A will on other occasions be

constant successes." This is not a defect in a particular theory, but in any theory of chances. No principle of evaluation can provide for such a case as that which the reviewer supposes. If an event has never once failed, in a number of trials sufficient to eliminate chance, it really has all the certainty which can be given by an empirical law; it *is* certain during the continuance of the same collocation of causes which existed during the observations. If it ever fails, it is in consequence of some change in that collocation. Now, no theory of chances will enable us to infer the future probability of an event from the past, if the causes in operation, capable of influencing the event, have intermediately undergone a change.

*[Chapter XXI of the eighth edition.]

followed by B is only allowable on the assumption that B must have some cause, that among its antecedents in any single instance in which it occurs, there must be one which has the capacity of producing it at other times. This being admitted, it is seen that in the case in question that antecedent can be no other than A; but that, if it be no other than A, it must be A is not proved, by these instances at least, but taken for granted. There is no need to spend time in proving that the same thing is true of the other inductive methods. The universality of the law of causation is assumed in them all.

But is this assumption warranted? Doubtless (it may be said) *most* phenomena are connected as effects with some antecedent or cause, that is, are never produced unless some assignable fact has preceded them, but the very circumstance that complicated processes of induction are sometimes necessary shows that cases exist in which this regular order of succession is not apparent to our unaided apprehension. If, then, the processes which bring these cases within the same category with the rest require that we should assume the universality of the very law which they do not at first sight appear to exemplify, is not this a *petitio principii?* Can we prove a proposition by an argument which takes it for granted? And if not so proved, on what evidence does it rest?

For this difficulty, which I have purposely stated in the strongest terms it will admit of, the school of metaphysicians who have long predominated in this country find a ready salvo. They affirm that the universality of causation is a truth which we cannot help believing, that the belief in it is an instinct, one of the laws of our believing faculty. As the proof of this, they say, and they have nothing else to say, that everybody does believe it, and they number it among the propositions, rather numerous in their catalogue, which may be logically argued against and perhaps cannot be logically proved, but which are of higher authority than logic, and so essentially inherent in the human mind that even he who denies them in speculation shows by his habitual practice that his arguments make no impression upon himself.

Into the merits of this question, considered as one of psychology, it would be foreign to my purpose to enter here, but I must protest against adducing, as evidence of the truth of a fact in external nature, the disposition, however strong or however general, of the human mind to believe it. . . .

Were we to suppose (what it is perfectly possible to imagine) that the present order of the universe were brought to an end, and that a chaos succeeded in which there was no fixed succession of events, and the past gave no assurance of the future; if a human being were miraculously kept alive to witness this change, he surely would soon cease to believe in any uniformity, the uniformity itself no longer existing. If this be admitted, the belief in uniformity either is not an instinct, or it is an instinct conquerable, like all other instincts, by acquired knowledge.

.   .   .   .

2. — but on an induction by simple enumeration

As was observed in a former place, the belief we entertain in the universality, throughout nature, of the law of cause and effect is itself an instance of induction, and by no means one of the earliest which any of us, or which mankind in general, can have made. We arrive at this universal law by generalization from many laws of inferior generality. We should never have had the notion of causation (in the philosophical meaning of the term) as a condition of all phenomena unless many cases of causation, or, in other words, many partial uniformities of sequence, had previously become familiar. The more obvious of the particular uniformities suggest and give evidence of the general uniformity, and the general uniformity, once established, enables us to prove the remainder of the particular uniformities of which it is made up. As, however, all rigorous processes of induction presuppose the general uniformity, our knowledge of the particular uniformities from which it was first inferred was not, of course, derived from rigorous induction, but from the loose and uncertain mode of induction *per enumerationem simplicem*, and the law of universal causation, being collected from results so obtained, cannot itself rest on any better foundation.

It would seem, therefore, that induction *per enumerationem simplicem* not only is not necessarily an illicit logical process, but is in reality the only kind of induction possible, since the more elaborate process depends for its validity on a law itself obtained in that inartificial mode. Is there not, then, an inconsistency in contrasting the looseness of one method with the rigidity of another, when that other is indebted to the looser method for its own foundation?

The inconsistency, however, is only apparent. Assuredly, if induction by simple enumeration were an invalid process, no process grounded on it could be valid; just as no reliance could be placed on telescopes if we could not trust our eyes. But though a valid process, it is a fallible one, and fallible in very different degrees; if, therefore, we can substitute for the more fallible forms of the process an operation grounded on the same process in a less fallible form, we shall have effected a very material improvement. And this is what scientific induction does.

. . . .

3. *In what cases such induction is allowable*

Now the precariousness of the method of simple enumeration is in an inverse ratio to the largeness of the generalization. The process is delusive and insufficient, exactly in proportion as the subject-matter of the observation is special and limited in extent. As the sphere widens, this unscientific method becomes less and less liable to mislead, and the most universal class of truths, the law of causation, for instance, and the principles of number and of geometry, are duly and satisfactorily proved by that method alone, nor are they susceptible of any other proof.

With respect to the whole class of generalizations of which we have recently treated, the uniformities which depend on causation, the truth of the remark just made follows by obvious inference from the principles laid down in the preceding chapters. When a fact has been observed a certain number of times to be true and is not in any instance known to be false, if we at once affirm that fact as a universal truth or law of nature without either testing it by any of the four methods of induction or deducing it from other known laws, we shall, in general, err grossly, but we are perfectly justified in affirming it as an empirical law, true within certain limits of time, place, and circumstance, provided the number of coincidences be greater than can with any probability be ascribed to chance. The reason for not extending it beyond those limits is that the fact of its holding true within them may be a consequence of collocations which cannot be concluded to exist in one place because they exist in another, or may be dependent on the accidental absence of counteracting agencies, which any variation of time or the smallest change of circumstances may possibly bring into play. If we suppose, then, the subject-matter of any generalization to be so widely diffused that there is no time, no place, and no combination of circumstances but must afford an example either of its truth or of its falsity, and if it be never found otherwise than true, its truth cannot be contingent on any collocations, unless such as exist at all times and places; nor can it be frustrated by any counteracting agencies, unless by such as never actually occur. It is, therefore, an empirical law co-extensive with all human experience; at which point the distinction between empirical laws and laws of nature vanishes, and the proposition takes its place among the most firmly established as well as largest truths accessible to science.

.   .   .   .

BOOK IV

Of Operations Subsidiary to Induction

"Clear and distinct ideas are terms which, though familiar and frequent in men's mouths, I have reason to think every one who uses does not perfectly understand. And possibly it is but here and there one who gives himself the trouble to consider them so far as to know what he himself or others precisely mean by them; I have, therefore, in most places, chose to put determinate or determined, instead of clear and distinct, as more likely to direct men's thoughts to my meaning in this matter." — LOCKE's *Essay on the Human Understanding;* Epistle to the Reader.

"Il ne peut y avoir qu'une méthode parfaite, qui est la *méthode naturelle;* on nomme ainsi un arrangement dans lequel les êtres du même genre seraient plus voisins entre eux que ceux de tous les autres genres; les genres du même ordre, plus que ceux de tous les autres ordres; et ainsi de suite. Cette méthode est l'idéal auquel l'histoire naturelle doit tendre; car il est évident que si l'on y parvenait, l'on aurait l'expression exacte et complète de la nature entière." — CUVIER, *Règne Animal*, Introduction.

"Deux grandes notions philosophiques dominent la théorie fondamentale de la méthode naturelle proprement dite, savoir la formation des groupes naturels, et ensuite leur succession hiérarchique." — COMTE, *Cours de Philosophie Positive,* 42me leçon.

CHAPTER I*

OF ABSTRACTION, OR THE FORMATION OF CONCEPTIONS

1. *The comparison which is a preliminary to induction implies general conceptions*

The metaphysical inquiry into the nature and composition of what have been called "abstract ideas," or, in other words, of the notions which answer in the mind to classes and to general names, belongs not to logic but to a different science, and our purpose

*[Chapter II of the eighth edition.]

292

does not require that we should enter upon it here. We are only concerned with the universally acknowledged fact that such notions or conceptions do exist. The mind can conceive a multitude of individual things as one assemblage or class, and general names do really suggest to us certain ideas or mental representations, otherwise we could not use the names with consciousness of a meaning. Whether the idea called up by a general name is composed of the various circumstances in which all the individuals denoted by the name agree, and of no others (which is the doctrine of Locke, Brown, and the Conceptualists), or whether it be the idea of some one of those individuals, clothed in its individualizing peculiarities, but with the accompanying knowledge that those peculiarities are not properties of the class (which is the doctrine of Berkeley, Mr. Bailey[1], and the modern Nominalists), or whether (as held by Mr. James Mill) the idea of the class is that of a miscellaneous assemblage of individuals belonging to the class, or whether, finally, it be any one or any other of all these, according to the accidental circumstances of the case, certain it is, that *some* idea or mental conception is suggested by a general name whenever we either hear it or employ it with consciousness of a meaning. And this, which we may call, if we please, a general idea, *represents* in our minds the whole class of things to which the name is applied. Whenever we think or reason concerning the class, we do so by means of this idea. And the voluntary power which the mind has of attending to one part of what is present to it at any moment and neglecting another part enables us to keep our reasonings and conclusions respecting the class unaffected by anything in the idea or mental image which is not really, or, at least, which we do not really believe to be common to the whole class.[2]

[1] Mr. Bailey has given the best statement of this theory. "The general name," he says, "raises up the image sometimes of one individual of the class formerly seen, sometimes of another, not unfrequently of many individuals in succession; and it sometimes suggests an image made of elements from several different objects, by a latent process of which I am not conscious." (Letters on the Philosophy of the Human Mind, 1st series, letter 22.) But Mr. Bailey must allow that we carry on inductions and ratiocinations respecting the class by means of this idea or conception of some one individual in it. This is all I require. The name of a class calls up some idea, through which we can, to all intents and purposes, think of the class as such and not solely of an individual member of it.

[2] I have entered rather fully into this question in chap. XVII of *An Examina-*

There are, then, such things as general conceptions, or conceptions by means of which we can think generally; and when we form a set of phenomena into a class, that is, when we compare them with one another to ascertain in what they agree, some general conception is implied in this mental operation. And inasmuch as such a comparison is a necessary preliminary to induction, it is most true that induction could not go on without general conceptions.

2. — *but these need not be pre-existent*

But it does not, therefore, follow that these general conceptions must have existed in the mind previously to the comparison. It is not a law of our intellect that in comparing things with each other and taking note of their agreement we merely recognize as realized in the outward world something that we already had in our minds. The conception originally found its way to us as the *result* of such a comparison. It was obtained (in metaphysical phrase) by *abstraction* from individual things. These things may be things which we perceived or thought of on former occasions, but they may also be the things which we are perceiving or thinking of on the very occasion. When Kepler compared the observed places of the planet Mars and found that they agreed in being points of an elliptic circumference, he applied a general conception which was already in his mind, having been derived from his former experience. But this is by no means universally the case. When we compare several objects and find them to agree in being white, or when we compare the various species of ruminating animals and find them to agree in being cloven-footed, we have just as much a general conception in our minds as Kepler had in his; we have the conception of "a white thing," or the conception of "a cloven-footed animal." But no one supposes that we necessarily bring these conceptions with us and *superinduce* them (to adopt Dr. Whewell's expression) upon the facts, because in these simple cases everybody sees that the very act of comparison which ends in our connecting the facts by means of the conception may be

tion of *Sir William Hamilton's Philosophy*, headed "The Doctrine of Concepts or General Notions," which contains my last views on the subject.

the source from which we derive the conception itself. If we had never seen any white object or had never seen any cloven-footed animal before, we should at the same time and by the same mental act acquire the idea and employ it for the colligation of the observed phenomena. Kepler, on the contrary, really had to bring the idea with him and superinduce it upon the facts; he could not evolve it out of them; if he had not already had the idea, he would not have been able to acquire it by a comparison of the planet's positions. But this inability was a mere accident; the idea of an ellipse could have been acquired from the paths of the planets as effectually as from anything else, if the paths had not happened to be invisible. If the planet had left a visible track, and we had been so placed that we could see it at the proper angle, we might have abstracted our original idea of an ellipse from the planetary orbit. Indeed, every conception which can be made the instrument for connecting a set of facts might have been originally evolved from those very facts. The conception is a conception *of* something, and that which it is a conception of is really *in* the facts and might, under some supposable circumstances or by some supposable extension of the faculties which we actually possess, have been detected in them. And not only is this always in itself possible, but it actually happens in almost all cases in which the obtaining of the right conception is a matter of any considerable difficulty. For if there be no new conception required, if one of those already familiar to mankind will serve the purpose, the accident of being the first to whom the right one occurs may happen to almost anybody, at least in the case of a set of phenomena which the whole scientific world are engaged in attempting to connect. The honor, in Kepler's case, was that of the accurate, patient, and toilsome calculations by which he compared the results that followed from his different guesses with the observations of Tycho Brahe, but the merit was very small of guessing an ellipse; the only wonder is that men had not guessed it before, nor could they have failed to do so if there had not existed an obstinate *a priori* prejudice that the heavenly bodies must move, if not in a circle, in some combination of circles.

The really difficult cases are those in which the conception destined to create light and order out of darkness and confusion has to be sought for among the very phenomena which it afterward serves to arrange. Why, according to Dr. Whewell himself, did the ancients fail in discovering the laws of mechanics, that is, of equilibrium and of the communication of motion? Because they had not or, at least, had not clearly the ideas or conceptions of pressure and resistance, momentum, and uniform and accelerating force. And whence could they have obtained these ideas except from the very facts of equilibrium and motion? The tardy development of several of the physical sciences, for example, of optics, electricity, magnetism, and the higher generalizations of chemistry, he ascribes to the fact that mankind had not yet possessed themselves of the idea of polarity, that is, the idea of opposite properties in opposite directions. But what was there to suggest such an idea until, by a separate examination of several of these different branches of knowledge, it was shown that the facts of each of them did present, in some instances at least, the curious phenomenon of opposite properties in opposite directions? The thing was superficially manifest only in two cases, those of the magnet and of electrified bodies, and there the conception was encumbered with the circumstance of material poles or fixed points in the body itself, in which points this opposition of properties seemed to be inherent. The first comparison and abstraction had led only to this conception of poles, and, if anything corresponding to that conception had existed in the phenomena of chemistry or optics, the difficulty now justly considered so great would have been extremely small. The obscurity arose from the fact that the polarities in chemistry and optics were distinct species, though of the same genus, with the polarities in electricity and magnetism, and that, in order to assimilate the phenomena to one another, it was necessary to compare a polarity without poles, such, for instance, as is exemplified in the polarization of light, and the polarity with (apparent) poles, which we see in the magnet, and to recognize that these polarities, while different in many other respects, agree in the one character which is expressed by the phrase opposite properties in opposite directions. From the result of such a comparison it was that the minds of scientific men formed this new general conception, between which and the first confused feeling of an analogy between some of the phenomena of light and those of electricity and magnetism, there is a long interval, filled up by the labors and more or less sagacious suggestions of many superior minds.

The conceptions, then, which we employ for the colligation and methodization of facts do not develop themselves from within, but are impressed upon the mind from without; they are never obtained otherwise than by way of comparison and abstraction and, in the most important and the most numerous cases, are evolved by abstraction from the very phenomena which it is their office to colligate. I am far, however, from wishing to imply that it is not often a very difficult thing to perform this process of abstraction well, or that the success of an inductive operation does not, in many cases, principally depend on the skill with which we perform it. Bacon was quite justified in designating as one of the principal obstacles to good induction general conceptions wrongly formed, "notiones temerè à rebus abstractae," to which Dr. Whewell adds that not only does bad abstraction make bad induction, but that, in order to perform induction well, we must have abstracted well; our general conceptions must be "clear" and "appropriate" to the matter in hand.

3. *A general conception, originally the result of a comparison, becomes itself the type of a comparison*

In attempting to show what the difficulty in this matter really is and how it is surmounted, I must beg the reader, once for all, to bear this in mind: that although, in discussing the opinions of a different school of philosophy, I am willing to adopt their language and to speak, therefore, of connecting facts through the instrumentality of a conception, this technical phraseology means neither more nor less than what is commonly called comparing the facts with one another and determining in what they agree. Nor has the technical expression even the advantage of being metaphysically correct. The facts are not *connected*, except in a merely metaphorical acceptation of the term. The *ideas* of the facts may become connected, that is, we may be led to think of them together, but this consequence is no more than what may be produced by any casual association. What really takes place is, I conceive, more philosophically expressed by the common word "comparison"

than by the phrases "to connect" or "to superinduce." For, as the
general conception is itself obtained by a comparison of particular
phenomena, so, when obtained, the mode in which we apply it to
other phenomena is again by comparison. We compare phenomena with each other to get the conception, and we then compare those and other phenomena *with* the conception. We get the
conception of an animal (for instance) by comparing different
animals, and when we afterward see a creature resembling an
animal, we compare it with our general conception of an animal,
and, if it agrees with that general conception, we include it in the
class. The conception becomes the type of comparison.

And we need only consider what comparison is to see that where
the objects are more than two, and still more when they are an
indefinite number, a type of some sort is an indispensable condition
of the comparison. When we have to arrange and classify a great
number of objects according to their agreements and differences,
we do not make a confused attempt to compare all with all. We
know that two things are as much as the mind can easily attend
to at a time, and we therefore fix upon one of the objects, either
at hazard or because it offers in a peculiarly striking manner some
important character, and, taking this as our standard, compare it
with one object after another. If we find a second object which
presents a remarkable agreement with the first, inducing us to
class them together, the question instantly arises, in what particular
circumstances do they agree? and to take notice of these circumstances is already a first stage of abstraction, giving rise to a
general conception. Having advanced thus far, when we now take
in hand a third object, we naturally ask ourselves the question, not
merely whether this third object agrees with the first, but whether
it agrees with it in the same circumstances in which the second did?
in other words, whether it agrees with the general conception which
has been obtained by abstraction from the first and second? Thus
we see the tendency of general conceptions, as soon as formed, to
substitute themselves as types for whatever individual objects
previously answered that purpose in our comparisons. We may,
perhaps, find that no considerable number of other objects agree
with this first general conception, and that we must drop the
conception and, beginning again with a different individual case,

proceed by fresh comparisons to a different general conception. Sometimes, again, we find that the same conception will serve by merely leaving out some of its circumstances, and, by this higher effort of abstraction, we obtain a still more general conception; as, in the case formerly referred to, the scientific world rose from the conception of poles to the general conception of opposite properties in opposite directions, or as those South-Sea islanders, whose conception of a quadruped had been abstracted from hogs (the only animals of that description which they had seen), when they afterward compared that conception with other quadrupeds, dropped some of the circumstances and arrived at the more general conception which Europeans associate with the term.

These brief remarks contain, I believe, all that is well grounded in the doctrine that the conception by which the mind arranges and gives unity to phenomena must be furnished by the mind itself, and that we find the right conception by a tentative process, trying first one and then another until we hit the mark. The conception is not furnished *by* the mind until it has been furnished *to* the mind, and the facts which supply it are sometimes extraneous facts, but more often the very facts which we are attempting to arrange by it. It is quite true, however, that, in endeavoring to arrange the facts, at whatever point we begin, we never advance three steps without forming a general conception, more or less distinct and precise, and that this general conception becomes the clue which we instantly endeavor to trace through the rest of the facts, or,.rather, becomes the standard with which we thenceforth compare them. If we are not satisfied with the agreements which we discover among the phenomena by comparing them with this type or with some still more general conception which by an additional stage of abstraction we can form from the type, we change our path and look out for other agreements; we recommence the comparison from a different starting-point and so generate a different set of general conceptions. This is the tentative process which Dr. Whewell speaks of, and which has not unnaturally suggested the theory that the conception is supplied by the mind itself, since the different conceptions which the mind successively tries it either already possessed from its previous experience, or they were supplied to it in the first stage of the corresponding act of comparison, so that, in the subsequent part of the process, the conception manifested itself as something compared with the phenomena, not evolved from them.

CHAPTER II*

OF CLASSIFICATION, AS SUBSIDIARY TO INDUCTION

1. *Theory of natural groups*

There is no property of objects which may not be taken, if we please, as the foundation for a classification or mental grouping of those objects, and in our first attempts we are likely to select for that purpose properties which are simple, easily conceived, and perceptible on a first view, without any previous process of thought. Thus Tournefort's arrangement of plants was founded on the shape and divisions of the corolla, and that which is commonly called the Linnaean (though Linnaeus also suggested another and more scientific arrangement) was grounded chiefly on the number of the stamens and pistils.

But these classifications, which are at first recommended by the facility they afford of ascertaining to what class any individual belongs, are seldom much adapted to the ends of that classification which is the subject of our present remarks. The Linnaean arrangement answers the purpose of making us think together of all those kinds of plants which possess the same number of stamens and pistils, but to think of them in that manner is of little use since we seldom have anything to affirm in common of the plants which have a given number of stamens and pistils. . . .

The ends of scientific classification are best answered when the objects are formed into groups respecting which a greater number

*[Chapter VII of the eighth edition.]

of general propositions can be made, and those propositions more important, than could be made respecting any other groups into which the same things could be distributed. The properties, therefore, according to which objects are classified should, if possible, be those which are causes of many other properties, or, at any rate, which are sure marks of them. Causes are preferable, both as being the surest and most direct of marks, and as being themselves the properties on which it is of most use that our attention should be strongly fixed. But the property which is the cause of the chief peculiarities of a class is unfortunately seldom fitted to serve also as the diagnostic of the class. Instead of the cause, we must generally select some of its more prominent effects which may serve as marks of the other effects and of the cause.

A classification thus formed is properly scientific or philosophical and is commonly called a natural, in contradistinction to a technical or artificial, classification or arrangement. The phrase "natural classification" seems most peculiarly appropriate to such arrangements as correspond, in the groups which they form, to the spontaneous tendencies of the mind, by placing together the objects most similar in their general aspect, in opposition to those technical systems which, arranging things according to their agreement in some circumstance arbitrarily selected, often throw into the same group objects which in the general aggregate of their properties present no resemblance, and into different and remote groups others which have the closest similarity. It is one of the most valid recommendations of any classification to the character of a scientific one that it shall be a natural classification in this sense also; for the test of its scientific character is the number and importance of the properties which can be asserted in common of all objects included in a group, and properties on which the general aspect of the things depends are, if only on that ground, important as well as, in most cases, numerous. But, though a strong recommendation, this circumstance is not a *sine qua non*, since the most obvious properties of things may be of trifling importance compared with others that are not obvious. I have seen it mentioned as a great absurdity in the Linnaean classification that it places (which, by the way, it does not) the violet by the side of the oak; it certainly dissevers natural affinities and brings together things quite as unlike as the oak and the violet are.   But the difference, apparently so wide, which renders the juxtaposition of those two vegetables so suitable an illustration of a bad arrangement depends, to the common eye, mainly on mere size and texture; now, if we made it our study to adopt the classification which would involve the least peril of similar *rapprochements*, we should return to the obsolete division into trees, shrubs, and herbs, which, though of primary importance with regard to mere general aspect, yet (compared even with so petty and unobvious a distinction as that into dicotyledons and monocotyledons) answers to so few differences in the other properties of plants that a classification founded on it (independently of the indistinctness of the lines of demarcation) would be as completely artificial and technical as the Linnaean.

Our natural groups, therefore, must often be founded, not on the obvious, but on the unobvious properties of things when these are of greater importance.   But in such cases it is essential that there should be some other property or set of properties, more readily recognizable by the observer, which co-exist with, and may be received as marks of, the properties which are the real groundwork of the classification. . . .

This shows, more strongly than ever, how extensive a knowledge of the properties of objects is necessary for making a good classification of them.   And as it is one of the uses of such a classification that, by drawing attention to the properties on which it is founded and which, if the classification be good, are marks of many others, it facilitates the discovery of those others; we see in what manner our knowledge of things and our classification of them tend mutually and indefinitely to the improvement of each other.

We said just now that the classification of objects should follow those of their properties which indicate not only the most numerous but also the most important peculiarities.   What is here meant by importance?   It has reference to the particular end in view, and the same objects, therefore, may admit with propriety of several different classifications.   Each science or art forms its classification of things according to the properties which fall within its special cognizance or of which it must take account in order to accomplish its peculiar practical end. . . .

These different classifications are all good for the purposes of their own particular departments of knowledge or practice. But when we are studying objects not for any special practical end, but for the sake of extending our knowledge of the whole of their properties and relations, we must consider as the most important attributes those which contribute most, either by themselves or by their effects, to render the things like one another and unlike other things, which give to the class composed of them the most marked individuality, which fill, as it were, the largest space in their existence and would most impress the attention of a spectator who knew all their properties but was not specially interested in any. Classes formed on this principle may be called, in a more emphatic manner than any others, natural groups.

2. *Kinds are natural groups*

The reader is by this time familiar with the general truth (which I restate so often on account of the great confusion in which it is commonly involved) that there are in nature distinctions of kind, distinctions not consisting in a given number of definite properties *plus* the effects which follow from those properties, but running through the whole nature, through the attributes generally, of the things so distinguished. Our knowledge of the properties of a kind is never complete. We are always discovering and expecting to discover new ones. Where the distinction between two classes of things is not one of kind, we expect to find their properties alike, except where there is some reason for their being different. On the contrary, when the distinction is in kind, we expect to find the properties different unless there be some cause for their being the same. All knowledge of a kind must be obtained by observation and experiment upon the kind itself; no inference respecting its properties from the properties of things not connected with it by kind goes for more than the sort of presumption usually characterized as an analogy, and generally in one of its fainter degrees.

Since the common properties of a true kind and, consequently, the general assertions which can be made respecting it, or which are certain to be made hereafter as our knowledge extends, are indefinite and inexhaustible; and since the very first principle of natural classification is that of forming the classes so that the objects composing each may have the greatest number of properties in common, this principle prescribes that every such classification shall recognize and adopt into itself all distinctions of kind which exist among the objects it professes to classify. To pass over any distinctions of kind and substitute definite distinctions which, however considerable they may be, do not point to ulterior unknown differences would be to replace classes with more by classes with fewer attributes in common, and would be subversive of the natural method of classification.

Accordingly all natural arrangements, whether the reality of the distinction of kinds was felt or not by their framers, have been led, by the mere pursuit of their own proper end, to conform themselves to the distinctions of kind so far as these have been ascertained at the time. The species of plants are not only real kinds, but are probably, all of them, real lowest kinds, infimae species, which, if we were to subdivide, as of course it is open to us to do, into subclasses, the subdivision would necessarily be founded on *definite* distinctions, not pointing (apart from what may be known of their causes or effects) to any difference beyond themselves.

In so far as a natural classification is grounded on real kinds, its groups are certainly not conventional; it is perfectly true that they do not depend upon an arbitrary choice of the naturalist. . . . They are determined by characters, but these are not arbitrary. The problem is to find a few definite characters which point to the multitude of indefinite ones. Kinds are classes between which there is an impassable barrier, and what we have to seek is marks whereby we may determine on which side of the barrier an object takes its place. The characters which will best do this should be chosen; if they are also important in themselves, so much the better. When we have selected the characters, we parcel out the objects according to those characters and not, I conceive, according to resemblance to a type. We do not compose the species Ranunculus acris of all plants which bear a satisfactory degree of resemblance to a model buttercup, but of those which possess certain characters selected as marks by which we might recognize the possibility of a common parentage, and the enumeration of those characters is the definition of the species.

The question next arises whether, as all kinds must have a place among the classes, so all the classes in a natural arrangement must be kinds? And to this I answer, certainly not. The distinctions of kinds are not numerous enough to make up the whole of a classification. Very few of the genera of plants or even of the families can be pronounced with certainty to be kinds. The great distinctions of vascular and cellular, dicotyledonous or exogenous and monocotyledonous or endogenous plants, are perhaps differences of kind; the lines of demarkation which divide those classes seem (though even on this I would not pronounce positively) to go through the whole nature of the plants. But the different species of a genus or genera of a family usually have in common only a limited number of characters. . . .

After the recognition and definition, then, of the *infimae species*, the next step is to arrange those *infimae species* into larger groups, making these groups correspond to kinds wherever it is possible, but in most cases without any such guidance. . . .

The truth is that every genus or family is framed with distinct reference to certain characters and is composed, first and principally, of species which agree in possessing all those characters. To these are added, as a sort of appendix, such other species, generally in small number, as possess *nearly* all the properties selected; wanting some of them one property, some another, and which, while they agree with the rest *almost* as much as these agree with one another, do not resemble in an equal degree any other group. Our conception of the class continues to be grounded on the characters; and the class might be defined: those things which *either* possess that set of characters *or* resemble the things that do so more than they resemble anything else.

And this resemblance itself is not, like resemblance between simple sensations, an ultimate fact, unsusceptible of analysis. Even the inferior degree of resemblance is created by the possession of common characters. Whatever resembles the genus "rose" more than it resembles any other genus does so because it possesses a greater number of the characters of that genus than of the characters of any other genus. Nor can there be any real difficulty in representing, by an enumeration of characters, the nature and degree of the resemblance which is strictly sufficient to include any object in the class. There are always some properties common to all things which are included. Others there often are to which some things, which are nevertheless included, are exceptions. But the objects which are exceptions to one character are not exceptions to another; the resemblance which fails in some particulars must be made up for in others. The class, therefore, is constituted by the possession of *all* the characters which are universal and *most* of those which admit of exceptions. . . .

Not only, therefore, are natural groups, no less than any artificial classes, determined by characters; they are constituted in contemplation of, and by reason of, characters. Put it is in contemplation not of those characters only which are rigorously common to all the objects included in the group, but of the entire body of characters, all of which are found in most of those objects and most of them in all. And hence our conception of the class, the image in our minds which is representative of it, is that of a specimen complete in all the characters, most naturally a specimen which, by possessing them all in the greatest degree in which they are ever found, is the best fitted to exhibit clearly and in a marked manner what they are. It is by a mental reference to this standard, not instead of, but in illustration of, the definition of the class, that we usually and advantageously determine whether any individual or species belongs to the class or not. . . .

BOOK V*

On the Logic of the Moral Sciences

"Si l'homme peut prédire, avec une assurance presque entière, les phénomènes dont il connaît les lois; si lors même qu'elles lui sont inconnues, il peut, d'après l'expérience, prévoir avec une grande probabilité les événements de l'avenir; pourquoi regarderait-on comme une entreprise chimérique, celle de tracer avec quelque vraisemblance le tableau des destinées futures de l'espèce humaine, d'après les résultats de son histoire? Le seul fondement de croyance dans les sciences naturelles, est cette idée, que les lois générales, connues ou ignorées, qui règlent les phénomènes de l'univers, sont nécessaires et constantes; et par quelle raison ce principe serait-il moins vrai pour le développement des facultés intellectuelles et morales de l'homme, que pour les autres opérations de la nature? Enfin, puisque des opinions formées d'après l'expérience . . . sont la seule règle de la conduite des hommes les plus sages, pourquoi interdirait-on au philosophe d'appuyer ses conjectures sur cette même base, pourvu qu'il ne leur attribue pas une certitude supérieure à celle qui peut naître du nombre, de la constance, de l'exactitude des observations?" — CON-DORCET, *Esquisse d'un Tableau Historique des Progrès de l'Esprit Humain.*

CHAPTER I

INTRODUCTORY REMARKS

1. *The backward state of the moral sciences can only be remedied by applying to them the methods of physical science, duly extended and generalized*

Principles of evidence and theories of method are not to be constructed *a priori*. The laws of our rational faculty, like those of every other natural agency, are only learned by seeing the agent at work. The earlier achievements of science were made without the conscious observance of any scientific method, and we should never have known by what process truth is to be ascertained if we

*[Book VI of the eighth edition.]

had not previously ascertained many truths. But it was only the easier problems which could be thus resolved; natural sagacity, when it tried its strength against the more difficult ones, either failed altogether, or, if it succeeded here and there in obtaining a solution, had no sure means of convincing others that its solution was correct. In scientific investigation, as in all other works of human skill, the way of obtaining the end is seen, as it were, instinctively by superior minds in some comparatively simple case and is then, by judicious generalization, adapted to the variety of complex cases. We learn to do a thing in difficult circumstances by attending to the manner in which we have spontaneously done the same thing in easier ones.

This truth is exemplified by the history of the various branches of knowledge which have successively, in the ascending order of their complication, assumed the character of sciences, and will doubtless receive fresh confirmation from those of which the final scientific constitution is yet to come and which are still abandoned to the uncertainties of vague and popular discussion. Although several other sciences have emerged from this state at a comparatively recent date, none now remain in it except those which relate to man himself, the most complex and most difficult subject of study on which the human mind can be engaged.

Concerning the physical nature of man as an organized being — though there is still much uncertainty and much controversy which can only be terminated by the general acknowledgment and employment of stricter rules of induction than are commonly recognized — there is, however, a considerable body of truths which all who have attended to the subject consider to be fully established; nor is there now any radical imperfection in the method observed in the department of science by its most distinguished modern teachers. But the laws of mind and, in even a greater degree, those of society are so far from having attained a similar state of even partial recognition that it is still a controversy whether they are capable of becoming subjects of science in the strict sense of the term, and among those who are agreed on this point there reigns the most irreconcilable diversity on almost every other. Here, therefore, if anywhere, the principles laid down in the preceding Books may be expected to be useful.

If, on matters so much the most important with which human intellect can occupy itself, a more general agreement is ever to exist among thinkers, if what has been pronounced "the proper study of mankind" is not destined to remain the only subject which philosophy cannot succeed in rescuing from empiricism, the same process through which the laws of many simpler phenomena have by general acknowledgment been placed beyond dispute must be consciously and deliberately applied to those more difficult inquiries. If there are some subjects on which the results obtained have finally received the unanimous assent of all who have attended to the proof, and others on which mankind have not yet been equally successful, on which the most sagacious minds have occupied themselves from the earliest date and have never succeeded in establishing any considerable body of truths so as to be beyond denial or doubt, it is by generalizing the methods successfully followed in the former inquiries and adapting them to the latter that we may hope to remove this blot on the face of science. The remaining chapters are an endeavor to facilitate this most desirable object.

CHAPTER II*

THAT THERE IS, OR MAY BE, A SCIENCE OF HUMAN NATURE

1. *There may be sciences which are not exact sciences*

It is a common notion, or, at least, it is implied in many common modes of speech, that the thoughts, feelings, and actions of sentient beings are not a subject of science in the same strict sense in which this is true of the objects of outward nature. This notion seems to involve some confusion of ideas which it is necessary to begin by clearing up.

*[Chapter III of the eighth edition.]

Any facts are fitted, in themselves, to be a subject of science which follow one another according to constant laws, although those laws may not have been discovered nor even be discoverable by our existing resources. Take, for instance, the most familiar class of meteorological phenomena, those of rain and sunshine. Scientific inquiry has not yet succeeded in ascertaining the order of antecedence and consequence among these phenomena, so as to be able, at least in our regions of the earth, to predict them with certainty or even with any high degree of probability. Yet no one doubts that the phenomena depend on laws, and that these must be derivative laws resulting from known ultimate laws, those of heat, electricity, vaporization and elastic fluids. Nor can it be doubted that if we were acquainted with all the antecedent circumstances, we could, even from those more general laws, predict (saving difficulties of calculation) the state of the weather at any future time. Meteorology, therefore, not only has in itself every natural requisite for being, but actually is, a science, though, from the difficulty of observing the facts on which the phenomena depend (a difficulty inherent in the peculiar nature of those phenomena), the science is extremely imperfect, and, were it perfect, might probably be of little avail in practice, since the data requisite for applying its principles to particular instances would rarely be procurable.

A case may be conceived of an intermediate character between the perfection of science and this its extreme imperfection. . . .

. . . No one doubts that tidology (as Dr. Whewell proposes to call it) is really a science. As much of the phenomena as depends on the attraction of the sun and moon is completely understood and may, in any, even unknown, part of the earth's surface, be foretold with certainty, and the far greater part of the phenomena depends on those causes. But circumstances of a local or casual nature, such as the configuration of the bottom of the ocean, the degree of confinement from shores, the direction of the wind, etc., influence, in many or in all places, the height and time of the tide; and, a portion of these circumstances being either not accurately knowable, not precisely measurable, or not capable of being certainly foreseen, the tide in known places commonly varies from the calculated result of general principles by some difference that we cannot explain, and in unknown ones may vary from it by a difference that we are not able to foresee or conjecture. Nevertheless, not only is it certain that these variations depend on causes and follow their causes by laws of unerring uniformity, not only, therefore, is tidology a science, like meteorology, but it is, what hitherto, at least, meteorology is not, a science largely available in practice. General laws may be laid down respecting the tides, predictions may be founded on those laws, and the result will in the main, though often not with complete accuracy, correspond to the predictions.

And this is what is or ought to be meant by those who speak of sciences which are not *exact* sciences. Astronomy was once a science, without being an exact science. It could not become exact until not only the general course of the planetary motions, but the perturbations also, were accounted for and referred to their causes. It has become an exact science because its phenomena have been brought under laws comprehending the whole of the causes by which the phenomena are influenced, whether in a great or only in a trifling degree, whether in all or only in some cases, and assigning to each of those causes the share of effect which really belongs to it. But in the theory of the tides the only laws as yet accurately ascertained are those of the causes which affect the phenomenon in all cases and in a considerable degree, while others which affect it in some cases only, or, if in all, only in a slight degree, have not been sufficiently ascertained and studied to enable us to lay down their laws, still less to deduce the completed law of the phenomenon by compounding the effects of the greater with those of the minor causes. Tidology, therefore, is not yet an exact science, not from any inherent incapacity of being so, but from the difficulty of ascertaining with complete precision the real derivative uniformities. By combining, however, the exact laws of the greater causes and of such of the minor ones as are sufficiently known with such empirical laws or such approximate generalizations respecting the miscellaneous variations as can be obtained by specific observation, we can lay down general propositions which will be true in the main, and on which, with allowance for the degree of their probable inaccuracy, we may safely ground our expectations and our conduct.

2. *To what scientific type the science of human nature corresponds*

The science of human nature is of this description. It falls far short of the standard of exactness now realized in astronomy, but there is no reason that it should not be as much a science as tidology is, or as astronomy was when its calculations had only mastered the main phenomena but not the perturbations.

The phenomena with which this science is conversant being the thoughts, feelings, and actions of human beings, it would have attained the ideal perfection of a science if it enabled us to foretell how an individual would think, feel, or act throughout life with the same certainty with which astronomy enables us to predict the places and the occultations of the heavenly bodies. It needs scarcely be stated that nothing approaching to this can be done. The actions of individuals could not be predicted with scientific accuracy, were it only because we cannot foresee the whole of the circumstances in which those individuals will be placed. But further, even in any given combination of (present) circumstances, no assertion which is both precise and universally true can be made respecting the manner in which human beings will think, feel, or act. This is not, however, because every person's modes of thinking, feeling, and acting do not depend on causes; nor can we doubt that, if, in the case of any individual, our data could be complete, we even now know enough of the ultimate laws by which mental phenomena are determined to enable us in many cases to predict with tolerable certainty what, in the greater number of supposable combinations of circumstances, his conduct or sentiments would be. But the impressions and actions of human beings are not solely the result of their present circumstances, but the joint result of those circumstances and of the characters of the individuals; and the agencies which determine human character are so numerous and diversified (nothing which has happened to the person throughout life being without its portion of influence) that in the aggregate they are never in any two cases exactly similar. Hence, even if our science of human nature were theoretically perfect, that is, if we could calculate any character as we can calculate the orbit of any planet, *from given data*, still, as the data are never all given nor ever precisely alike in different cases, we could neither make positive predictions nor lay down universal propositions.

Inasmuch, however, as many of those effects which it is of most importance to render amenable to human foresight and control are determined, like the tides, in an incomparably greater degree by general causes than by all partial causes taken together, depending in the main on those circumstances and qualities which are common to all mankind, or, at least, to large bodies of them, and only in a small degree on the idiosyncrasies of organization or the peculiar history of individuals, it is evidently possible with regard to all such effects to make predictions which will *almost* always be verified and general propositions which are almost always true. And whenever it is sufficient to know how the great majority of the human race or of some nation or class of persons will think, feel, and act, these propositions are equivalent to universal ones. For the purposes of political and social science this *is* sufficient. As we formerly remarked,* an approximate generalization is, in social inquiries, for most practical purposes equivalent to an exact one, that which is only probable when asserted of individual human beings indiscriminately selected being certain when affirmed of the character and collective conduct of masses.

It is no disparagement, therefore, to the science of human nature that those of its general propositions which descend sufficiently into detail to serve as a foundation for predicting phenomena in the concrete are for the most part only approximately true. But, in order to give a genuinely scientific character to the study, it is indispensable that these approximate generalizations, which in themselves would amount only to the lowest kind of empirical laws, should be connected deductively with the laws of nature from which they result, should be resolved into the properties of the causes on which the phenomena depend. In other words, the science of human nature may be said to exist in proportion as the approximate truths which compose a practical knowledge of mankind can be exhibited as corollaries from the universal laws of human nature on which they rest, whereby the proper limits of those approximate truths would be shown, and we should be enabled to deduce others for any new state of circumstances in anticipation of specific experience.

. . . .

* [Chapter II of the eighth edition, "Of Liberty and Necessity."]

CHAPTER III*

OF THE LAWS OF MIND

1. *What is meant by laws of mind*

What the mind is, as well as what matter is, or any other question respecting things in themselves as distinguished from their sensible manifestations, it would be foreign to the purposes of this treatise to consider. Here, as throughout our inquiry, we shall keep clear of all speculations respecting the mind's own nature and shall understand by the laws of mind those of mental phenomena, of the various feelings or states of consciousness of sentient beings. These, according to the classification we have uniformly followed, consist of thoughts, emotions, volitions, and sensations, the last being as truly states of mind as the three former. It is usual, indeed, to speak of sensations as states of body, not of mind. But this is the common confusion, of giving one and the same name to a phenomenon and to the approximate cause or conditions of the phenomenon. . . .

The phenomena of mind, then, are the various feelings of our nature, both those improperly called physical and those peculiarly designated as mental; and by the laws of mind, I mean the laws according to which those feelings generate one another.

2. *Is there a science of psychology?*

All states of mind are immediately caused either by other states of mind or by states of body. When a state of mind is produced by a state of mind, I call the law concerned in the case a law of mind. When a state of mind is produced directly by a state of body, the law is a law of body and belongs to physical science.

With regard to those states of mind which are called sensations, all are agreed that these have for their immediate antecedents states of body. Every sensation has for its proximate cause some affection of the portion of our frame called the nervous system, whether this affection originates in the action of some external

*[Chapter IV of the eighth edition.]

object or in some pathological condition of the nervous organization itself. The laws of this portion of our nature — the varieties of our sensations, and the physical conditions on which they proximately depend — manifestly belong to the province of physiology.

Whether the remainder of our mental states are similarly dependent on physical conditions is one of the *vexatae questiones* in the science of human nature. . . .

But, after all has been said which can be said, it remains incontestable that there exist uniformities of succession among states of mind and that these can be ascertained by observation and experiment. Further, that every mental state has a nervous state for its immediate antecedent and proximate cause, though extremely probable, cannot hitherto be said to be proved in the conclusive manner in which this can be proved of sensations, and, even were it certain, yet everyone must admit that we are wholly ignorant of the characteristics of these nervous states; we know not, and at present have no means of knowing, in what respect one of them differs from another; and our only mode of studying their successions or co-existences must be by observing the successions and co-existences of the mental states of which they are supposed to be the generators or causes. The successions, therefore, which obtain among mental phenomena do not admit of being deduced from the physiological laws of our nervous organization, and all real knowledge of them must continue, for a long time at least, if not always, to be sought in the direct study, by observation and experiment, of the mental successions themselves. Since, therefore, the order of our mental phenomena must be studied in those phenomena and not inferred from the laws of any phenomena more general, there is a distinct and separate science of mind.

The relations, indeed, of that science to the science of physiology must never be overlooked or undervalued. It must by no means be forgotten that the laws of mind may be derivative laws resulting from laws of animal life and that their truth, therefore, may ultimately depend on physical conditions; and the influence of physiological states or physiological changes in altering or counteracting the mental successions is one of the most important departments of psychological study. But, on the other hand, to reject the resource of psychological analysis and construct the theory of the mind solely on such data as physiology at present affords seems to me as great an error in principle and an even more serious one in practice. Imperfect as is the science of mind, I do not scruple to affirm that it is in a considerably more advanced state than the portion of physiology which corresponds to it, and to discard the former for the latter appears to me an infringement of the true canons of inductive philosophy, which must produce, and which does produce, erroneous conclusions in some very important departments of the science of human nature.

3. *The principal investigations of psychology characterized*

The subject, then, of psychology is the uniformities of succession, the laws, whether ultimate or derivative, according to which one mental state succeeds another, is caused by or, at least, is caused to follow another. Of these laws some are general, others more special. The following are examples of the most general laws:

First, whenever any state of consciousness has once been excited in us, no matter by what cause, an inferior degree of the same state of consciousness, a state of consciousness resembling the former but inferior in intensity, is capable of being reproduced in us without the presence of any such cause as excited it at first. Thus, if we have once seen or touched an object, we can afterward think of the object though it be absent from our sight or from our touch. . . . This law is expressed by saying, in the language of Hume, that every mental *impression* has its *idea*.

Secondly, these ideas, or secondary mental states, are excited by our impressions or by other ideas, according to certain laws which are called "laws of association." Of these laws the first is that similar ideas tend to excite one another. The second is that, when two impressions have been frequently experienced (or even thought of) either simultaneously or in immediate succession, then whenever one of these impressions, or the idea of it, recurs, it tends to excite the idea of the other. The third law is that greater intensity in either or both of the impressions is equivalent in rendering them excitable by one another to a greater frequency of conjunction. These are the laws of ideas, on which I shall not enlarge in this place but refer the reader to works professedly psychological, in particular to Mr. James Mill's *Analysis of the Phenomena of the Human Mind*, where the principal laws of association, along with many of their applications, are copiously exemplified, and with a masterly hand.

.   .   .   .

CHAPTER IV*

OF ETHOLOGY, OR THE SCIENCE OF THE FORMATION OF CHARACTER

1. *The empirical laws of human nature*

The laws of mind as characterized in the preceding chapter compose the universal or abstract portion of the philosophy of human nature, and all the truths of common experience, constituting a practical knowledge of mankind, must, to the extent to which they are truths, be results or consequences of these. Such familiar maxims, when collected *a posteriori* from observation of life, occupy among the truths of the science the place of what, in our analysis of induction, have so often been spoken of under the title of empirical laws.

An empirical law (it will be remembered) is a uniformity, whether of succession or of co-existence, which holds true in all instances within our limits of observation but is not of a nature to afford any assurance that it would hold beyond those limits. . . .

Now, the observations concerning human affairs collected from common experience are precisely of this nature. Even if they were universally and exactly true within the bounds of experience, which they never are, still they are not the ultimate laws of human action; they are not the principles of human nature, but results of those principles under the circumstances in which mankind have happened to be placed. . . .

*[Chapter V of the eighth edition.]

The really scientific truths, then, are not these empirical laws but the causal laws which explain them. The empirical laws of those phenomena which depend on known causes and of which a general theory can therefore be constructed have, whatever may be their value in practice, no other function in science than that of verifying the conclusions of theory. Still more must this be the case when most of the empirical laws amount, even within the limits of observation, only to approximate generalizations.

2. — are merely approximate generalizations. The universal laws are those of the formation of character

This, however, is not, so much as is sometimes supposed, a peculiarity of the sciences called moral. It is only in the simplest branches of science that empirical laws are ever exactly true, and not always in those. . . .

. . . Suppose that all which passes in the mind of man is determined by a few simple laws; still, if those laws be such that there is not one of the facts surrounding a human being or of the events which happen to him that does not influence in some mode or degree his subsequent mental history and if the circumstances of different human beings are extremely different, it will be no wonder if very few propositions can be made respecting the details of their conduct or feelings which will be true of all mankind.

Now, without deciding whether the ultimate laws of our mental nature are few or many, it is at least certain that they are of the above description. It is certain that our mental states and our mental capacities and susceptibilities are modified, either for a time or permanently, by everything which happens to us in life. Considering, therefore, how much these modifying causes differ in the case of any two individuals, it would be unreasonable to expect that the empirical laws of the human mind, the generalizations which can be made respecting the feelings or actions of mankind without reference to the causes that determine them, should be anything but approximate generalizations. They are the common wisdom of common life and, as such, are invaluable, especially as they are mostly to be applied to cases not very dissimilar to those from which they were collected. But when maxims of this sort, collected from Englishmen, come to be applied to Frenchmen, or when those collected from the present day are applied to past or future generations, they are apt to be very much at fault. Unless we have resolved the empirical law into the laws of the causes on which it depends and ascertained that those causes extend to the case which we have in view, there can be no reliance placed in our inferences. For every individual is surrounded by circumstances different from those of every other individual, every nation or generation of mankind from every other nation or generation, and none of these differences are without their influence in forming a different type of character. There is, indeed, also a certain general resemblance, but peculiarities of circumstances are continually constituting exceptions even to the propositions which are true in the great majority of cases.

Although, however, there is scarcely any mode of feeling or conduct which is, in the absolute sense, common to all mankind, and though the generalizations which assert that any given variety of conduct or feeling will be found universally (however nearly they may approximate to truth within given limits of observation) will be considered as scientific propositions by no one who is at all familiar with scientific investigation, yet all modes of feeling and conduct met with among mankind have causes which produce them; and in the propositions which assign those causes will be found the explanation of the empirical laws and the limiting principle of our reliance on them. Human beings do not all feel and act alike in the same circumstances, but it is possible to determine what makes one person, in a given position, feel or act in one way, another in another, how any given mode of feeling and conduct compatible with the general laws (physical and mental) of human nature has been, or may be, formed. In other words, mankind have not one universal character, but there exist universal laws of the formation of character. And since it is by these laws, combined with the facts of each particular case, that the whole of the phenomena of human action and feeling are produced, it is on these that every rational attempt to construct the science of human nature in the concrete and for practical purposes must proceed.

3. *The laws of the formation of character cannot be ascertained by observation and experiment*

The laws, then, of the formation of character being the principal object of scientific inquiry into human nature, it remains to determine the method of investigation best fitted for ascertaining them. And the logical principles according to which this question is to be decided must be those which preside over every other attempt to investigate the laws of very complex phenomena. For it is evident that both the character of any human being and the aggregate of the circumstances by which that character has been formed are facts of a high order of complexity. Now to such cases we have seen that the deductive method, setting out from general laws and verifying their consequences by specific experience, is alone applicable. The grounds of this great logical doctrine have formerly been stated, and its truth will derive additional support from a brief examination of the specialties of the present case.

There are only two modes in which laws of nature can be ascertained — deductively and experimentally, including under the denomination of experimental inquiry observation as well as artificial experiment. Are the laws of the formation of character susceptible of a satisfactory investigation by the method of experimentation? Evidently not, because, even if we suppose unlimited power of varying the experiment (which is abstractedly possible, though no one but an Oriental despot has that power, or, if he had, would probably be disposed to exercise it), a still more essential condition is wanting — the power of performing any of the experiments with scientific accuracy.

. . . .

Under this impossibility of studying the laws of the formation of character by experiments purposely contrived to elucidate them, there remains the resource of simple observation. But if it be impossible to ascertain the influencing circumstances with any approach to completeness even when we have the shaping of them ourselves, much more impossible is it when the cases are further removed from our observation and altogether out of our control. . . .

. . . .

4. — *but must be studied deductively*

Since, then, it is impossible to obtain really accurate propositions respecting the formation of character from observation and experiment alone, we are driven perforce to that which, even if it had not been the indispensable, would have been the most perfect mode of investigation, and which it is one of the principal aims of philosophy to extend, namely, that which tries its experiments not on the complex facts, but on the simple ones of which they are compounded, and, after ascertaining the laws of the causes the composition of which gives rise to the complex phenomena, then considers whether these will not explain and account for the approximate generalizations which have been framed empirically respecting the sequences of those complex phenomena. The laws of the formation of character are, in short, derivative laws, resulting from the general laws of mind, and are to be obtained by deducing them from those general laws by supposing any given set of circumstances and then considering what, according to the laws of mind, will be the influence of those circumstances on the formation of character.

A science is thus formed to which I would propose to give the name of ethology, or the science of character, from ἦθος, a word more nearly corresponding to the term "character" as I here use it than any other word in the same language. The name is perhaps etymologically applicable to the entire science of our mental and moral nature; but if, as is usual and convenient, we employ the name psychology for the science of the elementary laws of mind, ethology will serve for the ulterior science which determines the kind of character produced in conformity to those general laws by any set of circumstances, physical and moral. According to this definition, ethology is the science which corresponds to the art of education in the widest sense of the term, including the formation of national or collective character as well as individual. It would, indeed, be vain to expect (however completely the laws of the formation of character might be ascertained) that we could know so accurately the circumstances of any given case as to be able positively to predict the character that would be produced in that case. But we must remember that a degree of knowledge far short of the power of actual prediction is often of much practical value. There may be great power of influencing phenomena with a very imperfect knowledge of the causes by which they are in any given instance determined. It is enough that we know that certain means have a *tendency* to produce a given effect and that others have a tendency to frustrate it. When the circumstances of an individual or of a nation are in any considerable degree under our control, we may, by our knowledge of tendencies, be enabled to shape those circumstances in a manner much more favorable to the ends we desire than the shape which they would of themselves assume. This is the limit of our power, but within this limit the power is a most important one.

This science of ethology may be called the "exact science of human nature," for its truths are not, like the empirical laws which depend on them, approximate generalizations, but real laws. It is, however (as in all cases of complex phenomena), necessary to the exactness of the propositions that they should be hypothetical only and affirm tendencies, not facts. They must not assert that something will always, or certainly, happen, but only that such and such will be the effect of a given cause, so far as it operates uncounteracted. It is a scientific proposition that bodily strength tends to make men courageous, not that it always makes them so; that an interest on one side of a question tends to bias the judgment, not that it invariably does so; that experience tends to give wisdom, not that such is always its effect. These propositions, being assertive only of tendencies, are not the less universally true because the tendencies may be frustrated.

5. *The principles of ethology are the* axiomata media *of mental science*

While, on the one hand, psychology is altogether, or principally, a science of observation and experiment, ethology, as I have conceived it, is, as I have already remarked, altogether deductive. The one ascertains the simple laws of mind in general; the other traces their operation in complex combinations of circumstances. Ethology stands to psychology in a relation very similar to that in which the various branches of natural philosophy stand to mechanics. The principles of ethology are properly the middle principles, the *axiomata media* (as Bacon would have said), of the science of mind, as distinguished, on the one hand, from the empirical laws resulting from simple observation and, on the other, from the highest generalizations.

.   .   .   .

. . . The science of the formation of character is a science of causes. The subject is one to which those among the canons of induction by which laws of causation are ascertained can be rigorously applied. It is, therefore, both natural and advisable to ascertain the simplest, which are necessarily the most general, laws of causation first and to deduce the middle principles from them. In other words, ethology, the deductive science, is a system of corollaries from psychology, the experimental science.

6. *Ethology characterized*

Of these, the earlier alone has been, as yet, really conceived or studied as a science; the other, ethology, is still to be created. But its creation has at length become practicable. . . . A science of ethology, founded on the laws of psychology, is therefore possible, though little has yet been done, and that little not at all systematically, toward forming it. The progress of this important but most imperfect science will depend on a double process: first, that of deducing theoretically the ethological consequences of particular circumstances of position and comparing them with the recognized results of common experience; and, secondly, the reverse operation, increased study of the various types of human nature that are to be found in the world, conducted by persons not only capable of analyzing and recording the circumstances in which these types severally prevail, but also sufficiently acquainted with psychological laws to be able to explain and account for the characteristics of the type by the peculiarities of the circumstances, the residuum alone, when there proves to be any, being set down to the account of congenital predispositions.

.   .   .   .

It is hardly necessary again to repeat that, as in every other deductive science, verification *a posteriori* must proceed *pari passu* with deduction *a priori*. The inference given by theory as to the type of character which would be formed by any given circumstances must be tested by specific experience of those circumstances whenever obtainable, and the conclusions of the science as a whole must undergo a perpetual verification and correction from the general remarks afforded by common experience respecting human nature in our own age and by history respecting times gone by. The conclusions of theory cannot be trusted unless confirmed by observation; nor those of observation unless they can be affiliated to theory by deducing them from the laws of human nature and from a close analysis of the circumstances of the particular situation. It is the accordance of these two kinds of evidence separately taken — the consilience of *a priori* reasoning and specific experience — which forms the only sufficient ground for the principles of any science so "immersed in matter," dealing with such complex and concrete phenomena, as ethology.

CHAPTER V*

OF THE CHEMICAL, OR EXPERIMENTAL, METHOD IN THE SOCIAL SCIENCE

1. *Characters of the mode of thinking which deduces political doctrines from specific experience*

The laws of the phenomena of society are and can be nothing but the laws of the actions and passions of human beings united together in the social state. Men, however, in a state of society are still men; their actions and passions are obedient to the laws of individual human nature. Men are not, when brought together, converted into another kind of substance with different properties, as hydrogen and oxygen are different from water, or as hydrogen, oxygen, carbon, and azote are different from nerves, muscles, and tendons. Human beings in society have no properties but those

*[Chapter VII of the eighth edition.]

which are derived from, and may be resolved into, the laws of the nature of individual man. In social phenomena the composition of causes is the universal law.

Now, the method of philosophizing which may be termed chemical overlooks this fact and proceeds as if the nature of man as an individual were not concerned at all, or were concerned in a very inferior degree, in the operations of human beings in society. All reasoning in political or social affairs, grounded on principles of human nature, is objected to by reasoners of this sort under such names as "abstract theory." For the direction of their opinions and conduct, they profess to demand, in all cases without exception, specific experience.

This mode of thinking is not only general with practitioners in politics and with that very numerous class who (on a subject which no one, however ignorant, thinks himself incompetent to discuss) profess to guide themselves by common sense rather than by science, but is often countenanced by persons with greater pretensions to instruction — persons who, having sufficient acquaintance with books and with the current ideas to have heard that Bacon taught mankind to follow experience and to ground their conclusions on facts instead of metaphysical dogmas, think that, by treating political facts in as directly experimental a method as chemical facts, they are showing themselves true Baconians and proving their adversaries to be mere syllogizers and schoolmen. As, however, the notion of the applicability of experimental methods to political philosophy cannot co-exist with any just conception of these methods themselves, the kind of arguments from experience which the chemical theory brings forth as its fruits (and which form the staple, in this country especially, of parliamentary and hustings oratory) are such as, at no time since Bacon, would have been admitted to be valid in chemistry itself or in any other branch of experimental science. They are such as these: that the prohibition of foreign commodities must conduce to national wealth because England has flourished under it, or because countries in general which have adopted it have flourished; that our laws or our internal administration or our constitution are excellent for a similar reason; and the eternal arguments from historical examples, from Athens or Rome, from the fires in Smithfield or the French Revolution.

I will not waste time in contending against modes of argumentation which no person with the smallest practice in estimating evidence could possibly be betrayed into, which draw conclusions of general application from a single unanalyzed instance, or arbitrarily refer an effect to some one among its antecedents, without any process of elimination or comparison of instances. It is a rule both of justice and of good sense to grapple not with the absurdest, but with the most reasonable form of a wrong opinion. We shall suppose our inquirer acquainted with the true conditions of experimental investigation and competent in point of acquirements for realizing them, so far as they can be realized. He shall know as much of the facts of history as mere erudition can teach — as much as can be proved by testimony, without the assistance of any theory—and, if those mere facts, properly collated, can fulfill the conditions of a real induction, he shall be qualified for the task.

But that no such attempt can have the smallest chance of success, has been abundantly shown in the tenth chapter of the Third Book. We there examined whether effects which depend on a complication of causes can be made the subject of a true induction by observation and experiment, and concluded, on the most convincing grounds, that they cannot. . . .

CHAPTER VI*

OF THE GEOMETRICAL, OR ABSTRACT, METHOD

1. *Characters of this mode of thinking*

The misconception discussed in the preceding chapter is, as we said, chiefly committed by persons not much accustomed to scientific investigation, practitioners in politics who rather employ the commonplaces of philosophy to justify their practice than seek to guide their practice by philosophic principles, or imperfectly

*[Chapter VIII of the eighth edition.]

educated persons who, in ignorance of the careful selection and elaborate comparison of instances required for the formation of a sound theory, attempt to found one upon a few coincidences which they have casually noticed.

The erroneous method of which we are now to treat is, on the contrary, peculiar to thinking and studious minds. It never could have suggested itself but to persons of some familiarity with the nature of scientific research, who, being aware of the impossibility of establishing, by casual observation or direct experimentation, a true theory of sequences so complex as are those of the social phenomena, have recourse to the simpler laws which are immediately operative in those phenomena and which are no other than the laws of the nature of the human beings therein concerned. These thinkers perceive (what the partisans of the chemical or experimental theory do not) that the science of society must necessarily be deductive. But, from an insufficient consideration of the specific nature of the subject-matter — and often because (their own scientific education having stopped short in too early a stage) geometry stands in their minds as the type of all deductive science — it is to geometry rather than to astronomy and natural philosophy that they unconsciously assimilate the deductive science of society.

Among the differences between geometry (a science of co-existent facts, altogether independent of the laws of the succession of phenomena) and those physical sciences of causation which have been rendered deductive, the following is one of the most conspicuous: that geometry affords no room for what so constantly occurs in mechanics and its applications, the case of conflicting forces, of causes which counteract or modify one another. In mechanics we continually find two or more moving forces producing not motion, but rest, or motion in a different direction from that which would have been produced by either of the generating forces. It is true that the effect of the joint forces is the same when they act simultaneously as if they had acted one after another or by turns, and it is in this that the difference between mechanical and chemical laws consists. But still the effects, whether produced by successive or by simultaneous action, do, wholly or in part, cancel one another; what the one force does the other partly or altogether undoes.

There is no similar state of things in geometry. The result which follows from one geometrical principle has nothing that conflicts with the result which follows from another. What is proved true from one geometrical theorem, what would be true if no other geometrical principles existed, cannot be altered and made no longer true by reason of some other geometrical principle. What is once proved true is true in all cases, whatever supposition may be made in regard to any other matter.

Now a conception similar to this last would appear to have been formed of the social science in the minds of the earlier of those who have attempted to cultivate it by a deductive method. Mechanics would be a science very similar to geometry if every motion resulted from one force alone and not from a conflict of forces. In the geometrical theory of society, it seems to be supposed that this is really the case with the social phenomena, that each of them results always from only one force, one single property of human nature.

At the point which we have now reached, it cannot be necessary to say anything either in proof or in illustration of the assertion that such is not the true character of the social phenomena. There is not, among these most complex and (for that reason) most modifiable of all phenomena, any one over which innumerable forces do not exercise influence, which does not depend on a conjunction of very many causes. We have not, therefore, to prove the notion in question to be an error, but to prove that the error has been committed, that so mistaken a conception of the mode in which the phenomena of society are produced has actually been ascertained.

2. *The interest-philosophy of the Bentham school*

Passing over less important instances, I shall come at once to the most remarkable example afforded by our own times of the geometrical method in politics, emanating from persons who are well aware of the distinction between science and art, who knew that rules of conduct must follow, not precede, the ascertainment of laws of nature, and that the latter, not the former, is the legitimate field for the application of the deductive method. I allude to the interest-philosophy of the Bentham school.

The profound and original thinkers who are commonly known under this description founded their general theory of government on one comprehensive premise, namely, that men's actions are always determined by their interests. There is an ambiguity in this last expression; for, as the same philosophers, especially Bentham, gave the name of an interest to anything which a person likes, the proposition may be understood to mean only this, that men's actions are always determined by their wishes. In this sense, however, it would not bear out any of the consequences which these writers drew from it, and the word, therefore, in their political reasonings, must be understood to mean (which is also the explanation they themselves, on such occasions, gave of it) what is commonly termed private or worldly interest.

Taking the doctrine, then, in this sense, an objection presents itself *in limine* which might be deemed a fatal one, namely, that so sweeping a proposition is far from being universally true. Human beings are not governed in all their actions by their worldly interests. This, however, is by no means so conclusive an objection as it at first appears, because in politics we are for the most part concerned with the conduct not of individual persons, but either of a series of persons (as a succession of kings), or a body or mass of persons, as a nation, an aristocracy, or a representative assembly. And whatever is true of a large majority of mankind may without much error be taken for true of any succession of persons, considered as a whole, or of any collection of persons in which the act of the majority becomes the act of the whole body. Although, therefore, the maxim is sometimes expressed in a manner unnecessarily paradoxical, the consequences drawn from it will hold equally good if the assertion be limited as follows: Any succession of persons, or the majority of any body of persons, will be governed in the bulk of their conduct by their personal interests. We are bound to allow to this school of thinkers the benefit of this more rational statement of their fundamental maxim which is also in strict conformity to the explanations which, when considered to be called for, have been given by themselves.

The theory goes on to infer, quite correctly, that if the actions of mankind are determined in the main by their selfish interests, the only rulers who will govern according to the interest of the governed, are those whose selfish interests are in accordance with it. And to this is added a third proposition, namely, that no rulers have their selfish interest identical with that of the governed unless it be rendered so by accountability, that is, by dependence on the will of the governed. In other words (and as the result of the whole), that the desire of retaining or the fear of losing their power and whatever is thereon consequent is the sole motive which can be relied on for producing on the part of rulers a course of conduct in accordance with the general interest.

We have thus a fundamental theorem of political science, consisting of three syllogisms and depending chiefly on two general premises, in each of which a certain effect is considered as determined only by one cause, not by a concurrence of causes. In the one, it is assumed that the actions of average rulers are determined solely by self-interest; in the other, that the sense of identity of interest with the governed is produced and producible by no other cause than responsibility.

Neither of these propositions is by any means true; the last is extremely wide of the truth.

. . . .

I am not here attempting to establish a theory of government and am not called upon to determine the proportional weight which ought to be given to the circumstances which this school of geometrical politicians left out of their system and those which they took into it. I am only concerned to show that their method was unscientific, not to measure the amount of error which may have affected their practical conclusions.

. . . .

It is not to be imagined possible, nor is it true in point of fact, that these philosophers regarded the few premises of their theory as including all that is required for explaining social phenomena or for determining the choice of forms of government and measures of legislation and administration. They were too highly instructed, of too comprehensive intellect, and some of them of too sober and

practical a character for such an error. They would have applied
and did apply their principles with innumerable allowances. But
it is not allowances that are wanted.   There is little chance of
making due amends in the superstructure of a theory for the want
of sufficient breadth in its foundations.   It is unphilosophical to
construct a science out of a few of the agencies by which the phenomena are determined and leave the rest to the routine of practice or the sagacity of conjecture.   We either ought not to pretend
to scientific forms, or we ought to study all the determining agencies
equally and endeavor, so far as it can be done, to include all of
them within the pale of the science, else we shall infallibly bestow a
disproportionate attention upon those which our theory takes into
account while we misestimate the rest and probably underrate
their importance.   That the deductions should be from the whole
and not from a part only of the laws of nature that are concerned
would be desirable even if those omitted were so insignificant in
comparison with the others that they might, for most purposes
and on most occasions, be left out of the account.   But this is far
indeed from being true in the social science.   The phenomena of
society do not depend, in essentials, on some one agency or law of
human nature with only inconsiderable modifications from others.
The whole of the qualities of human nature influence those phenomena, and there is not one which influences them in a small
degree.   There is not one the removal or any great alteration of
which would not materially affect the whole aspect of society and
change more or less the sequences of social phenomena generally.

.   .   .   .

CHAPTER VII*

OF THE PHYSICAL, OR CONCRETE DEDUCTIVE, METHOD

1. *The direct and inverse deductive methods*

After what has been said to illustrate the nature of the inquiry into social phenomena, the general character of the method proper to that inquiry is sufficiently evident and needs only to be recapitulated, not proved. However complex the phenomena, all their sequences and co-existences result from the laws of the separate elements. The effect produced, in social phenomena, by any complex set of circumstances amounts precisely to the sum of the effects of the circumstances taken singly, and the complexity does not arise from the number of the laws themselves, which is not remarkably great, but from the extraordinary number and variety of the data or elements — of the agents which, in obedience to that small number of laws, co-operate toward the effect. The social science, therefore (which, by a convenient barbarism, has been termed sociology), is a deductive science, not, indeed, after the model of geometry, but after that of the more complex physical sciences. It infers the law of each effect from the laws of causation on which that effect depends, not, however, from the law merely of one cause, as in the geometrical method, but by considering all the causes which conjunctly influence the effect and compounding their laws with one another. Its method, in short, is the concrete deductive method, that of which astronomy furnishes the most perfect, natural philosophy a somewhat less perfect, example, and the employment of which, with the adaptations and precautions required by the subject, is beginning to regenerate physiology.

Nor does it admit of doubt that similar adaptations and precautions are indispensable in sociology. In applying to that most complex of all studies what is demonstrably the sole method capable of throwing the light of science even upon phenomena of a far inferior degree of complication, we ought to be aware that the same superior complexity which renders the instrument of

*[Chapter IX of the eighth edition.]

deduction more necessary renders it also more precarious, and we must be prepared to meet, by appropriate contrivances, this increase of difficulty.

The actions and feelings of human beings in the social state are, no doubt, entirely governed by psychological and ethological laws; whatever influence any cause exercises upon the social phenomena, it exercises through those laws. Supposing, therefore, the laws of human actions and feelings to be sufficiently known, there is no extraordinary difficulty in determining from those laws the nature of the social effects which any given cause tends to produce. But when the question is that of compounding several tendencies together and computing the aggregate result of many co-existent causes, and especially when, by attempting to predict what will actually occur in a given case, we incur the obligation of estimating and compounding the influences of all the causes which happen to exist in that case, we attempt a task to proceed far in which surpasses the compass of the human faculties.

. . . .

But, without dissembling the necessary imperfections of the *a priori* method when applied to such a subject, neither ought we, on the other hand, to exaggerate them. The same objections which apply to the method of deduction in this its most difficult employment apply to it, as we formerly showed, in its easiest, and would even there have been insuperable if there had not existed, as was then fully explained, an appropriate remedy. This remedy consists in the process which, under the name of "verification," we have characterized as the third essential constituent part of the deductive method, that of collating the conclusions of the ratiocination either with the concrete phenomena themselves or, when such are obtainable, with their empirical laws. The ground of confidence in any concrete deductive science is not the *a priori* reasoning itself but the accordance between its results and those of observation *a posteriori*. Either of these processes, apart from the other, diminishes in value as the subject increases in complication, and this is in so rapid a ratio as soon to become entirely worthless, but the reliance to be placed in the concurrence of the two sorts of evidence not only does not diminish in anything like the same proportion but is not necessarily much diminished at all. Nothing more results than a disturbance in the order of precedency of the two processes, sometimes amounting to its actual inversion; insomuch that, instead of deducing our conclusions by reasoning and verifying them by observation, we in some cases begin by obtaining them provisionally from specific experience, and afterward connect them with the principles of human nature by *a priori* reasonings, which reasonings are thus a real verification.

. . . .

We shall begin, then, by looking at the social science as a science of direct deduction and considering what can be accomplished in it, and under what limitations, by that mode of investigation. We shall, then, in a separate chapter, examine and endeavor to characterize the inverse process.

2. *Difficulties of the direct deductive method in the social science*

It is evident, in the first place, that sociology, considered as a system of deductions *a priori*, cannot be a science of positive predictions but only of tendencies. We may be able to conclude, from the laws of human nature applied to the circumstances of a given state of society, that a particular cause will operate in a certain manner unless counteracted, but we can never be assured to what extent or amount it will so operate or affirm with certainty that it will not be counteracted, because we can seldom know, even approximately, all the agencies which may co-exist with it and still less calculate the collective result of so many combined elements. The remark, however, must here be once more repeated that knowledge insufficient for prediction may be most valuable for guidance. It is not necessary for the wise conduct of the affairs of society, no more than of anyone's private concerns, that we should be able to foresee infallibly the results of what we do. We must seek our objects by means which may perhaps be defeated and take precautions against dangers which possibly may never be realized. The aim of practical politics is to surround any given society with the greatest possible number of circumstances of which the tendencies are beneficial and to remove or counteract, as far as practicable, those of which the tendencies are injurious. A knowledge of the tendencies only, though without the power of accurately predicting their conjunct result, gives us to a considerable extent this power.

It would, however, be an error to suppose that even with respect to tendencies we could arrive in this manner at any great number of propositions which will be true in all societies without exception. Such a supposition would be inconsistent with the eminently modifiable nature of the social phenomena and the multitude and variety of the circumstances by which they are modified — circumstances never the same, or even nearly the same, in two different societies or in two different periods of the same society. This would not be so serious an obstacle if, though the causes acting upon society in general are numerous, those which influence any one feature of society were limited in number, for we might then insulate any particular social phenomenon and investigate its laws without disturbance from the rest. But the truth is the very opposite of this. Whatever affects, in an appreciable degree, any one element of the social state affects through it all the other elements. The mode of production of all social phenomena is one great case of intermixture of laws. We can never either understand in theory or command in practice the condition of a society in any one respect without taking into consideration its condition in all other respects. There is no social phenomenon which is not more or less influenced by every other part of the condition of the same society and, therefore, by every cause which is influencing any other of the contemporaneous social phenomena. There is, in short, what physiologists term a *consensus*, similar to that existing among the various organs and functions of the physical frame of man and the more perfect animals, and constituting one of the many analogies which have rendered universal such expressions as the "body politic" and "body natural." It follows from this *consensus* that, unless two societies could be alike in all the circumstances which surround and influence them (which would imply their being alike in their previous history), no portion whatever of the phenomena will, unless by accident, precisely correspond; no one cause will produce exactly the same effects in both. Every cause, as its effect spreads through society, comes somewhere in contact with different sets of agencies and thus has its effects on some of the social phenomena differently modified; and these differences, by their reaction, produce a difference even in those of the effects which would otherwise have been the same. We can never, therefore, affirm with certainty that a cause which has a particular tendency in one people or in one age will have exactly the same tendency in another, without referring back to our premises and performing over again for the second age or nation that analysis of the whole of its influencing circumstances which we had already performed for the first. The deductive science of society will not lay down a theorem asserting in a universal manner the effect of any cause, but will rather teach us how to frame the proper theorem for the circumstances of any given case. It will not give the laws of society in general, but the means of determining the phenomena of any given society from the particular elements or data of that society.

All the general propositions which can be framed by the deductive science are, therefore, in the strictest sense of the word, hypothetical. They are grounded on some suppositious set of circumstances and declare how some given cause would operate in those circumstances, supposing that no others were combined with them. If the set of circumstances supposed have been copied from those of any existing society, the conclusions will be true of that society, provided, and in as far as, the effect of those circumstances shall not be modified by others which have not been taken into the account. If we desire a nearer approach to concrete truth, we can only aim at it by taking, or endeavoring to take, a greater number of individualizing circumstances into the computation.

. . . .

3. *To what extent the different branches of sociological speculation can be studied apart. Political economy characterized*

Notwithstanding the universal *consensus* of the social phenomena, whereby nothing which takes place in any part of the operations of society is without its share of influence on every other part, and notwithstanding the paramount ascendancy which the general state of civilization and social progress in any given society must hence exercise over all the partial and subordinate phenomena, it is not the less true that different species of social facts are in the main dependent, immediately and in the first resort, on different kinds of causes, and, therefore, not only may with advantage, but must, be studied apart, just as in the natural body we study separately the physiology and pathology of each of the principal organs and tissues, though every one is acted upon by the state of all the others, and though the peculiar constitution and general state of health of the organism co-operates with, and often preponderates over, the local causes in determining the state of any particular organ.

On these considerations is grounded the existence of distinct and separate though not independent branches or departments of sociological speculation

There is, for example, one large class of social phenomena in which the immediately determining causes are principally those which act through the desire of wealth, and in which the psychological law mainly concerned is the familiar one that a greater gain is preferred to a smaller. I mean, of course, that portion of the phenomena of society which emanate from the industrial or productive operations of mankind, and from those of their acts through which the distribution of the products of those industrial operations takes place, in so far as not effected by force or modified by voluntary gift. By reasoning from that one law of human nature and from the principal outward circumstances (whether universal or confined to particular states of society) which operate upon the human mind through that law, we may be enabled to explain and predict this portion of the phenomena of society, so far as they depend on that class of circumstances only, overlooking the influence of any other of the circumstances of society and, therefore, neither tracing back the circumstances which we do take into account to their possible origin in some other facts in the social state nor making allowance for the manner in which any of those other circumstances may interfere with and counteract or modify the effect of the former. A department of science may thus be constructed which has received the name of political economy.

The motive which suggests the separation of this portion of the social phenomena from the rest, and the creation of a distinct branch of science relating to them is — that they do *mainly* depend, at least in the first resort, on one class of circumstances only, and that, even when other circumstances interfere, the ascertainment of the effect due to the one class of circumstances alone is a sufficiently intricate and difficult business to make it expedient to perform it once for all and then allow for the effect of the modifying circumstances; especially as certain fixed combinations of the former are apt to recur often, in conjunction with ever-varying circumstances of the latter class.

. . . .

4. *The empirical laws of the social science*

We have seen that, in most deductive sciences, and among the rest in ethology itself, which is the immediate foundation of the social science, a preliminary work of preparation is performed on the observed facts to fit them for being rapidly and accurately collated (sometimes even for being collated at all) with the conclusions of theory. This preparatory treatment consists in finding general propositions which express concisely what is common to large classes of observed facts, and these are called the empirical laws of the phenomena. We have, therefore, to inquire whether any similar preparatory process can be performed on the facts of the social science; whether there are any empirical laws in history or statistics.

In statistics, it is evident that empirical laws may sometimes be traced, and the tracing them forms an important part of that system of indirect observation on which we must often rely for the data of the deductive science. The process of the science consists in inferring effects from their causes, but we have often no means of observing the causes except through the medium of their effects. In such cases the deductive science is unable to predict the effects for want of the necessary data; it can determine what causes are capable of producing any given effect, but not with what frequency and in what quantities those causes exist. An instance in point is afforded by a newspaper now lying before me. A statement was furnished by one of the official assignees in bankruptcy showing, among the various bankruptcies which it had been his duty to investigate, in how many cases the losses had been caused by misconduct of different kinds, and in how many by unavoidable misfortunes. The result was, that the number of failures caused by misconduct greatly preponderated over those arising from all other causes whatever. Nothing but specific experience could have given sufficient ground for a conclusion to this purport. To collect, therefore, such empirical laws (which are never more than approximate generalizations) from direct observation is an important part of the process of sociological inquiry.

The experimental process is not here to be regarded as a distinct road to the truth, but as a means (happening accidentally to be the only, or the best, available) for obtaining the necessary data for the deductive science. When the immediate causes of social facts are not open to direct observation, the empirical law of the effects gives us the empirical law (which in that case is all that we can obtain) of the causes likewise. But those immediate causes depend on remote causes, and the empirical law, obtained by this indirect mode of observation, can only be relied on as applicable to unobserved cases so long as there is reason to think that no change has taken place in any of the remote causes on which the immediate causes depend. In making use, therefore, of even the best statistical generalizations for the purpose of inferring (though it be only conjecturally) that the same empirical laws will hold in any new case, it is necessary that we be well acquainted with the remoter causes, in order that we may avoid applying the empirical law to cases which differ in any of the circumstances on which the truth of the law ultimately depends. And thus, even where conclusions derived from specific observation are available for practical inferences in new cases, it is necessary that the deductive science should stand sentinel over the whole process, that it should be constantly referred to, and its sanction obtained to every inference.

The same thing holds true of all generalizations which can be grounded on history. Not only there are such generalizations, but it will presently be shown that the general science of society, which inquires into the laws of succession and co-existence of the great facts constituting the state of society and civilization at any time, can proceed in no other manner than by making such generalizations — afterward to be confirmed by connecting them with the psychological and ethological laws on which they must really depend.

5. *The verification of the social science*

But (reserving this question for its proper place) in those more special inquiries which form the subject of the separate branches of the social science, this twofold logical process and reciprocal verification is not possible; specific experience affords nothing amounting to empirical laws. This is particularly the case where the object is to determine the effect of any one social cause among a great number acting simultaneously, the effect, for example, of corn laws, or of a prohibitive commercial system generally. Though it may be perfectly certain, from theory, what *kind* of effects corn laws must produce and in what general direction their influence must tell upon industrial prosperity, their effect is yet of necessity so much disguised by the similar or contrary effects of other influencing agents that specific experience can at most only show that, on the average of some great number of instances, the cases where there were corn laws exhibited the effect in a greater degree than those where there were not. Now the number of instances necessary to exhaust the whole round of combinations of the various influential circumstances and thus afford a fair average never can be obtained. Not only we can never learn with sufficient authenticity the facts of so many instances, but the world itself does not afford them in sufficient numbers, within the limits of the given state of society and civilization which such inquiries always presuppose. Having thus no previous empirical generalizations with which to collate the conclusions of theory, the only mode of direct verification which remains is to compare those conclusions with the result of an individual experiment or instance. But here the difficulty is equally great. For in order to verify a theory by an experiment, the circumstances of the experiment must be exactly the same with those contemplated in the theory. But in social phenomena the circumstances of no two cases are exactly alike. A trial of corn laws in another country or in a former generation would go a very little way toward verifying a conclusion drawn respecting their effect in this generation and in this country. It thus happens, in most cases, that the only individual instance really fitted to verify the predictions of theory is the very instance for which the predictions were made, and the verification comes too late to be of any avail for practical guidance.

Although, however, direct verification is impossible, there is an indirect verification, which is scarcely of less value, and which is always practicable. The conclusion drawn as to the individual case can only be directly verified in that case, but it is verified indirectly, by the verification of other conclusions drawn in other individual cases from the same laws. The experience which comes too late to verify the particular proposition to which it refers is not too late to help toward verifying the general sufficiency of the theory. The test of the degree in which the science affords safe ground for predicting (and consequently for practically dealing with) what has not yet happened is the degree in which it would have enabled us to predict what has actually occurred. Before our theory of the influence of a particular cause, in a given state of circumstances, can be entirely trusted, we must be able to explain and account for the existing state of all that portion of the social phenomena which that cause has a tendency to influence. . . .

To prove, in short, that our science and our knowledge of the particular case render us competent to predict the future, we must show that they would have enabled us to predict the present and the past. If there be anything which we could not have predicted, this constitutes a residual phenomenon, requiring further study for the purpose of explanation, and we must either search among the circumstances of the particular case until we find one which, on the principles of our existing theory, accounts for the unexplained phenomenon, or we must turn back and seek the explanation by an extension and improvement of the theory itself.

CHAPTER VIII*

OF THE INVERSE DEDUCTIVE, OR HISTORICAL, METHOD

1. *Distinction between the general science of society and special sociological inquiries*

There are two kinds of sociological inquiry. In the first kind, the question proposed is what effect will follow from a given cause, a certain general condition of social circumstances being presupposed. As, for example, what would be the effect of imposing or of repealing corn laws, of abolishing monarchy or introducing universal suffrage, in the present condition of society and civilization in any European country, or under any other given supposition with regard to the circumstances of society in general, without reference to the changes which might take place, or which may already be in progress, in those circumstances. But there is also a second inquiry, namely, what are the laws which determine those general circumstances themselves. In this last the question is not what will be the effect of a given cause in a certain state of society, but what are the causes which produce and the phenomena which characterize states of society generally. In the solution of this question consists the general science of society, by which the conclusions of the other and more special kind of inquiry must be limited and controlled.

2. *What is meant by a state of society?*

In order to conceive correctly the scope of this general science and distinguish it from the subordinate departments of sociological speculation, it is necessary to fix the ideas attached to the phrase, "A State of Society." What is called a state of society is the simultaneous state of all the greater social facts or phenomena. Such are: the degree of knowledge and of intellectual and moral culture existing in the community and in every class of it; the state of industry, of wealth and its distribution; the habitual occupations

*[Chapter X of the eighth edition.]

of the community; their division into classes and the relations of those classes to one another; the common beliefs which they entertain on all the subjects most important to mankind, and the degree of assurance with which those beliefs are held; their tastes, and the character and degree of their aesthetic development; their form of government, and the more important of their laws and customs. The condition of all these things and of many more which will readily suggest themselves constitute the state of society or the state of civilization at any given time.

When states of society and the causes which produce them are spoken of as a subject of science, it is implied that there exists a natural correlation among these different elements, that not every variety of combination of these general social facts is possible, but only certain combinations, that, in short, there exist uniformities of co-existence between the states of the various social phenomena. And such is the truth; as is indeed a necessary consequence of the influence exercised by every one of those phenomena over every other. It is a fact implied in the *consensus* of the various parts of the social body.

States of society are like different constitutions or different ages in the physical frame; they are conditions not of one or a few organs or functions, but of the whole organism. Accordingly, the information which we possess respecting past ages and respecting the various states of society now existing in different regions of the earth does, when duly analyzed, exhibit uniformities. It is found that when one of the features of society is in a particular state, a state of many other features, more or less precisely determinate, always or usually co-exists with it.

But the uniformities of co-existence obtaining among phenomena which are effects of causes must (as we have so often observed) be corollaries from the laws of causation by which these phenomena are really determined. The mutual correlation between the different elements of each state of society is, therefore, a derivative law, resulting from the laws which regulate the succession between one state of society and another, for the proximate cause of every state of society is the state of society immediately preceding it. The fundamental problem, therefore, of the social science is to find the laws according to which any state of society produces the state which succeeds it and takes its place. This opens the great and vexed question of the progressiveness of man and society, an idea involved in every just conception of social phenomena as the subject of a science.

3. *The progressiveness of man and society*

It is one of the characters, not absolutely peculiar to the sciences of human nature and society, but belonging to them in a peculiar degree, to be conversant with a subject matter whose properties are changeable. I do not mean changeable from day to day, but from age to age, so that not only the qualities of individuals vary, but those of the majority are not the same in one age as in another.

The principal cause of this peculiarity is the extensive and constant reaction of the effects upon their causes. The circumstances in which mankind are placed, operating according to their own laws and to the laws of human nature, form the characters of the human beings, but the human beings, in their turn, mold and shape the circumstances for themselves and for those who come after them. From this reciprocal action there must necessarily result either a cycle or a progress. . . .

. . . .

The words "progress" and "progressiveness" are not here to be understood as synonymous with improvement and tendency to improvement. It is conceivable that the laws of human nature might determine and even necessitate a certain series of changes in man and society, which might not in every case, or which might not on the whole, be improvements. It is my belief, indeed, that the general tendency is and will continue to be, saving occasional and temporary exceptions, one of improvement, a tendency toward a better and happier state. This, however, is not a question of the method of the social science, but a theorem of the science itself. For our purpose it is sufficient that there is a progressive change both in the character of the human race and in their outward circumstances, so far as molded by themselves; that in each successive age the principal phenomena of society are different from what they were in the age preceding, and still more different from any previous age, the periods which most distinctly mark these successive changes being intervals of one generation, during which a new set of human beings have been educated, have grown up from childhood, and taken possession of society.

The progressiveness of the human race is the foundation on which a method of philosophizing in the social science has been of late years erected, far superior to either of the two modes which had previously been prevalent, the chemical or experimental, and the geometrical modes. This method, which is now generally adopted by the most advanced thinkers on the Continent, consists in attempting, by a study and analysis of the general facts of history, to discover (what these philosophers term) the law of progress; which law, once ascertained, must according to them enable us to predict future events, just as after a few terms of an infinite series in algebra we are able to detect the principle of regularity in their formation, and to predict the rest of the series to any number of terms we please. The principal aim of historical speculation in France, of late years, has been to ascertain this law. But while I gladly acknowledge the great services which have been rendered to historical knowledge by this school, I cannot but deem them to be mostly chargeable with a fundamental misconception of the true method of social philosophy. The misconception consists in supposing that the order of succession which we may be able to trace among the different states of society and civilization which history presents to us, even if that order were more rigidly uniform than it has yet been proved to be, could ever amount to a law of nature. It can only be an empirical law. The succession of states of the human mind and of human society cannot have an independent law of its own; it must depend on the psychological and ethological laws which govern the action of circumstances on men and of men on circumstances. It is conceivable that those laws might be such and the general circumstances of the human race such as to determine the successive transformations of man and society to one given and unvarying order. But even if the case were so, it cannot be the ultimate aim of science to discover an empirical law. Until that law could be connected with the psychological and ethological laws on which it must depend and, by the consilience of deduction a priori with historical evidence, could be converted from an empirical law into a scientific one, it could not be relied on for the prediction of future events beyond, at most, strictly adjacent cases. M. Comte alone, among the new historical school, has seen the necessity of thus connecting all our generalizations from history with the laws of human nature.

4. *The laws of the succession of states of society can only be ascertained by the inverse deductive method*

But, while it is an imperative rule never to introduce any generalization from history into the social science unless sufficient grounds can be pointed out for it in human nature, I do not think anyone will contend that it would have been possible, setting out from the principles of human nature and from the general circumstances of the position of our species, to determine *a priori* the order in which human development must take place and to predict, consequently, the general facts of history up to the present time. After the first few terms of the series, the influence exercised over each generation by the generations which preceded it becomes (as is well observed by the writer last referred to) more and more preponderant over all other influences, until at length what we now are and do is in a very small degree the result of the universal circumstances of the human race or even of our own circumstances acting through the original qualities of our species, but mainly of the qualities produced in us by the whole previous history of humanity. . . .

If, therefore, the series of the effects themselves did not, when examined as a whole, manifest any regularity, we should in vain attempt to construct a general science of society. We must in that case have contented ourselves with that subordinate order of sociological speculation formerly noticed, namely, with endeavoring to ascertain what would be the effect of the introduction of any new cause in a state of society supposed to be fixed — a knowledge sufficient for the more common exigencies of daily political practice, but liable to fail in all cases in which the progressive movement of society is one of the influencing elements, and, therefore, more precarious in proportion as the case is more important. But, since both the natural varieties of mankind and the original diversities of local circumstances are much less considerable than the points of agreement, there will naturally be a certain degree of uniformity in the progressive development of the species and of its works. And this uniformity tends to become greater, not less, as society advances, since the evolution of each people, which is at first determined exclusively by the nature and circumstances of that people, is gradually brought under the influence (which becomes stronger as civilization advances) of the other nations of the earth and of the circumstances by which they have been influenced. History accordingly does, when judiciously examined, afford empirical laws of society. And the problem of general sociology is to ascertain these and connect them with the laws of human nature, by deductions showing that such were the derivative laws naturally to be expected as the consequences of those ultimate ones.

It is, indeed, hardly ever possible, even after history has suggested the derivative law, to demonstrate *a priori* that such was the only order of succession or of co-existence in which the effects could, consistently with the laws of human nature, have been produced. We can at most make out that there were strong *a priori* reasons for expecting it, and that no other order of succession or co-existence would have been so likely to result from the nature of man and the general circumstances of his position. Often we cannot do even this; we cannot even show that what did take place was probable *a priori*, but only that it was possible. This, however — which, in the inverse deductive method that we are now characterizing, is a real process of verification — is as indispensable as verification by specific experience has been shown to be where the conclusion is originally obtained by the direct way of deduction. . . .

5. *Social statics, or the science of the co-existences of social phenomena*

The empirical laws of society are of two kinds: some are uniformities of co-existence, some of succession. According as the science is occupied in ascertaining and verifying the former sort of uniformities or the latter, M. Comte gives it the title of "social statics" or of "social dynamics," conformably to the distinction in mechanics between the conditions of equilibrium and those of movement, or in biology, between the laws of organization and those of life. The first branch of the science ascertains the conditions of stability in the social union; the second, the laws of progress. Social dynamics is the theory of society considered in a state of progressive movement, while social statics is the theory of the *consensus* already spoken of as existing among the different parts of the social organism, in other words, the theory of the mutual actions and reactions of contemporaneous social phenomena. . . .

. . . .

6. *Social dynamics, or the science of the successions of social phenomena*

While the derivative laws of social statics are ascertained by analyzing different states of society and comparing them with one another, without regard to the order of their succession, the consideration of the successive order is, on the contrary, predominant in the study of social dynamics, of which the aim is to observe and explain the sequences of social conditions. This branch of the social science would be as complete as it can be made if every one of the leading general circumstances of each generation were traced to its causes in the generation immediately preceding. But the *consensus* is so complete (especially in modern history) that, in the filiation of one generation and another, it is the whole which produces the whole, rather than any part a part. Little progress, therefore, can be made in establishing the filiation directly from laws of human nature, without having first ascertained the immediate or derivative laws according to which social states generate one another as society advances, the *axiomata media* of general sociology.

The empirical laws which are most readily obtained by generalization from history do not amount to this. They are not the "middle principles" themselves, but only evidence toward the establishment of such principles. They consist of certain general tendencies which may be perceived in society, a progressive increase of some social elements and diminution of others, or a gradual change in the general character of certain elements. It is easily seen, for instance, that, as society advances, mental tend more and more to prevail over bodily qualities, and masses over individuals; that the occupation of all that portion of mankind who are not under external restraint is at first chiefly military, but society becomes progressively more and more engrossed with productive pursuits, and the military spirit gradually gives way to the industrial; to which many similar truths might be added. And with generalizations of this description ordinary inquirers, even of the historical school now predominant on the Continent, are satisfied. But these and all such results are still at too great a distance from the elementary laws of human nature on which they depend — too many links intervene, and the concurrence of causes at each link is far too complicated — to enable these propositions to be presented as direct corollaries from those elementary principles. They have, therefore, in the minds of most inquirers, remained in the state of empirical laws, applicable only within the bounds of actual observation, without any means of determining their real limits and of judging whether the changes which have hitherto been in progress are destined to continue indefinitely, or to terminate, or even to be reversed.

7. Outlines of the historical method

In order to obtain better empirical laws, we must not rest satisfied with noting the progressive changes which manifest themselves in the separate elements of society and in which nothing is indicated but the relation of fragments of the effect to corresponding fragments of the cause. It is necessary to combine the statical view of social phenomena with the dynamical, considering not only the progressive changes of the different elements, but the contemporaneous condition of each, and thus obtain empirically the law of correspondence not only between the simultaneous states, but between the simultaneous changes, of those elements. This law of correspondence it is which, duly verified a priori, would become the real scientific derivative law of the development of humanity and human affairs.

In the difficult process of observation and comparison which is here required, it would evidently be a great assistance if it should happen to be the fact that some one element in the complex existence of social man is pre-eminent over all others as the prime agent of the social movement. For we could then take the progress of that one element as the central chain, to each successive link of which the corresponding links of all the other progressions being appended, the succession of the facts would by this alone be presented in a kind of spontaneous order, far more nearly approaching to the real order of their filiation than could be obtained by any other merely empirical process.

Now, the evidence of history and that of human nature combine, by a striking instance of consilience, to show that there really is one social element which is thus predominant and almost paramount among the agents of the social progression. This is the state of the speculative faculties of mankind, including the nature of the beliefs which by any means they have arrived at concerning themselves and the world by which they are surrounded.

It would be a great error, and one very little likely to be committed, to assert that speculation, intellectual activity, the pursuit of truth, is among the more powerful propensities of human nature, or holds a predominating place in the lives of any save decidedly exceptional individuals. But, notwithstanding the relative weakness of this principle among other sociological agents, its influence is the main determining cause of the social progress, all the other dispositions of our nature which contribute to that progress being dependent on it for the means of accomplishing their share of the work. Thus (to take the most obvious case first), the impelling force to most of the improvements effected in the arts of life is the desire of increased material comfort; but, as we can only act upon external objects in proportion to our knowledge of them, the state of knowledge at any time is the limit of the industrial improvements possible at that time, and the progress of industry must follow and depend on the progress of knowledge. The same thing may be shown to be true, though it is not quite so obvious, of the progress of the fine arts. Further, as the strongest propensities of uncultivated or half-cultivated human nature (being the purely selfish ones, and those of a sympathetic character which partake most of the nature of selfishness) evidently tend in themselves to disunite mankind, not to unite them — to make them rivals, not confederates — social existence is only possible by a disciplining of those more powerful propensities, which consists in subordinating them to a common system of opinions. The degree of this sub-ordination is the measure of the completeness of the social union, and the nature of the common opinions determines its kind. But in order that mankind should conform their actions to any set of opinions, these opinions must exist, must be believed by them. And thus, the state of the speculative faculties, the character of the propositions assented to by the intellect, essentially determines the moral and political state of the community, as we have already seen that it determines the physical.

These conclusions, deduced from the laws of human nature, are in entire accordance with the general facts of history. Every considerable change historically known to us in the condition of any portion of mankind, when not brought about by external force, has been preceded by a change, of proportional extent, in the state of their knowledge or in their prevalent beliefs. As between any given state of speculation and the correlative state of everything else, it was almost always the former which first showed itself, though the effects, no doubt, reacted potently upon the cause. Every considerable advance in material civilization has been preceded by an advance in knowledge; and when any great social change has come to pass, either in the way of gradual development or of sudden conflict, it has had for its precursor a great change in the opinions and modes of thinking of society. Polytheism, Judaism, Christianity, Protestantism, the critical philosophy of modern Europe, and its positive science — each of these has been a primary agent in making society what it was at each successive period while society was but secondarily instrumental in making *them*, each of them (so far as causes can be assigned for its existence) being mainly an emanation not from the practical life of the period but from the previous state of belief and thought. The weakness of the speculative propensity in mankind generally has not, there-fore, prevented the progress of speculation from governing that of society at large; it has only, and too often, prevented progress altogether, where the intellectual progression has come to an early stand for want of sufficiently favorable circumstances.

From this accumulated evidence, we are justified in concluding that the order of human progression in all respects will mainly depend on the order of progression in the intellectual convictions of mankind, that is, on the law of the successive transformations of human opinions. The question remains whether this law can be determined, at first, from history as an empirical law, then, converted into a scientific theorem by deducing it *a priori*, from the principles of human nature. As the progress of knowledge and the changes in the opinions of mankind are very slow and manifest themselves in a well-defined manner only at long intervals, it cannot be expected that the general order of sequence should be discoverable from the examination of less than a very considerable part of the duration of the social progress. It is necessary to take into consideration the whole of past time, from the first recorded condition of the human race to the memorable phenomena of the last and present generations.

CHAPTER IX*

OF THE LOGIC OF PRACTICE, OR ART; INCLUDING MORALITY AND POLICY

1. *Morality not a science but an art*

In the preceding chapters we have endeavored to characterize the present state of those among the branches of knowledge called "moral" which are sciences in the only proper sense of the term, that is, inquiries into the course of nature. It is customary, however, to include under the term moral knowledge and even (though improperly) under that of moral science an inquiry the results of which do not express themselves in the indicative but in the imperative mood, or in periphrases equivalent to it; what is called the knowledge of duties: practical ethics, or morality.

Now, the imperative mood is the characteristic of art, as distinguished from science. Whatever speaks in rules or precepts,

*[Chapter XII of the eighth edition.]

not in assertions respecting matters of fact, is art; and ethics, or morality, is properly a portion of the art corresponding to the sciences of human nature and society.[1]

The method, therefore, of ethics can be no other than that of art, or practice, in general; and the portion yet uncompleted of the task which we proposed to ourselves in the concluding Book is to characterize the general method of art, as distinguished from science.

2. *Relation between rules of art and the theorems of the corresponding science*

. . . .

The relation in which rules of art stand to doctrines of science may be thus characterized: The art proposes to itself an end to be attained, defines the end, and hands it over to the science. The science receives it, considers it as a phenomenon or effect to be studied, and, having investigated its causes and conditions, sends it back to art with a theorem of the combination of circumstances by which it could be produced. Art then examines these combinations of circumstances and, according as any of them are or are not in human power, pronounces the end attainable or not. The only one of the premises, therefore, which art supplies is the original major premise, which asserts that the attainment of the given end is desirable. Science then lends to art the proposition (obtained by a series of inductions or of deductions) that the performance of certain actions will attain the end. From these premises art concludes that the performance of these actions is desirable, and finding it also practicable, converts the theorem into a rule or precept.

3. *Art cannot be deductive*

The error is, therefore, apparent of those who would deduce the line of conduct proper to particular cases from supposed universal

[1] It is almost superfluous to observe, that there is another meaning of the word Art, in which it may be said to denote the poetical department or aspect of things in general, in contradistinction to the scientific. In the text, the word is used in its older and, I hope, not yet obsolete sense.

practical maxims, overlooking the necessity of constantly referring back to the principles of the speculative science in order to be sure of attaining even the specific end which the rules have in view. How much greater still, then, must the error be of setting up such unbending principles not merely as universal rules for attaining a given end, but as rules of conduct generally, without regard to the possibility not only that some modifying cause may prevent the attainment of the given end by the means which the rule prescribes, but that success itself may conflict with some other end which may possibly chance to be more desirable.

.   .   .   .

4. *Every art consists of truths of science, arranged in the order suitable for some practical use*

The grounds, then, of every rule of art are to be found in the theorems of science. An art or a body of art consists of the rules, together with as much of the speculative propositions as comprises the justification of those rules. The complete art of any matter includes a selection of such a portion from the science as is necessary to show on what conditions the effects which the art aims at producing depend. And art in general consists of the truths of science, arranged in the most convenient order for practice instead of the order which is the most convenient for thought. Science groups and arranges its truths so as to enable us to take in at one view as much as possible of the general order of the universe. Art, though it must assume the same general laws, follows them only into such of their detailed consequences as have led to the formation of rules of conduct, and brings together from parts of the field of science most remote from one another the truths relating to the production of the different and heterogeneous conditions necessary to each effect which the exigencies of practical life require to be produced.

.   .   .   .

5. *Teleology, or the doctrine of ends*

But though the reasonings which connect the end or purpose of every art with its means belong to the domain of science, the definition of the end itself belongs exclusively to art and forms its peculiar province. Every art has one first principle or general major premise not borrowed from science, that which enunciates the object aimed at and affirms it to be a desirable object. The builder's art assumes that it is desirable to have buildings; architecture, as one of the fine arts, that it is desirable to have them beautiful or imposing. The hygienic and medical arts assume, the one that the preservation of health, the other that the cure of disease, are fitting and desirable ends. These are not propositions of science. Propositions of science assert a matter of fact: an existence, a co-existence, a succession, or a resemblance. The propositions now spoken of do not assert that anything is, but enjoin or recommend that something should be. They are a class by themselves. A proposition of which the predicate is expressed by the words *ought* or *should be* is generically different from one which is expressed by *is* or *will be*. It is true that, in the largest sense of the words, even these propositions assert something as a matter of fact. The fact affirmed in them is that the conduct recommended excites in the speaker's mind the feeling of approbation. This, however, does not go to the bottom of the matter; for the speaker's approbation is no sufficient reason why other people should approve, nor ought it to be a conclusive reason even with himself. For the purposes of practice, everyone must be required to justify his approbation; and for this there is need of general premises determining what are the proper objects of approbation and what the proper order of precedence among those objects.

These general premises, together with the principal conclusions which may be deduced from them, form (or rather might form) a body of doctrine which is properly the art of life, in its three departments, morality, prudence or policy, and aesthetics — the right, the expedient, and the beautiful or noble, in human conduct and works. To this art (which, in the main, is unfortunately still to be created) all other arts are subordinate, since its principles are those which must determine whether the special aim of any particular art is worthy and desirable and what is its place in the scale of desirable things. Every art is thus a joint result of laws of nature disclosed by science and of the general principles of what has been called teleology, or the doctrine of ends,[2] which, borrowing the language of the German metaphysicians, may also be termed, not improperly, the principles of practical reason.

A scientific observer or reasoner, merely as such, is not an adviser for practice. His part is only to show that certain consequences follow from certain causes and that, to obtain certain ends, certain means are the most effectual. Whether the ends themselves are such as ought to be pursued, and if so, in what cases and to how great a length, it is no part of his business as a cultivator of science to decide, and science alone will never qualify him for the decision. In purely physical science, there is not much temptation to assume this ulterior office, but those who treat of human nature and society invariably claim it; they always undertake to say not merely what is, but what ought to be. To entitle them to do this, a complete doctrine of teleology is indispensable. A scientific theory, however perfect, of the subject matter considered merely as part of the order of nature, can in no degree serve as a substitute. In this respect the various subordinate arts afford a misleading analogy. In them there is seldom any visible necessity for justifying the end, since in general its desirableness is denied by nobody, and it is only when the question of precedence is to be decided between that end and some other that the general principles of teleology have to be called in; but a writer on morals and politics requires those principles at every step. The most elaborate and well-digested exposition of the laws of succession and co-existence among mental or social phenomena and of their relation to one another as causes and effects will be of no avail toward the art of life or of society, if the ends to be aimed at by that art are left to the vague suggestions of the *intellectus sibi permissus*, or are taken for granted without analysis or questioning.

6. *Necessity of an ultimate standard, or first principle of teleology*

There is, then, a *philosophia prima* peculiar to art as there is one which belongs to science. There are not only first principles of knowledge, but first principles of conduct. There must be some

[2] The word "teleology" is also, but inconveniently and improperly, employed by some writers as a name for the attempt to explain the phenomena of the universe from final causes.

standard by which to determine the goodness or badness, absolute and comparative, of ends or objects of desire. And whatever that standard is, there can be but one; for, if there were several ultimate principles of conduct, the same conduct might be approved by one of those principles and condemned by another, and there would be needed some more general principle as umpire between them.

Accordingly, writers on moral philosophy have mostly felt the necessity not only of referring all rules of conduct and all judgments of praise and blame to principles, but of referring them to some one principle, some rule or standard with which all other rules of conduct were required to be consistent, and from which by ultimate consequence they could all be deduced. Those who have dispensed with the assumption of such a universal standard have only been enabled to do so by supposing that a moral sense or instinct, inherent in our constitution, informs us both what principles of conduct we are bound to observe and also in what order these should be subordinated to one another.

The theory of the foundations of morality is a subject which it would be out of place, in a work like this, to discuss at large, and which could not to any useful purpose be treated incidentally. I shall content myself, therefore, with saying that the doctrine of intuitive moral principles, even if true, would provide only for that portion of the field of conduct which is properly called moral. For the remainder of the practice of life some general principle or standard must still be sought, and if that principle be rightly chosen, it will be found, I apprehend, to serve quite as well for the ultimate principle of morality, as for that of prudence, policy, or taste.

Without attempting in this place to justify my opinion or even to define the kind of justification which it admits of, I merely declare my conviction that the general principle to which all rules of practice ought to conform and the test by which they should be tried is that of conduciveness to the happiness of mankind, or, rather, of all sentient beings; in other words, that the promotion of happiness is the ultimate principle of teleology.*

*For an express discussion and vindication of this principle, see the little volume entitled "Utilitarianism." [Reprinted in the "Little Library of Liberal Arts.]

I do not mean to assert that the promotion of happiness should be itself the end of all actions or even of all rules of action. It is the justification and ought to be the controller of all ends, but it is not itself the sole end. There are many virtuous actions and even virtuous modes of action (though the cases are, I think, less frequent than is often supposed) by which happiness in the particular instance is sacrificed, more pain being produced than pleasure. But conduct of which this can be truly asserted admits of justification only because it can be shown that, on the whole, more happiness will exist in the world if feelings are cultivated which will make people, in certain cases, regardless of happiness. I fully admit that this is true, that the cultivation of an ideal nobleness of will and conduct should be to individual human beings an end to which the specific pursuit either of their own happiness or of that of others (except so far as included in that idea) should, in any case of conflict, give way. But I hold that the very question what constitutes this elevation of character is itself to be decided by a reference to happiness as the standard. The character itself should be, to the individual, a paramount end, simply because the existence of this ideal nobleness of character or of a near approach to it, in any abundance, would go farther than all things else toward making human life happy, both in the comparatively humble sense of pleasure and freedom from pain, and in the higher meaning of rendering life not what it now is almost universally, puerile and insignificant, but such as human beings with highly developed faculties can care to have.

Selections from

AN EXAMINATION OF

SIR WILLIAM HAMILTON'S

PHILOSOPHY

[THIRD EDITION]

CHAPTER I

OF THE INTERPRETATION OF CONSCIOUSNESS

According to all philosophers, the evidence of consciousness, if only we can obtain it pure, is conclusive. This is an obvious but by no means a mere identical proposition. If consciousness be defined as intuitive knowledge, it is indeed an identical proposition to say that if we intuitively know anything, we do know it and are sure of it. But the meaning lies in the implied assertion that we do know some things immediately, or intuitively. That we must do so is evident if we know anything; for what we know mediately depends for its evidence on our previous knowledge of something else; unless, therefore, we knew something immediately we could not know anything mediately, and consequently could not know anything at all. That imaginary being, a complete skeptic, might be supposed to answer that perhaps we do not know anything at all. I shall not reply to this problematical antagonist in the usual manner, by telling him that if he does not know anything, I do. I put to him the simplest case conceivable of immediate knowledge and ask if we ever feel anything? If so, then, at the moment of feeling, do we know that we feel? Or if he will not call this knowledge, will he deny that when we have a feeling we have at least some sort of assurance or conviction of having it? This assurance or conviction is what other people mean by knowledge. If he dislikes the word, I am willing in discussing with him to employ some other. By whatever name this assurance is called, it is the test to which we bring all our other convictions. He may say it is not certain; but such as it may be, it is our model of certainty. We consider all our other assurances and convictions as more or less certain, according as they approach the standard of this. I have a conviction that there are icebergs in the Arctic seas. I have not had the evidence of my senses for it; I never saw an iceberg. Neither do I intuitively believe it by a law of my mind. My conviction is

* [Chapter IX of the third edition.]

mediate, grounded on testimony and on inferences from physical laws. When I say I am convinced of it, I mean that the evidence is equal to that of my senses. I am as certain of the fact as if I had seen it. And, on a more complete analysis, when I say I am convinced of it, what I am convinced of is that if I were in the Arctic seas I should see it. We mean by knowledge and by certainty an assurance similar and equal to that afforded by our senses; if the evidence in any other case can be brought up to this, we desire no more. If a person is not satisfied with this evidence, it is no concern of anybody but himself, nor, practically, of himself, since it is admitted that this evidence is what we must, and may with full confidence, act upon. Absolute skepticism, if there be such a thing, may be dismissed from discussion as raising an irrelevant issue, for in denying all knowledge it denies none. The dogmatist may be quite satisfied if the doctrine he maintains can be attacked by no arguments but those which apply to the evidence of the senses. If his evidence is equal to that, he needs no more; nay, it is philosophically maintainable that by the laws of psychology we can conceive no more, and that this is the certainty which we call perfect.

The verdict, then, of consciousness or, in other words, our immediate and intuitive conviction is admitted, on all hands, to be a decision without appeal. The next question is, *to what* does consciousness bear witness?

. . . .

. . . Among the facts which Sir W. Hamilton considers as revelations of consciousness, there is one kind which, as he truly says, no one does or can doubt, another kind which they can and do. The facts which cannot be doubted are those to which the word "consciousness" is by most philosophers confined: the facts of internal consciousness, "the mind's own acts and affections." What we feel, we cannot doubt that we feel. It is impossible to us to feel and to think that perhaps we feel not, or to feel not and think that perhaps we feel. What admits of being doubted is the revelation which consciousness is supposed to make (and which our author considers as itself consciousness) of an external reality. But according to him, though we may doubt this external reality, we are compelled to admit that consciousness testifies to it. We may disbelieve our consciousness, but we cannot doubt what its testimony is. This assertion cannot be granted in the same unqualified manner as the others. It is true that I cannot doubt my present impression; I cannot doubt that when I perceive color or weight, I perceive them as in an object. Neither can I doubt that when I look at two fields, I perceive which of them is the farthest off. The majority of philosophers, however, would not say that perception of distance by the eye is testified by consciousness, because although we really do so perceive distance, they believe it to be an acquired perception. It is at least possible to think that the reference of our sensible impressions to an external object is, in like manner, acquired; and if so, though a fact of our consciousness in its present artificial state, it would have no claim to the title of a fact of consciousness generally, not having been in consciousness from the beginning. This point of psychology we shall have to discuss farther on.

. . . .

At first sight it might seem as if there could not possibly be any doubt whether our consciousness does or does not affirm any given thing. Nor can there, if consciousness means, as it usually does, self-consciousness. If consciousness tells me that I have a certain thought or sensation, I assuredly have that thought or sensation. But if consciousness, as with Sir W. Hamilton, means a power which can tell me things that are not phenomena of my own mind, there is immediately the broadest divergence of opinion as to what are the things to which consciousness testifies. There is nothing which people do not think and say that they know by consciousness, provided they do not remember any time when they did not know or believe it, and are not aware in what manner they came by the belief. For consciousness, in this extended sense, is, as I have so often observed, but another word for "intuitive knowledge," and whatever other things we may know in that manner, we certainly do not know by intuition what knowledge is intuitive. It is a subject on which both the vulgar and the ablest thinkers are constantly making mistakes. . . .

. . . It is not enough to say that something is testified by consciousness, and refer all dissentients to consciousness to prove it. Substitute for consciousness the equivalent phrase (in our author's acceptation at least) intuitive knowledge, and it is seen that this is not a thing which can be proved by mere introspection of ourselves. Introspection can show us a present belief or conviction, attended with a greater or a less difficulty in accommodating the thoughts to a different view of the subject; but that this belief, or conviction, or knowledge, if we call it so, is intuitive, no mere introspection can ever show, unless we are at liberty to assume that every mental process which is now as unhesitating and as rapid as intuition was intuitive at its outset. . . .

So far, good. But now, it being conceded that the question, what do we know intuitively, or, in Sir W. Hamilton's phraseology, what does our consciousness testify, is not, as might be supposed, a matter of simple self-examination but of science, it has still to be determined in what manner science should set about it. And here emerges the distinction between two different methods of studying the problems of metaphysics, forming the radical difference between the two great schools into which metaphysicians are fundamentally divided. One of these I shall call, for distinction, the "introspective method"; the other, the "psychological."

. . . The difference between these methods will now be exemplified by showing them at work on a particular question, the most fundamental one in philosophy, the distinction between the Ego and the Non-ego.

CHAPTER II*

THE PSYCHOLOGICAL THEORY OF THE BELIEF IN AN EXTERNAL WORLD

. . . I proceed to state the case of those who hold that the belief in an external world is not intuitive but an acquired product.

*[Chapter XI of the third edition.]

This theory postulates the following psychological truths, all of which are proved by experience, and are not contested, though their force is seldom adequately felt by Sir W. Hamilton and the other thinkers of the introspective school.

It postulates, first, that the human mind is capable of "expectation." In other words, that after having had actual sensations, we are capable of forming the conception of *possible* sensations; sensations which we are not feeling at the present moment, but which we might feel and should feel if certain conditions were present, the nature of which conditions we have, in many cases, learned by experience.

It postulates, secondly, the laws of the "association of ideas." So far as we are here concerned, these laws are the following: first, similar phenomena tend to be thought of together. Secondly, phenomena which have either been experienced or conceived in close contiguity to one another tend to be thought of together. The contiguity is of two kinds: simultaneity and immediate succession. Facts which have been experienced or thought of simultaneously recall the thought of one another. Of facts which have been experienced or thought of in immediate succession, the antecedent, or the thought of it, recalls the thought of the consequent, but not conversely. Thirdly, associations produced by contiguity become more certain and rapid by repetition. When two phenomena have been very often experienced in conjunction, and have not, in any single instance, occurred separately either in experience or in thought, there is produced between them what has been called "inseparable," or less correctly, "indissoluble association"; by which is not meant that the association must inevitably last to the end of life — that no subsequent experience or process of thought can possibly avail to dissolve it—but only that as long as no such experience or process of thought has taken place, the association is irresistible; it is impossible for us to think the one thing disjoined from the other. Fourthly, when an association has acquired this character of inseparability — when the bond between the two ideas has been thus firmly riveted—not only does the idea called up by association become, in our consciousness, inseparable from the idea which suggested it, but the facts or phenomena answering to those ideas come at last to seem inseparable in existence; things which we are unable to conceive apart appear incapable of existing apart, and the belief we have in their coexistence, though really a product of experience, seems intuitive. Innumerable examples might be given of this law. One of the most familiar, as well as the most striking, is that of our acquired perceptions of sight. Even those who, with Mr. Bailey, consider the perception of distance by the eye as not acquired but intuitive, admit that there are many perceptions of sight which, though instantaneous and unhesitating, are not intuitive. What we see is a very minute fragment of what we think we see. We see artificially that one thing is hard, another soft. We see artificially that one thing is hot, another cold. We see artificially that what we see is a book, or a stone, each of these being not merely an inference, but a heap of inferences, from the signs which we see to things not visible. We see, and cannot help seeing, what we have learned to infer, even when we know that the inference is erroneous, and that the apparent perception is deceptive. We cannot help seeing the moon larger when near the horizon, though we know that she is of precisely her usual size. We cannot help seeing a mountain as nearer to us and of less height when we see it through a more than ordinarily transparent atmosphere.

Setting out from these premises, the psychological theory maintains that there are associations naturally and even necessarily generated by the order of our sensations and of our reminiscences of sensation which, supposing no intuition of an external world to have existed in consciousness, would inevitably generate the belief, and would cause it to be regarded as an intuition.

What is it we mean, or what is it which leads us to say, that the objects we perceive are external to us and not a part of our own thoughts? We mean that there is concerned in our perceptions something which exists when we are not thinking of it, which existed before we had ever thought of it, and would exist if we were annihilated; and further, that there exist things which we never saw, touched, or otherwise perceived, and things which never have been perceived by man. This idea of something which is distinguished from our fleeting impressions by what, in Kantian language, is called "perdurability"; something which is fixed and the same, while our impressions vary; something which exists whether we are aware of it or not, and which is always square (or of some other given figure) whether it appears to us square or round — constitutes altogether our idea of external substance. Whoever can assign an origin to this complex conception has accounted for what we mean by the belief in matter. Now all this, according to the psychological theory, is but the form impressed by the known laws of association upon the conception or notion, obtained by experience, of "contingent sensations"; by which are meant sensations that are not in our present consciousness, and individually never were in our consciousness at all, but which in virtue of the laws to which we have learned by experience that our sensations are subject, we know that we should have felt under given supposable circumstances, and under these same circumstances might still feel.

I see a piece of white paper on a table. I go into another room. If the phenomenon always followed me, or if, when it did not follow me, I believed it to disappear *e rerum natura*, I should not believe it to be an external object. I should consider it as a phantom — a mere affection of my senses; I should not believe that there had been anybody there. But, though I have ceased to see it, I am persuaded that the paper is still there. I no longer have the sensations which it gave me, but I believe that when I again place myself in the circumstances in which I had those sensations — that is, when I go again into the room — I shall again have them; and further, that there has been no intervening moment at which this would not have been the case. Owing to this property of my mind, my conception of the world at any given instant consists, in only a small proportion, of present sensations. Of these I may at the time have none at all, and they are in any case a most insignificant portion of the whole which I apprehend. The conception I form of the world existing at any moment comprises, along with the sensations I am feeling, a countless variety of possibilities of sensation — namely, the whole of those which past observation tells me that I could, under any supposable circumstances, experience at this moment, together with an indefinite and illimitable multitude of others which though I do not know that I could, yet it is possible that I might, experience in circumstances not known to me. These various possibilities are the important thing to me in the world. My present sensations are generally of little importance and are, moreover, fugitive; the possibilities, on the contrary, are permanent, which is the character that mainly distinguishes our idea of substance or matter from our notion of sensation. These possibilities, which are conditional certainties, need a special name to distinguish them from mere vague possibilities which experience gives no warrant for reckoning upon. Now, as soon as a distinguishing name is given, though it be only to the same thing regarded in a different aspect, one of the most familiar experiences of our mental nature teaches us that the different name comes to be considered as the name of a different thing.

There is another important peculiarity of these certified or guaranteed possibilities of sensation — namely, that they have reference, not to single sensations, but to sensations joined together in groups. When we think of anything as a material substance or body, we either have had, or we think that on some given supposition we should have, not some *one* sensation, but a great and even an indefinite number and variety of sensations, generally belonging to different senses but so linked together that the presence of one announces the possible presence at the very same instant of any or all of the rest. In our mind, therefore, not only is this particular possibility of sensation invested with the quality of permanence when we are not actually feeling any of the sensations at all; but when we are feeling some of them, the remaining sensations of the group are conceived by us in the form of present possibilities, which might be realized at the very moment. And as this happens in turn to all of them, the group as a whole presents itself to the mind as permanent, in contrast not solely with the temporariness of my bodily presence, but also with the temporary character of each of the sensations composing the group; in other words, as a kind of permanent substratum, under a set of passing experiences or manifestations, which is another leading character of our idea of substance or matter, as distinguished from sensation.

Let us now take into consideration another of the general characters of our experience, namely, that in addition to fixed groups we also recognize a fixed order in our sensations; an order of succession which, when ascertained by observation, gives rise to the ideas of cause and effect, according to what I hold to be the true theory of that relation, and is on any theory the source of all our knowledge what causes produce what effects. Now, of what nature is this fixed order among our sensations? It is a constancy of antecedence and sequence. But the constant antecedence and sequence do not generally exist between one actual sensation and another. Very few such sequences are presented to us by experience. In almost all the constant sequences which occur in nature, the antecedence and consequence do not obtain between sensations, but between the groups we have been speaking about, of which a very small portion is actual sensation, the greater part being permanent possibilities of sensation evidenced to us by a small and variable number of sensations actually present. Hence our ideas of causation, power, activity do not become connected in thought with our sensations as *actual* at all, save in the few physiological cases where these figure by themselves as the antecedents in some uniform sequence. Those ideas become connected, not with sensations, but with groups of possibilities of sensation. The sensations conceived do not, to our habitual thoughts, present themselves as sensations actually experienced, inasmuch as not only any one or any number of them may be supposed absent, but none of them need be present. We find that the modifications which are taking place more or less regularly in our possibilities of sensation are mostly quite independent of our consciousness and of our presence or absence. Whether we are asleep or awake, the fire goes out and puts an end to one particular possibility of warmth and light. Whether we are present or absent, the corn ripens and brings a new possibility of food. Hence we speedily learn to think of nature as made up solely of these groups of possibilities, and the active force in nature as manifested in the modification of some of these by others. The sensations, though the original foundation of the whole, come to be looked upon as a sort of accident depending on us, and the possibilities as much more real than the actual sensations, nay, as the very realities of which these are only the representations, appearances, or effects. When this state of mind has been arrived at, then, and from that time forward, we are never conscious of a present sensation without instantaneously referring it to some one of the groups of possibilities into which a sensation of that particular description enters; and if we do not yet know to what group to refer it, we at least feel an irresistible conviction that it must belong to some group or other; that is, that its presence proves the existence, here and now, of a great number and variety of possibilities of sensation without which it would not have been. The whole set of sensations as possible form a permanent background to any one or more of them that are, at a given moment, actual; and the possibilities are conceived as standing to the actual sensations in the relation of a cause to its effects, or of canvas to the figures painted on it, or of a root to the trunk, leaves, and flowers, or of a substratum to that which is spread over it, or, in transcendental language, of matter to form.

When this point has been reached, the permanent possibilities in question have assumed such unlikeness of aspect, and such difference of apparent relation to us, from any sensations, that it would be contrary to all we know of the constitution of human nature that they should not be conceived as, and believed to be, at least as different from sensations as sensations are from one another. Their groundwork in sensation is forgotten, and they are supposed to be something intrinsically distinct from it. We can withdraw ourselves from any of our (external) sensations or we can be withdrawn from them by some other agency. But though the sensations cease, the possibilities remain in existence; they are independent of our will, our presence, and everything which belongs to us. We find, too, that they belong as much to other human or sentient beings as to ourselves. We find other people grounding their expectations and conduct upon the same permanent possibilities on which we ground ours. But we do not find them experiencing the same actual sensations. Other people do not have our sensations exactly when and as we have them, but they have our possibilities of sensation; whatever indicates a present possibility of sensations to ourselves, indicates a present possibility of similar sensations to them, except so far as their organs of sensation may vary from the type of ours. This puts the final seal to our conception of the groups of possibilities as the fundamental reality in nature. The permanent possibilities are common to us and to our fellow-creatures; the actual sensations are not. That which other people become aware of when and on the same grounds as I do, seems more real to me than that which they do not know of unless

I tell them. The world of possible sensations succeeding one another according to laws is as much in other beings as it is in me; it has therefore an existence outside me; it is an external world.

If this explanation of the origin and growth of the idea of matter or external nature contains nothing at variance with natural laws, it is at least an admissible supposition that the element of non-ego which Sir W. Hamilton regards as an original datum of consciousness, and which we certainly do find in our present consciousness, may not be one of its primitive elements — may not have existed at all in its first manifestations. But if this supposition be admissible, it ought, on Sir W. Hamilton's principles, to be received as true. The first of the laws laid down by him for the interpretation of consciousness, the law (as he terms it) of "parsimony," forbids to suppose an original principle of our nature in order to account for phenomena which admit of possible explanation from known causes. If the supposed ingredient of consciousness be one which might grow up (though we cannot prove that it did grow up) through later experience; and if, when it had so grown up, it would, by known laws of our nature, appear as completely intuitive as our sensations themselves; we are bound, according to Sir W. Hamilton's and all sound philosophy, to assign to it that origin. Where there is a known cause adequate to account for a phenomenon, there is no justification for ascribing it to an unknown one. And what evidence does consciousness furnish of the intuitiveness of an impression except instantaneousness, apparent simplicity, and unconsciousness on our part of how the impression came into our minds? These features can only prove the impression to be intuitive on the hypothesis that there are no means of accounting for them otherwise. If they not only might, but naturally would, exist, even on the supposition that it is not intuitive, we must accept the conclusion to which we are led by the psychological method, and which the introspective method furnishes absolutely nothing to contradict.

Matter, then, may be defined a "permanent possibility" of sensation. If I am asked whether I believe in matter, I ask whether the questioner accepts this definition of it. If he does, I believe in matter; and so do all Berkeleians. In any other sense than this, I do not. But I affirm with confidence that this conception of matter includes the whole meaning attached to it by the common world, apart from philosophical and sometimes from theological theories. The reliance of mankind on the real existence of visible and tangible objects means reliance on the reality and permanence of possibilities of visual and tactual sensations, when no such sensations are actually experienced. We are warranted in believing that this is the meaning of matter in the minds of many of its most esteemed metaphysical champions, though they themselves would not admit as much; for example, of Reid, Stewart, and Brown. For these three philosophers alleged that all mankind, including Berkeley and Hume, really believed in matter, inasmuch as unless they did they would not have turned aside to save themselves from running against a post. Now all which this maneuver really proved is that they believed in permanent possibilities of sensation. We have therefore the unintentional sanction of these three eminent defenders of the existence of matter, for affirming that to believe in permanent possibilities of sensation is believing in matter. It is hardly necessary, after such authorities, to mention Dr. Johnson or any one else who resorts to the *argumentum baculinum* of knocking a stick against the ground. Sir W. Hamilton, a far subtler thinker than any of these, never reasons in this manner. He never supposes that a disbeliever in what he means by matter ought in consistency to act in any different mode from those who believe in it. He knew that the belief on which all the practical consequences depend is the belief in permanent possibilities of sensation, and that if nobody believed in a material universe in any other sense, life would go on exactly as it now does. He, however, did believe in more than this, but, I think, only because it had never occurred to him that mere possibilities of sensation could, to our artificialized consciousness, present the character of objectivity which, as we have now shown, they not only can but, unless the known laws of the human mind were suspended, must necessarily present.

Perhaps it may be objected that the very possibility of framing such a notion of matter as Sir W. Hamilton's — the capacity in the human mind of imagining an external world which is anything more than what the psychological theory makes it — amounts to a disproof of the theory. If (it may be said) we had no revelation in consciousness of a world which is not in some way or other identified with sensation, we should be unable to have the notion of such a world. If the only ideas we had of external objects were ideas of our sensations, supplemented by an acquired notion of permanent possibilities of sensation, we must (it is thought) be incapable of conceiving, and therefore still more incapable of fancying that we perceive, things which are not sensations at all. It being evident however that some philosophers believe this, and it being maintainable that the mass of mankind do so, the existence of a perdurable basis of sensations, distinct from sensations themselves, is proved, it might be said, by the possibility of believing it.

Let me first restate what I apprehend the belief to be. We believe that we perceive a something closely related to all our sensations, but different from those which we are feeling at any particular minute, and distinguished from sensations altogether by being permanent and always the same, while these are fugitive, variable, and alternately displace one another. But these attributes of the object of perception are properties belonging to all the possibilities of sensation which experience guarantees. The belief in such permanent possibilities seems to me to include all that is essential or characteristic in the belief in substance. I believe that Calcutta exists, though I do not perceive it, and that it would still exist if every percipient inhabitant were suddenly to leave the place or be struck dead. But when I analyze the belief, all I find in it is that were these events to take place, the permanent possibility of sensation which I call Calcutta would still remain; that if I were suddenly transported to the banks of the Hoogly, I should still have the sensations which, if now present, would lead me to affirm that Calcutta exists here and now. We may infer, therefore, that both philosophers and the world at large, when they think of matter, conceive it really as a permanent possibility of sensation. But the majority of philosophers fancy that it is something more; and the world at large, though they have really, as I conceive, nothing in their minds but a permanent possibility of sensation, would, if asked the question, undoubtedly agree with the philosophers; and though this is sufficiently explained by the tendency of the human mind to infer difference of things from difference of names, I acknowledge the obligation of showing how it can be possible to believe in an existence transcending all possibilities of sensation, unless on the hypothesis that such an existence actually is and that we actually perceive it.

The explanation, however, is not difficult. It is an admitted fact that we are capable of all conceptions which can be formed by generalizing from the observed laws of our sensations. Whatever relation we find to exist between any one of our sensations and something different from *it*, that same relation we have no difficulty in conceiving to exist between the sum of all our sensations and something different from *them*. The differences which our consciousness recognizes between one sensation and another give us the general notion of difference, and inseparably associate with every sensation we have the feeling of its being different from other things; and when once this association has been formed, we can no longer conceive anything without being able, and even being compelled, to form also the conception of something different from it. This familiarity with the idea of something different from *each* thing we know makes it natural and easy to form the notion of something different from *all* things that we know, collectively as well as individually. It is true we can form no conception of what such a thing can be — our notion of it is merely negative — but the idea of a substance, apart from its relation to the impressions which we conceive it as making on our senses, *is* a merely negative one. There is thus no psychological obstacle to our forming the notion of a something which is neither a sensation nor a possibility of sensation, even if our consciousness does not testify to it; and nothing is more likely than that the permanent possibilities of sensation, to which our consciousness does testify, should be confounded in our minds with this imaginary conception. All experience attests the strength of the tendency to mistake mental abstractions, even negative ones, for substantive realities; and the permanent possibilities of sensation which experience guarantees are so extremely unlike in many of their properties to actual sensations that since we are capable of imagining something which transcends sensation, there is a great natural probability that we should suppose these to be it.

But this natural probability is converted into certainty when we take into consideration that universal law of our experience which is termed the "law of causation," and which makes us mentally connect with the beginning of everything, some antecedent condition, or cause. The case of causation is one of the most marked of all the cases in which we extend to the sum total of our consciousness a notion derived from its parts. It is a striking example of our power to conceive, and our tendency to believe, that a relation which subsists between every individual item of our experience and some other item subsists also between our experience as a whole and something not within the sphere of experience. By this extension to the sum of all our experiences of the internal relations obtaining between its several parts, we are led to consider sensation itself — the aggregate whole of our sensations — as deriving its origin from antecedent existences transcending sensation. That we should do this, is a consequence of the particular character of the uniform sequences, which experience discloses to us among our sensations. As already remarked, the constant antecedent of a sensation is seldom another sensation, or set of sensations, actually felt. It is much oftener the existence of a group of possibilities, not necessarily including any actual sensations except such as are required to show that the possibilities are really present. Nor are actual sensations indispensable even for this purpose; for the presence of the object (which is nothing more than the immediate presence of the possibilities) may be made known to us by the very sensation which we refer to it as its effect. Thus the real antecedent of an effect — the only antecedent which, being invariable and unconditional, we consider to be the cause — may be not any sensation really felt but solely the presence, at that or the immediately preceding moment, of a group of possibilities of sensation. Hence it is not with sensations as actually experienced, but with their permanent possibilities, that the idea of cause comes to be identified; and we, by one and the same process, acquire the habit of regarding sensation in general, like all our individual sensations, as an effect, and also that of conceiving as the causes of most of our individual sensations, not other sensations, but general possibilities of sensation. If all these considerations put together do not completely explain and account for our conceiving these *possibilities* as a class of independent and substantive entities, I know not what psychological analysis can be conclusive.

It may perhaps be said that the preceding theory gives, indeed, some account of the idea of permanent existence which forms part of our conception of matter, but gives no explanation of our believing these permanent objects to be external or out of ourselves. I apprehend, on the contrary, that the very idea of anything out of ourselves is derived solely from the knowledge experience gives us of the permanent possibilities. Our sensations we carry with us wherever we go, and they never exist where we are not; but when we change our place, we do not carry away with us the permanent possibilities of sensation; they remain until we return, or arise and cease under conditions with which our presence has in general nothing to do. And more than all — they are, and will be after we have ceased to feel, permanent possibilities of sensation to other beings than ourselves. Thus our actual sensations and the permanent possibilities of sensation stand out in obtrusive contrast to one another; and when the idea of cause has been acquired, and extended by generalization from the parts of our experience to its aggregate whole, nothing can be more natural than that the permanent possibilities should be classed by us as existences generically distinct from our sensations, but of which our sensations are the effect.[1]

[1] My able American critic, Dr. H. B. Smith, contends through several pages (152–157) that these facts afford no proofs that objects *are* external to us. I never pretended that they do. I am accounting for our conceiving, or representing to ourselves, the permanent possibilities as real objects external to us. I do not believe that the real externality to us of anything, except other minds, is capable of proof. But the permanent possibilities are external to us in the only sense we need care about; they are not constructed by the mind itself but merely recognized by it; in Kantian language, they are *given* to us and to other beings in common with us. "Men cannot act, cannot live," says Professor Fraser (p. 26), "without assuming an external world, in some conception of the term external. It is the business of the philosopher to explain what that conception ought to be. For ourselves we can conceive only — (1) An externality to our present and transient experience in *our own* possible experience past and future, and (2) An externality to our own conscious experience, in the contemporaneous, as well as in the past or future experience of *other minds*." The view I take of externality, in the sense in which I acknowledge it as real, could not be more accurately expressed than in Professor Fraser's words. Dr. Smith's criticisms continually go wide of the mark because he has somehow imagined that I am defending, instead of attacking, the belief in matter as an entity *per se*. As when he says (pp. 157–158) that my reasoning assumes, contrary

The same theory which accounts for our ascribing to an aggregate of possibilities of sensation a permanent existence which our sensations themselves do not possess, and consequently a greater reality than belongs to our sensations, also explains our attributing greater objectivity to the primary qualities of bodies than to the secondary. For the sensations which correspond to what are called the primary qualities (as soon at least as we come to apprehend them by two senses, the eye as well as the touch) are always present when any part of the group is so. But colors, tastes, smells, and the like, being, in comparison, fugacious, are not, in the same degree, conceived as being always there, even when nobody is present to perceive them. The sensations answering to the secondary qualities are only occasional; those to the primary, constant. The secondary, moreover, vary with different persons and with the temporary sensibility of our organs; the primary, when perceived at all, are, as far as we know, the same to all persons and at all times.

APPENDIX TO THE PRECEDING CHAPTER*

This attempt to bring out into distinctness the mode in which the notions of matter and mind, considered as substances, may have been generated in us by the mere order of our sensations, has naturally received from those whose metaphysical opinions were already made up a much greater amount of opposition than of assent. I think I have observed, however, that the repugnance shown to it by writers has been in tolerably correct proportion to the evidence they give of deficiency in that indispensable apti-

---

to my own opinion, "an *a priori* necessity and validity of the law of cause and effect, or invariable antecedence and consequence." This might fairly have been said if I were defending the belief in the supposed hidden cause of our sensations; but I am only accounting for it, and to do so I assume only the tendency, but not the legitimacy of the tendency, to extend all the laws of our own experience to a sphere beyond our experience.

* [In the third edition: "Appendix to the two preceding chapters," referring also to Chapter XII, which is here omitted.]

tude of a metaphysician — facility in placing himself at the point of view of a theory different from his own; and that those who have ever (if the expression may be pardoned) thought themselves into the Berkeleian or any other idealistic scheme of philosophy, however little favorable toward other parts of the present volume, have either let this part of it alone or expressed more or less approbation of it. Those who are completely satisfied with the popular everyday notion of matter, or whose metaphysics have been adopted from any of the realistic thinkers who undertake to legitimate that common notion, are usually content with going round the counter-theory on the outside and seldom place themselves sufficiently at the center of it to perceive what a person ought to think or do, who occupies that position. They no longer, indeed, commit so gross a blunder as that which, not very long ago, even Reid, Stewart, and Brown rushed blindly into — that of charging a Berkeleian with inconsistency if he did not walk into the water or into the fire. Acquaintance with the German metaphysicians and (it is but just to add) the teachings of Sir W. Hamilton have had that much of beneficial result. But if such thinkers as these three could pass judgment on Berkeley's doctrine while showing by such conclusive proof that they had never understood its very alphabet — that, however much consideration they may have given to the mere arguments of Berkeley, they had not begun to realize his doctrine in their own minds — to look at the sensible universe as he saw it, and see what consequences would follow; it is not wonderful that those who have got on a few steps further than this have still much to do before they are able to accommodate their conceptive faculties to the conditions of what I have called the psychological theory, and follow that theory correctly into the ramification of its applications.

In principle, I must admit that my opponents, as a body, have referred the psychological theory to the right test. They have aimed at showing that its attempt to account for the belief in matter (I say matter only because I do not profess to have adequately accounted for the belief in mind) implies or requires that the belief should already exist, as a condition of its own production. The objection, if true, is conclusive; but they are not very particular about the proof of its truth. They, one and all, think their case made out if I employ, in any part of the exposition, the language of common life — a language constructed on the basis of the notions into the origin of which I am inquiring. If I say that after we have seen a piece of paper on a table, our belief that it is still there during our absence means a belief that if we went again into the room we should see it, they cry out, Here is belief in matter already assumed; the idea of going into a room implies belief in matter. If, as a proof that modifications may take place in our possibilities of sensation while the sensations are not in actual consciousness, I say that whether we are asleep or awake the fire goes out, I am told that I am assuming a knowledge of ourselves as a substance and of the difference between being asleep and awake. They forget that to go into a room, to be asleep or awake, are expressions which have a meaning in the psychological theory as well as in theirs; that every assertion that can be made about the external world, which means anything on the realistic theory, has a parallel meaning on the psychological. Going into a room, on the psychological theory, is a mere series of sensations felt and possibilities of sensation inferred,[1] but distinguishable from every other combination of sensations and possibilities, and which, with others like to itself, forms as vast and variegated a picture of the universe as can be had on the other theory; indeed, as I maintain, the very same picture. The psychological theory requires that we should have a conception of this series of actual and contingent sensations, as distinct from any other; but it does not require that we should have referred these sensations to a substance ulterior to all sensation or possibility of sensation. To suppose so is to commit the same kind of misapprehension, though in a less extreme degree, which Reid, Stewart, and Brown committed.

When, in attempting an intelligible discussion of an abstruse metaphysical question, I have occasion to speak of any combination of physical facts, I must speak of it by the only names there are for it. I must employ language every word of which expresses, not things as we perceive them or as we may have conceived them originally, but things as we conceive them now. I was addressing

---

[1] This particular series includes volitions in addition to sensations, but the difference is of no consequence; and the theory would stand if we suppose ourselves carried into the room instead of walking into it.

readers all of whom had the acquired notion of matter, and nearly all of them the belief in it, and it was my business to show, to these believers in matter, a possible mode in which the notion and belief of it might have been acquired even if matter, in the metaphysical meaning of the term, did not exist. In endeavoring to point out to them by what facts the notion might have been generated, it was competent to me to state those facts in the language which was not only the most intelligible, but, to the minds I was addressing, the truest. The real paralogism would have been if I had said anything implying, not the existence of matter, but that the belief in it or the notion of it was part of the facts by which I was maintaining that this belief and notion may have been generated. But in no single instance have any adversaries whom I am aware of been able to show this; and if they fairly placed themselves at the point of view of the psychological explanation, they would see that I could not, in any circumstances whatever, have been reduced to this necessity, because there is, as I have said, for every statement which can be made concerning material phenomena in terms of the realistic theory, an equivalent meaning in terms of sensation and possibilities of sensation alone, and a meaning which would justify all the same processes of thought. In fact, almost all philosophers who have narrowly examined the subject have decided that substance need only be postulated as a support for phenomena or as a bond of connection to hold a group or series of otherwise unconnected phenomena together; let us only, then, think away the support and suppose the phenomena to remain and to be held together in the same groups and series by some other agency, or without any agency but an internal law, and every consequence follows without substance, for the sake of which substance was assumed. The Hindoos thought that the earth required to be supported by an elephant, but the earth turned out quite capable of supporting itself, and "hanging self-balanced" on its own "center." Descartes thought that a material medium filling the whole space between the earth and the sun was required to enable them to act on one another; but it has been found sufficient to suppose an immaterial law of attraction, and the medium and its vortices dropped off as superfluities.

To dispel some of the haze which seems still to hang about the data assumed by the psychological theory of the belief in matter, it will be well that, as I have stated what laws and capacities, in one word, what conditions, that theory postulates in the mind itself, I should also state what conditions it postulates in nature, in that which, to use the Kantian phraseology, is given to the mind, as distinguished from the mind's own constitution.

First, then, it postulates sensations and a certain order among sensations. And the order postulated is of more kinds than one.

In the first place, there is the mere fact of succession. Sensations exist before and after one another. This is as much a primordial fact as sensation itself; it is a feature always present in sensation, and we have the strongest ground that can ever be had for regarding it as ultimate, because every genesis we assign to any other fact of perception or thought includes it as a condition. I shall be told that this is postulating the reality of time; and it is so, if by "time" be understood an indefinite succession of successions, unequal in rapidity. But an entity called "Time," and regarded as not a succession of successions, but as something *in* which the successions take place, I do not and need not postulate.[2] Neither do I decide whether this inseparable attribute of our sensations is annexed to them by the laws of mind or given in the sensations themselves, nor whether, at this great height of abstraction, the distinction does not disappear. Let me say also that I have never pretended to account by association for the idea of time. It is the seeming infinity of time, as of space, which, after Mr. James Mill, I have tendered that explanation of; and that of this it is the true and sufficient one, is to me obvious.

Sensations are not only successive, they are also simultaneous;

[2]This objective conception of time, as *holding* the successions instead of *being* them, is probably suggested by our being able to measure time and number its parts. But what we call measuring time is only comparing successions, and measuring the length or rapidity of one series of successions by that of another. Rapidity of succession, indeed, is a phrase which derives all its meaning from such a comparison. I say that the words of a person to whom I am listening succeed one another more rapidly than the tickings of a clock, because, after I have heard a word and a ticking simultaneously, a second word occurs before a second ticking. The only ultimate facts or primitive elements in time are *before* and *after;* which (the knowledge of opposites being one) involve the notion of *neither* before *nor* after, that is, simultaneous.

it often happens that several of them are felt, apparently at the same instant. This attribute of sensations is not so evidently primordial as their succession. There are philosophers who think that the sensations deemed simultaneous are very rapidly successive, their distinction from other cases of succession being that they may succeed one another in any order. I do not agree in this opinion; but, even supposing it correct, we should equally have to postulate the distinction. We should have to assume that plurality of sensations exists in two modes, one consciously successive, the other felt as simultaneous, and that the mind is able to distinguish between the one sort and the other.

Besides this twofold order inherent in sensations, of being either successive or simultaneous, there is an order within that order; they are successive or simultaneous in constant combinations. The same antecedent sensation is followed by the same consequent sensation; the same sensation is accompanied by the same set of simultaneous sensations. I use these expressions for shortness, for the uniformity of order is not quite so simple as this. The consequent sensation is not always *actually* felt after the antecedent, nor are all the synchronous sensations actually felt whenever one of them is felt. But the one which is felt gives us assurance, grounded on experience, that each of the others, if not felt, is feelable, that is, will be felt if the other facts be present which are the known antecedent conditions of such a sensation as it is. For example, I have the sensations of color and of a visible disk, which are parts of our present conception of a cast-iron ball. I infer that there is now or presently to be had by me, simultaneously with those visual sensations, another feeling called the sensation of hardness. But I do not have this last sensation inevitably and at once. Why? Because (as I also know by experience) no sensation of hardness is ever felt unless preceded by a condition, the same in all cases, but itself sensational — the sensations of muscular exertion and pressure. The visual sensation is synchronous, not necessarily with the actual sensation of hardness, but with a present possibility of that sensation. When we feel the one, we are not always feeling the other, but we know that it is to be felt on the ordinary terms; we know that so soon as the muscular sensations take place which are the observed preliminary to *every* sensation of hardness, that particular sensation of hardness will certainly be had, simultaneously with the visual sensation. This is what is meant by saying that a body is a group of simultaneous possibilities of sensation, not of simultaneous sensations. It rarely happens that the sensations which enter into the group can all be experienced at once, because many of them are never had without a long series of antecedent sensations, including volitions, which may be incompatible with the sensations and volitions necessary for having others. The sensations which we receive when we study the internal structure of a closed body are not to be obtained without having previously the complex series of sensations and volitions concerned in the operation of opening it. The sensations we receive from the complicated process by which food nourishes us must be long waited for after our first sight of the food, and many of them are not even then to be had without our being led up to them through a long series of muscular and other sensations. But the very first sensations we have, that are sufficient to identify the group, guarantee to us the possibility or potentiality of all the others. The potentiality becomes actuality on the occurrence of certain known conditions *sine qua non* of each, which are conditions not of having that particular sensation at a given moment, but of having any sensation of that kind — conditions which, when analyzed, are themselves also merely sensational. Anyone who had thrown his mind, by an act of imagination, into the psychological theory, would see at a glance all these applications and developments of it, even if he did not follow them out into detail. But men will not, and mostly cannot, throw their minds into any theory with which they are not familiar; and the bearings and consequences of the psychological theory will have to be developed and minutely expounded innumerable times before it will be seen as it is and have whatever chance it deserves of being accepted as true.

I have postulated, first, sensations; secondly, succession and simultaneousness of sensations; thirdly, a uniform order in their succession and simultaneousness, such that they are united in groups the component sensations of which are in such a relation to one another that when we experience one, we are authorized to expect all the rest, conditionally on certain antecedent sensations called organic, belonging to the *kind* of each. This is all we need postulate with regard to the groups considered in themselves or considered in relation to the perceiving subject. Let us examine whether it is necessary to postulate anything additional respecting the groups considered in relation to one another.

In Dr. M'Cosh's opinion, the psychological theory overlooks this part of the subject.[3] In quoting the analysis of our conception of matter into resistance, extension, and figure, together with miscellaneous powers of exciting other sensations, he observes, "There is a palpable omission here, for it omits those powers by which one body operates upon another; thus the sun has a power to make wax white, and fire to make lead fluid." If Dr. M'Cosh had entered even a very little way into the mode of thought which he is combating, he must have seen that after mentioning the attribute of exciting sensations, it could not be necessary to add that of making something else excite sensations. If body altogether is only conceived as a power of exciting sensations, the action of one body upon another is simply the modification by one such power of the sensations excited by another; or, to use a different expression, the joint action of two powers of exciting sensations. It is easy for anyone competent to such inquiries who will make the attempt to understand how one group of possibilities of sensation can be conceived as destroying or modifying another such group.

Let there be granted a synchronous group connected by the contingent simultaneousness already described, which renders each of the component sensations a mark of the possibility of having all the others; while each, independently of the others, has conditions *sine qua non* of its own, also sensational, but of the kind which, in common language, we call organic and refer to an internal sense. Let us suppose that these organic conditions, instead of existing for one or more sensations of the group and not for the rest, do not at present exist for any of them. The whole of the possibilities of sensation which form the group, and which mutually testify to each other's presence, are now dormant; but they are ready to

---

[3] M'Cosh, p. 118. The same observation applies to another of my critics, the writer in *Blackwood's Magazine*, who says (p. 28) "The qualities by which they [Things] act upon each other, cannot be resolved into any receptivity or subjectivity of mine."

start into actuality at any moment, when the conditions *sine qua non* which belong to them separately are realized; and whenever any of them thus starts up, it informs us (so far as our experience happens to have reached) what others are ready to do so in the same manner. This dormancy of all the possibilities, while, as real possibilities guaranteeing one another, they continue to exist, constitutes, on the psychological theory, the fact which is at the bottom of the assertion that the body is in existence when we are not perceiving it. This fact is all that we need postulate to account for our conceiving the groups of possibilities of sensation as permanent and independent of us, for our projecting them into objectivity, and for our conceiving them as perhaps capable of being possibilities of sensation to other beings in like manner as to ourselves, as soon as we have conceived the idea of other sentient beings than ourselves. And since we do actually recognize other sentient beings as existing, and receive impressions from them which entirely accord with this hypothesis, we accept the hypothesis as a truth and believe that the permanent possibilities of sensation really are common to ourselves and other beings.

Having thus arrived at the conception of an absent group of possibilities, there is surely no more difficulty in conceiving the annihilation or alteration of the possibilities while absent, than of the sensations themselves when present. The log which I saw on the fire an hour ago has been consumed and has disappeared when I look again; the possibilities of sensation which I called by that name are possibilities no longer. The ice which I placed in front of the fire at the same time is now water; such possibilities of sensation as form part of the groups called ice and not of the groups called water have ceased and given place to others. All this is intelligible without supposing the wood, the ice, or the water to be anything underneath or beyond permanent possibilities of sensation. Why, then, when I ascribe the disappearance of the wood and the conversion of the ice into water to the presence of the fire, must I suppose the fire to be something underneath a possibility of sensation? My experience informs me that those other possibilities of sensation do not vanish or change in the manner mentioned unless another possibility of sensation known by the name of fire has existed immediately before, and continued to exist simultaneously with, the change. Changes in the permanent possibilities I find to have always for their antecedent conditions other permanent possibilities and to be connected with them by an order or law as uniform as that which connects the elements of each group with one another; indeed, by a still stricter order, for the laws of succession, those of cause and effect, are laws of more rigid precision than those of simultaneousness. But the facts between which the observed uniformities of succession exist are facts of sense; that is, either actual sensations or possibilities of sensation inferred from the actual. Thus the whole variety of the facts of nature as we know it, is given in the mere existence of our sensations and in the laws or order of their occurrence.[4]

I have now given an exposition of the psychological theory and of the mode in which it accounts for what is supposed to be our natural conviction of the existence of matter, from the objective point of view, as I had previously done from the subjective; and I think it will be found that the exposition does not presuppose anything which I have not expressly postulated, and that I have not postulated any of the facts or notions which I undertake to explain. It may be said that I postulate an ego — the sentient subject of the sensations. I have stated what subjective, as well

[4] Mr. O'Hanlon, in his little pamphlet (pp. 12 and 14) puts his difficulty on this subject in the following terms: "Your permanent possibilities of sensation are, so long as they are not felt, nothing actual. Yet you speak of change taking place in them, and that independently of our consciousness and of our presence or absence. . . . If the fire, apart from any consciousness, be some positive condition or conditions of warmth and light, if the corn be some positive condition or conditions of food, my thesis is made out, and your Pure Idealism falls to the ground. If, on the other hand, the fire be nothing positive apart from any consciousness, then, since it is nothing at all when so apart, you can have no right to speak of modifications taking place in it whether we are asleep or awake, present or absent."

I give great credit to my young antagonist, not only for the neatness of his dilemma, but for having gone so directly to the point at which is the real stress of the dispute. But I think he will perceive, from what I have said in the text, in what manner one may have a right to speak of modifications as taking place in a possibility. And I think he will be able to see that the condition of a phenomenon needs not necessarily be anything positive, in his sense of the word, or objective; it may be anything, positive or negative, actuality or possibility, without which the phenomenon would not have occurred, and which may therefore be justly inferred from its occurrence.

as what objective, data I postulate. Expectation being one of these, in so far as reference to an ego is implied in expectation I do postulate an ego. But I am entitled to do so, for up to this stage it is not self, but body, that I have been endeavoring to trace to its origin as an acquired notion.[5]

. . . .

Having shown that in order to account for the belief in matter, or, in other words, in a non-ego supposed to be presented in or along with sensation, it is not necessary to suppose anything but sensations and possibilities of sensation connected in groups; it was natural and necessary to inquire whether the ego, supposed to be presented in or along with all consciousness whatever, is also an acquired notion, explicable in the same manner. I therefore stated this phenomenal theory of the ego, freed it from the prejudice which attaches to it on the score of consequences to which it does not lead, the non-existence, first, of our fellow-creatures, and

[5]Mr. O'Hanlon says (p. 14): "Conceding the entire truth of the position, that there are associations naturally and even necessarily generated by the order of our sensations, and of our reminiscences of sensation, which, supposing no intuition of an external world to have existed in consciousness, would inevitably generate the belief, and would cause it to be regarded as an intuition;—conceding, I say, for argument's sake, the entire truth of this position, it may still be true that though we have no intuition of the external world, the inference that such a world exists is a legitimate one." Undoubtedly it may. Malebranche, for instance, according to whose system matter is not perceived, nor in any way cognized, nor capable of being cognized, by our minds, all the things that we see or feel existing only as ideas in the Divine Mind, nevertheless fully believed in the reality of this superfluous wheel in the mechanism of the universe, which merely revolves while the machinery does its work independently of it — because he thought that God himself had asserted its existence in the Scriptures; and whoever agrees with Malebranche in his premises is likely to agree with him in his conclusion. But with most people, whether philosophers or common men, the evidence on which matter is believed to exist independently of our minds is either that we perceive it by our senses or that the notion and belief of it come to us by an original law of our nature. If it be shown that there is no ground for either of these opinions — that all we are conscious of may be accounted for without supposing that we perceive matter by our senses, and that the notion and belief in matter may have come to us by the laws of our constitution without being a revelation of any objective reality—the main evidences of matter are at an end; and though I am perfectly willing to listen to any other evidence, Malebranche's argument is, I must confess, quite as conclusive as any that I expect to find.

secondly, of God;[6] but showed that it has intrinsic difficulties

[6]Some of my critics have impugned the arguments of the preceding chapter on this particular point. They have said (Mr. O'Hanlon is the one who has said it with the greatest compactness and force) that persons, equally with inanimate things, may be conceived as mere states of my own consciousness; that the same processes of thought which, according to the psychological theory, can generate the belief in matter even if it does not exist, must be equally competent to engender the belief of the existence of other minds; and that the principles of the theory require us, under the law of parsimony, to conclude that if the belief may have been, it has been, thus generated; consequently the theory takes away all evidence of the existence of other minds or of other threads of consciousness than our own.

It would undoubtedly do so if the only evidence of the existence of other threads of consciousness was a natural belief, as a natural belief is the only evidence which rational persons now acknowledge of the existence of matter. But there is other evidence which does not exist in the case of matter, and which is as conclusive as the other is inconclusive. The nature of this has been stated, with sufficient fulness of development, in the preceding chapter, and Mr. O'Hanlon has rightly understood it to be a simple extension of "the principles of inductive evidence, which experience shows hold good of my states of consciousness, to a sphere without my consciousness." But he objects (p. 7): "The doing so postulates two things: (a) That there is a sphere beyond my consciousness; the very thing to be proved. (b) That the laws which obtain in my consciousness, also obtain in the sphere beyond it."

To this I reply that it does not postulate these two things, but, to the extent required by the present question, proves them. There is nothing in the nature of the inductive principle that confines it within the limits of my own consciousness, when it exceptionally happens that an inference surpassing the limits of my consciousness can conform to inductive conditions.

I am aware, by experience, of a group of permanent possibilities of sensation which I call my body, and which my experience shows to be an universal condition of every part of my thread of consciousness. I am also aware of a great number of other groups, resembling the one that I call my body, but which have no connection, such as that has, with the remainder of my thread of consciousness. This disposes me to draw an inductive inference, that those other groups are connected with other threads of consciousness, as mine is with my own. If the evidence stopped here, the inference would be but an hypothesis; reaching only to the inferior degree of inductive evidence called analogy. The evidence, however, does not stop here; for — having made the supposition that real feelings, though not experienced by myself, lie behind those phenomena of my own consciousness which, from their resemblance to my body, I call other human bodies — I find that my subsequent consciousness presents those very sensations, of speech heard, of movements and other outward demeanor seen, and so forth, which, being the effects or consequents of actual feelings in my own case, I should expect to follow upon those other hypothetical feelings if which no one has been able to remove; since certain of the attributes comprised in our notion of the ego, and which are at the very foundation of it, namely, memory and expectation, have no equivalent in matter and cannot be reduced to any elements similar to those into which matter is resolved by the psychological theory. Having stated these facts, as inexplicable by the psychological theory, I left them to stand as facts, without any theory whatever, not adopting the permanent possibility hypothesis as a sufficient theory of self, in spite of the objections to it, as some of

they really exist; and thus the hypothesis is verified. It is thus proved inductively that there is a sphere beyond my consciousness; that is, that there are other consciousnesses beyond it, for there exists no parallel evidence in regard to matter. And it is proved inductively that so far as respects those other consciousnesses, linked to as many groups of permanent possibilities of sensation similar to my own body, the laws which obtain in my consciousness also obtain in the sphere beyond it; that those other threads of consciousness are beings similar to myself.

The legitimacy of this process is open to no objections, either real or imaginary, but such as may equally be made against inductive inferences within the sphere of our own actual or possible consciousness. Facts of which I never *have* had consciousness are as much unknown facts, as much apart from my actual experience, as facts of which I cannot have consciousness. When I conclude, from facts that I immediately perceive, to the existence of other facts such as *might* come into my actual consciousness (which the feelings of other people never can) but which never *did* come into it, and of which I have no evidence but an induction from experience, how do I know that I am concluding rightly — that the inference is warranted, from an actual consciousness to a contingent possibility of consciousness which has never become actual? Surely because this conclusion from experience is verified by further experience; because those other experiences which I ought to have if my inference was correct really present themselves. This verification, which is the source of all my reliance on induction, justifies the same reliance wherever it is found. The alien threads of consciousness of which I presume the existence from the analogy of my own body manifest the truth of the presumption by visual and tactual effects within my own consciousness, resembling those which follow from sensations, thoughts, or emotions felt by myself. The reality beyond the sphere of my consciousness rests on the twofold evidence, of its antecedents and its consequents. It is an inference upward from the manifestations, and downward from the antecedent conditions; and whichever of these inferences is first drawn, the other is its verification.

I venture to hope that these considerations may remove Mr. O'Hanlon's difficulty. But whatever the difficulty may be, it is not peculiar to the psychological theory, but has equally to be encountered on every other. For no my critics have imagined and have wasted no small amount of argument and sarcasm in exposing the untenability of such a position; neither, on the other hand, did I, as others have supposed, accept the common theory of mind as a so-called substance. Since the state in which I profess to leave the question has been so ill understood, it is incumbent on me to explain myself more fully.

Since the fact which alone necessitates the belief in an ego, the one fact which the psychological theory cannot explain, is the fact of memory (for expectation I hold to be, both psychologically and

one supposes that other people's feelings or states of consciousness are a matter of direct intuition to us, or of natural belief. We do not directly perceive other minds; their reality is not known to us immediately, but by means of evidence. And there is no evidence by which it can be proved to me that there is a conscious being within each of the human bodies that I see, without a process of induction involving the very same assumptions which are required by the psychological theory.

I will delay the reader a few moments more while I reply to a minor difficulty of Mr. O'Hanlon. He urges that the psychological theory inserts an alien consciousness between two consciousnesses of my own, as the effect of one of them and the cause of the other. "A boy cuts his finger and screams. The knife, the blood, and the boy's body are only (in Mr. Mill's view) actual and possible groups of my sensations, and the scream is an actual sensation. I infer, continuing to accept Mr. Mill's theory, that between the scream and the other sensations, namely, between two sets of states of my own consciousness, a foreign consciousness had the feeling I call pain, and also that the sensations of cutting its finger, the same sensations, belong as much to it as to me, combined with certain additions, and in a very peculiar manner. Yet if I was not by, the boy, the knife, the blood, the scream, would only exist potentially" (pp. 8, 9). Whatever seeming absurdity and real confusion exist here are only attributable to the fact that Mr. O'Hanlon, notwithstanding his acuteness, has not yet sufficiently thought himself into the theory he denies. On the same evidence on which I recognize foreign threads of consciousness, I believe that the permanent possibilities of sensation are common to them and to me; but not the actual sensations. The evidence proves to me that, although the knife, the blood, and the boy's body would, if I were absent, be mere potentialities of sensation relatively to me, the similar potentialities which I infer to exist in him have been realized as actual sensations; and it is as conditions of the sensations in him, and not of sensations in me, that they form a part of the series of causes and effects which take place out of my consciousness. The chain of causation is the following: (1) A modification in a set of permanent possibilities of sensation common to the boy and me. (2) A sensation of pain in the boy, not felt by me. (3) The scream, which is a sensation in me.

logically, a consequence of memory), I see no reason to think that there is any cognizance of an ego until memory commences. There seems no ground for believing, with Sir W. Hamilton and Mr. Mansel, that the ego is an original presentation of consciousness; that the mere impression on our senses involves, or carries with it, any consciousness of a self, any more than I believe it to do of a not-self. Our very notion of a self takes its commencement, there is every reason to suppose, from the representation of a sensation in memory, when awakened by the only thing there is to awaken it before any associations have been formed, namely, the occurrence of a subsequent sensation similar to the former one. The fact of recognizing a sensation, of being reminded of it, and, as we say, remembering that it has been felt before, is the simplest and most elementary fact of memory; and the inexplicable tie, or law, the organic union (as Professor Masson calls it) which connects the present consciousness with the past one, of which it reminds me, is as near as I think we can get to a positive conception of self. That there is something real in this tie, real as the sensations themselves, and not a mere product of the laws of thought without any fact corresponding to it, I hold to be indubitable. The precise nature of the process by which we cognize it, is open to much dispute. Whether we are directly conscious of it in the act of remembrance, as we are of succession in the fact of having successive sensations, or whether, according to the opinion of Kant, we are not conscious of a self at all, but are compelled to assume it as a necessary condition of memory,[7] I do not undertake to decide. But this original element which has no community of nature with any of the things answering to our names, and to which we cannot give any name but its own peculiar one without implying some false or ungrounded theory, is the ego, or self. As such, I ascribe a reality to the ego — to my own mind — different from that real

[7]Mr. Mahaffy thinks that the question may be decided in favor of Kant on the evidence of consciousness itself. "Are you," he asks (p. lvi.), "conscious of being presented with yourself as a substance? or are you only conscious that in every act of thought you must presuppose a permanent self, and always refer it to self, while still that self you cannot grasp, and it remains a hidden basis upon which you erect the structure of your thoughts? Which of these opinions will most men adopt? After all, Kant's view is the simpler, and the more consistent with the ordinary language."

existence as a permanent possibility which is the only reality I acknowledge in matter; and by fair experiential inference from that one ego, I ascribe the same reality to other egoes or minds.

Having thus, as I hope, more clearly defined my position in regard to the reality of the ego considered as a question of ontology, I return to my first starting point, the relativity of human knowledge and affirm (being here in entire accordance with Sir W. Hamilton) that whatever be the nature of the real existence we are compelled to acknowledge in mind, the mind is only known to itself phenomenally as the series of its feelings or consciousnesses. We are forced to apprehend every part of the series as linked with the other parts by something in common, which is not the feelings themselves, any more than the succession of the feelings is the feelings themselves; and as that which is the same in the first as in the second, in the second as in the third, in the third as in the fourth, and so on, must be the same in the first and in the fiftieth, this common element is a permanent element. But beyond this, we can affirm nothing of it except the states of consciousness themselves. The feelings or consciousnesses which belong or have belonged to it, and its possibilities of having more, are the only facts there are to be asserted of self — the only positive attributes, except permanence, which we can ascribe to it. In consequence of this, I occasionally use the words "mind" and "thread of consciousness" interchangeably, and treat "mind as existing" and "mind as known to itself" as convertible; but this is only for brevity, and the explanations which I have now given must always be taken as implied.

CHAPTER III

THE DOCTRINE OF CONCEPTS, OR GENERAL NOTIONS

We now arrive at the questions which form the transition from psychology to logic — from the analysis and laws of the mental operations to the theory of the ascertainment of objective truth — the natural link between the two being the theory of the particular mental operations whereby truth is ascertained or authenticated. According to the common classification . . . these operations are three: conception or the formation of general notions, judgment, and reasoning. We begin with the first.

On this subject two questions present themselves: first, whether there are such things as general notions, and secondly, what they are. If there are general notions, they must be the notions which are expressed by general terms; and concerning general terms, all who have the most elementary knowledge of the history of metaphysics are aware that there are, or once were, three different opinions.

The first is that of the realists, who maintained that general names are the names of general things. Besides individual things, they recognized another kind of things, not individual, which they technically called "second substances," or universals *a parte rei*. Over and above all individual men and women, there was an entity called man — man in general, which inhered in the individual men and women and communicated to them its essence. These universal substances they considered to be a much more dignified kind of beings than individual substances, and the only ones the cognizance of which deserved the names of science and knowledge. Individual existences were fleeting and perishable, but the beings called genera and species were immortal and unchangeable.

This, the most prevalent philosophical doctrine of the middle ages, is now universally abandoned, but remains a fact of great significance in the history of philosophy; being one of the most

* [Chapter XVII of the third edition.]

striking examples of the tendency of the human mind to infer difference of things from difference of names — to suppose that every different class of names implied a corresponding class of real entities to be denoted by them. Having two such different names as "man" and "Socrates," these inquirers thought it quite out of the question that man should only be a name for Socrates and others like him, regarded in a particular light. Man, being a name common to many, must be the name of a substance common to many and in mystic union with the individual substances, Socrates and the rest.

In the later middle ages there grew up a rival school of metaphysicians, termed nominalists, who, repudiating universal substances, held that there is nothing general except names. A name, they said, is general if it is applied in the same acceptation to a plurality of things; but every one of the things is individual. The dispute between these two sects of philosophers was very bitter and assumed the character of a religious quarrel: authority, too, interfered in it, and as usual on the wrong side. The Realist theory was represented as the orthodox doctrine, and belief in it was imposed as a religious duty. It could not, however, permanently resist philosophical criticism, and it perished. But it did not leave nominalism in possession of the field. A third doctrine arose, which endeavored to steer between the two. According to this, which is known by the name of conceptualism, generality is not an attribute solely of names, but also of thoughts. External objects indeed are all individual, but to every general name corresponds a "general notion," or "conception," called by Locke and others an "abstract idea." General names are the names of these abstract ideas.

Realism being no longer extant, nor likely to be revived, the contest at present is between nominalism and conceptualism; each of which counts illustrious names among its modern adherents. . . .

. . . .

The formation . . . of a concept does not consist in separating the attributes which are said to compose it from all other attributes of the same object, and enabling us to conceive those attributes, disjoined from any others. We neither conceive them, nor think them, nor cognize them in any way, as a thing apart, but solely as forming, in combination with numerous other attributes, the idea of an individual object. But, though thinking them only as part of a larger agglomeration, we have the power of fixing our attention on them, to the neglect of the other attributes with which we think them combined. While the concentration of attention actually lasts, if it is sufficiently intense, we may be temporarily unconscious of any of the other attributes, and may really, for a brief interval, have nothing present to our mind but the attributes constituent of the concept. In general, however, the attention is not so completely exclusive as this; it leaves room in consciousness for other elements of the concrete idea, though of these the consciousness is faint, in proportion to the energy of the concentrative effort; and the moment the attention relaxes, if the same concrete idea continues to be contemplated, its other constituents come out into consciousness. General concepts, therefore, we have, properly speaking, none; we have only complex ideas of objects in the concrete; but we are able to attend exclusively to certain parts of the concrete idea, and by that exclusive attention we enable those parts to determine exclusively the course of our thoughts as subsequently called up by association; and are in a condition to carry on a train of meditation or reasoning relating to those parts only, exactly as if we were able to conceive them separately from the rest.

What principally enables us to do this is the employment of signs, and particularly the most efficient and familiar kind of signs, *viz.*, names. This is a point which Sir W. Hamilton puts well and strongly, and there are many reasons for stating it in his own language.[1]

The concept thus formed by an abstraction of the resembling from the non-resembling qualities of objects, would again fall back into the confusion and infinitude from which it has been called out, were it not rendered permanent for consciousness, by being fixed and ratified in a verbal sign. Considered in general, thought and language are reciprocally dependent; each bears all the imperfections and perfections of the other; but without language there could be no knowledge realized of the essential properties of things, and of the connexion of their accidental states.

[1] Lectures, iii. 137.

The rationale of this is that when we wish to be able to think of objects in respect of certain of their attributes — to recall no objects but such as are invested with those attributes, and to recall them with our attention directed to those attributes exclusively — we effect this by giving to that combination of attributes, or to the class of objects which possess them, a specific name. We create an artificial association between those attributes and a certain combination of articulate sounds which guarantees to us that when we hear the sound, or see the written characters corresponding to it, there will be raised in the mind an idea of some object possessing those attributes, in which idea those attributes alone will be suggested vividly to the mind, our consciousness of the remainder of the concrete idea being faint. As the name has been directly associated only with those attributes, it is as likely, in itself, to recall them in any one concrete combination as in any other. What combination it shall recall in the particular case depends on recency of experience, accidents of memory, or the influence of other thoughts which have been passing, or are even then passing, through the mind; accordingly, the combination is far from being always the same, and seldom gets itself strongly associated with the name which suggests it, while the association of the name with the attributes that form its conventional signification is constantly becoming stronger. The association of that particular set of attributes with a given word is what keeps them together in the mind by a stronger tie than that with which they are associated with the remainder of the concrete image. To express the meaning in Sir W. Hamilton's phraseology, this association gives them a unity[2] in our consciousness. It is only when this has been accom-

[2]One of the best and profoundest passages in all Sir W. Hamilton's writings is that in which he points out (though only incidentally) what are the conditions of our ascribing unity to any aggregate: "Though it is only by experience we come to attribute an external unity to aught continuously extended, that is, consider it as a system or constituted whole; still, in so far as we do so consider it, *we think the parts as held together by a certain force*, and the whole, therefore, as endowed with a power of resisting their distraction. It is, indeed, only by finding that a material continuity resists distraction, that we view it as more than a fortuitous aggregation of many bodies, that is, as a single body. The material universe, for example, though not *de facto* continuously extended, we consider as one system in so far, but only in so far, as we find all bodies tending together by reciprocal attraction." *Dissertations on Reid*, pp. 852, 853.

plished, that we possess what Sir W. Hamilton terms a "concept"; and this is the whole of the mental phenomenon involved in the matter. We have a concrete representation, certain of the component elements of which are distinguished by a mark, designating them for special attention; and this attention, in cases of exceptional intensity, excludes all consciousness of the others.

.   .   .   .

In summary: if the doctrine, that we think by concepts, means that a concept is the only thing present to the mind along with the individual object which (to use Sir W. Hamilton's language) we think under the concept, this is not true, since there is always present a concrete idea or image of which the attributes comprehended in the concept are only, and cannot be conceived as anything but, a part. Again, if it be meant that the concept, though only a part of what is present to the mind, is the part which is operative in the act of thought, neither is this true; for what is operative is, in a great majority of cases, much less than the entire concept, being that portion only which we have retained the habit of distinctly attending to. In neither of these senses, therefore, do we think by means of the concept; and all that is true is that when we refer any object or set of objects to a class, some at least of the attributes included in the concept are present to the mind, being recalled to consciousness and fixed in attention through their association with the class name.

.   .   .   .

CHAPTER IV*

OF REASONING

In common with the majority of modern writers on logic, whose language is generally that of the conceptualist school, Sir W. Hamilton considers reasoning, as he considers judgment, to consist

* [Chapter XIX of the third edition.]

in a comparison of notions: either of concepts with one another or of concepts with the mental representations of individual objects. Only in simple judgment two notions are compared immediately; in reasoning, mediately. Reasoning is the comparison of two notions by means of a third. As thus: "Reasoning is an act of mediate Comparison or Judgment; for to reason is to recognize that two notions stand to each other in the relation of a whole and its parts, through a recognition that those notions severally stand in the same relation to a third."[1] The foundation, therefore, of all reasoning is "the self-evident principle that a part of the part is a part of the whole."[2] "Without reasoning we should have been limited to a knowledge of what is given by immediate intuition; we should have been unable to draw any inference from this knowledge, and have been shut out from the discovery of that countless multitude of truths which, though of high, of paramount importance, are not self-evident."[3] This recognition that we discover a "countless multitude of truths" composing a vast proportion of all our real knowledge by mere reasoning, will be found to jar considerably with our author's theory of the reasoning process, and with his whole view of the nature and functions of logic, the science of reasoning; but this inconsistency is common to him with nearly all the writers on logic, because, like him, they teach a theory of the science too small and narrow to contain their own facts.

Notwithstanding the great number of philosophers who have considered the definition cited above to be a correct account of reasoning, the objections to it are so manifest that until after much meditation on the subject, one can scarcely prevail on oneself to utter them, so impossible does it seem that difficulties so obvious should always be passed over unnoticed unless they admitted of an easy answer. Reasoning, we are told, is a mode of ascertaining that one notion is a part of another; and the use of reasoning is to enable us to discover truths which are not self-evident. But how is it possible that a truth which consists in one notion being part of another, should not be self-evident? The notions, by supposition, are both of them in our mind. To perceive what parts they

[1]Lectures, iii. 274.   [2]Ibid., p. 271.   [3]Ibid., p. 277.

are composed of, nothing surely can be necessary but to fix our attention on them. We cannot surely concentrate our consciousness on two ideas in our own mind without knowing with certainty whether one of them as a whole includes the other as a part. If we have the notion "biped" and the notion "man," and know what they are, we must know whether the notion of a "biped" is part of the notion we form to ourselves of a "man." In this case the simply introspective method is in its place. We cannot need to go beyond our consciousness of the notions themselves.

Moreover, if it were really the case that we can compare two notions and fail to discover whether one of them is a part of the other, it is impossible to understand how we could be enabled to accomplish this by comparing each of them with a third. A, B, and C are three concepts of which we are supposed to know that A is a part of B, and B of C, but until we put these two propositions together we do not know that A is a part of C. We have perceived B in C intuitively, by direct comparison; but what is B? By supposition it is, and is perceived to be, A and something more. We have therefore, by direct intuition, perceived that A and something more is a part of C, without perceiving that A is a part of C. Surely there is here a great psychological difficulty to be got over, to which logicians of the conceptualist school have been surprisingly blind.

Endeavoring, not to understand what they say, for they never face the question, but to imagine what they might say, to relieve this apparent absurdity, two things occur to the mind. It may be said that when a notion is in our consciousness, but we do not know whether something is or is not a part of it, the reason is that we have forgotten some of its parts. We possess the notion but are only conscious of part of it, and it does its work in our trains of thought only symbolically. Or, again, it may be said that all the parts of the notion are in our consciousness, but are in our consciousness indistinctly. The meaning of having a distinct notion, according to Sir W. Hamilton, is that we can discriminate the characters or attributes of which it is composed. The admitted fact, therefore, that we can have indistinct notions may be adduced as proof that we can possess a notion and not be able to say positively what is included in it. These are the best or rather the only presentable arguments I am able to invent in support of the paradox involved in the conceptualist theory of reasoning.

It is a great deal easier to refute these arguments than it was to discover them. The refutation, like the original difficulty, is two deep. To begin, a notion part of which has been forgotten is to that extent a lost notion, and is as if we had never had it. The parts which we can no longer discern in it are not in it, and cannot, therefore, be proved to be in it, by reasoning any more than by intuition. We may be able to discover by reasoning that they ought to be there, and may, in consequence, put them there; but that is not recognizing them to be there already. As a notion in part forgotten is a partially lost notion, so an indistinct notion is a notion not yet formed, but in process of formation. We have an indistinct notion of a class when we perceive in a general way that certain objects differ from others, but do not as yet perceive in what; or perceive some of the points of difference, but have not yet perceived, or have not yet generalized, the others. In this case our notion is not yet a completed notion, and the parts which we cannot discern in it are undiscernible because they are not yet there. As in the former case, the result of reasoning may be to put them there; but it certainly does not effect this by proving them to be there already.

But even if these explanations had solved the mystery of our being conscious of a whole and unable to be directly conscious of its part, they would yet fail to make intelligible how, not having this knowledge directly, we are able to acquire it through a third notion. By hypothesis we have forgotten that A is a part of C, until we again become aware of it through the relation of each of them to B. We therefore had not forgotten that A is a part of B, nor that B is a part of C. When we conceived B, we conceived A as a part of it; when we conceived C, we conceived B as a part of it. In the mere fact, therefore, of conceiving C, we were conscious of B in it, and consciousness of A is a necessary part of that consciousness of B, and yet our consciousness of C did not enable us to find in it our consciousness of A, though it was really there, and though they both were distinctly present. If anyone can believe this, no contradiction and no impossibility in any theory of consciousness need stagger him. Let us now substitute for the hypothesis of forgetfulness the hypothesis of indistinctness. We had a notion of C, which was so indistinct that we could not discriminate A from the other parts of the notion. But it was not too indistinct to enable us to discriminate B, otherwise the reasoning would break down as well as the intuition. The notion of B, again, indistinct as it may have been in other respects, must have been such that we could with assurance discriminate A as contained in it. Here then returns the same absurdity: A is distinctly present in B, which is distinctly present in C, therefore A, if there be any force in reasoning, is distinctly present in C; yet A cannot be discriminated or perceived in the consciousness in which it is distinctly present, so that, before our reasoning commenced, we were at once distinctly conscious of A and entirely unconscious of it. There is no such thing as a reduction to absurdity if this is not one.

The reason why a judgment which is not intuitively evident can be arrived at through the medium of premises, is that judgments which are not intuitively evident do not consist in recognizing that one notion is part of another. When that is the case, the conclusion is as well known to us *ab initio* as the premises, which is really the case in analytical judgments. When reasoning really leads to the "countless multitudes of truths" not self-evident, which our author speaks of — that is, when the judgments are synthetical — we learn, not that A is part of C, because A is part of B and B of C, but that A is conjoined with C because A is conjoined with B, and B with C. The principle of the reasoning is not, a part of the part is a part of the whole, but, a mark of the mark is a mark of the thing marked, *Nota notae est nota rei ipsius.* It means that two things which constantly co-exist with the same third thing constantly co-exist with one another; the things meant not being our concepts, but the facts of experience on which our concepts ought to be grounded.

This theory of reasoning is free from the objections which are fatal to the conceptualist theory. We cannot discover that A is a part of C through its being a part of B, since if it really is so, the one truth must be as much a matter of direct consciousness as the other. But we can discover that A is conjoined with C through its being conjoined with B; since our knowledge that it is conjoined with B may have been obtained by a series of observations in which C was not perceptible. C, we must remember, stands for an attribute, that is, not an actual presentation of sense, but a power of producing such presentations; and that a power may have been present without being apparent is in the common course of things, implying nothing more than that the conditions necessary to determine it into act were not all present. This power or potentiality, C, may in like manner have been ascertained to be conjoined with B by another set of observations in which it was A's turn to be dormant or, perhaps, to be active but not attended to. By combining the two sets of observations, we are enabled to discover what was not contained in either of them, namely, a constancy of conjunction between C and A, such that one of them comes to be a mark of the other, though, in neither of the two sets of observations, nor in any others, may C and A have been actually observed together; or, if observed, not with the frequency or under the experimental conditions which would warrant us in generalizing the fact. This is the process by which we do, in reality, acquire the greater part of our knowledge — all of it (as our author says) which is not "given by immediate intuition." But no part of this process is at all like the operation of recognizing parts and a whole, or of recognizing any relation whatever between concepts which have nothing to do with the matter, more than is implied in the fact that we cannot reason about things without conceiving them or representing them to the mind.

The theory which supposes judgment and reasoning to be the comparison of concepts is obliged to make the term concept stand for, not the thinker's or reasoner's own notion of a thing, but a sort of normal notion which is understood as being owned by everybody, though everybody does not always use it; and it is this tacit substitution of a concept floating in the air for the very concept I have in my own mind, which makes it possible to fancy that we can, by reasoning, find out something to be in a concept which we are not able to discover in it by consciousness, because, in truth, *that* concept is not in our consciousness. But a concept of a thing which is not that whereby I conceive it, is to me as much an external fact as a presentation of the senses can be: it is another person's concept, not mine. It may be the conventional concept of the world at large — that which it has been tacitly agreed to associate with the class; in other words, it may be the connotation of the class name; and if so, it may very possibly contain elements which I cannot directly recognize in it, but may have to learn from external evidence; but this is because I do not know the signification of the word, the attributes which determine its application — and what I have to do is to learn them; when I have done this, I shall have no difficulty in directly recognizing, as a part of them, anything which really is so. But with regard to all attributes not included in the signification of the name, not only I do not find them in the concept, but they do not even become part of it after I have learned them by experience; unless we understand by the concept, not, with philosophers in general, only the essence of the class, but, with Sir W. Hamilton, all its known attributes. Even in Sir W. Hamilton's sense, they are not found in the concept, but added to it; and not until we have already assented to them as objective facts — subsequently, therefore, to the reasoning by which they were ascertained.

Take such a case as this: Here are two properties of circles. One is that a circle is bounded by a line, every point of which is equally distant from a certain point within the circle. This attribute is connoted by the name, and is, on both theories, a part of the concept. Another property of the circle is that the length of its circumference is to that of its diameter in the approximate ratio of 3.14159 to 1. This attribute was discovered, and is now known, as a result of reasoning. Now, is there any sense, consistent with the meaning of the terms, in which it can be said that this recondite property formed part of the concept "circle," before it had been discovered by mathematicians? Even in Sir W. Hamilton's meaning of concept, it is in nobody's but a mathematician's concept even now; and if we concede that mathematicians are to determine the normal concept of a circle for mankind at large, mathematicians themselves did not find the ratio of the diameter to the circumference in the concept, but put it there; and could not have done so until the long train of difficult reasoning which culminated in the discovery was complete.

It is impossible, therefore, rationally to hold both the opinions professed simultaneously by Sir W. Hamilton — that reasoning is the comparison of two notions through the medium of a third, and that reasoning is a source from which we derive new truths. And the truth of the latter proposition being indisputable, it is the former which must give way. The theory of reasoning which attempts to unite them both has the same defect which we have shown to vitiate the corresponding theory of judgment: it makes the process consist in eliciting something out of a concept which never was in the concept, and if it ever finds its way there, does so after the process, and as a consequence of its having taken place.

ON THE DEFINITION OF

POLITICAL ECONOMY

AND ON THE

METHOD OF INVESTIGATION

PROPER TO IT

ON THE DEFINITION OF POLITICAL ECONOMY AND ON THE METHOD OF INVESTIGATION PROPER TO IT[1]

It might be imagined, on a superficial view of the nature and objects of definition, that the definition of a science would occupy the same place in the chronological which it commonly does in the didactic order. As a treatise on any science usually commences with an attempt to express, in a brief formula, what the science is and wherein it differs from other sciences, so, it might be supposed, did the framing of such a formula naturally precede the successful cultivation of the science.

This, however, is far from having been the case. The definition of a science has almost invariably not preceded, but followed, the creation of the science itself. Like the wall of a city, it has usually been erected, not to be a receptacle for such edifices as might afterwards spring up, but to circumscribe an aggregation already in existence. Mankind did not measure out the ground for intellectual cultivation before they began to plant it; they did not divide the field of human investigation into regular compartments first, and then begin to collect truths for the purpose of being therein deposited; they proceeded in a less systematic manner. As discoveries were gathered in, either one by one or in groups resulting from the continued prosecution of some uniform course of inquiry, the truths which were successively brought into store cohered and became agglomerated according to their individual affinities. Without any intentional classification, the facts classed themselves. They became associated in the mind, according to their general and obvious resemblances; and the aggregates thus formed, having to be frequently spoken of as aggregates, came to be denoted by a common name. Any body of truths which had thus acquired a collective denomination was called a *science*. It was long before

[1] [This essay was originally published in the *Westminster Review* of October, 1836. Here the latter part of the title ran: "the Method of Philosophical Investigation in that Science."]

this fortuitous classification was felt not to be sufficiently precise. It was in a more advanced stage of the progress of knowledge that mankind became sensible of the advantage of ascertaining whether the facts which they had thus grouped together were distinguished from all other facts by any common properties, and what these were. The first attempts to answer this question were commonly very unskilful, and the consequent definitions extremely imperfect.

And, in truth, there is scarcely any investigation in the whole body of a science requiring so high a degree of analysis and abstraction as the inquiry what the science itself is; in other words, what are the properties common to all the truths composing it and distinguishing them from all other truths. Many persons, accordingly, who are profoundly conversant with the details of a science would be very much at a loss to supply such a definition of the science itself as should not be liable to well-grounded logical objections. From this remark we cannot except the authors of elementary scientific treatises. The definitions which those works furnish of the sciences, for the most part either do not fit them — some being too wide, some too narrow — or do not go deep enough into them, but define a science by its accidents, not its essentials; by some one of its properties which may, indeed, serve the purpose of a distinguishing mark, but which is of too little importance to have ever of itself led mankind to give the science a name and rank as a separate object of study.

The definition of a science must, indeed, be placed among that class of truths which Dugald Stewart had in view when he observed that the first principles of all sciences belong to the philosophy of the human mind. The observation is just; and the first principles of all sciences, including the definitions of them, have consequently participated hitherto in the vagueness and uncertainty which has pervaded that most difficult and unsettled of all branches of knowledge. If we open any book, even of mathematics or natural philosophy, it is impossible not to be struck with the mistiness of what we find represented as preliminary and fundamental notions, and the very insufficient manner in which the propositions which are palmed upon us as first principles seem to be made out, contrasted with the lucidity of the explanations and the conclusiveness of the proofs as soon as the writer enters upon the details of his object. Whence comes this anomaly? Why is the admitted certainty of the results of those sciences in no way prejudiced by the want of solidity in their premises? How happens it that a firm superstructure has been erected upon an unstable foundation? The solution of the paradox is that what are called first principles are in truth *last* principles. Instead of being the fixed point from whence the chain of proof which supports all the rest of the science hangs suspended, they are themselves the remotest links of the chain. Though presented as if all other truths were to be deduced from them, they are the truths which are last arrived at; the result of the last stage of generalization, or of the last and subtlest process of analysis, to which the particular truths of the science can be subjected; those particular truths having previously been ascertained by the evidence proper to their own nature.

Like other sciences, political economy has remained destitute of a definition framed on strictly logical principles, or even of, what is more easily to be had, a definition exactly co-extensive with the thing defined. This has not, perhaps, caused the real bounds of the science to be, in this country at least, practically mistaken or overpassed; but it has occasioned — perhaps we should rather say it is connected with — indefinite and often erroneous conceptions of the mode in which the science should be studied.

We proceed to verify these assertions by an examination of the most generally received definitions of the science.

1. First, as to the vulgar notion of the nature and object of political economy, we shall not be wide of the mark if we state it to be something to this effect: That political economy is a science which teaches, or professes to teach, in what manner a nation may be made rich. This notion of what constitutes the science is in some degree countenanced by the title and arrangement which Adam Smith gave to his invaluable work. A systematic treatise on political economy, he chose to call an *Inquiry into the Nature and Causes of the Wealth of Nations;* and the topics are introduced in an order suitable to that view of the purpose of his book.

With respect to the definition in question, if definition it can be called which is not found in any set form of words but left to be arrived at by a process of abstraction from a hundred current modes of speaking on the subject, it seems liable to the conclusive objection that it confounds the essentially distinct, though closely connected, ideas of *science* and *art*. These two ideas differ from one another as the understanding differs from the will, or as the indicative mood in grammar differs from the imperative. The one deals in facts, the other in precepts. Science is a collection of *truths;* art, a body of *rules* or directions for conduct. The language of science is, This is, or this is not; this does, or does not, happen. The language of art is, Do this; avoid that. Science takes cognizance of a *phenomenon*, and endeavors to discover its *law;* art proposes to itself an *end* and looks out for *means* to effect it.

If, therefore, political economy be a science, it cannot be a collection of practical rules, though, unless it be altogether a useless science, practical rules must be capable of being founded upon it. The science of mechanics, a branch of natural philosophy, lays down the laws of motion and the properties of what are called the mechanical powers. The art of practical mechanics teaches how we may avail ourselves of those laws and properties to increase our command over external nature. An art would not be an art unless it were founded upon a scientific knowledge of the properties of the subject matter; without this, it would not be philosophy, but empiricism; ἐμπειρία, not τέχνη, in Plato's sense. Rules, therefore, for making a nation increase in wealth are not a science, but they are the results of science. Political economy does not of itself instruct how to make a nation rich; but whoever would be qualified to judge of the means of making a nation rich must first be a political economist.

2. The definition most generally received among instructed persons, and laid down in the commencement of most of the professed treatises on the subject, is to the following effect: That political economy informs us of the laws which regulate the production, distribution, and consumption of wealth. To this definition is frequently appended a familiar illustration. Political economy, it is said, is to the state what domestic economy is to the family.

This definition is free from the fault which we pointed out in the former one. It distinctly takes notice that political economy is a science and not an art; that it is conversant with laws of nature, not with maxims of conduct, and teaches us how things take place of themselves, not in what manner it is advisable for us to shape them, in order to attain some particular end.

But though the definition is, with regard to this particular point, unobjectionable, so much can scarcely be said for the accompanying illustration, which rather sends back the mind to the current loose notion of political economy already disposed of. Political economy is really, and is stated in the definition to be, a science; but domestic economy, so far as it is capable of being reduced to principles, is an art. It consists of rules or maxims of prudence for keeping the family regularly supplied with what its wants require, and securing, with any given amount of means, the greatest possible quantity of physical comfort and enjoyment. Undoubtedly the beneficial *result*, the great practical *application* of political economy would be to accomplish for a nation something like what the most perfect domestic economy accomplishes for a single household; but supposing this purpose realized, there would be the same difference between the rules by which it might be effected and political economy, which there is between the art of gunnery and the theory of projectiles or between the rules of mathematical land-surveying and the science of trigonometry.

The definition, though not liable to the same objection as the illustration which is annexed to it, is itself far from unexceptionable. To neither of them, considered as standing at the head of a treatise, have we much to object. At a very early age in the study of the science, anything more accurate would be useless and therefore pedantic. In a merely initiatory definition, scientific precision is not required: the object is to insinuate into the learner's mind — it is scarcely material by what means — some general preconception of what are the uses of the pursuit, and what the series of topics through which he is about to travel. As a mere anticipation or *ébauche* of a definition, intended to indicate to a learner as much as he is able to understand before he begins, of the nature of what is about to be taught to him, we do not quarrel with the received formula. But if it claims to be admitted as that complete *definitio* or boundary line which results from a thorough exploring of the whole extent of the subject, and is intended to mark the exact place of political economy among the sciences, its pretension cannot be allowed.

"The science of the laws which regulate the production, distribution, and consumption of wealth." The term "wealth" is surrounded by a haze of floating and vapory associations, which will let nothing that is seen through them be shown distinctly. Let us supply its place by a periphrasis. Wealth is defined, all objects useful or agreeable to mankind, except such as can be obtained in indefinite quantity without labor. Instead of all objects, some authorities say "all material objects"; the distinction is of no moment for the present purpose.

To confine ourselves to production: if the laws of the production of all objects, or even of all material objects, which are useful or agreeable to mankind, were comprised in political economy, it would be difficult to say where the science would end; at the least, all or nearly all physical knowledge would be included in it. Corn and cattle are material objects in a high degree useful to mankind. The laws of the production of the one include the principles of agriculture; the production of the other is the subject of the art of cattle breeding, which, in so far as really an art, must be built upon the science of physiology. The laws of the production of manufactured articles involve the whole of chemistry and the whole of mechanics. The laws of the production of the wealth which is extracted from the bowels of the earth cannot be set forth without taking in a large part of geology.

When a definition so manifestly surpasses in extent what it professes to define, we must suppose that it is not meant to be interpreted literally, though the limitations with which it is to be understood are not stated.

Perhaps it will be said that political economy is conversant with such only of the laws of the production of wealth as are applicable to *all* kinds of wealth; those which relate to the details of particular trades or employments forming the subject of other and totally distinct sciences.

If, however, there were no more in the distinction between political economy and physical science than this, the distinction, we may venture to affirm, would never have been made. No similar division exists in any other department of knowledge. We do not break up zoology or mineralogy into two parts, one treating of the properties common to all animals or to all minerals, another conversant with the properties peculiar to each particular species of animals or minerals. The reason is obvious; there is no distinction *in kind* between the general laws of animal or of mineral nature and the peculiar properties of particular species. There is as close an analogy between the general laws and the particular ones as there is between one of the general laws and another; most commonly, indeed, the particular laws are but the complex result of a plurality of general laws modifying each other. A separation, therefore, between the general laws and the particular ones, merely because the former are general and the latter particular, would run counter both to the strongest motives of convenience and the natural tendencies of the mind. If the case is different with the laws of the production of wealth, it must be because, in this case, the general laws differ in kind from the particular ones. But if so, the difference in kind is the radical distinction, and we should find out what that is, and found our definition upon it.

But, further, the recognized boundaries which separate the field of political economy from that of physical science, by no means correspond with the distinction between the truths which concern all kinds of wealth and those which relate only to some kinds. The three laws of motion and the law of gravitation are common, as far as human observation has yet extended, to all matter; and these, therefore, as being among the laws of the production of all wealth, should form part of political economy. There are hardly any of the processes of industry which do not partly depend upon the properties of the lever; but it would be a strange classification which included those properties among the truths of political economy. Again, the latter science has many inquiries altogether as special, and relating as exclusively to particular sorts of material objects as any of the branches of physical science. The investigation of some of the circumstances which regulate the price of corn has as little to do with the laws common to the production of all wealth as any part of the knowledge of the agriculturist. The inquiry into the rent of mines or fisheries, or into the value of the precious metals, elicits truths which have immediate reference to the production solely of peculiar kinds of wealth; yet these are admitted to be correctly placed in the science of political economy.

The real distinction between political economy and physical

science must be sought in something deeper than the nature of the subject matter; which, indeed, is for the most part common to both. Political economy and the scientific grounds of all the useful arts have in truth one and the same subject matter — namely, the objects which conduce the man's convenience and enjoyment, but they are, nevertheless, perfectly distinct branches of knowledge.

If we contemplate the whole field of human knowledge, attained or attainable, we find that it separates itself obviously, and as it were spontaneously, into two divisions which stand so strikingly in opposition and contradistinction to one another that in all classifications of our knowledge they have been kept apart. These are *physical* science and *moral* or psychological science. The difference between these two departments of our knowledge does not reside in the subject matter with which they are conversant; for although of the simplest and most elementary parts of each, it may be said, with an approach to truth, that they are concerned with different subject matters — namely, the one with the human mind, the other with all things whatever except the mind; this distinction does not hold between the higher regions of the two. Take the science of politics, for instance, or that of law: who will say that these are physical sciences? And yet is it not obvious that they are conversant fully as much with matter as with mind? Take, again, the theory of music, of painting, of any other of the fine arts, and who will venture to pronounce that the facts they are conversant with belong either wholly to the class of matter or wholly to that of mind?

The following seems to be the *rationale* of the distinction between physical and moral science.

In all the intercourse of man with nature, whether we consider him as acting upon it or as receiving impressions from it, the effect or phenomenon depends upon causes of two kinds: the properties of the object acting, and those of the object acted upon. Everything which can possibly happen in which man and external things are jointly concerned, results from the joint operation of a law or laws of matter and a law or laws of the human mind. Thus the production of corn by human labor is the result of a law of mind and many laws of matter. The laws of matter are those properties of the soil and of vegetable life which cause the seed to germinate in the ground, and those properties of the human body which render food necessary to its support. The law of mind is that man desires to possess subsistence and consequently wills the necessary means of procuring it.

Laws of mind and laws of matter are so dissimilar in their nature that it would be contrary to all principles of rational arrangement to mix them up as part of the same study. In all scientific methods, therefore, they are placed apart. Any compound effect or phenomenon which depends both on the properties of matter and on those of mind may thus become the subject of two completely distinct sciences or branches of science: one, treating of the phenomenon in so far as it depends upon the laws of matter only; the other treating of it in so far as it depends upon the laws of mind.

The physical sciences are those which treat of the laws of matter and of all complex phenomena in so far as dependent upon the laws of matter. The mental or moral sciences are those which treat of the laws of mind and of all complex phenomena in so far as dependent upon the laws of mind.

Most of the moral sciences presuppose physical science, but few of the physical sciences presuppose moral science. The reason is obvious. There are many phenomena (an earthquake, for example, or the motions of the planets) which depend upon the laws of matter exclusively and have nothing whatever to do with the laws of mind. Many, therefore, of the physical sciences may be treated of without any reference to mind, and as if the mind existed as a recipient of knowledge only, not as a cause producing effects. But there are no phenomena which depend exclusively upon the laws of mind; even the phenomena of the mind itself being partially dependent upon the physiological laws of the body. All the mental sciences, therefore, not excepting the pure science of mind, must take account of great variety of physical truths, and (as physical science is commonly and very properly studied first) may be said to presuppose them, taking up the complex phenomena where physical science leaves them.

Now this, it will be found, is a precise statement of the relation in which political economy stands to the various sciences which are tributary to the arts of production.

The laws of the production of the objects which constitute wealth are the subject matter both of political economy and of almost all the physical sciences. Such, however, of those laws as are purely laws of matter belong to physical science, and to that exclusively. Such of them as are laws of the human mind, and no others, belong to political economy, which finally sums up the result of both combined.

Political economy, therefore, presupposes all the physical sciences; it takes for granted all such of the truths of those sciences as are concerned in the production of the objects demanded by the wants of mankind; or at least it takes for granted that the physical part of the process takes place somehow. It then inquires what are the phenomena of *mind* which are concerned in the production and distribution of those same objects; it borrows from the pure science of mind the laws of those phenomena, and inquires what effects follow from these mental laws acting in concurrence with those physical ones.[2]

---

[2] We say, the *production* and *distribution*, not, as is usual with writers on this science, the production, distribution, and *consumption*. For we contend that political economy, as conceived by those very writers, has nothing to do with the consumption of wealth, further than as the consideration of it is inseparable from that of production or from that of distribution. We know not of any *laws* of the *consumption* of wealth as the subject of a distinct science; they can be no other than the laws of human enjoyment. Political economists have never treated of consumption on its own account, but always for the purpose of the inquiry in what manner different kinds of consumption affect the production and distribution of wealth. Under the head of consumption, in professed treatises on the science, the following are the subjects treated of: first, the distinction between *productive* and *unproductive* consumption; secondly, the inquiry whether it is possible for *too much* wealth to be *produced*, and for too great a portion of what has been produced to be applied to the purpose of further *production;* thirdly, the theory of taxation, that is to say, the following two questions: by whom each particular tax is paid (a question of *distribution*), and in what manner particular taxes affect *production*.

The physical laws of the production of useful objects are all equally presupposed by the science of political economy: most of them, however, it presupposes in the gross, seeming to say nothing about them. A few (such, for instance, as the decreasing ratio in which the produce of the soil is increased by an increased application of labor) it is obliged particularly to specify, and thus seems to borrow those truths from the physical sciences to which they properly belong, and include them among its own.

From the above considerations the following seems to come out as the correct and complete definition of political economy: "The science which treats of the production and distribution of wealth, so far as they depend upon the laws of human nature." Or thus: "The science relating to the moral or psychological laws of the production and distribution of wealth."

For popular use this definition is amply sufficient, but it still falls short of the complete accuracy required for the purposes of the philosopher. Political economy does not treat of the production and distribution of wealth in all states of mankind, but only in what is termed the social state; nor so far as they depend upon the laws of human nature, but only so far as they depend upon a certain portion of those laws. This, at least, is the view which must be taken of political economy if we mean it to find any place in an encyclopedical division of the field of science. On any other view, it either is not science at all or it is several sciences. This will appear clearly if, on the one hand, we take a general survey of the moral sciences, with a view to assign the exact place of political economy among them, while, on the other, we consider attentively the nature of the methods or processes by which the truths which are the object of those sciences are arrived at.

Man, who, considered as a being having a moral or mental nature, is the subject matter of all the moral sciences, may, with reference to that part of his nature, form the subject of philosophical inquiry under several distinct hypotheses. We may inquire what belongs to man considered individually, and as if no human being existed besides himself; we may next consider him as coming into contact with other individuals; and finally, as living in a state of *society*, that is, forming part of a body or aggregation of human beings, systematically co-operating for common purposes. Of this last state, political government, or subjection to a common superior, is an ordinary ingredient but forms no necessary part of the conception, and, with respect to our present purpose, needs not be further adverted to.

Those laws or properties of human nature which appertain to man as a mere individual and do not presuppose, as a necessary condition, the existence of other individuals (except, perhaps, as mere instruments or means), form a part of the subject of pure mental philosophy. They comprise all the laws of the mere intellect, and those of the purely self-regarding desires.

Those laws of human nature which relate to the feelings called forth in a human being by other individual human or intelligent beings as such—namely, the *affections*, the *conscience* or feeling of duty, and the love of *approbation*; and to the conduct of man, so far as it depends upon, or has relation to, these parts of his nature — form the subject of another portion of pure mental philosophy, namely, that portion of it on which *morals*, or *ethics*, are founded. For morality itself is not a science but an art; not truths but rules. The truths on which the rules are founded are drawn (as is the case in all arts) from a variety of sciences; but the principal of them, and those which are most nearly peculiar to this particular art, belong to a branch of the science of mind.

Finally, there are certain principles of human nature which are peculiarly connected with the ideas and feelings generated in man by living in a state of *society*, that is, by forming part of a union or aggregation of human beings for a common purpose or purposes. Few, indeed, of the elementary laws of the human mind are peculiar to this state, almost all being called into action in the two other states. But those simple laws of human nature, operating in that wider field, give rise to results of a sufficiently universal character, and even (when compared with the still more complex phenomena of which they are the determining causes) sufficiently simple, to admit of being called, though in a somewhat looser sense, *laws* of society or laws of human nature in the social state. These laws or general truths form the subject of a branch of science which may be aptly designated from the title of *social economy;* somewhat less happily by that of *speculative politics* or the *science* of politics, as contradistinguished from the art. This science stands in the same relation to the social as anatomy and physiology to the physical body. It shows by what principles of his nature man is induced to enter into a state of society; how this feature in his position acts upon his interests and feelings, and through them upon his conduct; how the association tends progressively to become closer, and the co-operation extends itself to more and more purposes; what those purposes are, and what the varieties of means most generally adopted for furthering them;

what are the various relations which establish themselves among human beings as the ordinary consequence of the social union; what those which are different in different states of society; in what historical order those states tend to succeed one another; and what are the effects of each upon the conduct and character of man.

This branch of science, whether we prefer to call it social economy, speculative politics, or the natural history of society, presupposes the whole science of the nature of the individual mind; since all the laws of which the latter science takes cognizance are brought into play in a state of society, and the truths of the social science are but statements of the manner in which those simple laws take effect in complicated circumstances. Pure mental philosophy, therefore, is an essential part, or preliminary, of political philosophy. The science of social economy embraces every part of man's nature, in so far as influencing the conduct or condition of man in society; and therefore may it be termed "speculative politics" or "the art of government," of which the art of legislation is a part.[3]

It is to *this* important division of the field of science that one of the writers who have most correctly conceived and copiously illustrated its nature and limits — we mean M. Say — has chosen to give the name "political economy." And, indeed, this large extension of the signification of that term is countenanced by its etymology. But the words "political economy" have long ceased to have so large a meaning. Every writer is entitled to use the words which are his tools in the manner which he judges most conducive to the general purposes of the exposition of truth; but he exercises this discretion under liability to criticism; and M. Say seems to have done in this instance what should never be done without strong reasons — to have altered the meaning of a name which was appropriated to a particular purpose (and for which, therefore, a substitute must be provided) in order to transfer it

[3] The *science* of legislation is an incorrect and misleading expression. Legislation is *making laws*. We do not talk of the *science* of *making* anything. Even the *science* of *government* would be an objectionable expression were it not that *government* is often loosely taken to signify, not the act of governing, but the state or condition of being *governed* or of living under a government. A preferable expression would be the "science of *political society*"; a principal branch of the more extensive science of society, characterized in the text.

to an object for which it was easy to find a more characteristic denomination.

What is now commonly understood by the term "political economy" is not the science of speculative politics, but a branch of that science. It does not treat of the whole of man's nature as modified by the social state, nor of the whole conduct of man in society. It is concerned with him solely as a being who desires to possess wealth, and who is capable of judging of the comparative efficacy of means for obtaining that end. It predicts only such of the phenomena of the social state as take place in consequence of the pursuit of wealth. It makes entire abstraction of every other human passion or motive, except those which may be regarded as perpetually antagonizing principles to the desire of wealth, namely, aversion to labor and desire of the present enjoyment of costly indulgences. These it takes, to a certain extent, into its calculations, because these do not merely, like other desires, occasionally conflict with the pursuit of wealth, but accompany it always as a drag or impediment, and are therefore inseparably mixed up in the consideration of it. Political economy considers mankind as occupied solely in acquiring and consuming wealth; and aims at showing what is the course of action into which mankind, living in a state of society, would be impelled if that motive, except in the degree in which it is checked by the two perpetual countermotives above adverted to, were absolute rulers of all their actions. Under the influence of this desire it shows mankind accumulating wealth and employing that wealth in the production of other wealth; sanctioning by mutual agreement the institution of property; establishing laws to prevent individuals from encroaching upon the property of others by force or fraud; adopting various contrivances for increasing the productiveness of their labor; settling the division of the produce by agreement, under the influence of competition (competition itself being governed by certain laws, which laws are therefore the ultimate regulators of the division of the produce); and employing certain expedients (as money, credit, etc.) to facilitate the distribution. All these operations, though many of them are really the result of a plurality of motives, are considered by political economy as flowing solely from the desire of wealth. The science then proceeds to investigate the laws which govern these several operations, under the supposition that man is a being who is determined, by the necessity of his nature, to prefer a greater portion of wealth to a smaller in all cases, without any other exception than that constituted by the two countermotives already specified. Not that any political economist was ever so absurd as to suppose that mankind are really thus constituted, but because this is the mode in which science must necessarily proceed. When an effect depends upon a concurrence of causes, those causes must be studied one at a time and their laws separately investigated if we wish, through the causes, to obtain the power of either predicting or controlling the effect, since the law of the effect is compounded of the laws of all the causes which determine it. The law of the centripetal and that of the tangential force must have been known before the motions of the earth and planets could be explained or many of them predicted. The same is the case with the conduct of man in society. In order to judge how he will act under the variety of desires and aversions which are concurrently operating upon him, we must know how he would act under the exclusive influence of each one in particular. There is, perhaps, no action of a man's life in which he is neither under the immediate nor under the remote influence of any impulse but the mere desire of wealth. With respects to those parts of human conduct of which wealth is not even the principal object, to these political economy does not pretend that its conclusions are applicable. But there are also certain departments of human affairs in which the acquisition of wealth is the main and acknowledged end. It is only of these that political economy takes notice. The manner in which it necessarily proceeds is that of treating the main and acknowledged end as if it were the sole end; which, of all hypotheses equally simple, is the nearest to the truth. The political economist inquires, what are the actions which would be produced by this desire if, within the departments in question, it were unimpeded by any other. In this way a nearer approximation is obtained than would otherwise be practicable, to the real order of human affairs in those departments. This approximation is then to be corrected by making proper allowance for the effects of any impulses of a different description which can be shown to interfere with the result in any particular case. Only in a few of the most striking cases (such as the important one of the principle of population) are these corrections interpolated into the expositions of political economy itself; the strictness of purely scientific arrangement being thereby somewhat departed from, for the sake of practical utility. So far as it is known, or may be presumed, that the conduct of mankind in the pursuit of wealth is under the collateral influence of any other of the properties of our nature than the desire of obtaining the greatest quantity of wealth with the least labor and self-denial, the conclusions of political economy will so far fail of being applicable to the explanation or prediction of real events until they are modified by a correct allowance for the degree of influence exercised by the other cause.

Political economy, then, may be defined as follows, and the definition seems to be complete:

The science which traces the laws of such of the phenomena of society as arise from the combined operations of mankind for the production of wealth, in so far as those phenomena are not modified by the pursuit of any other objects.

But while this is a correct definition of political economy as a portion of the field of science, the didactic writer on the subject will naturally combine in his exposition, with the truths of the pure science, as many of the practical modifications as will, in his estimation, be most conducive to the usefulness of his work.

The above attempt to frame a stricter definition of the science than what are commonly received as such may be thought to be of little use or, at best, to be chiefly useful in a general survey and classification of the sciences rather than as conducing to the more successful pursuit of the particular science in question. We think otherwise, and for this reason that with the consideration of the definition of a science is inseparably connected that of the *philosophic method* of the science, the nature of the process by which its investigations are to be carried on, its truths to be arrived at.

Now, in whatever science there are systematic differences of opinion — which is as much as to say, in all the moral or mental sciences, and in political economy among the rest; in whatever science there exist, among those who have attended to the subject, what are commonly called differences of principle, as distinguished from differences of matter-of-fact or detail — the cause will be found to be a difference in their conceptions of the philosophic method of the science. The parties who differ are guided, either knowingly or unconsciously, by different views concerning the nature of the evidence appropriate to the subject. They differ not solely in what they believe themselves to see, but in the quarter whence they obtained the light by which they think they see it.

The most universal of the forms in which this difference of method is accustomed to present itself is the ancient feud between what is called theory and what is called practice or experience. There are, on social and political questions, two kinds of reasoners: there is one portion who term themselves practical men, and call the others theorists — a title which the latter do not reject, though they by no means recognize it as peculiar to them. The distinction between the two is a very broad one, though it is one of which the language employed is a most incorrect exponent. It has been again and again demonstrated that those who are accused of despising facts and disregarding experience build and profess to build wholly upon facts and experience; while those who disavow theory cannot make one step without theorizing. But, although both classes of inquirers do nothing but theorize, and both of them consult no other guide than experience, there is this difference between them, and a most important difference it is: that those who are called practical men require *specific* experience and argue wholly *upwards* from particular facts to a general conclusion; while those who are called theorists aim at embracing a wider field of experience, and, having argued upwards from particular facts to a general principle including a much wider range than that of the question under discussion, then argue *downwards* from that general principle to a variety of specific conclusions.

Suppose, for example, that the question were whether absolute kings were likely to employ the powers of government for the welfare or for the oppression of their subjects. The practicals would endeavor to determine this question by a direct induction from the conduct of particular despotic monarchs, as testified by history. The theorists would refer the question to be decided by the test not solely of our experience of kings, but of our experience of men. They would contend that an observation of the tendencies which nature has manifested in the variety of situations in which human beings have been placed, and especially observation of what passes in our own minds, warrants us in inferring that a human being in the situation of a despotic king will make a bad use of power; and that this conclusion would lose nothing of its certainty even if absolute kings had never existed or if history furnished us with no information of the manner in which they had conducted themselves.

The first of these methods is a method of induction, merely; the last a mixed method of induction and ratiocination. The first may be called the method *a posteriori;* the latter, the method *a priori.* We are aware that this last expression is sometimes used to characterize a supposed mode of philosophizing which does not profess to be founded upon experience at all. But we are not acquainted with any mode of philosophizing, on political subjects at least, to which such a description is fairly applicable. By the method *a posteriori* we mean that which requires, as the basis of its conclusions, not experience merely, but specific experience. By the method *a priori* we mean (what has commonly been meant) reasoning from an assumed hypothesis; which is not a practice confined to mathematics but is of the essence of all science which admits of general reason at all. To verify the hypothesis itself *a posteriori,* that is, to examine whether the facts of any actual case are in accordance with it, is no part of the business of science at all, but of the *application* of science.

In the definition which we have attempted to frame of the science of political economy, we have characterized it as essentially an *abstract* science and its method as the method *a priori.* Such is undoubtedly its character as it has been understood and taught by all its most distinguished teachers. It reasons and, as we contend, must necessarily reason from assumptions, not from facts. It is built upon hypothesis strictly analogous to those which under the name of definitions are the foundation of the other abstract sciences. Geometry presupposes an arbitrary definition of a line — "that which has length but not breadth." Just in the same manner does political economy presuppose an arbitrary definition of man as a being who invariably does that by which he may obtain the greatest amount of necessaries, conveniences, and luxuries with the smallest quantity of labor and physical self-denial with which they can be obtained in the existing state of knowledge. It is true that this definition of man is not formally prefixed to any work on political economy, as the definition of a line is prefixed to Euclid's *Elements;* and in proportion as by being so prefixed it would be less in danger of being forgotten we may see ground for regret that this is not done. It is proper that what is assumed in every particular case should once for all be brought before the mind in its full extent, by being somewhere formally stated as a general maxim. Now no one who is conversant with systematic treatises on political economy will question that whenever a political economist has shown that by acting in a particular manner a laborer may obviously obtain higher wages, a capitalist larger profits, or a landlord higher rent, he concludes as a matter of course that they will certainly act in that manner. Political economy, therefore, reasons from *assumed* premises — from premises which might be totally without foundation in fact and which are not pretended to be universally in accordance with it. The conclusions of political economy consequently, like those of geometry, are only true as the common phrase is *in the abstract,* that is, they are only true under certain suppositions in which none but general causes — causes common to the *whole class* of cases under consideration — are taken into the account.

This ought not to be denied by the political economist. If he deny it, then, and then only, he places himself in the wrong. The *a priori* method which is laid to his charge, as if his employment of it proved his whole science to be worthless, is, as we shall presently show, the only method by which truth can possibly be attained in any department of the social science. All that is requisite is that he be on his guard not to ascribe to conclusions which are grounded upon an hypothesis, a different kind of certainty from that which really belongs to them. They would be true without qualification only in a case which is purely imaginary. In proportion as the actual facts recede from the hypothesis, he must allow a corresponding deviation from the strict letter of his conclusion; otherwise it will be true only of things such as he has arbitrarily supposed, not of such things as really exist. That which is true in the abstract is always true in the concrete, with proper *allowances.* When a certain cause really exists and if left to itself would infallibly produce a certain effect, that same effect *modified* by all the other concurrent causes will correctly correspond to the result really produced.

The conclusions of geometry are not strictly true of such lines, angles, and figures as human hands can construct. But no one, therefore, contends that the conclusions of geometry are of no utility or that it would be better to shut up Euclid's Elements and content ourselves with "practice" and "experience."

No mathematician ever thought that his definition of a line corresponded to an actual line. As little did any political economist ever imagine that real men had no object of desire but wealth or none which would not give way to the slightest motive of a pecuniary kind. But they were justified in assuming this for the purposes of their argument, because they had to do only with those parts of human conduct which have pecuniary advantage for their direct and principal object and because, as no two individual cases are exactly alike, no *general* maxims could ever be laid down unless *some* of the circumstances of the particular case were left out of consideration.

But we go farther than to affirm that the method *a priori* is a legitimate mode of philosophical investigation in the moral sciences; we contend that it is the only mode. We affirm that the method *a posteriori* or that of specific experience is altogether inefficacious in those sciences as a means of arriving at any considerable body of valuable truth, though it admits of being usefully applied in aid of the method *a priori*, and even forms an indispensable supplement to it.

There is a property common to almost all the moral sciences, and by which they are distinguished from many of the physical; this is, that it is seldom in our power to make experiments in them. In chemistry and natural philosophy we cannot only observe what happens under all the combinations of circumstances which nature brings together, but we may also try an indefinite number of new combinations. This we can seldom do in ethical, and scarcely ever in political, science. We cannot try forms of government and systems of national policy on a diminutive scale in our laboratories, shaping our experiments as we think they may most conduce to the advancement of knowledge. We therefore study nature under circumstances of great disadvantage in these sciences, being confined to the limited number of experiments which take place (if we may so speak) of their own accord, without any preparation or management of ours, in circumstances, moreover, of great complexity and never perfectly known to us, and with the far greater part of the processes concealed from our observation.

The consequence of this unavoidable defect in the materials of the induction is that we can rarely obtain what Bacon has quaintly but most unaptly, termed an *experimentum crucis*.

In any science which admits of an unlimited range of arbitrary experiments, an *experimentum crucis* may always be obtained. Being able to vary all the circumstances, we can always take effectual means of ascertaining which of them are and which are not material. Call the effect B, and let the question be whether the cause A in any way contributes to it. We try an experiment in which all the surrounding circumstances are altered except A alone; if the effect B is nevertheless produced, A is the cause of it. Or instead of leaving A and changing the other circumstances, we leave all the other circumstances and change A; if the effect B in that case does not take place, then again A is a necessary condition of its existence. Either of these experiments, if accurately performed, is an *experimentum crucis;* it converts the presumption we had before of the existence of a connection between A and B into proof by negativing every other hypothesis which would account for the appearances.

But this can seldom be done in the moral sciences, owing to the immense multitude of the influencing circumstances and our very scanty means of varying the experiment. Even in operating upon an individual mind, which is the case affording greatest room for experimenting, we cannot often obtain a *crucial* experiment. The effect, for example, of a particular circumstance in education upon the formation of character may be tried in a variety of cases, but we can hardly ever be certain that any two of those cases differ in all their circumstances except the solitary one of which we wish to estimate the influence. In how much greater a degree must this difficulty exist in the affairs of states, where even the *number* of recorded experiments is so scanty in comparison with the variety and multitude of the circumstances concerned in each. How, for example, can we obtain a crucial experiment on the effect of a restrictive commercial policy upon national wealth? We must find two nations alike in every other respect or at least possessed in a degree exactly equal of everything which conduces to national opulence and adopting exactly the same policy in all their other affairs, but differing in this only that one of them adopts a system of commercial restrictions and the other adopts free trade. This would be a decisive experiment, similar to those which can almost always obtain in experimental physics. Doubtless this would be the most conclusive evidence of all if we could get it. But let anyone consider how infinitely numerous and various are the circumstances which either directly or indirectly do or may influence the amount of the national wealth, and then ask himself what are the probabilities that in the longest revolution of ages two nations will be found which agree, and can be shown to agree, in all those circumstances except one?

Since, therefore, it is vain to hope that truth can be arrived at either in political economy or in any other department of the social science while we look at the facts in the concrete clothed in all the complexity with which nature has surrounded them, and endeavor to elicit a general law by a process of induction from a comparison of details, there remains no other method than the *a priori* one or that of "abstract speculation."

Although sufficiently ample grounds are not afforded in the field of politics for a satisfactory induction by a comparison of the effects, the causes may in all cases be made the subject of specific experiment. These causes are laws of human nature and external circumstances capable of exciting the human will to action. The desires of man and the nature of the conduct to which they prompt him are within the reach of our observation. We can also observe what are the objects which excite those desires. The materials of this knowledge everyone can principally collect within himself, with reasonable consideration of the differences of which experience discloses to him the existence, between himself and other people. Knowing therefore accurately the properties of the substances concerned, we may reason with as much certainty as in the most demonstrative parts of physics, from any assumed set of circumstances. This will be mere trifling if the assumed circumstances bear no sort of resemblance of any real ones; but if the assumption is correct as far as it goes, and differs from the truth no otherwise than as a part differs from the whole, then the conclusions which are correctly deduced from the assumption constitute *abstract* truth; and when completed by adding or subtracting the effect of the non-calculated circumstances, they are true in the concrete and may be applied to practice.

Of this character is the science of political economy in the writings of its best teachers. To render it perfect as an abstract science, the combinations of circumstances which it assumes in order to trace their effects should embody all the circumstances that are common to all cases whatever, and likewise all the circumstances that are common to any important class of cases. The conclusions correctly deduced from these assumptions would be as true in the abstract as those of mathematics, and would be as near an approximation as abstract truth can ever be to truth in the concrete.

When the principles of political economy are to be applied to a particular case, then it is necessary to take into account all the individual circumstances of that case, not only examining to which of the sets of circumstances contemplated by the abstract science the circumstances of the case in question correspond, but likewise what other circumstances may exist in that case which, not being common to it with any large and strongly-marked class of cases, have not fallen under the cognizance of the science. These circumstances have been called "disturbing causes." And here only it is that an element of uncertainty enters into the process — an uncertainty inherent in the nature of these complex phenomena, and arising from the impossibility of being quite sure that all the circumstances of the particular case are known to us sufficiently in detail and that our attention is not unduly diverted from any of them.

This constitutes the only uncertainty of political economy; and not of it alone, but of the moral sciences in general. When the disturbing causes are known, the allowance necessary to be made for them detracts in no way from scientific precision, nor constitutes any deviation from the *a priori* method. The disturbing causes are not handed over to be dealt with by mere conjecture. Like *friction* in mechanics to which they have been often compared, they may at first have been considered merely as a non-assignable deduction to be made by guess from the result given by the general principles of science; but in time many of them are brought within the pale of the abstract science itself; and their effect is found to admit of as accurate an estimation as those more striking effects which they modify. The disturbing causes have their laws, as the causes which are thereby disturbed have theirs; and from the laws of the disturbing causes, the nature and amount of the disturbance may be predicted *a priori*, like the operation of the more general laws which they are said to modify or disturb, but with which they might more properly be said to be concurrent. The effect of the special causes is then to be added to, or subtracted from, the effect of the general ones.

These disturbing causes are sometimes circumstances which operate upon human conduct through the same principle of human nature with which political economy is conversant, namely, the desire of wealth, but which are not general enough to be taken into account in the abstract science. Of disturbances of this description every political economist can produce many examples. In other instances, the disturbing cause is some other law of human nature. In the latter case, it never can fall within the province of political economy; it belongs to some other science; and here the mere political economist, he who has studied no science but political economy, if he attempt to apply his science to practice, will fail.[4]

[4] One of the strongest reasons for drawing the line of separation clearly and broadly between science and art is the following: that the principle of classification in science most conveniently follows the classification of *causes*, while arts must necessarily be classified according to the classification of the *effects*, the production of which is their appropriate end. Now an effect, whether in physics or morals, commonly depends upon a concurrence of causes, and it frequently happens that several of these causes belong to different sciences. Thus in the construction of engines, upon the principles of the science of *mechanics* it is necessary to bear in mind the *chemical* properties of the material, such as its liability to oxydize; its electrical and magnetic properties, and so forth. From this it follows that although the necessary foundation of all art is science, that is, the knowledge of the properties or laws of the objects upon which, and with which, the art does its work, it is not equally true that every

As for the other kind of disturbing causes, namely, those which operate through the same law of human nature out of which the general principles of the science arise, these might always be brought within the pale of the abstract science if it were worth while; and when we make the necessary allowances for them in practice, if we are doing anything but guess, we are following out the method of the abstract science into minuter details, inserting among its hypotheses a fresh and still more complex combination of circumstances and so adding pro *hac vice* a supplementary chapter or appendix or at least a supplementary theorem to the abstract science.

Having now shown that the method *a priori* in political economy, and in all the other branches of moral science, is the only certain or scientific mode of investigation, and that the *a posteriori* method or that of specific experience as a means of arriving at truth is inapplicable to these subjects, we shall be able to show that the latter method is notwithstanding of great value in the moral sciences, namely, not as a means of discovering truth, but of verifying it and reducing to the lowest point that uncertainty before alluded to as arising from the complexity of every particular case and from the difficulty (not to say impossibility) of our being assured *a priori* that we have taken into account all the material circumstances.

If we could be quite certain that we knew all the facts of the particular case we could derive little additional advantage from specific experience. The causes being given, we may know what will be their effect, without an actual trial of every possible combination; since the causes are human feelings and outward circumstances fitted to excite them, and as these for the most part are or at least might be familiar to us, we can more surely judge of their combined effect from that familiarity than from any evidence which can be elicited from the complicated and entangled circumstances of an actual experiment. If the knowledge what are the particular causes operating in any given instance were revealed to us by infallible authority, then, if our abstract science were perfect, we should become prophets. But the causes are not so

art corresponds to one particular science. Each art presupposes, not one science, but sciences in general or, at least, many distinct sciences.

revealed; they are to be collected by observation, and observation in circumstances of complexity is apt to be imperfect. Some of the causes may lie beyond observation; many are apt to escape it unless we are on the look-out for them; and it is only the habit of long and accurate observation which can give us so correct a preconception what causes we are likely to find, as shall induce us to look for them in the right quarter. But such is the nature of the human understanding — that the very fact of attending with intensity to one part of a thing has a tendency to withdraw the attention from the other parts. We are consequently in great danger of adverting to a portion only of the causes which are actually at work. And if we are in this predicament, the more accurate our deductions and the more certain our conclusions in the abstract (that is making abstraction of all circumstances except those which form part of the hypothesis), the less we are likely to suspect that we are in error; for no one can have looked closely into the sources of fallacious thinking without being deeply conscious that the coherence and neat concatenation of our philosophical systems is more apt than we are commonly aware to pass with us as evidence of their truth.

We cannot therefore too carefully endeavor to verify our theory by comparing, in the particular cases to which we have access, the results which it would have led us to predict with the most trustworthy accounts we can obtain of those which have been actually realized. The discrepancies between our anticipations and the actual fact is often the only circumstance which would have drawn our attention to some important disturbing cause which we had overlooked. Nay, it often discloses to us errors in thought still more serious than the omission of what can with any propriety be termed a disturbing cause. It often reveals to us that the basis itself of our whole argument is insufficient, that the data from which we had reasoned comprise only a part, and not always the most important part, of the circumstances by which the result is really determined. Such oversights are committed by very good reasoners, and even by a still rarer class, that of good observers. It is a kind of error to which those are particularly liable whose views are the largest and most philosophical; for exactly in that ratio are their minds more accustomed to dwell upon those laws, qualities, and tendencies which are common to large classes of cases and which belong to all place and all time, while it often happens that circumstances almost peculiar to the particular case or era have a far greater share in governing that one case.

Although, therefore, a philosopher be convinced that no general truths can be attained in the affairs of nations by the *a posteriori* road, it does not the less behove him, according to the measure of his opportunities, to sift and scrutinize the details of every specific experiment. Without this he may be an excellent professor of abstract science; for a person may be of great use who points out correctly what effects will follow from certain combinations of possible circumstances, in whatever tract of the extensive region of hypothetical cases those combinations may be found. He stands in the same relation to the legislator as the mere geographer to the practical navigator, telling him the latitude and longitude of all sorts of places, but not how to find whereabouts he himself is sailing. If, however, he does no more than this, he must rest contented to take no share in practical politics; to have no opinion, or to hold it with extreme modesty, on the applications which should be made of his doctrines to existing circumstances.

No one who attempts to lay down propositions for the guidance of mankind, however perfect his scientific acquirements, can dispense with a practical knowledge of the actual modes in which the affairs of the world are carried on, and an extensive personal experience of the actual ideas, feelings, and intellectual and moral tendencies of his own country and of his own age. The true practical statesman is he who combines this experience with a profound knowledge of abstract political philosophy. Either acquirement without the other leaves him lame and impotent if he is sensible of the deficiency, renders him obstinate and presumptuous if, as is more probable, he is entirely unconscious of it.[5]

[5] [In the "Westminster Review" the author concluded this paragraph thus: "Knowledge of what is called history, so commonly regarded as the sole fountain of political experience, is useful only in the third degree. History by itself, if we knew it ten times better than we do, could, for the reasons already given, prove little or nothing; but the study of it is a corrective to the narrow and exclusive views which are apt to be engendered by observation on a more limited scale. Those who never look backwards, seldom look far forwards: their notions of human affairs, and of human nature itself, are circumscribed

Such then are the respective offices and uses of the *a priori* and the *a posteriori* methods — the method of abstract science and that of specific experiment — as well in political economy as in all the other branches of social philosophy. Truth compels us to express our conviction that, whether among those who have written on these subjects or among those for whose use they wrote, few can be pointed out who have allowed to each of these methods its just value and systematically kept each to its proper objects and functions. One of the peculiarities of modern times, the separation of theory from practice — of the studies of the closet from the outward business of the world — has given a wrong bias to the ideas and feelings both of the student and of the man of business. Each undervalues the part of the materials of thought with which he is not familiar. The one despises all comprehensive views, the other neglects details. The one draws his notion of the universe from the few objects with which his course of life has happened to render him familiar; the other, having got demonstration on his side and forgetting that it is only a demonstration *nisi* — a proof at all times liable to be set aside by the addition of a single new fact to the hypothesis — denies, instead of examining and sifting, the allegations which are opposed to him. For this he has considerable excuse in the worthlessness of the testimony on which the facts brought forward to invalidate the conclusions of theory usually rest. In these complex matters, men see with their preconceived opinions, not with their eyes; an interested or a passionate man's statistics are of little worth; and a year seldom passes without examples of the astounding falsehoods which large bodies of respectable men will back each other in publishing to the world as facts within their personal knowledge. It is not because a thing is *asserted* to be true, but because in its nature it *may* be true, that a sincere and patient inquirer will feel himself called upon to investigate it. He will use the assertions of opponents not as evidence but indications leading to evidence; suggestions of the most proper course of his own inquiries.

within the conditions of their own country and their own times. But the uses of history, and the spirit in which it ought to be studied, are subjects which have never yet had justice done them, and which involve considerations more multifarious than can be pertinently introduced in this place."]

But while the philosopher and the practical man bandy half truths with one another, we may seek far without finding one who, placed on a higher eminence of thought, comprehends as a whole what they see only in separate parts, who can make the anticipations of the philosopher guide the observation of the practical man, and the specific experience of the practical man warn the philosopher where something is to be added to his theory.

The most memorable example in modern times of a man who united the spirit of philosophy with the pursuits of active life and kept wholly clear from the partialities and prejudices both of the student and the practical statesman was Turgot, the wonder not only of his age but of history, for his astonishing combination of the most opposite and, judging from common experience, almost incompatible excellences.

Though it is impossible to furnish any test by which a speculative thinker, either in political economy or in any other branch of social philosophy, may know that he is competent to judge of the application of his principles to the existing condition of his own or any other country, indications may be suggested by the absence of which he may well and surely know that he is not competent. His knowledge must at least enable him to explain and account for what *is;* or he is an insufficient judge of what ought to be. If a political economist, for instance, finds himself puzzled by any recent or present commercial phenomena, if there is any mystery to him in the late or present state of the productive industry of the country, which his knowledge of principle does not enable him to unriddle, he may be sure that something is wanting to render his system of opinions a safe guide in existing circumstances. Either some of the facts which influence the situation of the country and the course of events are not known to him or, knowing them, he knows not what ought to be their effects. In the latter case, his system is imperfect even as an abstract system; it does not enable him to trace correctly all the consequences even of assumed premises. Though he succeed in throwing doubts upon the reality of some of the phenomena which he is required to explain, his task is not yet completed; even then he is called upon to show how the belief which he deems unfounded arose, and what is the real nature of the appearance which gave a color of probability to allegations which examination proves to be untrue.

When the speculative politician has gone through this labor — has gone through it conscientiously, not with the desire of finding his system complete but of making it so — he may deem himself qualified to apply his principles to the guidance of practice; but he must still continue to exercise the same discipline upon every new combination of facts as it arises; he must make a large allowance for the disturbing influence of unforeseen causes and must carefully watch the result of every experiment in order that any residuum of facts which his principles did not lead him to expect and do not enable him to explain may become the subject of a fresh analysis and furnish the occasion for a consequent enlargement or correction of his general views.

The method of the practical philosopher consists therefore of two processes: the one, analytical; the other, synthetical. He must *analyze* the existing state of *society* into its elements, not dropping and losing any of them by the way. After referring to the experience of individual man to learn the *law* of each of these elements, that is, to learn what are its natural effects and how much of the effects follow from so much of the cause when not counteracted by any other cause, there remains an operation of synthesis: to put all these effects together and, from what they are separately, to collect what would be effect of all the causes acting at once. If these various operations could be correctly performed, the result would be prophecy; but as they can be performed only with a certain approximation to correctness, mankind can never predict with absolute certainty, but only with a less or greater degree of probability, according as they are better or worse apprised what the causes are, have learned with more or less accuracy from experience the law to which each of those causes, when acting separately, conforms, and have summed up the aggregate effect more or less carefully.

With all the precautions which have been indicated, there will still be some danger of falling into partial views, but we shall at least have taken the best securities against it. All that we can do more is to endeavor to be impartial critics of our own theories and to free ourselves, as far as we are able, from that reluctance from which few inquirers are altogether exempt: to admit the reality or relevancy of any facts which they have not previously either taken into, or left a place open for, in their systems.

If, indeed, every phenomenon was generally the effect of no more than one cause, a knowledge of the law of that cause would, unless there was a logical error in our reasoning, enable us confidently to predict all the circumstances of the phenomenon. We might then, if we had carefully examined our premises and our reasoning, and found no flaw, venture to disbelieve the testimony which might be brought to show that matters had turned out differently from what we should have predicted. If the causes of erroneous conclusions were always patent on the face of the reasonings which lead to them, the human understanding would be a far more trustworthy instrument than it is. But the narrowest examination of the process itself will help us little toward discovering that we have omitted part of the premises which we ought to have taken into our reasoning. Effects are commonly determined by a *concurrence* of causes. If we have overlooked any one cause, we may reason justly from all the others, and only be the further wrong. Our premises will be true and our reasoning correct, and yet the result of no value in the particular case. There is, therefore, almost always room for a modest doubt as to our practical conclusions. Against false premises and unsound reasoning a good mental discipline may effectually secure us; but against the danger of *overlooking* something, neither strength of understanding nor intellectual cultivation can be more than a very imperfect protection. A person may be warranted in feeling confident that whatever he has carefully contemplated with his mind's eye he has seen correctly; but no one can be sure that there is not something in existence which he has not seen at all. He can do no more than satisfy himself that he has seen all that is visible to any other persons who have concerned themselves with the subject. For this purpose he must endeavor to place himself at their point of view and strive earnestly to see the object as they see it, nor give up the attempt until he has either added the appearance which is floating before them to his own stock of realities or made out clearly that it is an optical deception.

The principles which we have now stated are by no means alien to common apprehension; they are not absolutely hidden, perhaps, from anyone, but are commonly seen through a mist. We might have presented the latter part of them in a phraseology in which they would have seemed the most familiar of truisms: we might have cautioned inquirers against too extensive *generalization*, and reminded them that there are *exceptions* to all rules. Such is the current language of those who distrust comprehensive thinking, without having any clear notion why or where it ought to be distrusted. We have avoided the use of these expressions purposely because we deem them superficial and inaccurate. The error, when there is error, does *not* arise from generalizing too extensively, that is, from including too wide a range of particular cases in a single proposition. Doubtless, a man often asserts of an entire class what is only true of a part of it; but his error generally consists not in making too wide an assertion, but in making the wrong *kind* of assertion; he predicated an actual result when he should only have predicated a *tendency* to that result — a power acting with a certain intensity in that direction. With regard to exceptions in any tolerably advanced science, there is properly no such thing as an exception. What is thought to be an exception to a principle is always some other and distinct principle cutting into the former, some other force which impinges against the first force and deflects it from its direction. There are not a *law* and an *exception* to that law—the law acting in ninety-nine cases, and the exception in one. There are two laws, each possibly acting in the whole hundred cases and bringing about a common effect by their conjunct operation. If the force which, being the less conspicuous of the two, is called the disturbing force prevails sufficiently over the other force in some one case to constitute that case what is commonly called an exception, the same disturbing force probably acts as a modifying cause in many other cases which no one will call exceptions.

Thus, if it were stated to be a law of nature that all heavy bodies fall to the ground, it would probably be said that the resistance of the atmosphere which prevents a balloon from falling constitutes the balloon an exception to that pretended law of nature. But the real law is that all heavy bodies *tend* to fall, and to this there is no exception, not even the sun and moon; for even they, as every astronomer knows, tend toward the earth with a force exactly equal to that with which the earth tends toward them. The resistance of the atmosphere might in the particular case of the balloon, from a misapprehension of what the law of gravitation is, be said to *prevail* over the law, but its disturbing effect is quite as real in every other case, since, though it does not prevent, it retards the fall of all bodies whatever. The rule and the so-called exception do not divide the cases between them; each of them is a comprehensive rule extending to all cases. To call one of these concurrent principles an exception to the other is superficial and contrary to the correct principles of nomenclature and arrangement. An effect of precisely the same kind, and arising from the same cause, ought not to be placed in two different categories, merely as there does or does not exist another cause preponderating over it.

It is only in art, as distinguished from science, that we can with propriety speak of exceptions. Art, the immediate end of which is practice, has nothing to do with causes except as the means of bringing about effects. However heterogeneous the causes, it carries the effects of them all into one single reckoning; and according as the sum-total is *plus* or *minus*, according as it falls above or below a certain line, Art says, Do this or abstain from doing it. The exception does not run by insensible degrees into the rule, like what are called exceptions in science. In a question of practice, it frequently happens that a certain thing is either fit to be done or fit to be altogether abstained from, there being no medium. If in the majority of cases it is fit to be done, that is made the rule. When a case subsequently occurs in which the thing ought not to be done, an entirely new leaf is turned over: the rule is now done with and dismissed; a new train of ideas is introduced between which and those involved in the rule there is a broad line of demarcation, as broad and *tranchant* as the difference between Ay and No. Very possibly, between the last case which comes within the rule and the first of the exception there is only the difference of a shade, but that shade probably makes the whole interval between acting in one way and in a totally different one. We may, therefore, in talking of art, *unobjectionably* speak of the *rule* and the *exception*, meaning by the rule the cases in which there exists a preponderance, however slight, of inducements for acting in a particular way; and by the exception, the cases in which the preponderance is on the contrary side.

A SYSTEM OF LOGIC[1]

Complete Table of Contents, Eighth Edition

INTRODUCTION

BOOK I: OF NAMES AND PROPOSITIONS

[1] For an explanation of the asterisks and the numerals in brackets see "Note on the Text," page xliii.

BOOK VI [Bk V]:
ON THE LOGIC OF THE MORAL SCIENCES

INDEX

459

DATE DUE

JUN 29 '76			
APR 23 2004			
	DISCARDED		
GAYLORD		PRINTED IN U.S.A.	